# Convolutional Codes

# Convolutional Codes

An Algebraic Approach

Ph. Piret

The MIT Press
Cambridge, Massachusetts
London, England

## PUBLISHER'S NOTE

This format is intended to reduce the cost of publishing certain works in book form and to shorten the gap between editorial preparation and final publication. Detailed editing and composition have been avoided by photographing the text of this book directly from the author's prepared copy.

Library of Congress Cataloging-in-Publication Data

Piret, Ph. (Phillipe)
    Convolutional codes.

    Bibliography: p.
    Includes index.
    1. Coding theory.  2. Convolutions (Mathematics)
I. Title.
QA268.P53  1988        519.4        88-2769
ISBN 0-262-16110-9

*To Marie-Thérèse, Frédéric and Denis.*

# Contents

# Preface

In this book, I study convolutional codes from an algebraic point of view and, to some extent, I apply to convolutional codes some methods that have already proved useful in the construction and discussion of block codes. However, this algebraic point of view is *not* taken because of the pleasant mathematics it leads to, but rather because of its efficiency in constructing and analyzing convolutional codes. In particular, it leads to constructions of codes with good error correcting capabilities as explained in chapters 10 and 11.

The structure of the book is more or less linear, and most chapters require the material of the preceding ones. One exception is chapter 5, which may be skipped at first reading. As for chapters 1 and 6, where some algebraic tools are described, they should be considered more as reference summaries than as introductory accounts.

I am grateful to J-M. Goethals, director of the Philips Research Laboratory of Brussels, for allowing me the time to write this book. Some colleagues and friends provided me with the opportunity to discuss the subject with them. Some of the results in this monograph go back to two papers coauthored with Ph. Delsarte, who suggested many improvements to the present text. N. Sloane and the referees have also given useful suggestions.

The text was typed by Mrs E. Moes, using the LaTeX document preparation system. I am indebted to P. Devijver, F. Heymans and D. Snyers, of PRLB, for having helped me find my way about this system.

*Brussels*                                                        Ph. Piret
*November 1987*

# Convolutional Codes

# Introduction

In a landmark paper [111], published in 1948, Shannon introduced a new discipline: probabilistic information theory. The goal of this discipline is to investigate the conditions under which information can be reliably represented, transmitted or approximated in agreement with a given fidelity criterion. Its central concepts are *reliability* and *rate*. When information is transmitted over a channel, the rate of transmission $R$ is the ratio between a certain measure of the amount of information contained in the message and the length of the physical signal that represents this message. A basic result of information theory is that reliable information transmission is possible over a noisy channel if and only if the rate $R$ is smaller than a certain quantity $C$ depending only on the channel characteristics and called the *capacity* of the channel. Thus it is not necessary to use a vanishingly small rate $R$ in order to transmit information reliably if one can use sufficiently complex devices at both ends of the channel. The interested reader will find in [43] and [115] a thorough discussion of the basic results of information theory.

By nature the theorems of information theory are existence theorems, stating what is possible or impossible; but they do not lead by themselves to any actual implementation. The need for methods to carry out these promises gave birth to coding theory, which rapidly became an independent branch of research. Coding theory is usually divided into two parts, the first concerned with block codes and the second with convolutional codes.

The main goal of this book is to develop mathematical methods to simplify the systematic construction of good convolutional codes.

While it was soon recognized that the construction of efficient block codes was made easier by the use of certain algebraic tools, those tools were only rarely used to construct convolutional codes. Let us briefly comment on what is usually acknowledged to be a remarkable achievement of block coding theory: the $BCH$-codes [12-13] and the closely related $RS$-codes [99]. The construction and the analysis of these codes are related to the properties of Vandermonde determinants [71, 87]. Equivalently, they depend upon the property that a polynomial of degree $r$ over a field $F$ has exactly $r$ zeros, which are in some extension field $F^*$ of $F$ [83]. The main characteristics of these codes include the following points.

1. Flexibility in the choice of the parameters of the codes.

2. Ease of enumerating the codes of this class.

3. High efficiency when used on a noisy channel.

4. An a priori bound (the $BCH$-bound) on their error correcting capability.

5. A simple implementation, compared to that needed for a general block code.

Unfortunately, no similar achievement is known to date for convolutional codes: most convolutional codes have been constructed by computer search, and algebraic structures that guarantee good efficiency have proved difficult to find [67]. The main part of this book is devoted to an attempt to fill part of this gap between the construction methods for block codes and for convolutional codes. More precisely, we shall analyze in some detail a construction scheme for convolutional codes that fulfils the first three of the five characteristics above and partially fulfils the fourth one. Although we obtain no equivalent of the $BCH$-bound, the structure of the codes considered will indeed make their analysis much easier than that of arbitrary codes having the same parameters.

The book is organized as follows.

In chapter 1 we recall some basic elements of algebra required for any mathematical treatment of coding problems. We also introduce some tools to represent sequences and vector spaces of sequences, and we make some of their properties explicit.

Chapter 2 is devoted to the algebraic study of convolutional encoders. The concepts of minimal encoder and of basic encoder are introduced and an algorithm is given which, starting from an arbitrary encoder of a code, produces a minimal encoder of the same code. This chapter is based on results obtained in [79] and [35-36] but the methods we use are often different.

In chapter 3 we introduce some quantities (among which is the important minimum symbol distance) that may be used as quality criteria for convolutional codes. These quantities reflect the structure of the distances between code sequences and we mention bounds on some of them. We then present a state diagram that can be associated with a convolutional encoder [114] and we use this diagram to describe several methods that find an estimate of the transmitted code sequence from its received noisy version. We discuss also the concept of distance profile and some properties of catastrophic (i.e., nonbasic) encoders. Then we mention several construction methods producing reasonably good codes. We conclude this chapter by two appendices discussing the possibility of obtaining stronger lower bounds on the symbol minimum distance of some binary codes.

In chapter 4, we begin to describe the properties of convolutional codes with automorphisms. To introduce the notion of automorphism of a convolutional code we need to consider what we call a sliding set. We then define the automorphism group of a convolutional code and we show how one obtains a precise characterization of this group, starting from a minimal encoder of the code.

In chapter 5, we investigate the properties of any group that is the automorphism group of a convolutional code. We also obtain necessary conditions that must be satisfied by the minimal encoders generating a code having an infinite automorphism group. As another result of this chapter, it appears that "most" convolutional codes have an automorphism group that has a very special structure. Groups having this structure are called $\alpha$-constant groups.

Chapter 6 is devoted to a presentation of more advanced mathematical notions that are used in the subsequent chapters. Among these are the concepts of centralizer and of normalizer of a group as well as several notions related to the regular representation of a group. We also recall the definition and the main properties of a module over a ring.

In chapter 7, we investigate the algebraic structure of convolutional codes the automorphism group of which contains a specified subgroup, and we show that these codes are modules over an algebra. We introduce the concept of normal sequence, and we study some properties of the modules generated by these sequences. Finally we prove that, for most codes, a minimal encoder can be constructed that contains only normal sequences generating an irreducible module. Besides being minimal, such an encoder is of interest because it mirrors the direct sum structure of the code it generates.

The equivalences between convolutional codes are studied in chapter 8, where we emphasize the equivalences that preserve the automorphism group of the original code or at least some of its properties.

In chapter 9, we define the class of semiregular convolutional codes. These codes have a nontrivial automorphism group of a special type, and they can be analyzed with relative ease. In particular, the form of the corresponding normal sequences is made explicit. This leads to an easy method of enumeration of nonequivalent codes.

Chapter 10 is the first of two chapters where the tools developed will prove their efficiency in the construction of very good convolutional codes. In this chapter we enumerate a pile of codes of reasonably small length that have a strong algebraic structure and a large minimum symbol distance. Many of these will be shown to achieve an upper bound on the minimum distance that was mentioned in chapter 3.

In chapter 11, we describe convolutional codes that are efficient on channels where the errors have a clustered distribution or where the error-producing process is time-varying. We also describe codes that provide the information symbols with unequal error protection. Some of the codes considered in this chapter have the same algebraic structure as the codes described in chapter 10.

Our goal has not been to write an encyclopaedia of convolutional codes, but only to present some fundamental results and a first survey of the theory of convolutional codes with automorphisms. We hope that the reader will appreciate the efficiency of this approach for obtaining good convolutional codes. The study of convolutional codes with automorphisms may be seen as an extension of the study of cyclic block codes, but it needs the more advanced concepts presented in chapter 6.

The notation we use in this book is fairly standard. Some of it is as follows. If $S$ is a finite set, the number of elements in $S$ is denoted by $|S|$ and is called the cardinality or the order of $S$. If $s$ is an element of $S$, we write $s \in S$. The notation $S \supseteq T$ means that any element of the set $T$ is an element of $S$, whereas $S \supset T$ means that $S \supseteq T$ and that at least one $s$ in $S$ is not an element of $T$. If property $A$ implies property $B$, we write $A \Rightarrow B$. If the expression $B$ is the definition of the object $A$ we write $A := B$. If for integers $n_1, n_2$ and $n$, the difference $n_1 - n_2$ is a multiple of $n$, we say that $n_1$ is congruent to $n_2$ modulo $n$ and we write $n_1 = n_2 \bmod n$ or $n_1 \equiv n_2(n)$. The $k \times k$ identity matrix is denoted by $I_k$. If $x$ is a real number, $\lfloor x \rfloor$ denotes the largest integer $n$ satisfying $n \leq x$, and $\lceil x \rceil$ denotes the smallest integer $n$ satisfying $n \geq x$; thus $\lfloor x \rfloor = \lceil x \rceil$

implies that $x$ is an integer. For real numbers $x_1 \leq x_2$, $[x_1, x_2]$ denotes the set of real $x$ satisfying $x_1 \leq x \leq x_2$. The Stirling approximation to the factorial $n! = n(n-1)(n-2)...1$ is given by

$$n! = (2\pi n)^{1/2}(n/e)^n \exp(\frac{1}{12n} - \frac{1}{360n^2} + \cdots);$$

this leads to

$$(2\pi n)^{1/2}(n/e)^n \leq n! \leq (2\pi n)^{1/2}(n/e)^n \exp(\frac{1}{12n}).$$

For more information the reader may consult [87].

The binomial coefficient $n!/(n-k)!n!$ is denoted by $\binom{n}{k}$. By use of the Stirling approximation, one obtains, for $0 \leq \alpha \leq 1$,

$$\lim_{n \to \infty} n^{-1} \log \binom{n}{\lfloor \alpha n \rfloor} = -\alpha \log \alpha - (1-\alpha) \log(1-\alpha).$$

The right hand side of this equation is called the binary entropy function, denoted by $\mathcal{H}(\alpha)$. Its value depends on which basis is used for the computation of the logarithms. If nothing else is mentioned, natural logarithms are assumed. If base 2 logarithms are used, we denote the entropy function by $\mathcal{H}_2(\alpha)$.

Let $A$ be a set containing a zero and let $a(x) = \sum_{i=0}^{r} a_i x^i$, $a_i \in A$, be a polynomial over $A$. The integer $r$ is called the *formal degree* of the polynomial $a(x)$ and if not all $a_i$ are zero, the largest $i$ such that $a_i$ is nonzero is simply called the *degree* of $a(x)$. If all $a_i$ are zero we sometimes follow the convention that the degree of $a(x)$ is also zero. Some familiarity is assumed with the concepts of homomorphism, endomorphism, isomorphism and automorphism, (see for example [69]) but these concepts are recalled in the sequel.

# Chapter 1

# Mathematical background

To present a mathematical approach to convolutional codes we need some appropriate tools. As mentioned in the introduction, chapters 1 and 6 of this book are devoted to a description of these tools. In the first section of this chapter, we give an elementary survey of some basic mathematical structures: groups, rings, fields, vector spaces and associative algebras. The goal of this section is not to give the reader an in-depth introduction to these topics, but only to summarize the minimal background that is necessary to read the book to good purpose. In the second section of this chapter we introduce tools to represent sequences over the sets having the structures mentioned above. Some basic theorems are proved that are needed later.

## 1.1 Some algebraic structures

### 1.1.1 Groups

A *group* $H$ is a set of elements on which an operation is defined that satisfies the four axioms below. This operation associates a well-defined element $h$ of $H$ with any ordered pair $(h_1, h_2)$ of elements of $H$. It may be represented as a multiplication: $h = h_1 h_2$, as an addition: $h = h_1 + h_2$, or by any other convenient notation. In the first case the group is called a multiplicative group and in the second case it is called an additive group. Let us enumerate the axioms of a group $H$ in terms of the multiplicative notation.

(i) Closure: for any $h_1, h_2$ in $H$, $h = h_1 h_2$ is also an element of $H$.

(ii) Associativity: any three elements $h_1, h_2, h_3$ in $H$, satisfy

$$(h_1 h_2)h_3 = h_1(h_2 h_3).$$

(iii) Identity element: $H$ contains an identity element $u$ satisfying $hu = uh = h$, for all $h$ in $H$.

(iv) Existence of an inverse: for all $h$ in $H$ there exists $h^{-1}$ in $H$ such that $h^{-1}h = hh^{-1} = u$.

One shows that the identity element of a group $H$ is unique and that the inverse $h^{-1}$ of any element $h$ of a group $H$ is also unique. The inverse $(h_1 h_2)^{-1}$ of $h_1 h_2$ is $h_2^{-1} h_1^{-1}$. When $h_1 h_2 = h_2 h_1$ holds for all $h_1, h_2$ in the group $H$, this group is called a *commutative* or *Abelian* group.

If the additive notation is used for the group operation, the four group axioms remain the same with multiplication replaced by addition everywhere. In this case the inverse of $h$ is denoted by $-h$. The choice of a notation to represent the group operation depends upon personal preference, but it has become common practice to use the additive notation only for Abelian groups. In the sequel, the word "group" means a multiplicative group if no mention is made of the group operation.

A subset $\tilde{H}$ of elements of a group $H$ is called a set of generators for $H$ if all $h \in H$ can be expressed as a product of elements of $\tilde{H}$.

If the number of elements of the group $H$ is finite, $H$ is called a finite group. The smallest positive integer $n$, if it exists, such that $h^n = u$ is called the *order* of $h$ and the smallest positive integer $m$, if it exists, such that one has $h^m = u$ for all $h \in H$ is called the *period* of $H$. If $H$ is a finite group, its period and the order of any of its elements divide $|H|$. If a subset $H^*$ of $H$ is also a group it is called a subgroup of $H$. For fixed $h$ in $H$, the set $H^*h = \{h^*h \mid h^* \in H^*\}$ is called a right *coset* of $H^*$ in $H$. Two right cosets either are disjoint or coincide. The number of distinct right cosets of $H^*$ in $H$ is called the (right) *index* of $H^*$ in $H$ and it is denoted by $[H : H^*]$. So the notation $[H : u]$ is simply another notation for $|H|$. Similar properties hold for the left cosets $hH^*$ of $H^*$ in $H$. The left index and the right index of $H^*$ in $H$ are equal. A subgroup of $H$ is called *proper* if it does not coincide with $H$ and *trivial* if it reduces to $\{u\}$.

The subgroup $H^*$ of $H$ is said to be a *normal* subgroup of $H$, which we denote by $H \rhd H^*$, if it satisfies $hH^*h^{-1} = H^*$ for all $h \in H$. This is equivalent to $hH^* = H^*h$, all $h \in H$. Thus $H^*$ is normal in $H$ if and only if every right coset is a left coset and vice versa. If one has $H \rhd H^*$, the set of cosets $hH^*$ of $H^*$ in $H$ is endowed with a group structure since one can write $(h_1H^*)(h_2H^*) = h_1(H^*h_2)H^* = h_1(h_2H^*)H^* = (h_1h_2)H^*$. This group of cosets is denoted by $H/H^*$ and it is called the *quotient group* of $H$ by $H^*$. If one has a chain of subgroups $H_0 := H \rhd H_1 \rhd H_2 \rhd \cdots \rhd H_m$ with $H_m = \{u\}$, $H \rhd H_i$, and $H_i$ a proper normal subgroup of $H_{i-1}$, $1 \leq i \leq m$, this chain is called a *normal series* of length $m$ of subgroups $H_i$ of $H$.

Let $H$ and $H^*$ be two finite groups satisfying $|H| \geq |H^*|$ and let $\alpha$ be a mapping (denoted exponentially) of $H$ onto $H^*$. If one has

$$(h_1 h_2)^\alpha = h_1^\alpha h_2^\alpha \; ; \text{ all } h_1, h_2 \in H,$$

then $\alpha$ is called a (group) *homomorphism* of $H$ onto $H^*$. The set of $h \in H$ satisfying $h^\alpha = u^*$, with $u^*$ the identity of $H^*$, is called the *kernel* of $\alpha$. The kernel of any group homomorphism $\alpha$ of $H$ onto $H^*$ is a normal subgroup of $H$. If $|H^*| = |H|$, the homomorphism $\alpha$ is called an *isomorphism*. If $H^* \subseteq H$ it is called an *endomorphism* and if $H^* = H$ it is called an *automorphism*. An automorphism of $H$ that can be represented by

$h \mapsto h^\alpha = h_0^{-1}hh_0$, with $h_0$ in $H$, is called an inner automorphism of $H$.

Let us give three examples of groups.

**(i)** Consider the set of powers of $x$ endowed with the multiplicative rule $x^i x^j = x^{i+j}$ and the identity $x^n = x^0$. Under these rules, $H_1 = \{u = x^0, x, x^2, \cdots, x^{n-1}\}$ is obviously a group. Since it has a unique generator, $x$ for example, it is called a *cyclic* group.

**(ii)** Consider the set of monomials $x^i y^j$ endowed with the multiplication $(x^i y^j)(x^k y^l) = x^{i+k} y^{j+l}$ and the identities $x^n = x^0$ and $y^n = y^0$. Under these rules, $H_2 = \{x^i y^j \mid 0 \le i, j \le n-1\}$ is a group of order $n^2$ with $u = x^0 y^0$ as identity element. Since one has $h_1 h_2 = h_2 h_1$ for all $h_1, h_2 \in H_2$, it is an *Abelian* group. It is not cyclic because it does not contain any $h$ such that the $n^2$ powers $h^i$, $0 \le i \le n^2 - 1$, are all different.

**(iii)** Consider the set of monomials $y^i x^j$ endowed with the multiplication

$$(y^i x^j)(y^k x^l) = y^{i+k} x^{l+j} \text{ for even } k \,,$$

$$(y^i x^j)(y^k x^l) = y^{i+k} x^{l-j} \text{ for odd } k \,,$$

and the identities $x^n = x^0$ and $y^2 = y^0$, where $n$ is $\ge 3$. Under these rules, $H_3 = \{y^i x^j \mid 0 \le i \le 1, 0 \le j \le n-1\}$ is a noncommutative group with $y^0 x^0$ as identity element. This group is called the *dihedral* group of order $2n$.

Groups of matrices are other examples of groups (see subsection 1.1.3).

## 1.1.2  Rings and fields

In this subsection we recall the definitions and some properties of two algebraic structures having more than one operation. A set $R$ with two operations, usually called addition and multiplication, is called a *ring* if the following axioms are satisfied.

**(i)** $R$ is an Abelian group for the addition.

**(ii)** $R$ is closed for the multiplication.

**(iii)** Multiplication in $R$ is associative: $(r_1 r_2) r_3 = r_1 (r_2 r_3)$.

**(iv)** Multiplication in $R$ is distributive with respect to addition: $r_1 (r_2 + r_3) = r_1 r_2 + r_1 r_3$, $(r_1 + r_2) r_3 = r_1 r_3 + r_2 r_3$.

All rings considered below are rings with a multiplicative identity element, which is often denoted by 1 (one) and is different from the additive identity denoted by 0 (zero). A ring $R$ in which the multiplication is commutative $(r_1 r_2 = r_2 r_1,$ all $r_1, r_2 \in R)$ is called a *commutative* ring. Any $r \in R$ having a multiplicative inverse is called a *unit*.

Examples of rings are the ring $\mathbb{Z}$ of the integers endowed with the usual addition and multiplication, and the ring

$$Z_n = \{0, 1, \cdots, n - 1\}$$

in which the addition and the multiplication are performed modulo $n$. These two rings are obviously commutative. Other examples will be considered later.

A right *ideal* $I$ in a ring $R$ is a subset of $R$ satisfying the following axioms.

**(i)** The difference $s_1 - s_2 := s_1 + (-s_2)$ between any two elements of $I$ is an element $s$ of $I$.

**(ii)** For any $s \in I$ and any $r \in R$, one has $sr \in I$.

Axiom (ii) expresses the absorption property of ideals. Left ideals are defined similarly using $rs$ in (ii) in place of $sr$. If $R$ is a commutative ring, left ideals coincide with right ideals. If there exists $s$ in $I$ such that $I = sR$, this $I$ is called a *principal* (right) ideal.

For fixed elements $s_1, \cdots, s_t \in R$, let $I = s_1 R + \cdots + s_t R$ be the set of sums $s_1 r_1 + \cdots + s_t r_t$, $r_i \in R$, all $i$. This set $I$ is a (right) ideal in $R$,

and the set of the fixed elements $s_i$ is called a set of generators of the ideal
$I$. Many of the right ideals considered in this book can be generated by a
unique generator. In this case one has $I = sR$ for some well chosen $s \in R$.
Similar definitions hold for left ideals.

A *field* $F$ is a ring in which the nonzero elements form an Abelian group
for the multiplication. Well known examples of fields are the real field $\mathbb{R}$
and the complex field $\mathbb{C}$. More interesting for coding purpose are finite
fields, i.e., fields with a finite number of elements. These are often called
Galois fields. For this reason a finite field containing $q$ elements is often
denoted by $GF(q)$. A finite field of order $q$ (i.e., containing $q$ elements)
exists if and only $q$ is a power $p^r$ of some prime $p$ [16, 68, 87]. All fields
containing $q$ elements are isomorphic.

Suppose first that $q$ is a prime: $q = p$. In this case $F = GF(p)$ is called
a prime field and it is isomorphic to the set $\mathbb{Z}_p = \{0, 1, \cdots, p-1\}$ in which
the addition and the multiplication are performed modulo $p$. This means
that the sum $f = f_1 + f_2$ in $F$ is given by the remainder of the division by
$p$ of the integer obtained when one adds $f_2$ to $f_1$ in $\mathbb{Z}$. A similar rule holds
for the multiplication.

To make the structure of $GF(p^r)$ explicit for $r \geq 2$, we represent its
elements by the $p^r$ polynomials $a(x) = \sum_{i=0}^{r-1} a_i x^i$, $a_i \in GF(p)$, of formal
degree $r - 1$ over $GF(p)$. The addition of two such polynomials is made
in agreement with the usual rules of algebra: for $b(x) = \sum_{i=0}^{r-1} b_i x^i$, $c(x) = \sum_{i=0}^{r-1} c_i x^i$, the sum $b(x) + c(x)$ is defined to be $\sum_{i=0}^{r-1} (b_i + c_i) x^i$ with $b_i + c_i$ computed in $GF(p)$. The multiplication of two such polynomials is
a bit more complicated because the usual rules of algebra may generate
polynomials of degree $\geq r$. We have thus to find a way to map such a
polynomial in the set of polynomials of degree at most $r - 1$.

To do that we introduce first the concept of *irreducible polynomial*: a
polynomial $a(x) = \sum_{i=0}^{r} a_i x^i$, $a_i \in GF(p)$, $a_r \neq 0$, of degree $r$ over $GF(p)$
is said to be irreducible over $GF(p)$ if it cannot be written as a product
$b(x)c(x)$ of polynomials $b(x)$ and $c(x)$ of degree at least 1 over $GF(p)$. For

any prime $p$ it is known [7, 16] that there exists at least one monic (with leading coefficient equal to 1) irreducible polynomial of any degree over $GF(p)$.

We use then the fact that the set of polynomials over any field $F$ form a Euclidean ring [69], i.e., a ring having a division with quotient and remainder. With any pair $(f(x), a(x))$ of polynomials over $F$ we may indeed associate a unique pair $(u(x), v(x))$ of polynomials that satisfy $f = au + v$, where $v$ is a polynomial of degree smaller than the degree of $a$. In this equality $u$ is called the quotient, and $v$ is called the remainder, of the division of $f$ by $a$.

If the multiplication $b(x)c(x)$ considered above gives as a result a polynomial $f(x)$ of degree $\geq r$, we use an irreducible monic polynomial $a(x) = x^r - \sum_{i=0}^{r-1} a_i x^i$ of degree $r$ over $GF(p)$ to reduce this degree: any polynomial $f(x)$ of degree larger than $r - 1$ over $GF(p)$ is identified with the element of $GF(p^r)$ represented by the remainder $v(x)$ of the division of $f(x)$ by $a(x)$. This remainder is called the residue of $f(x)$ modulo $a(x)$ and we write $v(x) = f(x) \bmod a(x)$. These rules endow the set of polynomials of degree at most $r - 1$ over $GF(p)$ with the structure of the field $GF(p^r)$. A proof of this statement may be found, for example, in [68].

Let us now consider a polynomial $a(x) = \sum_{i=0}^{t} a_i x^i$, $a_t \neq 0$, over $GF(p^s)$. It is called irreducible over $GF(p^s)$ if it cannot be written as a product of two polynomials over $GF(p^s)$ of degree at least 1. If $r$ is a multiple of $s$, another possible construction of $GF(p^r)$ is to consider it as an extension of $GF(p^s)$. In this case, with $r = st$, the elements of $GF(p^r)$ are represented by the polynomials of degree at most $t - 1$ over $GF(p^s)$. The addition is the usual addition of polynomials: with $b(x) = \sum_{i=0}^{t-1} b_i x^i$, $c(x) = \sum_{i=0}^{t-1} c_i x^i$, $(b_i, c_i \in GF(p^s))$, $b(x) + c(x)$ is defined to be $\sum_{i=0}^{t-1} (b_i + c_i) x^i$ with $b_i + c_i$ computed in $GF(p^s)$. Since the multiplication can generate polynomials of degree $t$ or more, one has to reduce this degree: one identifies $f(x) = b(x)c(x)$ with the element of $GF(p^{st})$ represented by the remainder of the division of $f(x)$ by some monic irreducible polynomial

$a(x)$ of degree $t$ over $GF(p^s)$. Such a polynomial actually exists for all $t$, all $p$ and all $s$ [7, 16]. This addition and this multiplication give to the set of polynomials of degree at most $t - 1$ over $GF(p^s)$ the structure of the field $GF(p^{st})$. Although all finite fields containing $p^r$ elements are isomorphic, it is sometimes useful to consider $GF(p^r)$ as an extension of a specific subfield $GF(p^s)$ where $s$ is a divisor of $r$.

The multiplicative group of any finite field $GF(q)$ is cyclic. In other words, $GF(q)$ contains a *primitive element*, i.e., an element $\alpha$ such that the set $\{1, \alpha, \alpha^2, \cdots, \alpha^{q-2}\}$ is the set of the $q - 1$ nonzero elements of $GF(q)$. This $\alpha$ satisfies $\alpha^{q-1} = 1$. The prime number $p$ is called the characteristic of $GF(p^r)$. For any $t$ and any set $\{r_1, \cdots, r_t\}$ of $t$ integers, there exist integers $r$ such that the fields $GF(p^r)$ contain all fields $GF(p^{r_i})$ as subfields. These integers $r$ are all multiples of the least common multiple (or l.c.m.) of the integers $r_i$. A recent book [66] gives a detailed account of the properties of finite fields.

The concepts of homomorphism, endomorphism, isomorphism and automorphism defined above for the group structure can also be defined for structures with two operations. For example, an endomorphism $\alpha$ of a ring $R$ has to satisfy

$$(r_1 + r_2)^\alpha = r_1^\alpha + r_2^\alpha, \ (r_1 r_2)^\alpha = r_1^\alpha r_2^\alpha$$

for all $r_1, r_2 \in R$.

### 1.1.3   Vector spaces, matrices and algebras

Let $F$ be a field with 1 as a multiplicative identity, and let $V$ be an additive Abelian group. By abuse of notation, we use the same symbol 0 to denote the additive identity in $V$ and in $F$. Suppose that a mapping $F \times V \rightarrow V$ represented as a multiplication is defined and satisfies the following properties.

**(i)** $1v = v$; all $v \in V$.

**(ii)** $a(bv) = (ab)v$; all $a, b \in F$, all $v \in V$.

**(iii)** $a(v_1 + v_2) = av_1 + av_2$; all $a \in F$, all $v_1, v_2 \in V$.

**(iv)** $(a + b)v = av + bv$; all $a, b \in F$, all $v \in V$.

In this case $V$ is said to be a *vector space* over the field $F$, or an $F$-space, and the elements $v$ of $V$ are called *vectors*. The $r$ vectors $v_1, \cdots, v_r$ of $V$ are said to be independent over $F$ if it is not possible to find $r$ elements $a_1, \cdots, a_r$ of $F$ that are not all zero and that satisfy $\sum_{i=1}^{r} a_i v_i = 0$. Let $k$ be the largest integer, if any, for which $k$ independent vectors can be found in $V$. In this case, $k$ is called the *dimension* of $V$ over $F$, which we denote by $\dim_F V = k$ (or simply by $\dim V = k$). The set of the $k$ corresponding vectors $v_1, \cdots, v_k$ of $V$ is then called a basis of $V$ over $F$, and any vector $v$ in $V$ can be represented in a unique way as $v = \sum_{i=1}^{k} a_i v_i$, $a_i \in F$. If no such integer $k$ exists, one says that $\dim_F V$ is infinite. The set $F^n$ of row $n$-tuples over $F$ is an example of a vector space of dimension $n$ over $F$.

If $V_1$ is an $F$-space and if $V_2$ is a subset of $V_1$, which inherits from $V_1$ the structure of an $F$-space, then $V_2$ is called an $F$-subspace of $V_1$. If $V_1$ is a vector space of finite dimension and if $V_2$ is a subspace of $V_1$, their dimensions satisfy $\dim_F(V_1) \geq \dim_F(V_2)$. Moreover $V_1 \supseteq V_2$ and $\dim_F(V_1) = \dim_F(V_2)$ implies $V_1 = V_2$. If $V_1$ and $V_2$ are two $F$-subspaces of a same $F$-space $V$, the set of all sums $v_1 + v_2$, $v_i \in V_i$, $i = 1, 2$, is called the sum of $V_1$ and $V_2$ and it is denoted by $V_1 + V_2$. If $v_1 + v_2 = 0$ is possible only with $v_1 = v_2 = 0$, the sum of $V_1$ and $V_2$ is called direct and is denoted by $V_1 \oplus V_2$.

Let $V$ be an $F$-space of dimension $n$ and $\mathcal{V}^* = \{v_1, v_2, \cdots\}$ be a set of elements of $V$. The set of vectors $v$ that can be written as $\sum_i a_i v_i$, $a_i \in F$, with a finite number of nonzero $a_i$, is a subspace $V^*$ of $V$, and $\mathcal{V}^*$ is called a generating set of $V^*$.

In the sequel we make use of two properties of the bases of finite dimensional spaces, stated here as lemmas.

**Lemma 1.1 :** Let $V$ be a finite dimensional vector space over the field $F$ and let $k$ be its dimension. In any generating set $\mathcal{V}$ of $V$ there exists at least one subset of $k$ vectors that is a basis of $V$.

**Lemma 1.2 :** Let $v_1, \cdots, v_i$, $i \leq k$, be $i$ independent vectors of the $F$-space $V$ of dimension $k$ over $F$. In any generating set $\mathcal{V}$ of $V$ there exists at least one subset of $k - i$ vectors $v_{i+1}, \cdots, v_k$ such that $\{v_i \mid 1 \leq i \leq k\}$ is a basis of $V$.

Let $V$ and $U$ be two $F$-spaces and let $\phi$ be a mapping of $V$ *onto* $U$, i.e., any $u \in U$ is the image $\phi(v)$ of at least one $v \in V$. Such a mapping is called a homomorphism of $V$ onto $U$ (or an epimorphism) if it satisfies $\phi(\alpha_1 v_1 + \alpha_2 v_2) = \alpha_1 \phi(v_1) + \alpha_2 \phi(v_2)$ for all $\alpha_1, \alpha_2 \in F$ and all $v_1, v_2 \in V$. The set of all $v \in V$ satisfying $\phi(v) = 0$ is called the kernel of the homomorphism $\phi$ and it is denoted by $\ker(\phi)$. This kernel is a subspace of $V$. If $V$ is a finite dimensional vector space, the $F$-dimensions of $V$, $U$ and $\ker(\phi)$ are related by $\dim(U) + \dim[\ker(\phi)] = \dim(V)$.

It is assumed that the reader is familiar with the basic rules of matrix calculus for matrices over a commutative ring $R$ (or $R$-matrices). Two matrices of the same dimension can be added or subtracted. A $k \times m$ matrix $G_1$ can be multiplied to the right by an $m \times n$ matrix $G_2$, and the result $G = G_1 G_2$ is a $k \times n$ matrix. Any $k \times k$ matrix $G$ over $R$ has a determinant, denoted by $\det G$, which is an element of $R$. If there exists in $R$ a multiplicative inverse of $\det G$, then $G$ is called a *unimodular* matrix. In this case, there exists a $k \times k$ matrix $G^{-1}$ over $R$ that satisfies $G^{-1}G = GG^{-1} = I_k$. If the inverse of $\det G$ exists and is not in $R$ but in some ring $F$ containing $R$ as a subring, then $G^{-1}$ exists but is now a matrix over $F$. In both cases the matrix $G^{-1}$ is called the (multiplicative) inverse of $G$. If $G_1$ and $G_2$ are two $k \times k$ matrices over $R$, $\det G_1 G_2$ is equal to $\det G_1 \det G_2$.

Let $G$ be a matrix over the commutative ring $R$. We denote the restriction of $G$ to the subset $P$ (resp. $Q$) of its rows (resp. columns) by $G^P$ (resp. $G^Q$). Suppose now that $G$ is a $k \times k$ matrix. Write $k = k_1 + k_2$, with $1 \leq k_1, k_2 \leq k - 1$. Let $P$ be some fixed $k_1$-tuple of rows of $G$, let $\bar{P}$ be the set of rows of $G$ that are not in $P$, let $Q$ be any $k_1$-tuple of columns of $G$ and let $\bar{Q}$ be the set of columns of $G$ that are not in $Q$. For any fixed $P$, the Laplace rule [62] expresses $\det G$ as

$$\det G = \sum_Q (-1)^{f(P)+f(Q)} \det G^{PQ} \det G^{\bar{P}\bar{Q}}, \qquad (1.1)$$

where the functions $f(P)$ and $f(Q)$ are defined as follows. Numbering the rows of $G$ by the integers $1, 2, \cdots, k$, we represent $P$ by a $k_1$-tuple $P = \{p(1), \cdots, p(k_1)\}$ of integers between 1 and $k$ and we define $f(P) = \sum_{i=1}^{k_1}(p(i) - i)$. A similar definition holds for $f(Q)$. In (1.1) the numbers $\det G^{PQ}$ and $\det G^{\bar{P}\bar{Q}}$ are called *minors* of the matrix $G$.

Let $G$ be a $k \times n$ matrix over a field $F$ (or $F$-matrix) with $g_{ij}$ as $(i,j)$ entry. We denote its $i^{\text{th}}$ row by $g_i = (g_{i1}, \cdots, g_{in})$ and its $j^{\text{th}}$ column by $g^j = (g_{1j}, \cdots, g_{kj})^T$, where $^T$ denotes transposition. The set of all linear combinations $\sum_{i=1}^{k} a_i g_i$, $a_i \in F$, is a vector space called the row space of $G$ over $F$. The set of linear combinations $\sum_{j=1}^{n} a_j g^j$, $a_j \in F$, is another vector space called the column space of $G$ over $F$. Note that for any field $F^*$ containing $F$ as a subfield, the $F^*$-row space (resp. $F^*$-column space) of $G$ has the same dimension. The $F$-row space and the $F$-column space of a $k \times n$ $F$-matrix $G$ have the same dimension, which is called the *rank* of $G$ and is denoted by $\text{rk}(G)$. If $\text{rk}(G)$ is $< k$ (resp. $< n$), there exists a linear combination $\sum a_i g_i$ (resp. $\sum a_j g^j$) of its rows (resp. columns) that is zero and has at least one nonzero coefficient.

Let $G$ be an $F$-matrix with $n$ columns, let $V$ be the $F$-row space of $G$ and let $k$ be the dimension of $V$ over $F$. The set $V^\perp$ of row $n$-tuples $u$ over $F$ satisfying $Gu^T = 0$ is also a vector space over $F$ satisfying $\dim_F(V^\perp) = n - \dim_F(V)$.

If $G$ is an $n \times n$ $F$-matrix, the three following properties are equivalent.

(i) det $G$ is nonzero.

(ii) $\mathrm{rk}(G) = n$.

(iii) There exists a multiplicative inverse of $G$, i.e., an $n \times n$ $F$-matrix $G^{-1}$ satisfying $G^{-1}G = GG^{-1} = I_n$.

Any square matrix $G$ that enjoys these properties is called a *nonsingular* $F$-matrix.

If $G_1$ and $G_2$ are $n \times n$ nonsingular $F$-matrices, $G = G_1 G_2$ is also a nonsingular $F$-matrix. This implies that the set of all $n \times n$ nonsingular $F$-matrices is a group. This group is denoted by $GL(n, F)$ where $GL$ means *general linear*. For large $n$ the group $GL(n, F)$ contains many subgroups. Two of these subgroups deserve special attention. The first one, denoted by $S_n$, is the set of all $n \times n$ matrices with entries in $\{0, 1\}$ and having one and only one 1 in each row and in each column. The second distinguished subgroup denoted by $M_n$, is the set of all $n \times n$ matrices over $F$ with one and only one nonzero element in each row and in each column. The order of $S_n$ is $n!$ and the order of $M_n$ is $n!(|F| - 1)^n$. We may let act $S_n$ on $F^n$ by right multiplication,

$$x \in S_n \ : \ F^n \to F^n \ : \ v \mapsto vx.$$

A similar action may of course be defined for $M_n$ and for all other subgroups of $GL(n, F)$. As subgroups of $GL(n, F)$, $S_n$ and $M_n$ may thus be considered as permutation groups acting on the elements $v$ of $F^n$. However, from another point of view, $S_n$ is an example of a permutation group acting on the coordinates (or components) $v_i$ of the elements $v = (v_1, \cdots, v_n)$ of $F^n$: for $x \in S_n$ the coordinates $(vx)_i$ of the $n$-tuple $vx$ are just a reordering of the coordinates $v_i$ of the $n$-tuple $v$. The number of objects that are permuted by the elements of a permutation group is called the *degree* of the permutation group. For this reason, when $S_n$ is considered in its natural action by permutation on an ordered set of cardinality $n$ (such as an $n$-tuple of coordinates, for example) it is usually called the *symmetric group* of degree $n$. As for $M_n$, it is called a *monomial group*.

Given an $F$-matrix $G$, it is always possible to find a set $P$ (or $Q$) of $\text{rk}(G)$ rows (or columns) of $G$ that are a basis for the row space (or column space) of $G$ over $F$. Using this possibility, first for the rows of $G$ and then for the columns of $G^P$, we obtain an $\text{rk}(G) \times \text{rk}(G)$ submatrix $G^{PQ}$ of $G$ that is nonsingular. In this case we say that $(P, Q)$ *achieves* the rank of $G$. If $(P, Q)$ achieves the rank of $G$ and if $P$ (or $Q$) is the set of all rows (or columns) of $G$, we also say that $Q$ (or $P$) achieves the rank of $G$. If $Q$ is a set of columns that achieves the rank of $G$ and if $v$ and $w$ are two vectors in the row space of $G$, then $v^Q = w^Q$ implies $v = w$, and $v^Q = 0$ implies $v = 0$.

Let $F^*$ be a field and let $F$ be a subfield of $F^*$. Suppose that $G_1$ and $G_2$ are $k \times n$ matrices of rank $k$ over $F$ that generate the same row space of dimension $k$ over $F^*$.

**Theorem 1.3 :** There exists a $k \times k$ matrix $S$ over $F$ such that the matrix $G_1$ is equal to the matrix $SG_2$.
**Proof :** Let $g_i$ be the $i^{\text{th}}$ row of $G_1$. Since it is in the $F^*$-row space of $G_2$, there exists $s_i \in (F^*)^k$ such that $g_i$ is equal to $s_iG$, so that the matrix $S$ having $s_i$ as $i^{\text{th}}$ row satisfies $G_1 = SG_2$. We now show that the entries of $S$ are in the subfield $F$ of $F^*$. Let $Q$ be a $k$-tuple of columns that achieve the rank of $G_2$ over $F$. The matrix $S = G_1^Q(G_2^Q)^{-1}$ is an $F$-matrix. To prove that $G_1 - SG_2$ is the zero matrix, we remark that any row $v$ of $G_1 - SG_2$ is in the $F$-row space of $G_2$, and that $v^Q$ is zero by construction. Hence $v$ is also zero since $Q$ achieves the rank of $G_2$. $\square$

Now let $A$ be a vector space over the field $F$, and let a multiplication $A \times A \to A$ be defined that satisfies the following axioms.

(i) Together with the addition in the vector space, this multiplication endows $A$ with a ring structure.

(ii) $(fa)b = a(fb)$, all $f \in F$, all $a, b \in A$.

In this case $A$ is said to be an *algebra* over the field $F$ or an $F$-algebra.

The set of $n \times n$ matrices over the field $F$ has the structure of an algebra. It is a vector space of dimension $n^2$ over $F$, the matrix multiplication endows it with the structure of a ring, and the multiplication of matrices by an element of $F$ satisfies (ii). A group algebra is another type of algebra that is very useful in coding theory. With $H$ a group and $F$ a field, the group algebra $A = FH$ is the set of all formal sums $a = \sum_{h \in H} a(h)h$ with a finite number of nonzero $a(h) \in F$ in which addition and multiplication are defined by

$$a + b = \sum_{h \in H} [a(h) + b(h)]\, h\,,$$

$$a\, b = \sum_{h^* \in H} [\sum_{h \in H} a(h)\, b(h^{-1}h^*)]\, h^*\,.$$

Let us give a simple example. Let $H = \{x^0, x, x^2, \cdots, x^6\}$ be endowed with the multiplication $x^r x^s = x^{(r+s) \bmod 7}$, which gives it the structure of a multiplicative group. With $F = GF(2)$, the set of elements of $A = FH$ is the set of polynomials in $x$ over $GF(2)$ of formal degree 6, i.e., $A = \{a = \sum_{i=0}^{6} a_i x^i \mid a_i \in GF(2)\}$ . In $A$, the addition is natural addition: $a + b = \sum_{i=0}^{6}(a_i + b_i)x^i$ where $a_i + b_i$ is computed in $GF(2)$. The multiplication is performed modulo $x^7 - x^0$. One has $ab = \sum_{i=0}^{6}(\sum_{j=0}^{6} a^*_{i-j}b_j)x^i$ where $a^*_{i-j}$ means $a_{i-j}$ for $j \leq i$, and $a_{i-j+7}$ for $j > i$.

The ring structure of an algebra permits one to define ideals. In the algebra $A = FH$ with $H$ the cyclic group of order 7 and $F = GF(2)$, the set $I$ of elements of $A$ that are multiples of $e = 1 + x + x^2 + x^4$ is an ideal that contains 8 polynomials: the zero polynomial and the seven polynomials $ex^i$, $0 \leq i \leq 6$. One verifies indeed that, for $0 \leq i, j \leq 6$, $i \neq j$, the element $ex^i + ex^j$ is equal to some $ex^k$. The set $\hat{I}$ of polynomials of $A$

that are multiples of $\hat{e} = 1 + x^2 + x^3$ is an other ideal that contains $I$ as a subideal. Besides the eight polynomials of $I$, the ideal $\hat{I}$ contains the seven polynomials $\hat{e}x^i$, $0 \leq i \leq 6$, and the polynomial $\sum_{i=0}^{6} x^i$. Further properties of ideals are mentioned in chapter 6.

In the group algebra $A = FH$, the multiplicative identity is the product $(1_F)u$ of $1_F$ (the multiplicative identity in $F$) and $u$ (the multiplicative identity in the group $H$). We thus have three multiplicative identities in this context. By abuse of notation we often denote them by the same symbol 1.

## 1.2  Sequences and spaces of sequences

Let $A$ be a finite nonempty set, let $\mathbb{Z}$ be the set of integers, and let $A^{\mathbb{Z}}$ be the set of mappings

$$a \; : \; \mathbb{Z} \; \to \; A \; : \; i \; \mapsto \; a_i. \tag{1.2}$$

We call such a mapping a *sequence* over $A$. To represent an element $a$ of $A^{\mathbb{Z}}$, one may write

$$a \; = \; (\cdots, a_{-i}, a_{-i+1}, \cdots, a_0, a_1, \cdots, a_j, \cdots). \tag{1.3}$$

However, it may be more useful to represent $a$ as a power series over $A$ in the indeterminate $D$ (which should be considered only as a marker)

$$a \; = \; \sum_{i \in \mathbb{Z}} a_i \, D^i \, . \tag{1.4}$$

When this last notation is used, the sequence $a$ will sometimes be denoted by $a(D)$. With any sequence $a$ over $A$ represented as in (1.4) we associate the sequence $\hat{a} = \sum_{i \in \mathbb{Z}} a_{-i} D^i$, and we call it the reciprocal sequence of $a$.

Suppose that $A$ contains a distinguished element denoted by 0 and called zero. If all $a_i$ are zero, $a$ itself is called the zero sequence. We need some concepts to describe the zero patterns of a sequence.

**Definition 1.4** : For any nonzero $a$ in $A^{\mathbb{Z}}$, the smallest $i$ (if any) for which $a_i$ is nonzero is called the *delay* of $a$. We denote this delay by $\text{del}(a)$.

**Definition 1.5** : For any nonzero $a$ in $A^{\mathbb{Z}}$, the largest $i$ (if any) for which $a_i$ is nonzero is called the *degree* of $a$. We denote this degree by $\deg(a)$.

This concept of degree was already used above in the context of polynomials over finite fields. The integers $\text{del}(a)$ and $\deg(a)$ may be positive, negative or zero. If there is no smallest (resp. largest) integer $i$ for which $a_i$ is nonzero, we say that the delay (resp. the degree) of $a$ is equal to $-\infty$ (resp. $+\infty$).

**Definition 1.6** : For any nonzero $a$ in $A^{\mathbb{Z}}$, the *length* $\ell(a)$ of $a$ is defined by $\ell(a) := \deg(a) - \text{del}(a) + 1$. If $a$ is zero, $\ell(a)$ is defined to be zero.

When $A$ contains a zero, some subsets of $A^{\mathbb{Z}}$ are of particular interest. Let us mention two of them here.

**(i)** The set $A((D))$ of *Laurent series* over $A$. It is defined to be the set of sequences $a$ in which only a finite number of coefficients $a_i$ with a negative index $i$ are nonzero. Any $a$ in $A((D))$ may be represented as $a = \sum_{i=r}^{\infty} a_i D^i$, $a_i \in A$, with $r \leq \text{del}(a)$.

**(ii)** The set $A[D]$ of *polynomials* over $A$. It is defined to be the set of sequences $a$ in which $a_i$ is zero for $i < 0$, and only a finite number of $a_i$ are nonzero.

The algebraic structure of $A((D))$ and of $A[D]$ depends on the structure of $A$ itself. Consider the case where $A$ is a field $F$. Any $a$ in $F((D))$ may be written as $\sum_{i=r}^{\infty} a_i D^i$ with $a_i \in F$ and $r \leq \text{del}(a)$. We can then define in $F((D))$ an addition and a multiplication. The addition satisfies

$$a + b = \sum_{i=r}^{\infty} (a_i + b_i) D^i , \tag{1.5}$$

where $a_i + b_i$ denotes the addition of $a_i$ and $b_i$ in $F$ and where $r$ has to be chosen not larger than the minimum of $\mathrm{del}(a)$ and $\mathrm{del}(b)$. The multiplication satisfies

$$ab = \sum_{i=r}^{\infty} \left( \sum_j a_{i-j} b_j \right) D^i \,, \tag{1.6}$$

where $\sum_j a_{i-j} b_j$ is performed in $F$. Since any $a$ in $F((D))$ contains only a finite number of nonzero coefficients $a_i$ for $i < 0$, all these sums $\sum_j a_{i-j} b_j$ contain only a finite number of nonzero terms. For all $i$, the coefficient of $D^i$ in (1.6) is thus a well defined quantity so that the multiplication $ab$ makes sense. To find the multiplicative inverse $a^{-1}$ of a nonzero $a$ in $F((D))$ we write $a = \sum_{i=r}^{\infty} a_i D^i$, $a_i \in F$, $a_r \neq 0$, thus choosing $r$ to be equal to $\mathrm{del}(a)$. The inverse $b = a^{-1}$ is then obtained by long division, which means that it may be written as $b = \sum_{j=-r}^{\infty} b_j D^j$, $b_j \in F$, where the $b_j$ are obtained as the solution of the infinite triangular system of linear equations

$$b_{-r} a_r = 1$$

$$b_{-r} a_{r+1} + b_{-r+1} a_r = 0$$

$$\vdots \tag{1.7}$$

$$\sum_{j=0}^{s} b_{-r+j} a_{r+s-j} = 0$$

$$\vdots$$

That the components $b_j$, $j \geq -r$, of $b$ are obtainable from (1.7) is obvious from $a_r \neq 0$.

It is now easy to check that $F((D))$ is an infinite Abelian group for the addition and that the set of its nonzero elements form a multiplicative Abelian group. Moreover this multiplication is distributive with respect to the addition. Hence $F((D))$ has the structure of a field that is called the field of Laurent series over $F$.

Let us now consider the set $F[D]$ of polynomials over $F$ in the indeterminate $D$. As a subset of $F((D))$, this set $F[D]$ can be endowed with the same addition (1.5) and multiplication (1.6) and, obviously, it satisfies the four axioms of a ring. The only units it contains are the nonzero elements of $F$. As mentioned above, $F[D]$ is a Euclidean ring, i.e., a ring that admits a division with a quotient and a remainder. Let $a(D) = \sum_{i=0}^{t} a_i D^i$, $a_t \neq 0$, be an element of degree $t$ in $F[D]$. It is called a monic polynomial if $a_t$ is the multiplicative identity of $F$. If $\beta$ is an element of an extension field $F^*$ of $F$ that satisfies $a(\beta) = 0$, this $\beta$ is called a *zero* of $a(D)$ or a root of $a(D) = 0$. In this case one has $a(D) = (D - \beta)\, \hat{a}(D)$, for some polynomial $\hat{a}(D)$ of degree $t - 1$ over $F^*$. A polynomial $a(D)$ of degree $t$ over $F$ has exactly $t$ zeros $\beta_i$, $1 \leq i \leq t$, and it can be written in a unique way (up to ordering) as $a(D) = a_t \prod_{i=1}^{t} (D - \beta_i)$. For $F = GF(p^s)$, all these $\beta_i$ are in finite fields of characteristic $p$ and the smallest field containing all these zeros is called the *splitting field* of $a(D)$.

Let $a(D)$ be an irreducible monic polynomial of degree $t$ over $GF(q)$ such that at least one of its coefficients $a_i$ is in $GF(q)$ and in no proper subfield. In this case the splitting field of $a(D)$ is $GF(q^t)$ and all zeros of $a(D)$ are simple. If one denotes any one of these zeros by $\beta$, the other ones are $\beta^q, \beta^{q^2}, \cdots, \beta^{q^{t-1}}$. These $t$ zeros are said to be *conjugate elements* of $GF(q^t)$ with respect to $GF(q)$.

Given any pair $(a, b)$ of elements of $F[D]$, with $b \neq 0$, we can compute the element $ab^{-1}$ of $F((D))$ obtained by the long division of $a$ by $b$. Not all elements of $F((D))$ are obtainable in this way. The subset of $F((D))$ containing only the elements of the form $ab^{-1}$ with $a, b \in F[D]$, $b \neq 0$, is denoted by $F(D)$. The set $F(D)$ is a subfield of $F((D))$ and it is the smallest field containing $F[D]$. It is called the field of *rational fractions* over $F$ or the quotient field of $F[D]$.

Let $A$ be the set $F^n$ of row $n$-tuples over some field $F$ and let $v = \sum_{i=r}^{\infty} v_i D^i$, $v_i = (v_i^1, \cdots, v_i^n)$, be an element of $F^n((D))$. In the sequel the coefficients $v_i$ of the monomials $D^i$ in $v$ are often called the *words* of $v$.

Defining $v^j := \sum_{i=r}^{\infty} v_i^j D^i$, $1 \leq j \leq n$, we may also represent $v$ as the element $(v^1, \cdots, v^n)$ of $[F((D))]^n$. The notations $F^n((D))$ and $[F((D))]^n$ are thus two ways of looking at the same thing, and in the sequel we shall feel free to use both of them in the same context. Similar remarks are of course true for $F^n[D]$ and $(F[D])^n$.

More generally, let $A$ be the set of $k \times n$ matrices over a field $F$. Any element $G$ of $A((D))$ can be written as a sum $G = \sum_{i=r}^{\infty} G_i D^i$, where the $G_i$ are elements of $A$. Another representation of $G$ is as a $k \times n$ matrix over $F((D))$. In this case, denoting by $g_{ij}(D)$ the element in position $(i, j)$ of $G$, we can write

$$G = \begin{bmatrix} g_{11}(D) & \cdots & g_{1n}(D) \\ g_{21}(D) & \cdots & g_{2n}(D) \\ \vdots & & \vdots \\ g_{k1}(D) & \cdots & g_{kn}(D) \end{bmatrix}.$$

Two other points of view are also useful when one considers such matrices. The first is to consider them as a $k$-tuple of row $n$-tuples over $F((D))$, and the second is to consider them as an $n$-tuple of column $k$-tuples. All these notations are used freely in the sequel. Similar remarks can be made for the elements $G$ of the set $A[D]$ of $k \times n$ polynomial matrices over $F$.

Being a book on convolutional codes, the present book is concerned with properties of $F((D))$-subspaces of $F^n((D))$ with $F$ a finite field. Hence the need of some specific notations. Since the notation $F((D))$ is repeatedly used throughout, we abbreviate it as $\mathcal{F}$. When $\mathcal{F}$ and $F[D]$ are used in the same context, both should be considered as being extensions of the same finite field $F$. The remarks made above about the equivalence of $F^n((D))$ and $[F((D))]^n$ will allow us to denote these two sets by $\mathcal{F}^n$. The $\mathcal{F}$-row space of a $k \times n$ matrix $G$ over $\mathcal{F}$ will be denoted by $E(G)$. The set of all $aG$ where $a$ varies over the set of polynomials of formal degree $r$ over $F^k$ is an $F$-space and it will be denoted by $E_r(G)$. In particular $E_0(G)$ denotes the $F$-space of $G$. These notations are generalized to any subset $\mathcal{V}$ of $\mathcal{F}$: thus $E(\mathcal{V})$ denotes the set of all $v = \sum_i a_i v^{[i]}$, $a_i \in \mathcal{F}$, $v^{[i]} \in \mathcal{V}$, with only a finite number of nonzero $a_i$, and $E_r(\mathcal{V})$ denotes the subset of $E(\mathcal{V})$ obtained when the $a_i$ are restricted to elements of $F[D]$ of formal degree $r$.

Let $G$ be a $k \times n$ matrix of rank $k$ over $\mathcal{F}$ and denote by $d_i$ the delay of its $i^{\text{th}}$ row.

**Theorem 1.7 :** For any $v$ in $\mathcal{F}^n$, not belonging to $E(G)$, there exists an integer $b(v)$ such that for all $a$ in $\mathcal{F}^k$, one has

$$\text{del}(v - aG) \leq b(v).$$

**Proof :** Append $v$ as a $(k+1)^{\text{st}}$ row to $G$. The obtained matrix $\overline{G}$ has rank $k+1$ over $\mathcal{F}$ so that for some $(k+1)$-tuple $Q$ of columns, $\overline{G}^Q$ is a nonsingular $(k+1) \times (k+1)$ matrix. The nonzero determinant $\det \bar{G}^Q$ is not modified if the row $v$ of $\bar{G}$ is replaced by $v - aG$. Since $\text{del}(\det \bar{G}^Q)$ is not less than the sum of the delays $d_i$ of the rows of $\bar{G}$, we have

$$\text{del}(\det \bar{G}^Q) \geq \sum_{i=1}^{k} d_i + \text{del}(v - aG).$$

This means that, for all $a$, $\text{del}(v - aG)$ is bounded from above by $b(v) = \text{del}(\det \bar{G}^Q) - \sum_{i=1}^{k} d_i$. $\square$

We use this property to prove the following theorem.

**Theorem 1.8 :** Given a $k \times n$ matrix $G$ of rank $k$ over $\mathcal{F}$, there exists a nonsingular $k \times k$ matrix $S$ over $\mathcal{F}$ such that $G^* = SG$ can be written as $G^* = \sum_{j=0}^{\infty} G_j^* D^j$, with $\text{rk}(G_0^*) = k$.

**Proof :** Let $g_i$ denote the $i^{\text{th}}$ row of $G$, let $d_i$ denote $\text{del}(g_i)$, and let $G^*$ be the matrix having $g_i^* := D^{-d_i} g_i$ as $i^{\text{th}}$ row. Write $G^* = \sum_{j=0}^{\infty} G_j^* D^j$ and denote by $G^{[i]} = \sum_{j=r}^{\infty} G_j^{[i]} D^j$ the matrix of the first $i$ rows of $G^*$, $1 \leq i \leq k$. If $\text{rk}(G_0^*) \leq k - 1$, let $i$ be the smallest integer such that $\text{rk}(G_0^{[i]}) = i - 1$, let $\Delta(i)$ be the maximum value of $\text{del}(g_i^* - a_{i-1} G^{[i-1]})$ for

$a_{i-1}$ in $\mathcal{F}^{i-1}$, and let $\gamma_i$ be $D^{-\Delta(i)}(g_i^* - a_{i-1}^* G^{[i-1]})$ where $a_{i-1}^*$ "achieves" $\Delta(i)$. Replace then $g_i^*$ by $\gamma_i$ in $G^*$. The new $G^*$ satisfies $\mathrm{rk}(G_0^{[i]}) = i$. If it does not satisfy $\mathrm{rk}(G_0^*) = k$ the procedure is iterated and, in at most $k - 1$ steps, one obtains a matrix $G^*$ satisfying $\mathrm{rk}(G_0^*) = k$. Since all these transformations can be expressed in matrix form, the existence of $S$ is proved. Moreover $\mathrm{rk}(G_0^*) = k$ implies $\mathrm{rk}(G^*) = k$, so that $S$ has to be a nonsingular matrix. $\square$

Let $\mathcal{V}$ be an infinite collection of elements $v^{[i]}$, $i = 0, 1, 2, \cdots$, in $\mathcal{F}^n$, where the $v^{[i]}$ do not need to be all different. In general the sum $\sum_{i=0}^{\infty} v^{[i]}$ does not make sense; however, in some cases it does. To make this explicit we write $v^{[i]} = \sum_j v_j^{[i]} D^j$ with $v_j^{[i]}$ in $F^n$. Since the coefficient of $D^j$ in $\sum_{i=0}^{\infty} v^{[i]}$ is $\sum_{i=0}^{\infty} v_j^{[i]}$, it is well defined if and only if the number of nonzero $v_j^{[i]}$, $i \geq 0$, is finite. Thus $\sum_{i=0}^{\infty} v^{[i]}$ makes sense if and only if for any $j$ the number of nonzero $v_j^{[i]}$ is finite.

**Definition 1.9 :** A collection $\mathcal{V}$ of elements $v^{[i]}$, $i = 0, 1, 2, \cdots$, in $\mathcal{F}^n$ is said to be *progressive* if, for every integer $r$, the number of nonzero $v^{[i]}$ in $\mathcal{V}$ satisfying $\mathrm{del}(v^{[i]}) \leq r$ is finite.

For any sum of elements in a progressive collection $\mathcal{V}$ the number of elements of $F^n$ to be added to compute the coefficient of any $D^j$ is finite even if the number of elements involved in the sum is infinite. Any sum over a progressive collection thus makes sense. Conversely, any collection $\mathcal{V}$ of $v^{[i]} \in \mathcal{F}^n$, such that $\sum_{i=0}^{\infty} v^{[i]}$ makes sense and all nonzero $v^{[i]}$ satisfy $\mathrm{del}\ v^{[i]} \geq r_0$ for some $r_0$ in $\mathbb{Z}$, has to be a progressive collection. The $\mathcal{F}$-space $E(\mathcal{V})$ was defined above to be the set of all sums $\sum_i a_i v_i$, $a_i \in \mathcal{F}, /, v_i \in \mathcal{V}$, with a finite number of nonzero $a_i$. However the following theorem shows that any infinite sum of elements in a progressive collection $\mathcal{V}$ is also in $E(\mathcal{V})$.

**Theorem 1.10 :** For any progressive collection $\mathcal{V}$ of elements $v^{[i]}$, $i = 0, 1, 2, \cdots$ in $\mathcal{F}^n$, the sum $v = \sum_{i=0}^{\infty} v^{[i]}$ is in $E(\mathcal{V})$.

**Proof :** Let $k$ be $\dim_{\mathcal{F}} E(\mathcal{V})$. From theorem 1.8, there exists a $k \times n$ basis $G = \sum_{i=r}^{\infty} G_j D^j$ of $E(\mathcal{V})$ such that $\text{rk}(G_0) = k$. Denote the $s^{\text{th}}$ row of $G$ by $\gamma_s$ and expand $v^{[i]}$ as $\sum_{s=1}^{k} b_{is} \gamma_s$, $b_{is} \in \mathcal{F}$. This leads to

$$v = \sum_{i=r}^{\infty} \sum_{s=1}^{k} b_{is}\, \gamma_s. \tag{1.8}$$

From $\text{rk}(G_0) = k$, one has

$$\text{del } b_{is} \geq \text{del } v^{[i]} \; ; \quad i = 0, 1, 2, \cdots, \; 1 \leq s \leq k \,.$$

It follows that the collection $\mathcal{B}$ of all $b_{is}$ contains at most $k$ times as many elements with delay at most $r$, as the collection $\mathcal{V}$. Hence, since $\mathcal{V}$ is progressive, so is $\mathcal{B}$ and any sum over $\mathcal{B}$ makes sense. We may thus define $b_s := \sum_{i=0}^{\infty} b_{is}$ and express $v$ as

$$v = \sum_{s=1}^{k} b_s\, \gamma_s,$$

which shows that $v$ is in $E(\mathcal{V})$ since it is obtained as a sum over $E(\mathcal{V})$ with a finite number of nonzero coefficients. $\square$

Consider some arbitrary subset $B$ of $\mathcal{F}^n$ and define $C(B)$ to be the set of all sums

$$w = \sum_{i=0}^{\infty} a_i v^{[i]}; \; a_i \in F, \; v^{[i]} \in B \,,$$

where $(v^{[0]}, v^{[1]}, v^{[2]}, \cdots)$ is a progressive collection. Clearly $C(B)$ is an $F$-subspace of $\mathcal{F}^n$, since it contains all finite sums $\sum_j b_j w^j$, $b_j \in F$, $w^j \in C(B)$. Is it also an $\mathcal{F}$-subspace of $\mathcal{F}^n$? To answer this question, we need to introduce a notation. We denote by $C(B)D^r$ the set of sequences $vD^r$ with $v$ in $C(B)$.

**Theorem 1.11 :** The $F$-subspace $C(B)$ of $\mathcal{F}^n$ is an $\mathcal{F}$-space if and only if one has $C(B)D = C(B)$.

**Proof :** The *only if* part of the theorem is trivial. To prove the *if* part of the theorem, we prove that

$$E(B) \;=\; C(B) \tag{1.9}$$

is true if $C(B)D = C(B)$. By theorem 1.10, we have

$$E(B) \;\supseteq\; C(B). \tag{1.10}$$

To prove

$$C(B) \;\supseteq\; E(B), \tag{1.11}$$

we show that any $w$ in $E(B)$ can be written as a sum over a progressive collection in $B$. Let $k$ $(\leq n)$ be the $\mathcal{F}$-dimension of $E(B)$. By lemma 1.1 there exist $k$ elements $\gamma_1, \cdots, \gamma_k$ in $B$ that are a basis of the $\mathcal{F}$-space $E(B)$ so that any $w$ in $E(B)$ can be written as $w = \sum_{i=1}^{k} b_i \gamma_i$, with $b_i = \sum_{j=r(i)}^{\infty} b_{ij} D^j \in \mathcal{F}$. Hence we can write $b_i \gamma_i = \sum_{j=r(i)}^{\infty} b_{ij} D^j \gamma_i$, with $b_{ij} \in F$ and $r(i) \in \mathbb{Z}$. The collection of $D^j \gamma_i$, with $j = r(i), r(i)+1, r(i)+2, \cdots$, is progressive. Hence the sequences $b_i \gamma_i$ belong to $C(B)$, and so does their (finite) sum $w$, which proves (1.11). Together with (1.10), this proves (1.9) so that $C(B)$ is an $\mathcal{F}$-space, namely $E(B)$. $\square$

## 1.3 Comments

The material presented in section 1.1 is standard background for which basic references are [16, 66, 69]. Most of the books on coding theory contain at least an introduction to these topics. Section 1.2 is more specialized. Part of [35] is concerned with similar matters.

Reference [11] is a nice introduction to the mathematical tools that may be useful to the coding theorist. Beside the references given above and in the next chapters, we would also like to mention [10, 17, 21, 84, 98].

# Chapter 2

# Convolutional encoders

Assume that some information is represented by a sequence of *symbols* $a_i$, $i \in \mathbb{Z}$, taken from a finite alphabet $F$, and that this sequence of symbols is transmitted to a receiver through a certain medium called a *channel*. If this channel is noisy (and to some extent all channels are noisy) the received symbols will be different from the transmitted ones, possibly to the point of being unrecognizable. To improve this situation one can use an encoding scheme that adds redundancy to the information and makes the receiver able to recover at least partially the transmitted sequence from the received one. Information transmission using such a scheme is represented in figure 2.1. The sequence $a$ of symbols $a_i$, $i \in \mathbb{Z}$, produced by a source is called the information sequence. It is divided into $k$-tuples $a_t^* = (a_{tk}, \cdots, a_{(t+1)k-1})$, $t \in \mathbb{Z}$, of symbols called information $k$-tuples. The $k$-tuples $a_t^*$ are used as successive inputs to a machine $\mathcal{E}$ called an encoder. Whenever $\mathcal{E}$ receives a $k$-tuple $a_t^*$ over $F$, it produces an $n$-tuple $v_t^* = (v_{tn}, \cdots, v_{(t+1)n-1})$, $(n \geq k)$, of symbols $v_i$, $i \in \mathbb{Z}$, over the same alphabet $F$.[1] These $n$-tuples $v_t^*$ are often called the *words* produced by the encoder $\mathcal{E}$. The number $R = k/n$ is called the *rate* of the encoding

---

[1] It is possible to use encoders in which the input and output alphabets are different. Such encoders are not considered in this book.

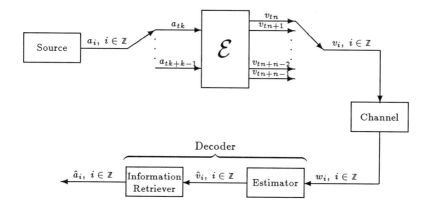

**Figure 2.1** : Transmission of encoded information.

operation performed by $\mathcal{E}$, and the sequence $v$ of the symbols $v_i$ is called an encoded sequence. This encoded sequence is transmitted over the channel and received as a sequence $w$ of symbols $w_i$ that are in some alphabet $F^*$ possibly different from $F$. The receiver has a *decoder* at disposal, to guess which information sequence $a$ the received sequence $w$ originates from. This guess is obtained by a two step operation. A first machine called the *estimator* obtains from $w$ an estimate $\hat{v}$ of the transmitted sequence $v$, and a second machine called the *information retriever* obtains from $\hat{v}$ an estimate $\hat{a}$ of $a$. In the next chapter we shall discuss which arguments can be used by the estimator to find from $w$ the estimate $\hat{v}$ of $v$.

Let us go back to the encoder $\mathcal{E}$. If $\mathcal{E}$ is a memoryless machine, i.e., if the $n$-tuple $v_t^*$ is a function only of the $k$-tuple $a_t^*$, it is called a *block* encoder and the set of all $n$-tuples that it can produce is called the *block code* generated by $\mathcal{E}$. For obvious reasons different information $k$-tuples should be encoded by a block encoder into different $n$-tuples. In this book we study the class of encoders called convolutional encoders. These encoders have a memory. The $n$-tuple $v_t^*$ produced by such an encoder is not only a function of the information $k$-tuple $a_t^*$ but also of some $k$-tuples $a_s^*$, $s < t$, produced by the source before the $k$-tuple $a_t^*$. Convolutional encoders are defined in section 2.1. Two specific classes of convolutional encoders, the minimal encoders and the basic encoders, are considered in sections 2.2 and 2.3 respectively. The encoders of some codes easily derived from other codes are discussed in section 2.4.

## 2.1    General properties of encoders of convolutional codes

A detailed discussion of the encoding procedures is difficult when no structure is given to the alphabet $F$ handled by the encoder. As is usual in coding theory we assume that $F$ can be endowed with the structure of a finite field. As a consequence the order of $F$ has to be a prime power. The advantage is that it is now possible to make use of powerful tools to define or to analyze codes and encoders. Suppose for example that a $k$-tuple $a$ represented as a row $k$-tuple over the finite field $F$ is presented as input to a block encoder $\mathcal{E}$ and that $\mathcal{E}$ delivers as output the $n$-tuple $v = aG$, with $G$ a $k \times n$ matrix of rank $k$ over $F$. In this case, the block encoder $\mathcal{E}$ is called a linear block encoder and the set of words $v$ that are possible outputs of $\mathcal{E}$ is called a linear block code. A linear block encoder may be realized as a memoryless (or combinatorial) linear circuit over $F$ with $k$ inputs and $n$ outputs that contains only adders and multipliers by fixed elements of $F$. In place of using only one $k$-tuple $a$ as input to $\mathcal{E}$, let us consider now an arbitrary sequence $a = \sum_{i=r}^{\infty} a_i D^i$ of $k$-tuples $a_i$ over $F$, "starting" at some arbitrary time unit $r$. This means that for $i < r$ all $a_i$ are zero. When this sequence is presented as input to a linear block encoder $\mathcal{E}$, the output of $\mathcal{E}$ is a sequence $v = \sum_{i=r}^{\infty} v_i D^i$ of $n$-tuples $v_i$ over $F$. This sequence satisfies $v = aG$ and its words $v_i$ satisfy $v_i = a_i G$. The input $a$ to the encoder is an element of $\mathcal{F}^k$ and the output $v$ is an element of $\mathcal{F}^n$, with the notation $\mathcal{F}$ as defined in chapter 1. However, the mapping of $\mathcal{F}^k$ into $\mathcal{F}^n$ realized by $G$ is a very particular one since the entries of $G$ are in the alphabet $F$ and not in $\mathcal{F}$. This suggests the following generalization.

**Definition 2.1 :** An encoder $\mathcal{E}$ is called a $k \times n$ *convolutional encoder* over $F$ if the mapping $\mathcal{F}^k \rightarrow \mathcal{F}^n : a \mapsto v$ realized by $\mathcal{E}$ can be represented by $v = aG$, where $G$ is a $k \times n$ matrix of rank $k$ with entries in the subset $F[D]$ of $\mathcal{F}$.

A $k \times n$ convolutional encoder is sketched in figure 2.2. The information $a \in \mathcal{F}^k$ is represented as a $k$-tuple of elements $a^j = \sum_{i=r}^{\infty} a_i^j D^i$, $a_i^j \in F$, $1 \leq j \leq k$, of $\mathcal{F}$, where $r$ denotes the arbitrary initial time unit of the information transmission. At the output of the $s^{\text{th}}$ delay element of the $j^{\text{th}}$ shift register, the $j^{\text{th}}$ input $a^j$ appears with a delay of $s$ time units and it can thus be represented by $D^s a^j$. The encoded sequence $v = aG$ is an element of $\mathcal{F}^n$, and we represent it as $v = \sum_{t=r}^{\infty} v_t D^t$, $v_t \in F^n$.

Let us denote by $m(j)$ the degree of the $j^{\text{th}}$ row of $G$ considered as a polynomial over $F^n$. For any $j$ the number $m(j)$ indicates how many information symbols $a_i^j$ from the past have to remain available at time unit $t$ to compute the new $n$-tuple $v_t$. The condition of definition 2.1 that all entries of $G$ are polynomials thus guarantees that, at any time unit $t$, only a finite number of past informations $a_i^j$ must remain available.

Since the mapping realized by the convolutional encoder $\mathcal{E}$ is specified as soon as $G$ is given, it is convenient to call $G$ itself a convolutional encoder.

**Definitions 2.2 :** An $(n, k)$ *convolutional code* $C$ over the finite field $F$ is the $\mathcal{F}$-row space of a $k \times n$ convolutional encoder $G$. The parameter $n$ is called the *length* of $C$ and the parameter $k$ is called its *dimension*. The ratio $R = k/n$ is called the *rate* of the encoder $G$ and of the code $C$.

The encoder $G$ is said to generate $C$ as an $\mathcal{F}$-space, and we shall use

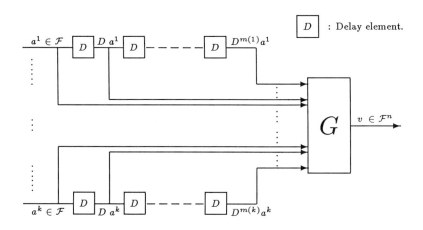

**Figure 2.2** : A $k \times n$ convolutional encoder.

the notation $C = E(G)$. In the particular case considered above where $G$ is an $F$-matrix, $C = E(G)$ is the set of Laurent series $v = \sum_{i=r}^{\infty} v_i D^i$ over $F^n$ that have all their words $v_i$ in the block code $E_0(G)$. In this case we say that the convolutional code $C$ is the Laurent extension of the block code $E_0(G)$.

To specify a convolutional code $C$ by means of one of its encoders $G$ may seem to be quite reasonable. However, $C$ admits many different encoders and to make a choice between them we have to consider in more details the encoding operation

$$v = aG \tag{2.1}$$

mentioned in definition 2.1. The mapping (2.1) of $\mathcal{F}^k$ into $\mathcal{F}^n$ is indeed not as innocent as it may seem to be, especially when $C$ is used to improve the information transmission over a noisy channel. To discuss this point we need some definitions. Let $v = (v^1, \cdots, v^n)$ and $u = (u^1, \cdots, u^n)$ be two arbitrary elements of $F^n$.

**Definitions 2.3 :** The *symbol weight* $sw(v)$ of $v$ is defined to be the number of its nonzero entries $v^i$. The *symbol distance* $sd(v, u)$ (often called the *Hamming* distance) between $v$ and $u$ is defined to be $sw(v - u)$.

These definitions are extended to elements of $\mathcal{F}^n$. Let $v = \sum_{i=r}^{\infty} v_i D^i$, $u = \sum_{i=r}^{\infty} u_i D^i$, with $v_i, u_i \in F^n$, $r \in \mathbb{Z}$, be two arbitrary elements of $\mathcal{F}^n$.

**Definitions 2.4 :** If $v$ contains a finite number of nonzero words $v_i$, its *symbol weight* $sw(v)$ is defined to be $\sum_{i=r}^{\infty} sw(v_i)$. If the number of nonzero words $v_i$ of $v$ is infinite, the symbol weight $sw(v)$ of $v$ is said to be infinite. The *symbol distance* $sd(v, u)$ between $v$ and $u$ is defined to be $sw(v - u)$.

Let us assume now that the encoding performed by $\mathcal{E}$ is convolutional and that the decoder can be divided as in figure 2.1 into an estimator and an information retriever. The different steps represented in this figure can be summarized by

$$a \rightarrow v \rightarrow w \rightarrow \hat{v} \rightarrow \hat{a} , \tag{2.2}$$

where $v = \sum_i v_i D^i$ and $\hat{v} = \sum_i \hat{v}_i D^i$ are the sequences of $C$ given by $v = aG$ and $\hat{v} = \hat{a}G$, for some $k \times n$ convolutional encoder $G$ over $F$. Consider the two central steps $v \rightarrow w \rightarrow \hat{v}$ in (2.2). Since the channel is noisy we may expect that the estimate $\hat{v}$ will not be identical to $v$: for some indices $i$ (hopefully very scarce) the word $\hat{v}_i$ will be different from the word $v_i$. However, what the receiver is really interested in is not $\hat{v}$ but the estimate $\hat{a}$ of $a$. For this reason, the decoding step $\hat{v} \rightarrow \hat{a}$ should be such that the number of erroneous symbols in the estimate $\hat{a}$ of $a$ depends reasonably on the number of erroneous symbols in the estimate $\hat{v}$ of $v$. In particular the situation where a finite number of erroneous symbols in $\hat{v}$ can generate an infinite number of erroneous symbols in the sequence $\hat{a}$ satisfying $\hat{v} = \hat{a}G$ is very unpleasant. To give a more formal treatment of these commonsense remarks, we denote $v - \hat{v}$ and $a - \hat{a}$ by $\bar{v}$ and $\bar{a}$. These two sequences satisfy

$\bar{v} = \bar{a}G$. The unpleasant event mentioned above can occur if and only if the mapping $\bar{a} \mapsto \bar{v} = \bar{a}G$ is such that for some $\bar{a} \in \mathcal{F}^k$ the symbol weight $sw(\bar{a})$ is infinite while the symbol weight $sw(\bar{a}G)$ is finite.

Thus the event that a finite number of errors in the estimate $\hat{v}$ of $v$ leads to an infinite number of errors in the estimate $\hat{a}$ of $a$ is a property of the encoder $G$. It was called *catastrophic error propagation* and an encoder for which this event is possible was called a *catastrophic encoder* [79] (see also [35]). The conditions on $G$ that guarantee

$$sw(\bar{a}) = \infty \Rightarrow sw(\bar{a}G) = \infty \tag{2.3}$$

will be investigated in sections 2.2 and 2.3. In subsection 3.3.4 of the next chapter, we discuss why a catastrophic encoder should be avoided even if the decoding method is not the 2-step method sketched above.

**Definition 2.5** : Two $k \times n$ convolutional encoders $G_1$ and $G_2$ are said to be *equivalent* if they generate the same code: $E(G_1) = E(G_2)$.

**Theorem 2.6** : If $G_1$ and $G_2$ are two equivalent $k \times n$ convolutional encoders, there exists a nonsingular $k \times k$ matrix $A$ over $F(D)$ such that $G_2$ is equal to $AG_1$.

**Proof** : Since $G_1$ and $G_2$ are convolutional encoders, they have entries in $F[D]$ which is a subset of $F(D)$. The existence of the matrix $A$ over $F(D)$ is then a direct application of theorem 1.3. $\square$

## 2.2 Minimal encoders

Let $G$ be a $k \times n$ convolutional encoder over the finite field $F$, and let $m(j)$ be the degree of the $j^{\text{th}}$ row of $G$ considered as a polynomial over $F^n$. When the $k$ integers $m(j)$ satisfy $m(j) \leq m(j+1)$ for $1 \leq j \leq k-1$, we say that the encoder $G$ is *ordered*. Any encoder can be ordered by a trivial permutation of its rows and we assume that all encoders considered in the sequel are ordered if nothing else is mentioned. With any convolutional encoder $G$ we associate the integer $M(G) := \sum_{j=1}^{k} m(j)$ which we call the complexity of $G$. By looking at the complexity of all convolutional encoders that generate the same code $C$, we can now define the complexity of the code $C$ itself.

**Definition 2.7 :** The *complexity* $\mu(C)$ of the convolutional code $C$ is defined to be the minimum value of $M(G)$ over all polynomial encoders $G$ that generate $C$.

It follows from this definition that any encoder $G$ generating $C$ satisfies

$$M(G) \geq \mu(C). \tag{2.4}$$

If $\mu(C)$ is zero, $C$ may be generated by at least one encoder $G$ having all its entries in $F$. This is the particular case mentioned above where $C$ is the Laurent extension of some block code.

**Definition 2.8 :** The convolutional encoder $G$ that generates the convolutional code $C$ is said to be *minimal* if it satisfies (2.4) with equality.

Being defined as encoders achieving the minimum of some parameter, namely $M(G)$, minimal encoders are attractive from a theoretical point of view. Moreover the "natural" implementation of $G$ represented in figure 2.2 needs $M(G)$ memory elements. The algebraic minimality of an encoder thus corresponds to some hardware minimality of the encoding device. As a last characteristic, minimal encoders are immune against catastrophic error propagation. All minimal encoders $G$ will indeed be shown to satisfy (2.3).

This section is divided into three subsections. In the first one we describe an algorithm that constructs, starting from any convolutional encoder $G$, a minimal convolutional encoder of $C = E(G)$. This algorithm is not very practical, and a more efficient algorithm will be given later in section 2.3. However, it gives insight on the properties of a minimal encoder, which is a sufficient reason to present it here. In the second subsection we introduce and discuss the concept of predictable span encoder. This concept was introduced by Forney [35] who showed that it is equivalent to the concept of minimal encoder. In the third subsection, we discuss several other properties of minimal encoders.

## 2.2.1   An algorithm that generates minimal encoders

Let us introduce some notation. If $C$ is an $(n, k)$ convolutional code over $F$ we denote by $L_s(C)$ the $F$-space generated by the polynomial sequences of $C$ that have degree at most $s$. The $\mathcal{F}$-space $E(L_s(C))$ is denoted by $C_s$ and $\dim_{\mathcal{F}}(C_s)$ is denoted by $k(s)$. In the present context, lemmas 1.1 and 1.2 become

**Lemma 2.9 :** There exists a set of $k(s)$ sequences of $L_s(C)$ that form a basis of $C_s$.

**Lemma 2.10 :** To any set of $u$ $(0 \leq u \leq k(s))$ polynomials of $C_s$ that are linearly independent over $\mathcal{F}$ one can append a set of $k(s) - u$ polynomials of $L_s(C)$ to obtain a basis of $C_s$.

Since an $(n, k)$ convolutional code $C$ is generated by $k$ polynomials over $F^n$, one has $C = C_s$ provided $s$ is sufficiently large.

**Definition 2.11 :** The smallest $s$ for which one has $C = C_s$ is called the *span* of $C$. We denote it by $\mathrm{sp}(C)$.

If $G$ is a $k \times n$ ordered convolutional encoder of $C$, one has $\mathrm{sp}(C) \leq m(k)$, with $m(k)$ the degree of the last row of $G$.

We now present an algorithmic procedure that constructs a minimal encoder for a convolutional code $C$ over the finite field $F$. This code is assumed to be specified by some $k \times n$ ordered convolutional encoder $G$.

The first step of this procedure is to draw up the list of the $|F|^{n[m(k)+1]}$ polynomials of $L_{m(k)}(\mathcal{F}^n)$ in the order of nondecreasing degrees, and to erase all polynomials of the list that are not in $E(G)$. (By convention, the degree of the zero polynomial is zero.) To do that, we need a way to verify whether an element $v$ of $F^n[D]$ is in $E(G)$ or not. This can be done if we append $v$ as a $(k+1)^{\text{st}}$ row to $G$. The polynomial $v$ over $F^n$ will be in $E(G)$ if and only if all $(k+1) \times (k+1)$ minors of this new matrix are zero. After the first step of the procedure, one obtains the list $L_{m(k)}(C) = \{g^0 = 0, g^1, g^2, \cdots\}$ which is ordered so as to satisfy $\deg(g^{i-1}) \leq \deg(g^i)$, $1 \leq i < |L_{m(k)}(C)| - 1$.

The second step of the procedure consists first of finding the smallest integer $s$ such that $L_s(C)$ contains at least one nonzero polynomial. Next, let $k(s)$ be the $\mathcal{F}$-dimension of $C_s = E[L_s(C)]$. By lemma 2.9, $C_s$ has a basis consisting of $k(s)$ polynomials of $L_s(C)$. Representing this basis by a $k(s) \times n$ polynomial matrix $G^s$, we can write $C_s = E(G^s)$. If $s$ is equal to $m(k)$, then $G^s$ is a basis of $E[L_{m(k)}(C)] = C$. Otherwise $m(k) - s$ matrices $G^{r+1}$ with $s \leq r \leq m(k) - 1$, are obtained recurrently as follows. For any integer $r$ satisfying $s \leq r \leq m(k)$, let $k(r)$ denote the dimension of the vector space $E[L_r(C)]$ over $\mathcal{F}$. Suppose that, for some integer $r \leq m(k) - 1$, we have constructed a $k(r) \times r$ basis $G^r$ of $C_r = E[L_r(C)]$, with all its rows in $L_r(C)$. From lemma 2.10, and from the obvious inclusion $L_r(C) \subseteq L_{r+1}(C)$, it follows that $k(r+1) - k(r)$ polynomials of $L_{r+1}(C)$ can be appended to $G^r$ to produce a basis of $C_{r+1} = E[L_{r+1}(C)]$. We denote this new matrix by $G^{r+1}$. It is equal to $G^r$ if and only if $k(r+1) = k(r)$ holds. Iterating $m(k) - s$ times the computation of $G^{r+1}$ from $G^r$, with $r = s, s+1, \cdots, m(k) - 1$, we obtain finally a matrix $G^{m(k)}$ which is a basis of $C = E[L_{m(k)}(C)] = E(G)$.

**Theorem 2.12 :** If one has $k(r+1) > k(r)$, the rows that are added to $G^r$ to form $G^{r+1}$ have degree exactly equal to $r + 1$.

**Proof :** By construction these rows are in $L_{r+1}(C)$ but not in $L_r(C)$. $\square$

Before proving that $G^{m(k)}$ is a minimal encoder we give an example of how the foregoing procedure works. Let $G$ be the following $2 \times 4$ matrix over $F[D]$ with $F = GF(2)$:

$$G = \begin{bmatrix} 1 + D & D^2 & D + D^2 & 1 + D + D^2 \\ D + D^2 & 1 & 1 + D & D^2 \end{bmatrix}.$$

Considering $G$ as a matrix over a field ($\mathcal{F}$, for example) containing $F[D]$ as a subring, we see that its rank is equal to 2. Thus $G$ may be used as an encoder of a $(4,2)$ convolutional code $C = E(G)$ over $GF(2)$, and its parameters $m(1)$ and $m(2)$ are both equal to 2. The first step of the procedure described above is to construct the list $L_2(C)$. Appending all elements of $L_2(\mathcal{F}^4)$ as a third row to $G$ and checking the rank of the resulting $3 \times 4$ matrices, one finds that $L_2(C)$ contains 8 polynomials. Here follows the list of these polynomials in the order of increasing degrees:

$$
\begin{array}{llcccc}
g^0 & = & [ \quad 0 & 0 & 0 & 0 \quad ], \\
g^1 & = & [ \quad 1 + D & 1 + D & 1 + D & 1 \quad ], \\
g^2 & = & [ \quad D + D^2 & D + D^2 & D + D^2 & D \quad ], \\
g^3 & = & [ \quad 1 + D^2 & 1 + D^2 & 1 + D^2 & 1 + D \quad ], \\
g^4 & = & [ \quad 1 + D^2 & D & 0 & 1 + D^2 \quad ], \\
g^5 & = & [ \quad 1 + D & D^2 & D + D^2 & 1 + D + D^2 \quad ], \\
g^6 & = & [ \quad 0 & 1 + D + D^2 & 1 + D^2 & D + D^2 \quad ], \\
g^7 & = & [ \quad D + D^2 & 1 & 1 + D & D^2 \quad ].
\end{array}
$$

Applying the second step of the procedure to the list $L_2(C) = \{g^0, \cdots, g^7\}$ one obtains first

$$G^1 = [1 + D \quad 1 + D \quad 1 + D \quad 1].$$

Then it appears that $g^2$ and $g^3$ are in $E(G^1)$, that $g^4$ is the first element of $L_2(C)$ not in $E(G^1)$, and that all elements of $L_2(C)$ are in the row space of the $2 \times 4$ matrix

$$G^2 = \begin{bmatrix} G^1 \\ g^4 \end{bmatrix}.$$

Let us now go back to the general case to prove that the encoder $\Gamma := G^{m(k)}$ obtained from the procedure above is minimal. We need a preliminary lemma. Let $\mu(j)$ denote the degree of the $j^{\text{th}}$ row of the ordered encoder $\Gamma$, let $G$ be any other ordered convolutional encoder of $C = E(\Gamma)$ and let $m(j)$ denote the degree of the $j^{\text{th}}$ row of $G$.

**Lemma 2.13 :** The degrees $\mu(j)$ and $m(j)$ satisfy

$$\mu(j) \leq m(j) ; \ \ 1 \leq j \leq k . \tag{2.5}$$

**Proof :** If $(2.5)$ is not true, let $i$ be the smallest integer for which one has

$$\mu(i) > m(i) . \tag{2.6}$$

By construction, the submatrix $G^{m(i)}$ of $\Gamma$ generates $C_{m(i)}$ as an $\mathcal{F}$-space. On the other hand $(2.6)$ implies that $G^{m(i)}$ contains at most $i-1$ rows so that $\dim_\mathcal{F}[C_{m(i)}]$ is $\leq i-1$. Conversely, since $G$ contains at least $i$ rows of degree $\leq m(i)$, one has $\dim_\mathcal{F}(C_{m(i)}) \geq i$. Hence the contradiction. $\square$

From $(2.5)$ one readily obtains

$$\sum_{j=1}^{k} \mu(j) \leq \sum_{j=1}^{k} m(j) , \tag{2.7}$$

which shows that any convolutional encoder $G$ that generates $E(\Gamma)$ satisfies $M(\Gamma) \leq M(G)$. This proves the following theorem.

**Theorem 2.14 :** The encoder $\Gamma$ produced by the algorithmic procedure described above is a minimal encoder.

**Corollary 2.15 :** If $G$ is another minimal encoder of $C = E(\Gamma)$, then $(2.5)$ is satisfied with equality.
**Proof :** The equality in $(2.5)$, for all $j$, is necessary to have equality in $(2.7)$. $\square$

This corollary implies that with any ordered minimal encoder of a given $(n, k)$ convolutional code $C$ there is associated the same $k$-tuple $\mu = [\mu(1), \cdots, \mu(k)]$ of degrees $\mu(i)$ achieving $\sum_{i=1}^{k} \mu(i) = \mu(C)$.

With any $k \times n$ convolutional encoder $G = \sum_{i=0}^{m(k)} G_i D^i$ over $F$, we associate now two $k \times n$ $F$-matrices. The first one is the matrix $G_0$. The second one is denoted by $G_f$. To specify it we write the $j^{\text{th}}$ row $g_j$ of $G$ as a polynomial over $F^n$ in the form $g_j = \sum_{i=0}^{m(j)} (g_j)_i D^i$, with $(g_j)_i \in F^n$, $(g_j)_{m(j)} \neq 0$. The $F$-matrix $G_f$ is then defined to be

$$G_f = \begin{bmatrix} (g_1)_{m(1)} \\ \vdots \\ (g_j)_{m(j)} \\ \vdots \\ (g_k)_{m(k)} \end{bmatrix}.$$

**Theorem 2.16 :** If $G$ is a minimal $(n, k)$ convolutional encoder over $F$, one has $\text{rk}(G_0) = \text{rk}(G_f) = k$.

**Proof :** If $\text{rk}(G_0) < k$, then, for some integer $r$ in the interval $[1, k]$, one has $(g_r)_0 + \sum_{j=1}^{r-1} a_j(g_j)_0 = 0$ for some elements $a_j$ of $F$. To replace the row $g_r$ of $G$ by $D^{-1}[g_r + \sum_{j=1}^{r-1} a_j g_j]$ does not modify $E(G)$ but makes $M(G)$ smaller. Similarly, if $\text{rk}(G_f) < k$, then, for some integer $r$ in $[1, k]$, one has $(g_r)_{m(r)} + \sum_{j=1}^{r-1} a_j(g_j)_{m(j)} = 0$ for some elements $a_j$ of $F$. To replace the row $g_r$ of $G$ by $g_r + \sum_{j=1}^{r-1} a_j g_j D^{m(r)-m(j)}$ does not modify $E(G)$ but makes $M(G)$ smaller. In both cases this contradicts the hypothesis that $G$ is a minimal encoder of $E(G)$. $\square$

**Definition 2.17 :** Let $v = \sum_{i=r}^{\infty} v_i D^i$ with $v_i \in F^n$, be an element of $\mathcal{F}^n$. The word $v_t$ is called an *initial* word of $v$ if $v_i$ is zero for $i \leq t - 1$. It is called a *final* word of $v$ if $v_i$ is zero for $i \geq t + 1$.

**Definitions 2.18 :** The block code $C^0$ of the initial words of the $(n, k)$

convolutional code $C$ over $F$ is defined to be

$$C^0 = \{v_r \in F^n \mid v = \sum_{j=r}^{\infty} v_j D^j \in C \,;\, r \in \mathbb{Z}\} \,.$$

The block code $C^f$ of the final words of the $(n, k)$ convolutional code $C$ over $F$ is defined to be

$$C^f = \{v_s \in F^n \mid v = \sum_{j=r}^{s} v_j D^j \in C \,;\, r, s \in \mathbb{Z}\} \,.$$

The following theorem gives a characterization of $C^0$.

**Theorem 2.19 :** If $G$ is a minimal $k \times n$ encoder of $C$, then one has $C^0 = E_0(G_0)$.

**Proof :** Write any $v \in C$ as $v = aG$ with $a = \sum_{j=r}^{\infty} a_j D^j$, $a_j \in F^k$, $a_r \neq 0$. Since, from theorem 2.16, $\mathrm{rk}(G_0)$ is equal to $k$, it follows that $a_r G_0$ is the nonzero initial word of $v = aG$. $\square$

A similar characterization of $C^f$ will be given in the next subsection. The proof of the following corollary is omitted.

**Corollary 2.20 :** The $\mathcal{F}$-dimension of $C$ and the $F$-dimension of $C^0$ are equal.

## 2.2.2 Minimal encoders have the predictable span property

Minimal $k \times n$ convolutional encoders $G$ over $F$ were defined above as encoders achieving the complexity of the codes they generate. In this subsection we take another point of view. We consider $G$ as achieving a mapping $\mathcal{F}^k \rightarrow \mathcal{F}^n : a \mapsto v = aG$ and we show that the minimality of $G$ can also be characterized by some properties of this mapping. We shall need the following definitions.

**Definition 2.21 :** The $k \times n$ convolutional encoder $G$ is said to have the *predictable delay* property if any nonzero $a \in \mathcal{F}^k$ satisfies

$$\text{del}(aG) = \text{del}(a) . \tag{2.8}$$

Representing $a \in \mathcal{F}^k$ as a row $k$-tuple $(a^1, \cdots, a^k)$ of elements $a^j = \sum_{i=r}^{\infty} a_i^j D^i$ of $\mathcal{F}$, we denote by $J(a)$ the set of integers $j$ for which $a^j$ is nonzero. Furthermore, we denote by $g_j$ the $j^{\text{th}}$ row of $G$.

**Definition 2.22 :** The encoder $G$ is said to have the *predictable degree* property if it satisfies

**(i)** for any nonzero $a \in \mathcal{F}$ of finite length

$$\deg(aG) = \max_{j \in J(a)} (\deg a^j + \deg g_j), \tag{2.9}$$

**(ii)** for any $a \in \mathcal{F}$

$$\ell(a) = \infty \;\Rightarrow\; \ell(aG) = \infty. \tag{2.10}$$

Obviously (2.10) is just another way to write (2.3) (see definition 1.6).

**Definition 2.23 :** The encoder $G$ is said to have the *predictable span* property if it satisfies (2.8), (2.9) and (2.10).

We prove now the main theorem of this subsection.

**Theorem 2.24 :** A $k \times n$ convolutional encoder $G$ is minimal if and only if it has the predictable span property.

**Proof :** We assume first that $G$ is minimal and we prove that it has the predictable span property. The statements (2.8) and (2.9) are easy consequences of theorem 2.16. Let us prove statement (2.10). We denote the $j^{\text{th}}$ row of $G$ by $g_j = \sum_{i=0}^{m(j)} (g_j)_i D^i$, $(g_j)_i \in F^n$, and, with any $a = (a^1, \cdots, a^k)$ in $\mathcal{F}^k$ satisfying $\ell(a) = \infty$, we associate the sequence

$$v_0 = \sum_{j \in J_{\infty}} a^j g_j \tag{2.11}$$

where $J_\infty$ denotes the set of $j$ such that $\ell(a^j) = \infty$. We have to prove that if $G$ is minimal and if $J_\infty$ is nonempty, then $\ell(aG) = \infty$, which is of course equivalent to $\ell(v_0) = \infty$. Assume that $\ell(v_0)$ is finite and denote by $h$ the maximum of the integers $j$ in $J_\infty$. Denote $\mathrm{del}(v_0)$ by $r$ and $\deg(v_0)$ by $s$ to write $v_0 = \sum_{i=r}^{s}(v_0)_i D^i$, $(v_0)_i \in F^n$. Compute then a sequence $w$ as follows. If the length $s - r + 1$ of $v_0$ is $< \ell(g_h)$, define $w := v_0$. Otherwise it follows from (2.11) and from $\mathrm{rk}\,(G_0) = k$ that the initial nonzero word $(v_0)_r$ of $v_0$ can be written as $(v_0)_r = \sum_{j \in J_\infty} a_r^j (g_j)_0$, where $a_r^j \in F$ is the coefficient of $D^r$ in $a^j$. We define then the sequence

$$v_1 := v_0 - D^r \sum_{j \in J_\infty} a_r^j g_j.$$

It satisfies clearly $\ell(v_1) \leq \ell(v_0) - 1$. We iterate this construction of $v_t$ from $v_{t-1}$ for $t = 1, 2, \cdots$, as long as

$$\ell(v_t) \geq \ell(g_h) \tag{2.12}$$

remains satisfied. Since $\ell(v_t) < \ell(v_{t-1})$ holds, we eventually obtain a sequence $v_t$ that does not satisfy (2.12). We call it $w$. By construction, $w$ satisfies

$$\ell(w) < \ell(g_h)\,. \tag{2.13}$$

Obviously, during the computation of $w$ from $v_0$, only a finite number of coefficients were modified in any of the sequences $a^j$ appearing in (2.11). As a consequence $w$ can be written as

$$w = \sum_{j \in J_\infty} \hat{a}^j g_j\,, \tag{2.14}$$

where all sequences $\hat{a}^j$ have yet infinite length. Moreover, it follows from (2.14) that $g_h$ is given by

$$g_h = (\hat{a}^h)^{-1}[w - \sum_{j \in J_\infty,\, j \neq h} \hat{a}^j g_j]\,.$$

Thus if we replace $g_h$ by $w$ in $G$, we do not modify the space generated by $G$ but we obtain a smaller complexity. This proves that $G$ would not be minimal. Hence the contradiction proving that $\ell(aG)$ is infinite.

Conversely, let us prove now that if $G$ has the predictable span property, then it is minimal. If it is not minimal, it follows from theorem 1.3 that there exists a nonsingular $k \times k$ matrix $T$ over $F(D)$, the field of rational fractions over $F$ that contains $F[D]$ as a subring, such that $G' = TG$ is minimal. Let $t_{ij}$ be the $(i, j)$ entry of $T$, and denote by $g'_i$ and $g_i$ the $i^{\text{th}}$ row of $G'$ and $G$ respectively. From the predictable span property of $G$, one has

$$\ell(g'_i) \geq \max[\ell(t_{ij}) + \ell(g_j)] - 1 \tag{2.15}$$

where the maximum is over all $j$ such that $t_{ij}$ is nonzero. Since there is at least one nonzero $t_{ij}$ in each row and each column of $T$, (2.15) implies

$$\sum_{i=1}^{k} \ell(g'_i) \geq \sum_{j=1}^{k} \ell(g_j)$$

It follows that one has $\mu(C) \geq M(G)$, which contradicts the assumption that $G$ is not minimal. $\square$

A consequence of theorem 2.24 is that any minimal encoder $G$ satisfies (2.10) or equivalently (2.3). In explicit words, the set of minimal encoders is a subset of the set of noncatastrophic encoders.

### 2.2.3   Other properties of minimal encoders

Let $G$ be a minimal encoder with $k_s$ rows of degree $m_s, 1 \leq s \leq S$. These parameters satisfy $\sum_{s=1}^{S} k_s = k$ and $\sum_{s=1}^{S} m_s k_s = \mu(C)$ with $C = E(G)$. Let $A_s$ be any $k_s \times k_s$ nonsingular matrix over $F$ and, for $r < s$, let $T_{sr}$ be any $k_s \times k_r$ matrix over $F[D]$ the nonzero elements of which have degree at most $m_s - m_r$. Then define $T$ to be the matrix

$$
T = \begin{bmatrix}
A_1 & 0 & 0 & \cdots & 0 \\
T_{21} & A_2 & 0 & \cdots & 0 \\
T_{31} & T_{32} & A_3 & & \vdots \\
\vdots & \vdots & \vdots & \ddots & \\
T_{s1} & T_{s2} & T_{s3} & & A_s
\end{bmatrix}.
\tag{2.16}
$$

**Corollary 2.25 :** The matrix $G_1$ is a minimal encoder of $C$ if and only if it can be written as $G_1 = TG$, where $T$ has the form (2.16).

**Proof :** If $G_1$ equals $TG$, $G_1$ is clearly minimal. Now assume that $G$ and $G_1$ are two minimal encoders of $C$. Since $E(G) = E(G_1)$, it follows from theorem 1.3 that there exists a $k \times k$ matrix $T$ over $F(D)$ such that $G_1$ is equal to $TG$. Being minimal, $G$ satisfies (2.8), (2.9) and (2.10). It follows from (2.8) that the delay of all entries of $T$ is zero, from (2.10) that $T$ is a matrix over the subset $F[D]$ of $F(D)$ and from (2.9) that the matrices $A_s$ and $T_{rs}$ have to satisfy the constraints above. $\square$

**Definition 2.26 :** The convolutional encoder $G^*$ is said to be a *subencoder* of the encoder $G$ if all rows of $G^*$ are rows of $G$.

A simple application of theorem 2.24 leads to

**Theorem 2.27 :** Any subencoder of a minimal encoder is minimal.

**Proof :** The predictable span property is preserved for all subencoders of a minimal encoder. $\square$

Let now $C$ be an $(n, k)$ convolutional code over $F$ and let $C^* \subset C$ be an $(n, k^*)$ convolutional code with $k^* < k$. In general it is not possible to construct a pair $(G, G^*)$ of minimal encoders satisfying $E(G) = C$ and $E(G^*) = C^*$ and such that $G^*$ is a subencoder of $G$. As an example let $F$

be $GF(2)$ and consider the two minimal encoders

$$G^* = \begin{bmatrix} 1 & 1+D & 1+D \end{bmatrix}, \quad G = \begin{bmatrix} 1 & 1 & 1 \\ 0 & 1 & 1 \end{bmatrix}.$$

Obviously $C^* = E(G^*)$ is contained in $C = E(G)$ but $\mu(C^*) = 1$ and $\mu(C) = 0$ preclude that any minimal encoder of $C$ contain a minimal encoder of $C^*$ as a subencoder.

**Theorem 2.28 :** The $(n, k)$ convolutional code $C$ is the Laurent extension of a block code if and only if all words of $C$ are initial words of some sequences of $C$.

**Proof :** Suppose that all words of $C$ are words of the block code $C^0$ of the initial words of $C$. Define $\overline{C}$ to be the $\mathcal{F}$-space of a matrix $G$ over $F$ for which $C^0$ is equal to $E_0(G)$. By corollary 2.20, $\overline{C}$ and $C$ have the same dimension. Since $\overline{C}$ contains $C$, one has $\overline{C} = C$. The converse property is immediate. $\square$

Let now $G$ be a $k \times n$ minimal encoder, let $C$ be $E(G)$ and let $G_f$ be as defined after corollary 2.15.

**Theorem 2.29 :** The block code $C^f$ of definition 2.18 satisfies $C^f = E_0(G_f)$.

**Proof.** Let $v = aG$ be a nonzero sequence of finite length in $C$, i.e., $v = \sum_{j=r}^{s} v_j D^j$ with $v_j \in F^n$, $v_s \neq 0$. Theorem 2.24 implies that $a$ itself has finite length. The proof is then a consequence of the property $\mathrm{rk}(G_f) = k$, which is proved in theorem 2.16. $\square$

## 2.3   Basic encoders: an intermediate step to obtain minimal encoders

In section 2.2 an algorithm was described that constructs a minimal encoder generating the same code as some given nonminimal encoder. This algorithm clarifies some algebraic properties of minimal encoders, but it is too slow to be of any practical value. Another algorithm will be presented in subsection 2.3.2. That one is more efficient and it puts into light some other properties of minimal encoders. Starting from an arbitrary (maybe nonminimal) encoder $G'$, it produces an encoder $G$ satisfying $E(G') = E(G)$ and also (2.8) and (2.10). As a consequence, $G$ satisfies (2.3) and is thus a noncatastrophic encoder. Modifications of reasonable complexity then produce from $G$ another encoder of $E(G')$ that besides satisfying (2.8) and (2.10) also satisfies (2.9). The first step of this algorithm appears as a generalization of Euclid's well known algorithm that computes the greatest common divisor of two polynomials and is recalled in subsection 2.3.1.

### 2.3.1   Euclid's algorithm

Consider the Euclidean ring $F[D]$ of polynomials in the indeterminate $D$ with coefficients in the field $F$. A greatest common divisor (or g.c.d.) of two elements $b_1$ and $b_2$ of $F[D]$ is a polynomial of the highest possible degree that divides $b_1$ and $b_2$. Two different g.c.d. of the same pair of polynomials differ only by a multiplicative nonzero factor of $F$. To obtain a g.c.d. of two nonzero polynomials $b_1$ and $b_2$, one uses Euclid's algorithm. With deg $b_1 \geq$ deg $b_2$ we can write

$$
\begin{aligned}
b_1 &= q_1 b_2 + b_3 , \\
b_2 &= q_2 b_3 + b_4 , \\
&\ \vdots \\
b_{r-2} &= q_{r-2} b_{r-1} + b_r , \\
b_{r-1} &= q_{r-1} b_r .
\end{aligned}
\tag{2.17}
$$

In (2.17), $q_{i-1}$ is the quotient and $b_{i+1}$ is the remainder of the division of $b_{i-1}$ by $b_i$. Thus one has deg $b_{i+1} <$ deg $b_i$, and $r$ is the smallest integer such that $b_{r+1}$ is zero. Obviously $b_r$ divides $b_{r-1}$ and $b_{r-2} - q_{r-2}b_{r-1}$. Hence it also divides $b_{r-2}$. By iteration of this remark it appears that $b_r$

divides all polynomials $b_i$, with $r - 1 \geq i \geq 1$, and is therefore a common
divisor of $b_1$ and $b_2$. Conversely any common divisor $b$ of $b_1$ and $b_2$ divides
$b_1 - q_1 b_2 = b_3$. By iteration, we see that $b$ is a divisor of all $b_i$, $1 \leq i \leq r$.
These remarks show that $b_r$ is a g.c.d. of $b_1$ and $b_2$, which we denote by
$b_r = \text{g.c.d.}(b_1, b_2)$. Since any common divisor $b$ of $b_1$ and $b_2$ divides $b_r$,
the set of greatest common divisors of $b_1$ and $b_2$ is the set of divisors of $b_r$
having maximal degree, i.e., the set of polynomials $\beta b_r$, with $\beta$ any nonzero
element of $F$. One polynomial in this set is monic. This monic polynomial
is usually called *the* g.c.d. of $b_1$ and $b_2$.

Going back to (2.17) we can use its first $r - 2$ equations to obtain

$$
\begin{aligned}
b_r &= b_{r-2} - q_{r-2} b_{r-1} , \\
b_{r-1} &= b_{r-3} - q_{r-3} b_{r-2} , \\
&\vdots \\
b_3 &= b_1 - q_2 b_2 .
\end{aligned}
\tag{2.18}
$$

In the first of these equations we use the expression of $b_{r-1}$ given by the
second equation, then the expression of $b_{r-2}$ given by the third equation,
and so on, up to

$$
b_r = Q_1 b_1 + Q_2 b_2 , \tag{2.19}
$$

where $Q_1$ and $Q_2$ are elements of $F[D]$ that are relatively prime and have
degree at most equal to deg $b_1 - 1$ [71]. Dividing both sides of (2.19) by $b_r$
we obtain

$$
1 = Q_1 \beta_1 + Q_2 \beta_2 , \tag{2.20}
$$

with $\beta_i = b_i / b_r$, $i = 1, 2$. The obvious equality

$$
0 = -\beta_2 b_1 + \beta_1 b_2 \tag{2.21}
$$

is then coupled to (2.13). This leads to

$$
(b_r, 0) = (b_1, b_2) Q \tag{2.22}
$$

with

$$Q = \begin{pmatrix} Q_1 & -\beta_2 \\ Q_2 & \beta_1 \end{pmatrix}.$$

It follows from (2.20) that this matrix $Q$ is unimodular: $\det Q \in F$, $\det Q \neq 0$.

Suppose now that we have $n$ elements $b_1, b_2, \cdots, b_n$ of $F[D]$. A g.c.d. of these $n$ polynomials $b_i$ is a polynomial of the highest possible degree that divides each of them. To compute such a g.c.d. we make a repeated use of Euclid's algorithm. Starting with $c_1 := b_1$ we compute successively

$$
\begin{aligned}
c_2 &= \text{g.c.d.}(c_1, b_2), \\
c_3 &= \text{g.c.d.}(c_2, b_3), \\
&\vdots \\
c_n &= \text{g.c.d.}(c_{n-1}, b_n).
\end{aligned}
\tag{2.23}
$$

Obviously $c_n$ is a common divisor of the $n$ polynomials $b_i$. Conversely any common divisor of the polynomials $b_i$ has to be a divisor of all polynomials $c_i$. Hence the polynomial $c_n$ is a g.c.d. of the polynomials $b_i$, which we denote by $c_n = \text{g.c.d.}(b_1, \cdots, b_n)$. The set of g.c.d.'s of the polynomials $b_i$, $1 \leq i \leq n$, is the set of polynomials $\gamma c_n$ with $\gamma$ any nonzero element of $F$. The unique monic polynomial in this set is usually called *the* g.c.d. of the $n$ polynomials $b_i$.

With the computation of g.c.d.$(b_1, b_2)$, we have associated the equations (2.19) and (2.22). Similarly, with the computation of $c_i = \text{g.c.d.}(c_{i-1}, b_i)$, we associate the equations

$$c_i = Q_1^{(i)} c_{i-1} + Q_2^{(i)} b_i, \quad (c_i, 0) = (c_{i-1}, b_i) Q^{(i)}, \tag{2.24}$$

where the polynomial matrix $Q^{(i)}$ is given by

$$Q^{(i)} = \begin{pmatrix} Q_1^{(i)} & -\beta_i \\ Q_2^{(i)} & \gamma_{i-1} \end{pmatrix} ; \quad i = 1, \cdots, t-1$$

with

$$\beta_i = b_i/c_i, \quad \gamma_{i-1} = c_{i-1}/c_i. \tag{2.25}$$

Dividing the two sides of the first equation of (2.24) by $c_i$ we obtain $1 = Q_1^{(i)}\gamma_{i-1} + Q_2^{(i)}\beta_i$. This makes clear that all matrices $Q^{(i)}$ are unimodular. Define $\overline{Q}^{(i)}$ to be the *direct sum* of $Q^{(i)}$ and of the $(n-2) \times (n-2)$ identity matrix $I_{n-2}$, i.e.,

$$\overline{Q}^{(i)} = \begin{pmatrix} Q^{(i)} & 0 \\ 0^T & I_{n-2} \end{pmatrix},$$

with 0, the $2 \times (n-2)$ zero matrix and $0^T$ the transpose of 0. Define $T^{(2)} = I_n$ and, for $i \geq 3$, define $T^{(i)}$ to be the $n \times n$ permutation matrix such that the $n$-tuple $(b_1, b_2, b_3, b_4, \cdots, b_{i-1}, b_i, b_{i+1}, \cdots, b_n)T^{(i)}$ is given by $(b_1, b_i, b_3, b_4, \cdots, b_{i-1}, b_2, b_{i+1}, \cdots, b_n)$. It is now clear that one has

$$(c_n, 0, 0, \cdots, 0) = (b_1, \cdots, b_n)S, \tag{2.26}$$

with $S = \Pi_{i=1}^{n-1}[T^{(i+1)}\overline{Q}^{(i)}]$. Since all matrices $T^{(i)}$ and $\overline{Q}^{(i)}$ are unimodular matrices, $S$ is also a unimodular matrix. We summarize these results in the following theorem.

**Theorem 2.30 :** Given any $n$-tuple $(b_1, \cdots, b_n)$ over $F[D]$, there exists a unimodular matrix $S$ such that (2.26) is true with $c_n$ a g.c.d. of the $n$ polynomials $b_i$, $1 \leq i \leq n$.

The algorithm used to compute this matrix $S$ can be seen as an iterative application of Euclid's algorithm that computes the g.c.d. of two polynomials. Of course a similar transformation is applicable to the column vector $\bar{b} = (b_1, \cdots, b_n)^T$:

$$\bar{c} = S^T \bar{b}$$

with $\bar{c} = (c_n, 0, 0, \cdots, 0)^T$, and $S$ a unimodular matrix.

## 2.3.2 A simple algorithm to construct minimal encoders

In subsection 2.2.1 an algorithm was presented that constructs a minimal encoder equivalent to an arbitrary $k \times n$ encoder $G$ over the finite field $F$. The complexity of this algorithm is high since one has to check whether the $|F|^{n(m+1)}$ elements of $F^n[D]$ having degree up to the largest degree $m$ of the rows of $G$ are in $E(G)$ or not. This makes the algorithm unpractical if $nm$ is large. To arrive at a more practical method we need first a definition.

**Definition 2.31 :** A $k \times n$ convolutional encoder $G$ over $F$ is called *basic* if it satisfies (2.8) and (2.10).

From theorem 2.24 it follows that the set of basic encoders contains the set of minimal encoders as a subset. For this reason, to construct a minimal encoder equivalent to a given encoder $G$, we first construct an equivalent basic encoder and we then modify this basic encoder to make it minimal. The complexity of this method remains reasonable for large $m$ and $n$.

The computation of a basic encoder equivalent to $G$ makes repeated use of Euclid's algorithm. Denote the first row of $G$ by $g_1 = (g_1^1, \cdots, g_1^n)$, $g_1^j \in F[D]$, and repeatedly apply Euclid's algorithm to the $n$ components $g_1^j$, $1 \le j \le n$, of $g_1$ to obtain an $n \times n$ polynomial unimodular matrix $S_1$ that satisfies

$$(\gamma_{11}, 0, \cdots, 0) = g_1 S_1 , \qquad (2.27)$$

where $\gamma_{11}$ is the g.c.d. of the elements $g_1^j$ of $g_1$. Thus we can write

$$GS_1 = \begin{bmatrix} \gamma_{11} & 0 & \cdots & 0 \\ * & & & \\ \vdots & & G_2 & \\ * & & & \end{bmatrix} ,$$

where * denotes an element of $F[D]$ and where $G_2$ is a $(k-1) \times (n-1)$ matrix over $F[D]$. Again apply Euclid's algorithm to the first row $g_2$ of $G_2$, to obtain an $(n-1) \times (n-1)$ polynomial unimodular matrix $S_2'$ satisfying

$$(\gamma_{22}, 0, \cdots, 0) = g_2 S_2' ,$$

where $\gamma_{22}$ is the g.c.d. of the elements $g_2^j$ of $g_2$. Defining $S_2$ by

$$S_2 := \begin{bmatrix} 1 & 0 & \cdots & 0 \\ 0 & & & \\ \vdots & & S_2' & \\ 0 & & & \end{bmatrix} ,$$

we can write

$$GS_1 S_2 = \begin{bmatrix} \gamma_{11} & 0 & 0 & \cdots & 0 \\ * & \gamma_{22} & 0 & \cdots & 0 \\ * & * & & & \\ \vdots & \vdots & & G_3 & \\ * & * & & & \end{bmatrix} ,$$

where $G_3$ is a $(k-2) \times (n-2)$ matrix over $F[D]$. Continuing in this manner we eventually obtain

$$GS = \begin{bmatrix} \gamma_{11} & 0 & 0 & 0 & \cdots & 0 & 0 & \cdots & 0 \\ * & \gamma_{22} & 0 & 0 & \cdots & 0 & 0 & \cdots & 0 \\ * & * & \gamma_{33} & 0 & \cdots & 0 & 0 & \cdots & 0 \\ \vdots & \vdots & \vdots & \vdots & & \vdots & \vdots & & \vdots \\ * & * & * & * & \cdots & \gamma_{kk} & 0 & \cdots & 0 \end{bmatrix} \qquad (2.28)$$

where $S = S_1 S_2 \cdots S_k$, being a product of $n \times n$ unimodular polynomial matrices $S_i$ over $F[D]$, is itself a unimodular polynomial matrix. As a consequence the inverse $T = S^{-1}$ of $S$ is also a polynomial unimodular matrix. Denoting the $k \times n$ matrix of the $k$ first rows of $T$ by $T^*$ we then write (2.28) as

$$G = \Gamma T^* , \qquad (2.29)$$

where $\Gamma$ is the $k \times k$ matrix formed by the $k$ first columns of $GS$. All its elements above the main diagonal are zero. Its diagonal elements $\gamma_{ii}$ are nonzero elements of $F[D]$, but some of them may be in the subset $F$ of $F[D]$. Suppose that not all $\gamma_{ii}$ are in $F$ and define $s$ to be the smallest integer such that $\gamma_{ss}$ is a proper element of $F[D]$ i.e., $\gamma_{ss} \notin F$.

**Lemma 2.32 :** There exists a unimodular $k \times k$ matrix $U_0$ over $F[D]$ satisfying the following properties.

**(i)** The $s - 1$ first rows of $\Gamma_0 = U_0 \Gamma$ constitute the matrix $(I_{s-1} \ 0)$ with 0 the $(s - 1) \times (k - s + 1)$ zero matrix.

**(ii)** The $s^{\text{th}}$ row of $\Gamma_0$ is $(0^{s-1}, \gamma_{ss}, 0^{k-s})$.

**Proof :** For $s = 1$, the result is obvious. For $s \geq 2$, let us denote by $\Gamma_{s-1}$ the upper left $(s - 1) \times (s - 1)$ submatrix of $\Gamma$. Since all its diagonal elements are in $F$ and all its elements above the main diagonal are zero, $\Gamma_{s-1}$ is unimodular and $(\Gamma_{s-1})^{-1}$ is a matrix over $F[D]$. Define then $U' = \begin{pmatrix} (\Gamma_{s-1})^{-1} & 0 \\ 0^T & I_{k-s+1} \end{pmatrix}$ with 0 the $(s - 1) \times (k - s + 1)$ zero matrix. The matrix $\Gamma' = U' \Gamma$ has the form

$$\Gamma' = \begin{bmatrix} I_{s-1} & & & 0 & & \\ \gamma_{s1} & \cdots & \gamma_{s,s-1} & \gamma_{ss} & 0 & \cdots & 0 \\ \vdots & & \vdots & \vdots & \vdots & & \vdots \\ \gamma_{k1} & \cdots & \gamma_{k,s-1} & \gamma_{ks} & \gamma_{k,s+1} & \cdots & \gamma_{kk} \end{bmatrix}.$$

Define then the $k \times k$ matrix $U$ by $u_{ii} = 1$ for all $i$, $u_{sj} = -\gamma_{sj}$, for all $j < s$, $u_{ij} = 0$ in the other cases. It is seen that $\Gamma_0 = UU' \Gamma$ satisfies the requirements of the theorem and that $U_0 = UU'$ is unimodular. $\square$

By theorem 2.6, the matrices $G = U_0^{-1} \Gamma_0 T^*$ and $T^*$ generate the same convolutional code. We claim that $T^*$ is a basic encoder of $E(G)$. To prove this result we need the following lemma.

**Lemma 2.33 :** There exists an $n \times k$ matrix $S^*$ over $F[D]$ that satisfies

$$T^* S^* = I_k. \tag{2.30}$$

**Proof :** Choose $S^*$ to be the matrix consisting of the first $k$ columns of $S = T^{-1}$. $\square$

A matrix $S^*$ over $F[D]$ that satisfies (2.30) is called a *polynomial right pseudoinverse* of $T^*$.

**Theorem 2.34 :** $T^*$ is a basic encoder.
**Proof :** Any $v = aT^*$, $a \in \mathcal{F}^k$, satisfies $vS^* = a$ with $S^*$ a polynomial right pseudoinverse of $T^*$. This implies

$$\ell(v) < \infty \Rightarrow \ell(a) < \infty \,.$$

As a consequence, the matrix $G := T^*$ satisfies (2.10). Write then $T^*$ and $S^*$ as $T^* = \sum_{i=0}^{m} T_i^* D^i$, $S^* = \sum_{i=0}^{m} S_i^* D^i$ for some $m$. From $T^* S^* = I_k$, one obtains $T_0^* S_0^* = I_k$, which proves $\mathrm{rk}(T_0^*) = k$. Hence $T^*$ satisfies (2.8). $\square$

We also have the following theorem.

**Theorem 2.35 :** If $G$ is a $k \times n$ basic encoder, all polynomials $\gamma_{ii}$ of (2.28) are elements of $F$.
**Proof :** Suppose that some $\gamma_{ii}$ are not in $F$ and denote by $s$ the smallest integer such that $\gamma_{ss}$ is not in $F$. Denote by $u$ the $s^{\text{th}}$ row of the matrix $U_0$ defined in lemma 2.32, and define $a := u/\gamma_{ss}$. Since $U_0$ is unimodular, it follows from problem 2.4 that the g.c.d. of the elements of any of its rows is in $F$. Since $\gamma_{ss}$ is not in $F$, the $k$-tuple $a$ is not a polynomial. On the other hand $v = aG$ being the $s^{\text{th}}$ row of the polynomial matrix $T^*$ is a polynomial. As a consequence the pair $(a, aG)$ would not satisfy simultaneously (2.8) and (2.10), so that the encoder $G$ would not be basic. Hence the contradiction, thus proving that all $\gamma_{ii}$ are in $F$. $\square$

**Corollary 2.36 :** For $k \leq n$, the three following properties are equivalent.

**(i)** $G$ is a basic $k \times n$ convolutional encoder.

**(ii)** The g.c.d. of the minors of order $k$ of the convolutional encoder $G$ is in $F$.

**(iii)** $G$ is a $k \times n$ convolutional encoder with a polynomial right pseudoinverse.

**Proof :** Compute the form (2.28) of $G$. We prove (i) $\Rightarrow$ (ii) $\Rightarrow$ (iii) $\Rightarrow$ (i).

(i) $\Rightarrow$ (ii) : The g.c.d. of the minors of order $k$ of $G$ is equal to the polynomial $\gamma_{11}\gamma_{22}\cdots\gamma_{kk}$ multiplied by the g.c.d. of the minors of order $k$ of $T^*$. Since $T$ is unimodular, we can prove by use of (1.1) that this g.c.d. is in $F$, and since $G$ is basic all $\gamma_{ii}$ are in $F$ by theorem 2.35.

(ii) $\Rightarrow$ (iii) : Property (ii) implies that in (2.29) all diagonal elements $\gamma_{ii}$ of $\Gamma$ are in $F$. As a consequence $\Gamma^{-1}$ is polynomial and the matrix $H := S^* \Gamma^{-1}$, with $S^*$ as in lemma 2.33, is a polynomial pseudoinverse of $G$.

(iii) $\Rightarrow$ (i) : See the proof of theorem 2.34. $\square$

We have devoted the first part of this subsection to obtaining a basic encoder equivalent to a given convolutional encoder. We have also investigated some properties of basic encoders. It is now time to describe how to modify a basic encoder to obtain a minimal encoder. Given a polynomial encoder $G$, let us denote by $G_f$ the final matrix of $G$ defined before theorem 2.16.

**Lemma 2.37 :** A $k \times n$ basic encoder $G$ is minimal if and only if $\mathrm{rk}(G_f)$ is equal to $k$.

**Proof :** A basic encoder is minimal if and only if it satisfies (2.9) which is equivalent to $\mathrm{rk}(G_f) = k$. $\square$

We use this lemma as a guide to modify the basic encoder $T^*$ of $E(G)$, to make it minimal. We denote the $i^{\text{th}}$ row of $T^*$ by $t_i = \sum_{j=0}^{m(i)}(t_i)_j D^j$, with $(t_i)_j \in F^n$, $(t_i)_{m(i)} \neq 0$. We define then $\overrightarrow{T^*}$ to be the $k \times n$ matrix having $D^{m(k)-m(i)}t_i$ as $i^{\text{th}}$ row and we define $\overrightarrow{T_f^*}$ to be the final matrix of $\overrightarrow{T^*}$. If $\text{rk}(\overrightarrow{T_f^*}) = k$, then $T^*$ is minimal by lemma 2.37. If $\text{rk}(\overrightarrow{T_f^*}) \leq k-1$, there exists a nonzero $a = (a^1, \cdots, a^k)$ in $F^k$ that satisfies

$$\sum_{i=1}^{k} a^i[(t_i)_{m(i)}] = 0 . \tag{2.31}$$

Define $s$ to be the largest $i$ such that $a^i$ is nonzero, and make the substitution

$$t_s \rightarrow t_s - (a^s)^{-1} \sum_{i=1}^{s-1} a^i D^{m(s)-m(i)} t_i , \tag{2.32}$$

which lowers $M(T^*)$ by at least 1. Ordering the rows of this new matrix, renaming it $T^*$ and iterating this procedure, we obtain in at most $M(T^*)$ steps a new encoder $T^*$ that satisfies

$$\text{rk}(T_f^*) = k. \tag{2.33}$$

**Theorem 2.38 :** The new encoder $T^*$ is mininal.
**Proof :** All substitutions (2.32) and all reorderings of the rows are representable by left multiplications by $k \times k$ unimodular matrices. This operation does not modify the g.c.d. of the $k \times k$ minors of $T^*$. Hence the new $T^*$ is a basic encoder, since it still satisfies property (ii) of corollary 2.36. Since it satisfies also (2.33), it is minimal by lemma 2.37. $\square$

Let us comment a bit on the complexity of this two-step algorithm. Obtaining the matrix $S_1$ in (2.27) needs a number of elementary operations (additions, multiplications and divisions) that is a polynomial function of $n$ and $m = m(k)$. There are less than $n$ matrices $S_i$ to be computed. The inversion of $S$ to obtain $T$ and the modification of $T^*$ are also operations of polynomial complexity. This is to be compared with the length of the list $L_{m(k)}(\mathcal{F}^n)$ used by the algorithm of subsection 2.2.1 which is an exponential function of $n$ and $m(k)$.

### 2.3.3   Equivalent basic encoders and basic encoders of subcodes

Let us first make explicit the relation between equivalent basic encoders.

**Theorem 2.39 :** Let $G_1$ be a basic $k \times n$ convolutional encoder over $F$. Any basic encoder $G_2$ is equivalent to $G_1$ if and only if it can be written as $G_2 = AG_1$ with $A$ a $k \times k$ polynomial unimodular matrix.

**Proof :** We prove first that $G_2 = AG_1$ with $A$ unimodular and $G_1$ basic implies that $G_2$ is also basic. Since $G_1$ is basic, it has a polynomial $n \times k$ right pseudoinverse $H_1$ thus satisfying $G_1 H_1 = I_k$. Consider then the $n \times k$ matrix $H_2 = H_1 A^{-1}$. Since $A$ is unimodular, $H_2$ is polynomial. Moreover it satisfies $G_2 H_2 = (AG_1)(H_1 A^{-1}) = A(G_1 H_1)A^{-1} = I_k$. Hence $G_2$ is basic since it has a polynomial right pseudoinverse.

Conversely, suppose that $G_1$ and $G_2$ are basic and generate the same code. From theorem 2.6 it follows that $G_2 = AG_1$ and, equivalently, $G_1 = A^{-1}G_2$, are true for some $k \times k$ nonsingular matrix $A$ over $F(D)$. Being basic, $G_1$ and $G_2$ satisfy (2.8) and (2.10), which implies that $A$ and $A^{-1}$ are polynomial matrices. Since $A$ is a polynomial matrix with a polynomial inverse, it is unimodular. $\square$

Let now $G_1$ be a $k_1 \times n$ basic encoder and let $G_2$ be a $k_2 \times n$ subencoder of $G_1$.

**Theorem 2.40 :** $G_2$ is a basic encoder.

**Proof :** We prove that the g.c.d. $\gamma_2$ of the $k_2 \times k_2$ minors of $G_2$ is in $F$. Assume that $\gamma_2$ is not in $F$. In this case it follows from (1.1) that the g.c.d. $\gamma_1$ of the $k_1 \times k_1$ minors of $G_1$ is not in $F$. By corollary 2.36, this contradicts the hypothesis that $G_1$ is a basic encoder. $\square$

To conclude this subsection, we prove the following theorem.

**Theorem 2.41 :** Let $C^*$ and $C$ be convolutional codes of length $n$ over $F$ satisfying dim $C^* = k^*$, dim $C = k^* + 1$ and $C^* \subset C$. It is possible to add a row to any basic $k^* \times n$ encoder $G^*$ of $C^*$ to obtain a $(k^* + 1) \times n$ basic encoder of $C$.

**Proof :** For any encoder $G$ of $C$, there exists a polynomial $k^* \times (k^* + 1)$ matrix $T$ satisfying $G^* = TG$. We note then that $T$ is a $k^* \times (k^* + 1)$ basic encoder. Indeed if it is not basic let $\tau(D)$ be the g.c.d. of its $k^* \times k^*$ minors. From $G^* = TG$ it follows that $\tau(D)$ divides all $k^* \times k^*$ minors of $G^*$, and since $G^*$ is basic it follows from corollary 2.36 that $\tau(D)$ is an element of $F$. Let now $t_i$ be the determinant of the $k^* \times k^*$ submatrix of $T$ obtained by suppression of its $i^{\text{th}}$ column. Since $\tau(D)$ is in $F$, there exists $u = (u_1, \cdots, u_{k^*+1}) \in F^{k^*+1}[D]$ satisfying

$$\sum_{i=1}^{k^*+1} u_i t_i = 1 . \tag{2.34}$$

Appending $u$ as a last row to $T$, we obtain a $(k^* + 1) \times (k^* + 1)$ matrix $U$ which is unimodular since, by (2.34), det $U$ is equal to 1. As a consequence of theorem 2.39, the matrix $UG$ is still a basic encoder, and since it contains $G^*$ as a subencoder the theorem is proved. $\square$

The statement of this last theorem should be compared with the comments made after theorem 2.27.

## 2.4    Encoders of dual codes and reciprocal codes

In subsection 2.3.2 we have described how to obtain a basic encoder $T^*$ equivalent to a given encoder $G$. This was done by consideration of $n \times n$ matrices $T$ and $S$ that we write now as

$$T = \begin{pmatrix} T_{11} & T_{12} \\ & \\ T_{21} & T_{22} \end{pmatrix}, S = \begin{pmatrix} S_{11} & S_{12} \\ & \\ S_{21} & S_{22} \end{pmatrix},$$

where $T_{11}$ and $S_{11}$ are $k \times k$ matrices, $T_{12}$ and $S_{12}$ are $k \times (n-k)$ matrices, $T_{21}$ and $S_{21}$ are $(n-k) \times k$ matrices and $T_{22}$ and $S_{22}$ are $(n-k) \times (n-k)$

matrices. The matrices $T^*$ and $S^*$ considered in subsection 2.3.2 are then

$$T^* = (T_{11} \ T_{12}) \, , \ S^* \ = \ \begin{pmatrix} S_{11} \\ \\ S_{21} \end{pmatrix} .$$

Denote then by $G^\perp$ the transpose of the matrix of the $n-k$ last columns of $S$ :

$$G^\perp \ = \ (S_{12}^T \ S_{22}^T).$$

Being an $(n-k) \times n$ polynomial matrix of rank $n-k$, $G^\perp$ is an $(n, n-k)$ convolutional encoder. Moreover, since the rows of $G^\perp$ are a subset $P$ of the $n$ rows of $S^T$, we can use (1.1) to write

$$\det S^T \ = \ \sum_Q (-1)^{f(P)+f(Q)} \det (S^T)^{PQ} \det (S^T)^{\bar{P}\bar{Q}} \tag{2.35}$$

where $Q$ runs through the set of all $(n-k)$-tuples of columns of $S^T$. Since $\det S^T$ is a nonzero element of $F$, (2.35) makes clear that the g.c.d. of the polynomials $\det (S^T)^{PQ}$, for all $Q$, is an element of $F$. Since the set of these polynomials is nothing but the set of all $(n-k) \times (n-k)$ minors of $G^\perp$, it follows from corollary 2.36 that $G^\perp$ is a basic encoder.

From $TS = I_n$ it follows that $T^*(G^\perp)^T$ is the zero matrix, which means that $C^\perp = E(G^\perp)$ is *orthogonal* to $C = E(T^*)$. Equivalently, any $u \in C^\perp$ satisfies

$$vu^T = 0 \, ; \ \text{all } v \in C \, . \tag{2.36}$$

Conversely, any $u \in \mathcal{F}^n$ satisfying (2.36) is in $E(G^\perp)$. Defining indeed $a$ and $w$ to be the unique elements of $\mathcal{F}^k$ and $\mathcal{F}^n$, that satisfy $v = aT^*$ and $u = wS^T$, we see that (2.36) is equivalent to

$$aT^* Sw^T = 0 \, ; \ \text{all } a \in \mathcal{F}^k. \tag{2.37}$$

Together with $TS = I_n$, this implies that the $k$ first components of $w$ are zero, or equivalently that $u = wS^T$ is in the row space of $G^\perp$ over $\mathcal{F}$.

Hence it follows that $C^\perp$ is the code formed by all sequences $u$ that satisfy (2.36). We call it the *dual* of $C$. Obviously the sum of the dimensions of the codes $C$ and $C^\perp$ viewed as vector spaces over $\mathcal{F}$ is equal to $n$.

**Lemma 2.42 :** The $(n-k) \times (n-k)$ minors of $G^\perp$ are equal to the $k \times k$ minors of $T^*$ within a nonzero factor in $F$.

**Proof :** We use the proof given in [35], based on the fact that $T^*$ consists of the $k$ first rows of $T$ and $(G^\perp)^T$ consists of the $n-k$ last columns of $S$ with $TS = I_n$. We prove only that the determinant of the $k \times k$ matrix formed by the first $k$ columns of $T^*$ is equal to the determinant of the $(n-k) \times (n-k)$ matrix formed by the last $n-k$ rows of $(G^\perp)^T$, multiplied by det $S$ which is an element of $F$. Consider the matrix product

$$
\begin{pmatrix} T_{11} & T_{12} \\ 0 & I_{n-k} \end{pmatrix} \begin{pmatrix} S_{11} & S_{12} \\ S_{21} & S_{22} \end{pmatrix} = \begin{pmatrix} I_k & 0 \\ S_{21} & S_{22} \end{pmatrix}.
$$

It makes clear that det $T_{11}$ det $S = $ det $S_{22}$ . To prove the general case it suffices to apply the same reasoning to the matrices $TX$ and $X^T S$, with $X$ an appropriate permutation matrix. $\square$

**Theorem 2.43 :** The codes $C$ and $C^\perp$ satisfy $\mu(C) = \mu(C^\perp)$.

**Proof :** It follows from theorem 2.39 that within a unit of $F[D]$, i.e., a nonzero factor in $F$, all basic encoders of $C$ (resp. $C^\perp$) have exactly the same set of $k \times k$ (resp. $(n-k) \times (n-k)$) minors. By lemma 2.42, these two sets are identical, again within a unit. Denote by $m$ the maximal degree of these minors. Any basic encoder $G$ of $C$ satisfies $M(G) \geq m$, with equality if and only if $\mathrm{rk}(G_f)$ is equal to $k$. In this case, by lemma 2.37, $G$ is minimal which implies $M(G) = \mu(C)$ and hence $m = \mu(C)$. In the same way, one proves $m = \mu(C^\perp)$. $\square$

Let us briefly discuss reciprocal codes. With any $k \times n$ convolutional encoder $G = \sum_{i=0}^m G_i D^i$, we associate the *reciprocal* matrix $\hat{G} = \sum_{i=0}^m G_i D^{-i}$

which is in general not a polynomial matrix. To obtain a polynomial matrix from $\hat{G}$, we multiply its $i^{\text{th}}$ row by $D^{m(i)}$ where $m(i)$ is the degree of the $i^{\text{th}}$ row of $G$. Let us denote the resulting convolutional encoder by $\hat{G}^*$.

**Theorem 2.44 :** Let $G$ be an encoder of a convolutional code over $F$, and let $v(D)$ be an element of finite length in $\mathcal{F}^n$. The sequence $v(D)$ is in $E(G)$ if and only if $v(D^{-1})$ is in $E(\hat{G}^*)$.

**Theorem 2.45 :** The encoder $\hat{G}^*$ is minimal if and only if the encoder $G$ is minimal. It is catastrophic if and only if $G$ is a catastrophic encoder.

The proofs of these two theorems are left to the reader (problem 2.1).

If $v$ is a sequence of infinite length in $C = E(G)$, then del$(\hat{v})$ is not finite, which implies that $\hat{v}$ is not a sequence of $E(\hat{G})$. For this reason $E(\hat{G})$ is *not* the set of all $\hat{v}$ such that $v$ is in $E(G)$. Despite this, we shall use the symbols $C$ and $\hat{C}$ to denote respectively $E(G)$ and $E(\hat{G}) = E(\hat{G}^*)$. The convolutional code $\hat{C}$ will be called the *reciprocal* code of the convolutional code $C$.

## 2.5   Comments

This chapter is based mainly on [79] and [35]. In particular Massey and Sain [79] have proved that a $k \times n$ convolutional encoder $G$ satisfies (2.10) if and only if the g.c.d. of the minors of order $k$ of $G$ is equal to some power of $D$. The distinction between basic and minimal encoders and the concept of predictable degree are due to Forney [35].

The treatment given above, however, is somewhat different. We have first defined the minimal encoders and we have shown that they are characterized by a triple of conditions. The larger class of basic encoders was then defined as the class of encoders satisfying the first and the third of these three conditions. This approach is due to Piret [92] (see also [103]). In this discussion no use is made of the *Smith canonical form* of a polynomial matrix [72] used by Forney [35]. Instead of using this form, we have transformed the encoder $G$ into a triangular form $\Gamma$ (see (2.28)). This form is called the Hermite canonical form of a polynomial matrix. The corresponding transformation matrix $S$ is more easily computed than the pair of transformation matrices that are used to obtain the Smith canonical form.

## PROBLEMS

**2.1** Prove theorems 2.44 and 2.45.

**2.2** Prove that a nonminimal encoder $G$ of an $(n, 1)$ convolutional code is catastrophic.

**2.3** Let $G = \sum_{i=0}^{m} G_i D^i$ be a $k \times n$ encoder over $F$ that satisfies $m \geq 1$ and $\mathrm{rk}(G_0) = \mathrm{rk}(G_m) = k$ and is such that all nonzero matrices $G_i$ satisfy $E_0(G_i) \subseteq E_0(G_0)$. Prove that $G$ does not satisfy (2.10).

**2.4** Prove that if $U$ is a unimodular square matrix over $F[D]$, the g.c.d. of the elements of any of its rows is an element of $F$.

**2.5** Show that the encoder

$$G = \begin{bmatrix} 1 & 1 & 1 \\ 1 & D & D^2 \end{bmatrix},$$

over $GF(2)$ does not satisfy (2.10). Compute an equivalent minimal encoder.

**2.6** Prove that any basic $1 \times n$ convolutional encoder is minimal.

# Chapter 3

# How to choose and to use a convolutional encoder

This chapter is devoted to several topics related to the distance properties of convolutional codes. These properties are important criteria when the codes are used as error correcting codes on a noisy channel. In section 3.1 we discuss two concepts of distance between elements of $\mathcal{F}^n$: the symbol distance, already defined in chapter 2, and the word distance. Then we define the minimum symbol distance and the minimum word distance of a convolutional code. Finally we combine these two concepts into a broader one: the distance repartition of a convolutional code. The symbol distance was much studied in the past and some bounds were obtained on which minimum symbol distance can (or cannot) be achieved by codes of specified parameters. In section 3.2, a state diagram is associated with any convolutional encoder and it is shown how to use this diagram to compute enumerators that give information on the distance structure of the code generated by this encoder. In section 3.3, several methods are described that find an estimate $\hat{v}$ of the transmitted code sequence $v$ from the received sequence $w$, and we sketch out why good distance properties are important in making a code an efficient error correcting code. In particular, we discuss in subsection 3.3.4 why the use of a catastrophic encoder should be avoided even if the decoding method does not fit the principles mentioned in chapter 2. The distance profile of a convolutional code is defined in section 3.4, where the asymptotically catastrophic classes of convolutional codes considered by Hemmati and Costello [53] are briefly discussed. In section 3.5 some constructions producing reasonably good codes are mentioned and in section 3.6 the zero run problem is considered. Section 3.7 is devoted to some comments. Sections 3.8 and 3.9 are appendices.

## 3.1  Distance measures for the evaluation of convolutional codes

As mentioned in the introduction to chapter 2, convolutional codes over a finite field $F = GF(q)$ are mainly used as error correcting codes on a noisy channel. In algebraic coding theory it is usual to express the error correcting capability of a code in terms of a distance concept. Let $X$ be a set and consider a function $d$ mapping $X^2$ into the set $\mathbb{R} \cup \{\infty\}$, with $\mathbb{R}$ the set of real numbers. This function $d(.,.)$ is called a *distance* over $X$ if it satisfies the following axioms.

(i)  $d(x_1, x_2)$ is nonnegative or infinite.

(ii)  $d(x_1, x_2) = 0$ if and only if $x_1 = x_2$.

(iii)  $d(x_1, x_2) = d(x_2, x_1)$.

(iv)  $d(x_1, x_2) + d(x_2, x_3) \geq d(x_1, x_3)$ :  this is the well-known *triangle inequality*.

As an example the symbol distance $sd(.,.)$ introduced in definitions 2.3 and 2.4 satisfies the foregoing axioms.

Given a block code $C$, the *minimum symbol distance* $sd(C)$ of $C$ is defined by

$$sd(C) := \min sd(u, v)\,;\ u, v \in C\,,\ u \neq v, \tag{3.1}$$

with $sd(u, v)$ as in definitions 2.3. Given a convolutional code $C$, its minimum symbol distance $sd(C)$ is also defined by (3.1) (with $sd(u, v)$ as in definition 2.4), and since a convolutional code is an $F$-space, this definition is equivalent to

$$sd(C) := \min sw(u)\,;\ u \in C\,,\ u \neq 0, \tag{3.2}$$

with $sw(u)$ as in definitions 2.4. This quantity $sd(C)$ is often called the *free distance* of $C$ [24, 78] and is then denoted by $d_f$.

Let us introduce another distance measure for convolutional codes. First let $u$ and $v$ be elements of $\mathcal{F}^n$. Define the *word weight* $ww(u)$ of $u = \sum_{i=r}^{\infty} u_i D^i$, $u_i \in F^n$, to be the number of nonzero words $u_i$ of $u$, and the *word distance* $wd(u, v)$ between $u$ and $v$ to be the word weight of $u - v$. It is not difficult to verify that this function $wd(.\,,.)$ satisfies the four axioms above.

Given any convolutional code $C$, we define its *minimum word distance* $wd(C)$ as

$$wd(C) := \min wd(u, v)\,;\ u, v \in C\,,\ u \neq v. \tag{3.3}$$

Since $C$ is an $F$-space, this definition is equivalent to

$$wd(C) := \min ww(u)\,;\ u \in C\,,\ u \neq 0. \tag{3.4}$$

These two concepts, $sd(C)$ and $wd(C)$, may now be merged into a more general notion, the distance repartition of a convolutional code. To introduce it, we need some preliminary definitions.

**Definition 3.1** : The *symbol weight of order* $s$ of any element $v = \sum_{i=r}^{\infty} v_i D^i$, $v_i \in F^n$, of $\mathcal{F}^n$ is defined to be the minimum symbol weight of all elements of $\mathcal{F}^n$ resulting from $v$ when one sets any $s$ of its words $v_i$ equal to zero.

If we denote this symbol weight of order $s$ by $sw(v \mid s)$, we thus have

$$sw(v \mid s) \;=\; \min \, sw(v^*) \,,$$

where the minimum is taken over all elements $v^*$ of $\mathcal{F}^n$ obtained from $v$ by cancellation of any $s$ of its words $v_i$. Clearly, for $s \geq ww(v)$, $sw(v \mid s)$ is zero, and for $s < ww(v)$, $sw(v \mid s)$ is achieved by setting to zero the $s$ words of $v$ having the largest symbol weight. In other words $sw(v \mid s) = d$ means that $v$ can be written as $v = v(1) + v(2)$ with $ww[v(1)] = s$ and $sw[v(2)] = d$ but that this decomposition is impossible if $ww[v(1)] \leq s$ and $sw[v(2)] < d$ are simultaneously true.

**Definition 3.2 :** The *symbol distance of order* $s$ between two elements $u$ and $v$ of $\mathcal{F}^n$ is defined to be $sw(u - v \mid s)$ and it is denoted by $sd(u, v \mid s)$.

Let us remark here that the quantity $sd(u, v \mid s)$ does not satisfy the axioms **(ii)** and **(iv)** of a distance. Thus calling it a distance is an abuse of terminology.

**Definitions 3.3 :** The *minimum symbol distance of order* $s$, denoted by $sd(C \mid s)$, of a convolutional code $C$ is defined by

$$sd(C \mid s) \;:=\; \min \, sd(u, v \mid s); \; u, v \in C \,, \; u \neq v.$$

Since $C$ is an $F$-space, $sd(C \mid s)$ is equivalently defined by

$$sd(C \mid s) \;:=\; \min \, sw(v \mid s); \; v \in C \,, \; v \neq 0.$$

We now use these definitions to introduce the concept of distance repartition.

**Definition 3.4 :** Let $C$ be a convolutional code that satisfies $wd(C) = w_0$. The *distance repartition* $dr(C)$ of $C$ is defined to be the $w_0$-tuple

$$dr(C) := [sd(C \mid 0), \ sd(C \mid 1), \cdots, \ sd(C \mid w_0 - 1)].$$

The distance repartition $dr(C)$ of $C$ gives more information about $C$ than the parameters $sd(C) = sd(C \mid 0)$ and $wd(C) = w_0$ defined above. Indeed, beside the values of these two quantities, it incorporates information on how the nonzero symbols are distributed among the words of the nonzero code sequences.

Later in this chapter we sketch why it is desirable to use a convolutional code $C$ with a large minimum symbol distance $sd(C)$ or with a good distance repartition $dr(C)$. In general, it is not an easy matter to compute the distance parameters of a code. To compute $sd(C)$, Forney has suggested in [37] (see also [2, 64]) the use of a modified version of the Viterbi decoder described in subsection 3.3.1. Several authors [26, 65] have obtained bounds on the largest value of $sd(C)$ that is achievable by the class of $(n, k)$ convolutional codes over $F$ and we give now a short survey of these bounds.

We consider first the problem of obtaining an upper bound on the minimum symbol distance of the codes generated by a $k \times n$ minimal encoder $G$, the rows of which have degrees respectively equal to $m(1), \cdots, m(k)$. We make the following simple remark. For $C = E(G)$, let $L_m(C)$ be the $F$-space of the polynomials of $C$ (over $F^n$) that have formal degree $m$ in the indeterminate $D$. Consider $L_m(C)$ as a linear block code of length $n(m + 1)$ over $F$, denote the dimension of this block code by $k[L_m(C)]$ and denote its minimum symbol distance by $sd[L_m(C)]$. Obviously this minimum distance $sd[L_m(C)]$ is an upper bound on $sd(C)$. It follows that for any upper bound $\bar{d}_m$ on $sd[L_m(C)]$ we have $sd(C) \le \bar{d}_m$. To find such bounds we compute the dimension $k[L_m(C)]$ of $L_m(C)$ viewed as an $F$-space and we use as $\bar{d}_m$ any known upper bound on the minimum distance of the $(n(m + 1), k[L_m(C)])$ block codes over $F$.

Let us give some examples. Let $C$ be the class of binary[2] convolutional codes of length $n = 10$ and dimension $k = 9$ that are generated by minimal encoders satisfying $m(i) = 1$ for all $i$. It follows from the remarks above that, for any $C \in C$, the binary block code $L_m(C)$ has length equal to $10(m+1)$ and dimension equal to $9m$. The following upper bounds $\overline{d}_m$ on $sd[L_m(C)]$ can be found in [50].

$$\overline{d}_1 = 7 , \ \overline{d}_m = 6 \text{ for } 2 \leq m \leq 5 , \ \overline{d}_m \geq 7 \text{ for } m \geq 6.$$

As a consequence the minimum symbol distance $sd(C)$ of any code $C$ in the class $C$ cannot be larger than 6.

As another example let $C$ be the class of binary codes generated by $3 \times 6$ minimal encoders satisfying $m(1) = 0$, $m(2) = m(3) = 2$. For any $C \in C$, the block code $L_m(C)$ has length $6(m+1)$. The $F$-dimension of $L_0(C)$ is 1, and, for $m \geq 1$, the $F$-dimension of $L_m(C)$ is $2 + 3(m-1)$. The following upper bounds $\overline{d}_m$ on $d_m$ were found in [50]: $\overline{d}_0 = \overline{d}_1 = 6$, $\overline{d}_m \geq 8$ for $m \geq 2$. As a result, the minimum symbol distance $sd(C)$ of any code $C$ in $C$ is at most 6.

We consider now the problem of obtaining for a class of binary convolutional codes, the largest possible integer $\underline{sd}$ such that $sd(C) \geq \underline{sd}$ is satisfied by at least one $C$ in the class. Several asymptotic results in this direction can be found in [26]. Among these are the following ones. Let $C(n, k, m)$ be the class of all binary convolutional codes that are generated by a $k \times n$ convolutional encoder $G$ the entries of which have degree $\leq m$. Let $\mathcal{H}_2(x)$ be the entropy function (in base 2) defined in the introduction and denote by $\mathcal{H}_2^{-1}$ the inverse function of $\mathcal{H}_2$ thus satisfying $\mathcal{H}_2^{-1}[\mathcal{H}_2(x)] = x$ for all $x \in [0, 1/2]$. Let also $\underline{sd}(n, k, m)$ be the largest minimum symbol distance achieved by a code in $C(n, k, m)$, and let $R := k/n$ be the *rate* of the codes in $C(n, k, m)$.

---

[2] A binary code is a code over the alphabet $F = GF(2)$.

For fixed $n$ and $k$, the quantity $\delta(m) := \underline{sd}(n, k, m)/(m + 1)$ can be shown to satisfy

$$\liminf_{m \to \infty} \delta(m) \geq 2n\, \mathcal{H}_2^{-1}(1 - R), \tag{3.5}$$

for $3/8 \leq R \leq 1$ and

$$\liminf_{m \to \infty} \delta(m) \geq 2nR(1 - 2^{2R-1})/[\mathcal{H}_2(2^{2R-1}) + 2R - 1],$$

for $0 \leq R \leq 3/8$.

A stronger bound was obtained by Costello for the larger class of *time-varying* codes. Although these codes are outside the scope of this book, it is worth examining them here. Instead of being specified by means of a unique $k \times n$ polynomial encoder $G$, the $(n, k)$ time-varying codes are specified by a collection of $k \times n$ polynomial encoders $G^{(j)} = \sum_{i=0}^{m} G_i^{(j)} D^i$ with $j \in \mathbb{Z}$, and the encoding of $a = \sum_{j=r}^{\infty} a_j D^j$ with $a_j \in F^k$, produces the encoded sequence $v = \sum_{j=r}^{\infty} a_j G^{(j)} D^j$. The time-varying code $C$ associated with this collection of $G^{(j)}$ is then defined to be the set of elements $v \in \mathcal{F}^n$ that can be obtained in this way, and its minimum symbol distance $sd(C)$ is defined by (3.1) or equivalently by (3.2). Denote by $C^*(n, k, m)$ the set of all time-varying $(n, k)$ codes defined by collections of encoders $G^{(j)}$ having entries of degree at most $m$ and let $\underline{sd}^*(n, k, m)$ be the largest value of $sd(C)$ for $C \in C^*$. It has been shown by Costello [26] that the quantity $\delta^*(m) := \underline{sd}^*(n, k, m)/(m + 1)$ satisfies, for $R = k/n$,

$$\liminf_{m \to \infty} \delta^*(m) \geq -nR/\log_2(2^{1-R} - 1). \tag{3.6}$$

It is tempting to make the conjecture that convolutional codes also satisfy (3.6). This conjecture is supported by the following recent result of Zigangirov [118] (to which we will return in section 3.9). Let $K$ and $N$ be relatively prime positive integers satisfying $K < N$ and, for a positive integer $r$, define $n = rN$, $k = rK$. As above, let $\underline{sd}(n, k, m)$ be the largest minimum distance achieved by a code in $\mathcal{C}(n, k, m)$ and let $\delta(m)$

be $\underline{sd}(n,k,m)/(m+1)$. Zigangirov proves that $\delta(m)$ satisfies

$$\liminf_{m\to\infty} \delta(m) \geq -nR/\log_2(2^{1-R}-1) - n\epsilon(r), \qquad (3.7)$$

where $\epsilon(r)$ satisfies $\lim_{r\to\infty} \epsilon(r) = 0$. Although this result is quite significant, the problem remains open to know whether (3.6) is also true for convolutional codes of short length $n$. In particular, any estimate for $\underline{sd}(2,1,m)$ would be welcome. In section 3.8, we sketch an argument that shows how the solution of this problem is related to the solution of two interesting open subproblems.

## 3.2   State diagrams and enumerators of convolutional encoders

Let $G$ be an ordered $k \times n$ convolutional encoder over $F = GF(q)$ and let $m(j)$ be the degree of its $j^{\text{th}}$ row considered as a polynomial over $F^n$. This encoder maps any $k$-tuple $a = (a^1, \cdots, a^k)$ over $\mathcal{F}$ to the $n$-tuple $v = (v^1, \cdots, v^n)$ over $\mathcal{F}$ given by $v = aG$. A possible realization of this mapping was sketched in figure 2.2. Let us write $a^j \in \mathcal{F}$ as $a^j = \sum_{i=r}^{\infty} a_i^j D^i$, $a_i^j \in F$, for some $r \leq \text{del}(a)$. At time $i$, the content of the $k$ input registers of the encoder is then as given in figure 3.1: the $j^{\text{th}}$ input register contains the $(1+m(j))$-tuple $a^j(i) = (a_i^j, a_{i-1}^j, \cdots, a_{i-m(j)}^j)$. We call the last of these symbols, $a_{i-m(j)}^j$, the *obsolete* symbol at time $i$ in the $j^{\text{th}}$ input register and we call the $m(j)$ first symbols $a_\ell^j$, $i \geq \ell \geq i - m(j) + 1$, of $a^j(i)$, the $j^{\text{th}}$ *partial state* of the encoder at time $i$. In particular, for all $j$ satisfying $m(j) = 0$, any symbol $a_i^j$, $i \in \mathbb{Z}$, transmitted to the $j^{\text{th}}$ input of the encoder at time $i$, becomes immediately obsolete without being included first in the $j^{\text{th}}$ partial state of the encoder. An information symbol that becomes obsolete at time unit $i$ may yet be used by the encoder at time unit $i$ but not later. At time unit $i+1$ a new symbol $a_{i+1}^j$, $1 \leq j \leq k$, enters each input register of the encoder and all symbols in these registers are shifted

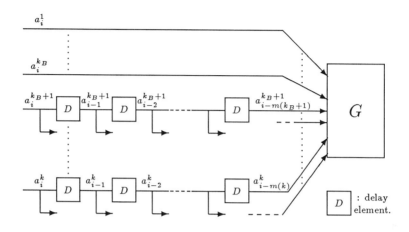

**Figure 3.1** : The inputs to a $k \times n$ convolutional encoder.

by one stage to the right. The obsolete symbols $a_{i-m(j)}^j$ of time unit $i$ are dismissed and the symbols $a_{i+1-m(j)}^j$ become the new obsolete symbols. We call the union of the partial states $(a_i^j, \cdots, a_{i+1-m(j)}^j)$, $1 \le j \le k$, the *state* of the encoder $G$ at time $i$, and we denote it by $s(i)$. If $k_B$ is the number of integers $m(j)$ that are equal to zero, the state $s(i)$ can be represented by a $(k - k_B)$-tuple of vectors over $F$, of lengths respectively equal to $m(1 + k_B)$, $m(2 + k_B)$, $\cdots$, $m(k)$:

$$s(i) = \begin{bmatrix} (a_i^{1+k_B}, & \cdots, & a_{i-m(1+k_B)+1}^{1+k_B}) \\ (a_i^{2+k_B}, & \cdots, & a_{i-m(2+k_B)+1}^{2+k_B}) \\ \vdots & & \vdots \\ (a_i^k, & \cdots, & a_{i-m(k)+1}^k) \end{bmatrix}. \qquad (3.8)$$

Obviously, the number of different states is $q^M$ with $M$ given by $\sum_{j=1}^k m(j)$. This definition implies that $s(i)$ has exactly $q^{k-k_B}$ possible successors $s(i+1)$. Beside a sequence of states $s(i)$, $i \in \mathbb{Z}$, the information sequence

$a = (a^1, \cdots, a^k)$ also induces an encoded sequence $v = aG$ of $n$-tuples $v_i = (v_i^1, \cdots .v_i^n)$ over $F$ with $i \in \mathbb{Z}$. Each $n$-tuple $v_i$ is computed by the encoder $G$ in terms of the $(1 + m(j))$-tuples $a^j(i)$, $1 \leq j \leq k$. Obviously the knowledge of these $k$ vectors $a^j(i)$ is equivalent to the simultaneous knowledge of $a_i^j$ for $1 \leq j \leq k_B$, of $s(i)$ and of $s(i-1)$. Conversely, if $k_B$ is nonzero, to specify an admissible pair $(s(i-1), s(i))$ of consecutive states is not equivalent to specifying which $n$-tuple $v_i$ is transmitted at time $i$. Indeed, $v_i$ will be specified only when the first $k_B$ elements $a_i^j$, $1 \leq j \leq k_B$, of the information at time unit $i$ will be given.

Let us now represent the $q^M$ possible states $s(i)$ of the encoder $G$ and the possible transitions between them by a directed graph $\Sigma(G)$. With any state $s(i)$ of $G$ is associated a vertex (or state) in $\Sigma(G)$ and there is an arc in $\Sigma(G)$ from the state $s(i-1)$ to the state $s(i)$ if and only if $(s(i-1), s(i))$ is a pair of consecutive states of the encoder $G$. We call the graph $\Sigma(G)$ the *state diagram* associated with $G$.

As an illustration we consider the $(6,3)$ code over $F = GF(2)$ generated by the encoder

$$G = \begin{bmatrix} 1 & 1 & 1 & 1 & 1 & 1 \\ 1+D & D & 1 & D & 1 & 0 \\ D & 1+D^2 & D+D^2 & D & 1+D+D^2 & 1+D \end{bmatrix}. \quad (3.9)$$

The parameters $m(j)$ of this encoder $G$ are $m(1) = 0$, $m(2) = 1$, $m(3) = 2$, and its parameter $k_B$ is equal to 1. Let us choose $a = (a^1, a^2, a^3) \in \mathcal{F}^3$ as being the information sequence to be encoded by $G$ and let us represent its components by $a^j = \sum_{i=r}^{\infty} a_i^j D^j$ with $a_i^j \in F$ and $1 \leq j \leq 3$. At time unit $i$, the state $s(i)$ of the encoder $G$ is

$$s(i) = \begin{bmatrix} (a_i^2) \\ (a_i^3, a_{i-1}^3) \end{bmatrix}$$

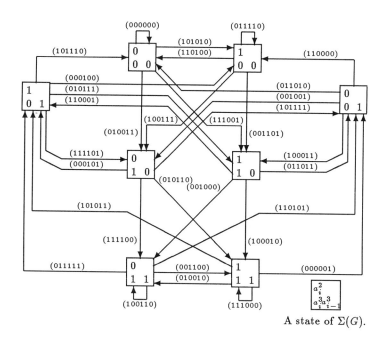

A state of $\Sigma(G)$.

**Figure 3.2** : The state diagram $\Sigma(G)$.

and the six components $v_i^j$, $1 \leq j \leq 6$, of the codeword $v_i$ produced at time $i$ are the elements of $GF(2)$ given by

$$
\begin{aligned}
v_i^1 &= a_i^1 + a_i^2 + a_{i-1}^2 + a_{i-1}^3, \\
v_i^2 &= a_i^1 + a_{i-1}^2 + a_i^3 + a_{i-2}^3, \\
v_i^3 &= a_i^1 + a_i^2 + a_{i-1}^3 + a_{i-2}^3, \\
v_i^4 &= a_i^1 + a_{i-1}^2 + a_{i-1}^3, \\
v_i^5 &= a_i^1 + a_i^2 + a_i^3 + a_{i-1}^3 + a_{i-2}^3, \\
v_i^6 &= a_i^1 + a_i^3 + a_{i-1}^3.
\end{aligned}
\tag{3.10}
$$

Since $k_B$ is equal to 1, with any state transition $s(i-1) \mapsto s(i)$ in $\Sigma(G)$, there are associated 2 $(= 2^{k_B})$ binary 6-tuples denoted by $v(0)$ and $v(1)$. Which of these two 6-tuples is transmitted depends on the value, 0 or 1, of $a_i^1$. In figure 3.2 are represented the eight states associated with the encoder $G$ specified by (3.9), together with the possible transitions $s(i-1) \mapsto s(i)$ and the 6-tuples $v(0)$ produced in these transitions when $a_i^1$ is zero. For all these transitions, the 6-tuple $v(1)$ is obtained from $v(0)$ by complementation: $v(1) = v(0) + (111111)$.

For a given encoder $G$ we are interested in describing the weight structure of $C = E(G)$. To do that we distinguish the state of $\Sigma(G)$ that is indexed by the all-zero $(\sum_{j=1}^{k} m(j))$-tuple. This distinguished state (denoted here by $s_0$) is one of its own successors, i.e., there is a self-loop around it. Then we modify $\Sigma(G)$ as follows. We split $s_0$ into two states: an initial state $s_I$ and a final state $s_F$. In this modified state diagram, denoted by $\Sigma^*(G)$, all arcs of $\Sigma(G)$ are unchanged except the ones that enter or leave the state $s_0$: the initial state $s_I$ is left by all arcs that leave $s_0$ in $\Sigma(G)$ and the final state $s_F$ is entered by all arcs that enter $s_0$ in $\Sigma(G)$. Conversely, $s_I$ has no arc entering it and $s_F$ has no arc leaving it.

With each arc $(s^*, s)$ of $\Sigma^*(G)$ is associated a *gain* $g(s^*, s)$ that gives information on the codewords that can be transmitted when, at any time unit $i$, the encoder makes the state transition $s(i-1) = s^* \mapsto s(i) = s$. This gain has a multiplicative property in the sense that the gain associated with a sequence of consecutive arcs is the product of the gains associated with the arcs of this sequence.

Before mentioning some gain functions that are in agreement with this rule, we give further comments on the use of these gain functions to obtain an analytical expression that describes some properties of $C = E(G)$.

Assume first that the encoder $G$ is in state $s_I$ at time unit $-1$ and that it reaches state $s_F$ for the first time at some integer time unit $t \geq 0$. Such a path from $s_I$ to $s_F$ is called a *simple path* and the piece of encoded sequence generated by $G$ along a simple path is called a *simple sequence*. Any code sequence can be seen as a succession of appropriately delayed simple sequences. The shortest simple sequences contain only one word. These words are nothing but the words of the block code generated by the $k_B$ first rows of $G$. When $k_B$ is zero, this block code contains only the zero $n$-tuple. The state diagram $\Sigma^*(G)$ is considered only to obtain descriptions of all simple sequences of the code $C = E(G)$. To obtain these descriptions, we attach to each arc $(s^*, s)$ of $\Sigma^*(G)$ a gain function $g(s^*, s)$ that has the multiplicative property mentioned above. Then we associate with any state $s$ of $\Sigma^*(G)$ a function $h(s)$ that is called the cumulative gain of $s$ and that satisfies, for $s \neq s_I$,

$$h(s) \;=\; \sum_{s^*} g(s^*, s)\, h(s^*)\,. \tag{3.11}$$

In (3.11) the sum is taken over all states $s^*$ such that $(s^*, s)$ is an arc in $\Sigma^*(G)$. There are $1 + q^M$ states (with $M = \sum_{j=1}^k m(j)$) in $\Sigma^*(G)$ and the relations (3.11) forms a system of $q^M$ equations that permit one to calculate the cumulative gain $h(s)$ of the state $s$ as a function of $h(s_I)$, for all $s \neq s_I$. We call the ratio $\eta^G := h(s_F)/h(s_I)$ an enumerator associated with the encoder $G$. Of course, the meaning of an enumerator $\eta^G$ depends on the gain functions $g(s^*, s)$ used in (3.11) so that we have now to be more specific.

Let us first remember that, to any state transition $s^* \mapsto s$ in $\Sigma^*(G)$, there is attached a set of $q^{k_B}$ $n$-tuples over $F$ that form a coset $C(s^*, s)$ of the block code generated by the first $k_B$ rows of $G$ and considered as an additive subgroup of $F^n$. (In particular, if $k_B$ is zero, the $k_B$ first rows of $G$ are considered as generating only the zero $n$-tuple, and the cosets $C(s^*, s)$ only contain one $n$-tuple.) The gain functions $g(s^*, s)$ that we use depend only on the coset $C(s^*, s)$ associated with the arc $(s^*, s)$ of $\Sigma^*(G)$. Here follow three examples.

(i) Define $g(s^*, s) = \sum_{v \in C(s^*, s)} x^{sw(v)}$. Since all gain functions $g(s^*, s)$ are polynomials in the indeterminate $x$ with integer coefficients, the enumerator $\eta^G$ is a rational fraction $n(x)/d(x)$ with integer coefficients. One can express it as a power series $\eta^G(x) = \sum_{j=0}^{\infty} \eta_j^G x^j$ obtained by long division of the polynomial $n(x)$ by the polynomial $d(x)$. The coefficient $\eta_j^G$ is then equal to the number of simple sequences $v$ in $C = E(G)$ that satisfy $sw(v) = j$. The power series $\eta^G(x)$ is called the *symbol weight enumerator* associated with the encoder $G$.

(ii) Define $g(s^*, s) = \sum_{v \in C(s^*, s)} y^{ww(v)}$. The enumerator $\eta^G$ is then a rational fraction $n(y)/d(y)$ in the indeterminate $y$ that can be expressed as a power series $\eta^G(y) = \sum_{j=0}^{\infty} \eta_j^G y^j$ in the indeterminate $y$. The coefficient $\eta_j^G$ is equal to the number of simple sequences $v$ in $C = E(G)$ that satisfy $ww(v) = j$. The power series $\eta^G(y)$ is called the *word weight enumerator* associated with the encoder $G$.

(iii) Index the $q$ elements of $F$ in any way by the $q$ integers $0, 1, \cdots, q-1$ and define $g(s^*, s) = \sum_{v \in C(s^*, s)} [\prod_{i=0}^{q-1} z_i^{n_i(v)}]$ where $n_i(v)$ is the number of entries of the $n$-tuple $v$ that are equal to the element of $F$ having index $i$. The enumerator $\eta^G$ is a rational fraction $n(z_0, \cdots, z_{q-1})/d(z_0, \cdots, z_{q-1})$ in the indeterminates $z_0, \cdots, z_{q-1}$, that can be expressed as a power series

$$\eta^G(z_0, \cdots, z_{q-1}) = \sum \eta_{j_0, \cdots, j_{q-1}} z_0^{j_0} z_1^{j_1} \cdots z_{q-1}^{j_{q-1}}.$$

The coefficient $\eta_{j_0, \cdots, j_{q-1}}$ is then equal to the number of simple sequences in $C$ that contain $j_r$ symbols indexed by $r$ for $0 \le r \le q - 1$. The power series $\eta^G(z_0, \cdots, z_{q-1})$ is called the *composition enumerator* of $G$.

In general, the computation of the enumerators $\eta^G$ is difficult. Here are two encoders for which the computation remains reasonably simple. Both are (2,1) encoders over $F = GF(2)$. The first one is $G = [1 + D^2, 1 + D + D^2]$. Its symbol weight enumerator is $\eta^G(x) = x^5/(1 - 2x)$ and its word weight enumerator is $\eta^G(y) = y^3/(1 - 2y)$. The second one is $G = [1 + D + D^3, 1 + D^2 + D^3]$. Its symbol weight enumerator is $\eta^G(x) = (x^6 + x^7 - x^8)/(1 - 2x - x^8)$ and its word weight enumerator is $\eta^G(y) = y^4/(1 - 2y - y^2)$. Some techniques to compute the enumerators $\eta^G$ are given in [67, 114, 115].

Due to the $F$-space structure of $E(G)$, these three enumerators $\eta^G(x)$, $\eta^G(y)$ and $\eta^G(z_0, \cdots, z_{q-1})$ describe the distance properties with respect to an arbitrary code sequence $v$ of the set of all code sequences $u$ such that $v - u$ is a simple sequence. This explains the use of such enumerators to evaluate for example [114] the performances of a binary code over the binary symmetric channels defined in subsection 3.3.1. Some other enumerators, beside giving a description of the encoded simple sequences, give a joint characterization of the encoded simple sequences and of the information sequences to which they correspond [114].

Let us emphasize here that, in general, the property of being a simple sequence depends on the encoder and not just on the code generated by this encoder. In particular, problem 3.3 specifies explicitly which sequences $v$ of a convolutional code $C$ can be rows of a basic encoder $G$ of $C$. Problem 3.4 is concerned with simple sequences relative to a minimal encoder. As a consequence of the property stated in this problem, the three enumerators given above as examples are the same for all minimal encoders of a same code $C$.

Viterbi was the first to associate enumerators with convolutional encoders and to use a state diagram to compute them. His paper [114] is a basic reference in this area.

## 3.3  Decoding of convolutional codes

Let $G$ be a convolutional encoder over the field $F = GF(q)$, and let $\Sigma(G)$ be the unmodified state diagram associated with $G$. Assuming that we use $G$ to encode some information to be transmitted on a noisy channel, we concentrate here on what is done at the receiving end of the channel. We find it useful to develop the state diagram $\Sigma(G)$ associated with $G$ as follows. With each time unit $j \in \mathbb{Z}$ we associate a copy $S(j)$ of the set $\{s_0, s_1, \cdots, s_{q^M-1}\}$ of all states of $\Sigma(G)$. At time unit $j-1$, the encoder is in some state $s(j-1)$ of $S(j-1)$ and, when receiving some information $k$-tuple

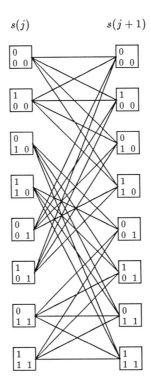

**Figure 3.3 :** The possible state transitions $s(i) \mapsto s(i+1)$ of the encoder $G$.

$a_j$ at time unit $j$, it is driven to some state $s(j)$ of $S(j)$ while producing some element $v_j$ of $F^n$. In figure 3.3 are represented the sets $S(j-1)$ and $S(j)$ of the encoder $G$ given in (3.9) together with the possible state transitions from states in $S(j-1)$ to states in $S(j)$. When this unfolding is made for all $i \in \mathbb{Z}$, we are left with what is called a *trellis diagram*. The trellis associated with $G$ is denoted by $\mathcal{T}(G)$. Part of it is represented in figure 3.4 for $G$ as given in (3.9). To be specific we assume now that the information sequence $a$ is a polynomial of fixed degree $\ell$. Thus we

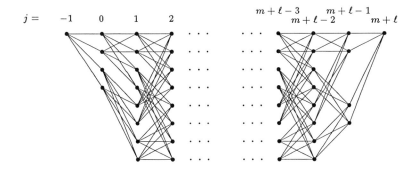

**Figure 3.4 :** The trellis $\mathcal{T}_{m+\ell}(G)$.

have $a = \sum_{j=0}^{\ell} a_j D^j$ with $a_j \in F^k$. This information $a$ is encoded by the encoder $G$ into the sequence $v = aG$ that we write as $v = \sum_{j=0}^{\ell+m} v_j D^j$ with $v_j \in F^n$ and $m$ the maximal degree of the entries of the matrix $G$. To the set of all these polynomial code sequences $v$ of degree $\leq \ell + m$, we attach a "subtrellis" $\mathcal{T}_{m+\ell}(G)$ of $\mathcal{T}(G)$, obtained by juxtaposition of $m + \ell + 2$ copies $S(j)$ with $-1 \leq j \leq m + \ell$, of the states of $\Sigma(G)$. Of course, when $a$ is known to be a polynomial of degree $\leq \ell$, we are sure that at time units $j = -1$ and $j = m + \ell$, the state of the encoder is the zero state $s_0$. For this reason $\mathcal{T}_{m+\ell}(G)$ does not contain all states of $S(j)$ for $-1 \leq j \leq m - 2$ and $\ell + 1 \leq j \leq \ell + m$. This is illustrated by figure 3.4 that represents the subtrellis $\mathcal{T}_{m+\ell}(G)$ associated with the encoder $G$ given in (3.9). As mentioned in the introduction to chapter 2, when a sequence $v$ in $E_\ell(G)$ is transmitted on a noisy channel and received as a sequence $w = \sum_{j=0}^{m+\ell} w_j D^j$ of $n$-tuples $w_j$ over some alphabet $F^*$ possibly different from $F$, the sequence $w$ is used by the decoder to find out an estimate $\hat{a}$ of the information sequence $a = \sum_{j=0}^{\ell} a_j D^j$, $a_j \in F^k$, satisfying $v = aG$. When the decoder works in two steps, first producing an estimate $\hat{v} \in C$ of the transmitted code sequence $v$ and then computing from $\hat{v}$ the estimate

$\hat{a}$ of the information $a$, we call it a *perfect* decoder. To obtain $\hat{a}$ the decoder multiplies $\hat{v}$ by an $n \times k$ matrix $G^*$ that is a right pseudoinverse of $G$ i.e., $GG^* = I_k$. The existence of $G^*$ follows from the property that the rank of the $k \times n$ matrix $G$ is equal to $k$. Since $G$ is a matrix over $F[D]$, the elements of $G^*$ generally belong to the field $F(D)$ of rational fractions over $F$, but it follows from corollary 2.36 that if $G$ is a basic encoder, then it has a polynomial pseudoinverse $G^*$. Perfect decoders were assumed throughout chapter 2 but there exist other decoders. We call them *nonperfect*. With nonperfect decoders, the estimates $\hat{a}_i$ of the information $k$-tuples $a_i$ are not computed from the complete received sequence $w$, so that these decoders do not use the total error correcting capability of the codes. However, their implementation is simpler. The amount of computation needed with these nonperfect decoders is in general much less than with the Viterbi decoders to be described in subsections 3.3.1 and 3.3.3, and the decoding effort is not a random variable as it is for the sequential decoding algorithms mentioned in subsection 3.3.2.

The next three subsections will describe some perfect decoders and the fourth one will describe nonperfect decoders. A perfect decoder obtains first an estimate $\hat{v}$ of the code sequence that was transmitted and received as $w$. As it follows from [43, 115], it is reasonable to choose the estimate $\hat{v}$ to be the code sequence that maximizes the probability $P(w \mid \hat{v})$ to receive $w$ when $\hat{v}$ is transmitted. This method of estimation is sometimes called *maximum likelihood decoding* (or MLD). Of course, to be carried out, it needs a reasonable probabilistic model of the channel. However, we do not go into details here about probabilistic models. What we do is to attach to any channel event $F^n \rightarrow (F^*)^n : v_j \mapsto w_j$ a positive cost $c(v_j, w_j)$. Our goal is then to find a polynomial $\hat{v}$ in $C = E(G)$, having degree $\leq m + \ell$, for which the total cost $c(\hat{v}, w) = \sum_{j=0}^{m+\ell} c(\hat{v}_j, w_j)$ is minimal or at least reasonably small. This goal can be interpreted as finding in $\mathcal{T}_{m+\ell}(G)$ a low cost path from the zero state in $S(-1)$ to the zero state in $S(m + \ell)$, when the cost of a path is the sum of the costs of its arcs, and when the cost of any arc $(s(j-1), s(j))$ with $s(j-1) \in S(j-1)$, $s(j) \in S(j)$ and $-1 \leq j \leq m+\ell-1$, is the minimum of $c(v_j, w_j)$ for all words $v_j$ in the coset $C(s(j-1), s(j))$ of the linear block code generated by the $k_B$ first rows of $G$ (see section 3.2).

## 3.3.1 The Viterbi algorithm

The first perfect decoding algorithm we describe is the Viterbi algorithm [39,113], which works as follows. Let $F = GF(q)$ and $F^*$ be respectively the input and output alphabet of the channel. Let $\ell$ be the degree of the polynomial information sequence $a = \sum_{j=0}^{\ell} a_j D^j$ with $a_j \in F^k$, and let $m$ be the maximum degree of the entries of $G$. The channel input sequence is represented by $v = \sum_{j=0}^{m+\ell} v_j D^j$, $v_j \in F^n$, and the channel output sequence is represented by $w = \sum_{j=0}^{m+\ell} w_j D^j$, $w_j \in (F^*)^n$. Assume that, for some $i \geq 0$, we know the following three things about all states $s^* \in S(i)$.

(i) A path $p(s^*)$ of minimum cost between the zero state $s_0 \in S(-1)$ and the state $s^*$.

(ii) The cost $c(s^*)$ of this path.

(iii) A sequence $v(s^*) = \sum_{j=0}^{i} v_j(s^*) D^j$, $v_j(s^*) \in F^n$, that achieves this minimum cost $c(s^*) = \sum_{j=0}^{i} c(v_j(s^*), w_j)$.

Let us show how to use this knowledge to compute the triples $t(s) = [p(s), c(s), v(s)]$ associated with all states $s$ of $S(i+1)$. To compute these triples we denote by $\mathcal{P}(s)$ the set of immediate predecessors $s^* \in S(i)$ of the state $s \in S(i+1)$. Thus $(s^*, s)$ is an arc in $\mathcal{T}_{m+\ell}(G)$ for every $s^* \in \mathcal{P}(s)$. Then, for all $s^* \in \mathcal{P}(s)$, we search in the block code $C(s^*, s)$ a word $v_{i+1}(s^*)$ that minimizes the cost $c(v_{i+1}(s^*), w_{i+1})$ and we denote this cost by $c_{i+1}(s^*, s)$. The cost $c(s)$ of the "best" path from $s_0 \in S(-1)$ to $s$ is then given by

$$c(s) = \min_{s^* \in \mathcal{P}(s)} [c(s^*) + c_{i+1}(s^*, s)], \qquad (3.12)$$

and using a state $s^*$ that achieves the minimum in (3.12) we define

$$p(s) \; = \; p(s^*) \cup (s^*, s) \,, \tag{3.13}$$

$$v(s) \; = \; v(s^*) \, + \, v_{i+1}(s^*) D^{i+1} \,. \tag{3.14}$$

Equations (3.12) to (3.14) are the *updating equations* of the Viterbi decoder. Due to the regularity of the trellis $\mathcal{T}_{m+\ell}(G)$, the updating method is identical for all time units $i$ satisfying $m \leq i \leq \ell$. The result of this iterative updating is to produce eventually a sequence $v(s_0)$, with $s_0$ the zero state in $S(m + \ell)$, that is chosen as the estimate $\hat{v}$ of $v$. As it was recognized by Forney [41], the path $p(s_0)$ associated with this sequence $v(s_0)$ has the minimum cost $c(s_0)$ among all paths from $s_0 \in S(-1)$ to $s_0 \in S(m + \ell)$. We state this as a theorem.

**Theorem 3.5 :** Let $w = \sum_{i=0}^{m+\ell} w_i D^i$ with $w_i \in (F^*)^n$, be the sequence received after transmission of a code sequence. The polynomial $\hat{v} = v(s_0)$ over $F^n$ (with $s_0$ the zero state in $S(m+\ell)$) that is produced by the Viterbi algorithm achieves the minimum value of $c(v, w)$ among all polynomials $v \in E(G)$ of degree $\leq m + \ell$.

**Proof :** The proof is by induction. If we know for all $s^* \in S(i)$ the triple $t(s^*) = [p(s^*), c(s^*), v(s^*)]$ for which $c(s^*)$ is minimal, the formulas (3.12), (3.13) and (3.14) produce for any $s \in S(i+1)$ a triple $t(s) = [p(s), c(s), v(s)]$ for which $c(s)$ is minimal. We omit the details. $\square$

The cost function can be given a probabilistic interpretation if it is defined to be

$$c(v_i, w_i) \; = \; -\alpha \, \log P(w_i \mid v_i) + \beta \,, \tag{3.15}$$

where $i$ is the time unit, $\alpha$ and $\beta$ are real numbers with $\alpha > 0$ such that all costs are nonnegative, and $P(w_i \mid v_i)$ is the probability to receive $w_i \in (F^*)^n$ when $v_i \in F^n$ is transmitted on the channel. For simplicity we assume here that the channel is memoryless at the word level, which means that the probabilities $P(w_i \mid v_i)$ are independent of the time unit $i$.

If one knows the probabilities $P(w_i \mid v_i)$ and if one uses the cost function (3.15), one can prove that the sequence $v(s_0)$ produced by the Viterbi algorithm maximizes the probability $P(w \mid v(s_0))$ to receive $w$ when $v(s_0)$ was transmitted [41]. Thus, in this case the Viterbi algorithm is a MLD algorithm.

Consider now the particular case where $F$ and $F^*$ are both $GF(2)$ and where the channel is the memoryless binary symmetric channel $BSC(p)$ with crossover probability $p$. On this channel, for $a, b \in GF(2)$, the probability $P(b \mid a)$ to receive the symbol $b$ when the symbol $a$ is transmitted is equal to $p$ for $a \neq b$ and to $1 - p$ for $a = b$. We assume $p < 1/2$. Choosing $\alpha = -1/\log[p/(1-p)]$ and $\beta = \alpha n \log(1-p)$ in (3.15) makes the cost $c(v_i, w_i)$ equal to the symbol distance between $v_i$ and $w_i$. Viterbi [114] has shown that on $BSC(p)$ the probability $P_f$ to make a first decoding error at any time $i$ with MLD satisfies

$$P_f \leq \left[ \eta^G(x) - 1 \right]_{x = 2\sqrt{p\,(1-p)}} ,$$

with $\eta^G(x)$ the symbol weight enumerator of the simple sequences of $E(G)$. Since the first nonzero coefficient in $\sum_{j=0}^{\infty} \eta_j^G x^j - 1$ is $\eta_{sd(C)}^G$, this clearly explains the influence of $sd(C)$ on $P_f$ and the reason why $sd(C)$ has been recognized as a quality criterion for binary convolutional codes at least for small values of $p$. To the author's knowledge no similar expression has been obtained to date for memoryless channels accepting symbols of an arbitrary Galois field $GF(q)$, although the significance of $sd(C)$ seems to be intuitively clear also in this case. Similar comments could be made on the importance of the parameter $wd(C)$ for a code used on a channel that modifies the codewords as a whole, rather than on a symbol by symbol basis. Such a channel is sometimes called a phased burst channel [67]. In the same way, it is reasonable to use $dr(C)$ as a quality criterion for a code $C$ used on a channel modifying the symbols *and* the codewords (see section 11.2).

Let us now briefly discuss the amount of storage space that is necessary

for the Viterbi algorithm. At each time unit $i$, the algorithm computes a
new set of costs $c(s)$, $s \in S(i)$, and it extends a set of paths $p(s^*)$ and
of code sequences $v(s^*)$, $s^* \in S(i-1)$. The explicit storage of the paths
$p(s^*)$ is not necessary to the algorithm and the space needed to store $c(s)$
increases only as a logarithmic function of $i$. The problem is different with
the $q^M$ sequences $v(s)$, $s \in S(i)$, because the space needed to store them
is proportional to $i$. Thus, if the degree $\ell$ of the information sequence $a$
is large, the required space may go beyond the available memory space
of the decoder. To overcome this problem one may decide to choose the
estimate $\hat{v}_i$ long before time unit $\ell + m$. For example one may decide to
choose, for some integer $b > 0$, the estimate $\hat{v}_i$ of $v_i$ to be the coefficient
of $D^i$ in any one of the sequence $v(s)$ with $s \in S(i+b)$. The integer
$b$ thus represents the fixed delay allowed to the decoder to produce its
estimates $\hat{v}_i$. It has been observed experimentally [67] that the choice of
a specific state $s \in S(i+b)$ and of the corresponding sequence $v(s)$ to
find $\hat{v}_i$ is not far from being irrelevant for sufficiently large $b$, and that
$b = 5m$ is a quite acceptable value, with $m$ the maximum degree of the
entries of $G$. The advantage of this *truncated* Viterbi algorithm is that,
at time $i$, only the $b + 1$ last words of all sequences $v(s)$, $s \in S(i)$, must
be kept into the memory. The price to be paid is that there may be some
integers $i$ for which the estimates $\hat{v}_i$ are different from those that would
have been chosen by the original Viterbi algorithm. Another property of
this truncated algorithm is that the sequence of the estimates $\hat{v}_i$ is not
necessarily a code sequence. Although the truncated Viterbi algorithm is
not a perfect decoder, the information retrieval $\hat{v} \mapsto \hat{a}$ may yet be achieved
by a matrix multiplication $\hat{a} = \hat{v} G^*$ with $G^*$ a pseudoinverse of the encoder
$G$.

### 3.3.2   The stack algorithm

In the Viterbi algorithm no triple $t(s) = [p(s), c(s), v(s)]$, $s \in S(i+1)$,
is computed before the evaluation of all triples $t(s^*)$, $s^* \in S(i)$. Since,

for any $i$, only one state $s$ in $S(i)$ is an intermediate state in the path selected by the Viterbi algorithm from $s_0 \in S(-1)$ to $s_0 \in S(\ell + m)$ , the work carried out by this algorithm may appear to be rather heavy with respect to the obtained result, and the temptation arises to find simpler algorithms. *Sequential decoding algorithms* like the Fano algorithm [33] and the stack algorithm [55, 117] are a step in this direction. As an illustration we describe here the stack algorithm. In this algorithm the triples $t(s)$ are not evaluated in the order of the time units $i$ $(0 \le i \le m + \ell)$ to which the states $s$ correspond, but in the order of the increasing value of the cost $c(s^*)$ of the predecessors $s^* \in P(s)$.

Suppose indeed that we have already drawn up a list $\mathcal{K}$ (called a *stack*) of triples $t(s)$ for some states $s$ in some of the sets $S(i)$ with $0 \le i \le m+\ell+1$. In such a triple $t(s)$, the path $p(s)$ is not necessarily the minimum cost path leading to $s$, but the cost $c(s)$ and the sequence $v(s)$ are of course the cost and the estimate associated with this path. Moreover, to draw up this list we did not use as such the costs $c(v_i, w_i) \ge 0$ introduced above (see (3.15) for example), but we subtracted from all of them some positive quantity $c_0$. As a consequence, some of these costs may become negative numbers. We call them the *modified costs*.

At the beginning of the decoding procedure, the stack $\mathcal{K}$ contains the unique triple $t(s_0)$, $s_0 \in S(-1)$, in which $c(s_0)$ and $v(s_0)$ are zero and $p(s_0)$ is empty. To extend the stack we assume that we have ordered the triples $t(s)$ of $\mathcal{K}$ according to the value of the cost function $c(s)$, thus putting at the top of the stack the triple $t(s)$ for which $c(s)$ has the smallest value. An elementary step of the stack algorithm consists in expanding the first triple $t(s^*)$ of $\mathcal{K}$ to obtain from it a set of $q^{k-k_B}$ new triples, one for each state $s$ such that $(s^*, s)$ is an arc of the trellis $\mathcal{T}(m+\ell)$, to delete then the triple $t(s^*)$ and to finally reorder the stack (which contains now $q^{k-k_B} - 1$ more states) according to the cost $c(s)$ of each triple $t(s)$. To obtain the $q^{k-k_B}$ new triples $t(s)$ is quite simple. Assume that $s^*$ is a state of $S(i)$ and let $s$ be any state in $S(i+1)$ having $s^*$ as predecessor i.e., $s^* \in \mathcal{P}(s)$. For each such $s$, find in the block code $C(s^*, s)$ the word $v_{i+1}$ that minimizes the modified cost $c(v_{i+1}, w_{i+1})$, with $w_{i+1}$ the word received at time unit $i+1$. Then define the entries of $t(s)$ by

$$
\begin{aligned}
c(s) &= c(s^*) + c(v_{i+1}, w_{i+1}), \\
p(s) &= p(s^*) \cup (s^*, s), \\
v(s) &= v(s^*) + D^{i+1} v_{i+1}.
\end{aligned}
$$

We iterate this step up to obtaining at the top of the stack $\mathcal{K}$ a triple $t(s_0)$ with $s_0$ the zero state in $S(m+\ell)$. The element $v(s_0)$ of this triple is the estimate $\hat{v}$ of the transmitted sequence $v$. The positive quantity $c_0$ subtracted from the initial costs $c(v_i, w_i) \geq 0$ is called the *bias*. It is of course an important parameter of the stack decoder, and it must be carefully selected because a bad choice may have unpleasant consequences. For example, if we choose $c_0$ sufficiently large to make all costs negative, the cost $c(s)$ of all successors $s$ of $s^*$ always satisfies $c(s) < c(s^*)$. As a consequence, the first triple of the stack is always obtained from the expansion of the preceding first triple $t(s^*)$: if at a certain instant the triple $t(s^*)$ occupies the first position in the stack, only those triples $t(s)$ such that $s$ can be reached from $s^*$ will possibly occupy later the first position in the stack. Conversely, if the bias $c_0$ is zero, the work performed by the stack algorithm will be essentially the same as the work performed by the Viterbi algorithm. The importance of $c_0$ was first recognized by Fano [33]. The value he suggested was later interpreted by Massey [81] in terms of a metric suitable to decoding variable length codes.

Any implementation of the stack decoding algorithm has to incorporate solutions to several practical problems such as the reordering of the stack and the possibility of stack overflow. We refer the reader to [67] and to the current literature (see [47], for example) for detailed information about these problems. Let us also mention that in place of using a cost function, several authors use a gain function. In this case the problem is of course to find a path of maximum gain in $\mathcal{T}(m+\ell)$.

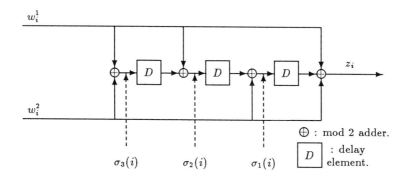

**Figure 3.5 :** The syndrome former associated
with $G^{\perp} = [1 + D^2 + D^3, 1 + D + D^3]$.

### 3.3.3   Perfect syndrome decoding

Both the Viterbi decoder and the stack algorithm make a direct use of
the received sequence $w$ to compute an estimate $\hat{v}$ of $v$. However, when
the output alphabet $F^*$ of the channel coincides with the input alphabet
$F = GF(q)$, it is possible to define a function of $w$ called the syndrome
and to use it in the decoding. From chapter 2, we know indeed that an
$(n, k)$ convolutional code $C = E(G)$, with $G$ a $k \times n$ polynomial matrix
of rank $k$, can be defined as the set of $v \in \mathcal{F}^n$ that satisfy $v(G^{\perp})^T = 0$,
where $G^{\perp}$ is an $(n - k) \times n$ polynomial matrix of rank $n - k$ that satisfies
$G(G^{\perp})^T = 0$. Such a matrix $G^{\perp}$ is called a *parity check matrix* of $C$ and,
for an arbitrary element $w$ of $\mathcal{F}^n$, the sequence $z = w(G^{\perp})^T$ is called the
*syndrome* of $w$ with respect to $G^{\perp}$. The circuit that computes $z = w(G^{\perp})^T$
is called *the syndrome former* associated with the parity check matrix
$G^{\perp}$. In [108-109] a decoding algorithm is presented that makes use of the
syndrome $z = w(G^{\perp})^T$ of the received sequence $w \in \mathcal{F}^n$. This algorithm
appears as a specific implementation of the Viterbi algorithm described in

subsection 3.3.1. Instead of describing it in the general case, we only give a simple example. Consider the $(2,1)$ convolutional code $C$ over $F = GF(2)$ generated by the encoder $G = [g_1, g_2]$ with

$$g_1 = 1 + D + D^3, \quad g_2 = 1 + D^2 + D^3 .$$

The syndrome former associated with the parity check matrix $G^\perp = [g_2, g_1]$ of $C$ is represented in figure 3.5. At time unit $i$, it receives the word $w_i = (w_i^1, w_i^2) \in F^2$ of the sequence $w$ and it computes a new symbol $z_i$ of the syndrome $z = \sum_i z_i D^i$. To compute $z_i$ it needs some information that is conveyed by the words $w_i$, $w_{i-1}$, $w_{i-2}$ and $w_{i-3}$. This information can be summarized in the triple $\sigma(i) = [\sigma_1(i), \sigma_2(i), \sigma_3(i)]$ of elements of $F$. This triple, represented in figure 3.5, is called the state of the syndrome former at time $i$ and its components satisfy

$$
\begin{aligned}
\sigma_3(i) &= w_i^1 + w_i^2 , \\
\sigma_2(i) &= \sigma_3(i-1) + w_i^1 , \\
\sigma_1(i) &= \sigma_2(i-1) + w_i^2 ,
\end{aligned}
$$

while the output $z_i$ of the syndrome former at time $i$ is given by

$$z_i = \sigma_1(i-1) + w_i^1 + w_i^2 .$$

Let us now denote by $m$ the maximum degree of the entries of $G$ and by $m^\perp$ the maximum degree of the entries of $G^\perp$. For basic $(2,1)$ encoders $G$ and $G^\perp$, one has $m = m^\perp$. If the degree of the information sequence $a$ is known to be $\leq \ell$, the degree of the received sequence $w$ is then known to be $\leq \ell + m$. For $i \in [m + \ell + 1, \, m + m^\perp + \ell]$, no word $w_i$ is received but the decoder fulfils $w$ with $m^\perp$ zero words $w_i$ in order to be able to calculate the last $m^\perp$ symbols of $z$. Figure 3.6 represents the state transitions $\sigma(i-1) \mapsto \sigma(i)$ that are compatible with $z_i = 0$ and $z_i = 1$ respectively, together with the pair $w_i = (w_i^1, w_i^2)$ that drives the syndrome former from state $\sigma(i-1)$ to state

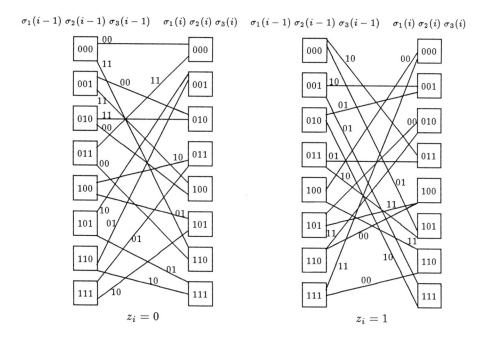

Figure 3.6 : The possible state transitions $\sigma(i-1) \mapsto \sigma(i)$ of the syndrome former $G^{\perp}$.

$\sigma(i)$ and produces the output $z_i$. If one subtracts from $w = \sum_{i=0}^{m+\ell} w_i D^i$ any sequence $e = \sum_{i=0}^{m+\ell} e_i D^i$, $e_i \in F^2$, that produces the same syndrome

$$e(G^{\perp})^T = w(G^{\perp})^T, \qquad (3.16)$$

the sequence $\hat{v} = w - e$ will satisfy $\hat{v}(G^{\perp})^T = 0$ and hence will be a sequence of $C$. The goal of the syndrome decoding algorithm is to find among all sequences $e$ that satisfy (3.16) a reasonable candidate to produce the estimate $\hat{v}$ of $v$, by subtraction from $w$.

Assume that the channel is a binary memoryless symmetric channel, as described in subsection 3.3.1. In this case it is reasonable (see for example

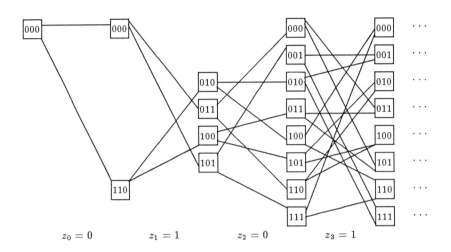

**Figure 3.7** : The trellis $T(z)$ for $z = D + D^3 + \dots$ .

[43]) to choose $e$ to be a sequence that satisfies (3.16) and contains the smallest number of 1's. To find this $e$, one associates with the syndrome $z$ a trellis $T(z)$. This trellis is obtained by the juxtaposition of elementary building blocks which are the two graphs of figure 3.6 : if $z_i$ is 0, one uses the left side of this figure and if $z_i$ is 1, one uses its right side. In figure 3.7 are represented the four first stages of $T(z)$ for $z = D + D^3 + \cdots$.

If one assumes that the information sequence $a$ is a polynomial of degree $\ell$, the trellis $T(z)$ then contains $m + m^\perp + \ell + 1$ building blocks taken for figure 3.6 and $m + m^\perp + \ell + 2$ sets of states corresponding to all time units $i$ from $i = -1$ to $i = m + m^\perp + \ell$. As in the classical Viterbi algorithm, the first and the last of these sets of states are not complete since one has assumed $\sigma(i) = 0$ for $i \leq -1$ and $i \geq m + m^\perp + \ell$. To find the sequence $e$ of minimum symbol weight compatible with $z$, we associate with each arc $(s^*, s)$ of $T(z)$ a cost $c(s^*, s)$ chosen to be the symbol weight of the pair $w_i$ associated with it. The Viterbi algorithm is then used to find in $\mathcal{T}(z)$ the path of minimum cost (and the associated sequence $e$) from the initial zero state to the final zero state. The advantages of this syndrome implementation of the Viterbi decoder are discussed in [108-109]. A syndrome implementation of the stack decoder is also possible, as suggested as problem 3.5.

### 3.3.4 Nonperfect decoding methods

The decoding methods described so far do need powerful computing devices, especially those based on the Viterbi algorithm. Other decoding methods exist that are nonperfect but more easily implemented. In these methods the decoder computes for any time unit $i$ an estimate $\hat{a}_i = f(w_{i-M}, \cdots, w_i, \cdots, w_{i+L})$; $M, L \geq 0$, of the information $k$-tuple $a_i$. This approach to decoding is called *definite decoding* [102].

Instead of using the received words $w_{i+j}$ with $-M \leq j \leq -1$, as the first $M$ arguments of $f$, the decoder can use the $M$ previous estimates $\hat{v}_{i+j}$ with $-M \leq j \leq -1$, of the transmitted words $v_{i+j}$. These estimates are indeed computable for each time unit $i$ just by reencoding the previous estimates $\hat{a}_{i+j}$ with $j < 0$. The corresponding decoding methods are then called *feedback decoding* methods.

A comparison of definite and feedback decoding methods was made in [85] (see also [67]). The *threshold* decoding method first developed by Massey [74] was a landmark in the development of the nonperfect feedback decoding methods. In this decoding method the function $f$ above is obtained as the result of a set of votes in which several estimates of $a_i$ participate.

Feedback decoding methods may suffer from a type of *noncatastrophic* error propagation due to the fact that some estimates $\hat{v}_{i+j}$ used as arguments of the function $f$ may be erroneous. This phenomenon is considered in [75]. A careful distinction has to be made between this type of error propagation, which is a decoder property, and the catastophic error propagation considered in chapter 2, which is an encoder property.

Let us notice here that catastrophic error propagation is not avoided by use of a nonperfect decoder in place of a perfect decoder. Let indeed $G = \sum_{j=0}^{m} G_j D^j$ be a catastrophic encoder and let $e \in \mathcal{F}^k$ be a sequence satisfying $sw(e) = \infty$ while $sw(eG)$ is finite. It follows that, for any $a \in \mathcal{F}^k$, there exists at least one $b := a + e \in \mathcal{F}^k$ that satisfies $sd(a, b) = \infty$ while $sd(aG, bG)$ is finite. Write $u := aG$ and $v := bG$ as $u = \sum_j u_j D^j$ and $v = \sum_j v_j D^j$ respectively. It follows that there exists $j_0 \in \mathbb{Z}$ such that for all $j \geq j_0$, one has $u_j = v_j$ while the number of $j \geq j_0$ for which $a_j$ is not equal to $b_j$ is infinite. Consider now the definite decoding method mentioned above and assume that the information $a$ was encoded and transmitted as $u = aG$. Whether $u$ or $v$ was transmitted, the word transmitted at time units $i \geq j_0$ (i.e., $u_i$ or $v_i$) will anyway be the same since these two sequences coincide after time unit $j_0$. As a consequence, for $i \geq j_0 + M$, it is impossible to decide, on the basis of the received words $w_{i+j}$, $-M \leq j \leq L$, whether $u_i$ or $v_i$ was transmitted. It follows that, for all $i$ such that $a_i$ is not equal to $b_i$, the estimate $\hat{a}_i$ of $a_i$ will be erroneous with probability $\geq .5$, which is a catastrophic situation for the decoder. On the other hand, if feedback decoding is used in place of definite decoding, the situation of the decoder will not be better, since a finite number of channel errors (in these words where $u_j \neq v_j$ holds) may lead to the decoding decision $\hat{a} = b$, thus causing an infinite number of errors in the estimated information sequence.

In this analysis we have considered infinite information sequences $a$ and $b$, but similar comments apply to polynomial information sequences.

## 3.4 Distance profile and column distance function of a convolutional encoder

Let us first consider two arbitrary elements $u$ and $v$ of $\mathcal{F}^n$, having delay $\geq 0$

$$u = \sum_{i=0}^{\infty} u_i D^i, \quad v = \sum_{i=0}^{\infty} v_i D^i; \quad u_i, v_i \in F^n.$$

For any integer $j \geq 0$ define the numbers

$$dp^{(j)}(u, v) := \sum_{i=0}^{j} sd(u_i, v_i), \tag{3.17}$$

which obviously satisfy $dp^{(j+1)}(u, v) \geq dp^{(j)}(u, v)$, all $j \geq 0$. These numbers $dp^{(j)}(u, v)$ may be thought of as being the symbol distances between the sequences $u \bmod D^{j+1}$ and $v \bmod D^{j+1}$, or equivalently as being the symbol weight of $(u - v) \bmod D^{j+1}$.

Let now $a = \sum_{i=0}^{\infty} a_i D^i$ and $b = \sum_{i=0}^{\infty} b_i D^i$, $a_i, b_i \in F^k$, be two elements of $\mathcal{F}^k$ having degree $\geq 0$. When considered as information sequences to be encoded by the encoder $G$, these two sequences induce in the state diagram $\mathcal{T}(G)$ associated with $G$ two sequences of states denoted by $s_a$ and $s_b$ respectively:

$$
\begin{aligned}
s_a &= [s_a(-1), s_a(0), \cdots, s_a(i), \cdots], \\
s_b &= [s_b(-1), s_b(0), \cdots, s_b(i), \cdots].
\end{aligned}
\tag{3.18}
$$

We call these two state sequences *disjoint* if $s_a(i) = s_b(i)$ implies $i = -1$. If $a$ and $b$ satisfy del $a \geq 0$, del $b \geq 0$ and if they induce disjoint state sequences, we call them disjoint information sequences with respect to $G$. In particular, if $a$ and $b$ are disjoint information sequences with respect to a convolutional encoder $G$, they satisfy $a_0 \neq b_0$.

With any $k \times n$ encoder $G$ and to any integer $j \geq 0$, we now associate two numbers. The first one $dp^{(j)}(G)$ is defined by

$$dp^{(j)}(G) := \min_{a,b} dp^{(j)}(aG, bG), \tag{3.19}$$

where the minimum is taken over all $a, b \in \mathcal{F}^k$ that are disjoint information sequences with respect to $G$. Equivalently we define $dp^{(j)}(G)$ by

$$dp^{(j)}(G) := \min_a dp^{(j)}(aG, 0), \qquad (3.20)$$

where the minimum is taken over all sequences $a$ that are disjoint from the zero sequence. If $G$ is a noncatastrophic encoder it follows from (2.3) that the sequence of the numbers $dp^{(j)}(G)$ has no upper bound for $j \to \infty$. Conversely, if $G$ is a catastrophic encoder, there exists $j_0$ such that $dp^{(j)}(G) = dp^{(j_0)}(G)$ is true for all $j \geq j_0$.

The second number $cdf^{(j)}(G)$ is defined by

$$cdf^{(j)}(G) := \min_{a,b} dp^{(j)}(aG, bG), \qquad (3.21)$$

where the minimum is taken over all polynomials $a, b$ over $F^k$ satisfying $a_0 \neq b_0$ without the requirement of being disjoint. Obviously, one has

$$dp^{(j)}(G) \geq cdf^{(j)}(G) \qquad (3.22)$$

and

$$cdf^{(j+1)}(G) \geq cdf^{(j)}(G) \qquad (3.23)$$

for all $j$. However, for $j_0$ sufficiently large, one has $cdf^{(j)}(G) = cdf^{(j_0)}(G)$ for all $j \geq j_0$. The smallest $j_0$ having this property is an interesting parameter of the encoder $G$. From these numbers $dp^{(j)}(G)$ and $cdf^{(j)}(G)$ we construct now two sequences of numbers.

The sequence

$$dp(G) = [dp^{(0)}(G), dp^{(1)}(G), \cdots, dp^{(j)}(G), \cdots] \qquad (3.24)$$

of all integers $dp^{(j)}(G)$ is called the *distance profile* associated with the encoder $G$. This concept was introduced by Johannesson [56-59], who actually considered only the $m + 1$ first components of $dp(G)$ with $m$ the largest degree of the entries of the encoder $G$. Upper bounds on $dp^{(m)}(G)$ are discussed in [1].

The sequence

$$cdf(G) = [cdf^{(0)}(G), cdf^{(1)}(G), \cdots, cdf^{(j)}(G), \cdots] \tag{3.25}$$

is called the *column distance function* [67] of the encoder $G$.

The distance measures $dp(G)$ and $cdf(G)$ give rise to two criteria for choosing between encoders generating codes with the same minimum symbol distance. The speed of increase of their components as a function of $j$ is indeed recognized [67] as a quality criterion for binary codes used on the channel $BSC(p)$ with a sequential decoder.

Some years ago, Hemmati and Costello [53] introduced the class of *asymptotically catastrophic $(n, k)$ encoders*. This concept is related to the concept of distance profile. Such a class can be characterized as follows. For fixed $F, n$ and $k$ and for any $m \geq 0$, let $\mathcal{G}_P(m)$ be the set of all $k \times n$ polynomial matrices over $F$ having entries of degree $\leq m$, and satisfying some property $P$ called the defining property. Define

$$\alpha_P(m) := \max_{G \in \mathcal{G}_P(m)} \left[ \limsup_{j \to \infty} dp^{(j)}(G)/j \right]. \tag{3.26}$$

It turns out that, for some choices of the defining property $P$, the limit of $\alpha_P(m)$ for $m \to \infty$ is zero. Following Hemmati and Costello, we shall say in this case that the defining property $P$ specifies an *asymptotically catastrophic class* of encoders. As an example, let $\mathcal{G}_P(m)$ be the class of $(2,1)$ encoders $G = [g_1, g_2]$ over $F = GF(2)$ that satisfy the following set $P$ of requirements.

**(i)** del $(g_1)$ = del $(g_2)$ = 0,

**(ii)** deg $(g_1)$ = deg $(g_2)$ = $m$,

**(iii)** $g_1 + g_2 = D + D^2 + \cdots + D^{m-2} + D^{m-1}$.

Hemmati and Costello have proved that $P$ specifies an asymptotically catastrophic class of encoders. They also argue that good encoders for large values of $m$ cannot be discovered in an asymptotically catastrophic class of encoders because such encoders generate codes that are ill-conditioned for sequential decoding algorithms, such as the stack algorithm considered in subsection 3.3.2.

## 3.5 Some constructions of binary convolutional codes

We first mention some code constructions for use with a perfect decoder. Let $\mathcal{G}(m)$ be the set of $1 \times 2$ convolutional encoders $G = [g_1, g_2]$ over $F = GF(2)$ that satisfy del $g_1 = $ del $g_2 = 0$, deg $g_1 = $ deg $g_2 = m$. For $g \in F[D]$ let $\mathcal{G}_g(m)$ be the subset of $\mathcal{G}(m)$ containing all $G$ satisfying $g_1 + g_2 = g$. The cardinalities of these sets are $|\mathcal{G}(m)| = 2^{2(m-1)}$, $|\mathcal{G}_g(m)| = 2^{m-1}$. Since the codes are linear, finding $sd(E(G))$ just requires finding the minimum value of $sw(aG) = sw(ag_1) + sw(ag_2)$ among all nonzero elements $a$ of $\mathcal{F}$. In computing $sw(ag_1) + sw(ag_2)$ we can use the following formula. Let $\gamma_1$ and $\gamma_2$ be polynomials over $F$ in the indeterminate $D$, define $\gamma := \gamma_1 + \gamma_2$ and denote by $\chi = \sum_i \chi_i D^i$ the element of $F[D]$ such that $\chi_i$ is 1 if and only if the coefficient of $D^i$ is 1 in both $\gamma_1$ and $\gamma_2$. In this case one has

$$sw(\gamma_1) + sw(\gamma_2) = sw(\gamma) + 2sw(\chi). \tag{3.27}$$

Using (3.27) and some more specific arguments, certain authors have investigated in detail some of these sets $\mathcal{G}_g(m)$ with the symbol distance $sd[E(G)]$ or the column distance function $cdf[E(G)]$ as the underlying criterion.

In particular, Bahl and Jelinek [3] investigated the sets $\mathcal{G}_g(m)$ with $g = D + D^2 + \cdots + D^{m-2} + D^{m-1}$ for $2 \le m \le 23$ to obtain noncatastrophic encoders specifying codes $C$ with a large value of $sd(G)$. For $m \le 16$ and

$m = 18$, they obtained codes satisfying $sd(C) = m + 3$. This is the maximum value of $sd(C)$ compatible with the structure and, for some values of $m$, it is even equal to some known upper bound on $sd(C)$. Unfortunately, as mentioned in section 3.4, these polynomials $g$ make $\mathcal{G}_g(m)$ an asymptotically catastrophic class of encoders: for large $m$ the encoders in $\mathcal{G}_g(m)$ have a poor distance profile $dp(G)$.

Other sets $\mathcal{G}_g(m)$ are obtained by choosing $g = D$. The corresponding codes were investigated by Massey and Costello [80] who called them "quick look in" (or QLI) codes. Using a QLI code on a binary input and binary output channel, one obtains a first quick estimate $\hat{a}$ of $a$ by computing $\hat{a} = D^{-1}(w_1 + w_2)$ from the received noisy sequence $w = (w_1, w_2)$.

Other constructions of encoders $G$ with a good $sd[E(G)]$ or a good $cdp(G)$ are given in [56-59, 63, 86]. Most of these constructions use an algorithmic procedure to select good codes in the investigated class. However, in [60-61, 82, 100], algebraic methods are used to evaluate the minimum symbol distance of convolutional codes. In [82], the authors prove and use the following property: if the polynomial $a = \sum_{j=0}^{\ell} a_j D^j$, $a_j \in F$ can be written as $a = (D^m - b)^s \alpha(D)$ with $b$ a nonzero element of $F$ and $\alpha(D)$ a polynomial relatively prime with $D^m - b$, the quantity $sw(a)$ is lower-bounded by $sw[(D^m - b)^s]$ times $sw(\alpha \bmod D^m - b)$. In [112], a connection is established between quasi-cyclic block codes and convolutional codes.

Another algebraic approach is followed by Seguin in [110]. He makes first the following remark. For $q$ a prime power and $k$ a divisor of $n$, the finite fields $F = GF(q)$, $F_k = GF(q^k)$ and $F_n = GF(q^n)$ are nested: $F \subseteq F_k \subseteq F_n$. To any polynomial $g$ over $F_n$, he associates the subset $C_g = \{ag : a \in F_k((D))\}$ of $F_n((D))$. Then he represents any element of $F_n$ as an $n$-tuple over $F$ and, more generally, any element of $F_n((D))$ as an $n$-tuple over $F((D))$. When applied to $C_g$, this representation produces an image $C$ of $C_g$ that is an $(n, k)$ convolutional code over $F$. In [110] the algebraic structure of these codes is discussed and several codes are found that have a good minimum symbol distance.

Let us now mention some references describing constructions of codes to be used with a nonperfect decoder. The landmark contribution in this area was the monograph [74] by Massey. Other contributions are [6, 15, 25, 76-77, 101-102, 106]. For a more complete survey of several construction methods of very good binary codes, we refer the reader to [67].

# 3.6   The zero run problem

Let $G$ be a $k \times n$ minimal encoder over $F$, let $\Sigma(G)$ be the state diagram associated with $G$ (see figure 3.2, for example), and let $v = \sum_{j=r}^{\infty} v_j D^j$, $v_j \in F^n$, be given by $v = aG$ where $a = \sum_{j=r}^{\infty} a_j D^j$, $a_j \in F^k$, is an element of $\mathcal{F}^k$. Assume that at time unit $i$, the encoder $G$ was lead by the $i - r + 1$ first words $a_j$ of $a$ into the state $s_i$ of the state diagram $\Sigma(G)$. This state $s_i$ takes into account the influence of the $k$-tuples $a_j$ with $j \leq i$, on the $n$-tuples $v_j$ for $j \geq i + 1$. As a result, for all $t \geq 1$, the $(t + 1)$-tuple $(s_i, a_{i+1}, \cdots, a_{i+t})$ specifies the words $v_j$ of $v$ for $i + 1 \leq j \leq t$. We call the $t$-tuple $v^* = (v_{i+1}, \cdots, v_{i+t})$ over $F^n$, a subsequence of length $t$ of the encoded sequence $v$. If in such a subsequence all $n$-tuples $v_j$ are zero, we say that the corresponding $(t + 1)$-tuple $(s_i, a_{i+1}, \cdots, a_{i+t})$ is a $t$-zero run of the convolutional code $C = E(G)$. In [40], Forney shows that when $G$ is a minimal encoder, the number of $t$-zero runs in the convolutional code $C = E(G)$ is a function only of the degrees $m(j)$ of $G$. He presents two proofs of this result, and we give now the more algebraic of these two proofs.

Denote by $\mathcal{Y}_t$ the set of all $(t + 1)$-tuples $y = (s_i, a_{i+1}, \cdots, a_{i+t})$ where $s_i$ is a state of $\Sigma(G)$ represented as in (3.8) and the $a_j$ are $k$-tuples over $F$. The set $\mathcal{Y}_t$ has the structure of an $F$-space: for all $y_1, y_2$ in $\mathcal{Y}_t$ and all $\alpha_1, \alpha_2 \in F$, one has indeed $\alpha_1 y_1 + \alpha_2 y_2 \in \mathcal{Y}_t$, when addition and multiplication by elements of $F$ are defined componentwise. Denote then by $\mathcal{V}_t$ the set of all subsequences $v^* = (v_{i+1}, \cdots, v_{i+t})$ that can be produced by $G$. Obviously this set $\mathcal{V}_t$ is also an $F$-space. If we denote by $\phi_t$ the mapping $\mathcal{Y}_t \to \mathcal{V}_t : (s_i, a_{i+1}, \cdots, a_{i+t}) \mapsto (v_{i+1}, \cdots, v_{i+t})$ induced by the encoder $G$, it follows from the linearity of the encoding operation that this mapping $\phi_t$ is a vector space homomorphism, i.e., $\phi_t(\alpha_1 y_1 + \alpha_2 y_2) = \alpha_1 \phi_t(y_1) + \alpha_2 \phi_t(y_2)$ is true for all $\alpha_1, \alpha_2 \in F$ and all $y_1, y_2 \in \mathcal{Y}_t$. The kernel $\ker(\phi_t)$ of this homomorphism (i.e., the set of all $y$ s.t. $\phi_t(y) = 0$) is an $F$-subspace of $\mathcal{Y}_t$, and as a consequence of subsection 1.1.3 we have the following relation between the dimensions of the $F$-spaces $\mathcal{Y}_t$, $\mathcal{V}_t$ and $\ker(\phi_t)$:

$$\dim[\ker(\phi_t)] + \dim(\mathcal{V}_t) = \dim(\mathcal{Y}_t). \tag{3.28}$$

By definition, the $(t+1)$-tuple $y$ is a zero run if and only if $\phi_t(y) = 0$, i.e., if and only if $y$ is in the kernel of $\phi_t$. To evaluate the number of zero runs is thus equivalent to evaluating $\dim[\ker(\phi_t)] = \dim(\mathcal{Y}_t) - \dim(\mathcal{V}_t)$. Since no restriction exists on the elements $y$ of $\mathcal{Y}_t$ one has

$$\dim(\mathcal{Y}_t) = \sum_{i=1}^{k} m(i) + kt, \tag{3.29}$$

where $m(i)$ is the degree of the $i^{\text{th}}$ row of $G$.

Let us now consider the quantity $\dim(\mathcal{V}_t)$. Since it is an $F$-subspace of $F^{nt}$, one has

$$\dim(\mathcal{V}_t) + \dim(\mathcal{V}_t^{\perp}) = nt, \tag{3.30}$$

where $\mathcal{V}_t^{\perp}$ denotes the vector space of all $t$-tuples $u^* = (u_1, \cdots, u_t)$, $u_i \in F^n$, that are orthogonal to $\mathcal{V}_t$. Associating to such a $u^*$ the element $u(D) = \sum_{j=0}^{t-1} u_{t-j} D^j$ of $F^n[D]$, we see that $u^* \in \mathcal{V}_t$ is equivalent to $u(D) \in E(G^{\perp})$ with $G^{\perp}$ a minimal encoder of $C^{\perp}$, the dual code of $C$. Let us denote by $m^{\perp}(i)$, $i = 1, \cdots, n - k$, the degrees of the rows of $G^{\perp}$. Since a minimal encoder has the predictable span property (see theorem 2.24), the quantity $\dim(\mathcal{V}_t)$ is given by

$$\dim(\mathcal{V}_t^{\perp}) = \sum_{i:t \geq m^{\perp}(i)} (t - m^{\perp}(i)). \tag{3.31}$$

We use (3.31) in (3.30) to obtain

$$\dim(\mathcal{V}_t) = nt - \sum_{i:t \geq m^\perp(i)} (t - m^\perp(i)). \qquad (3.32)$$

We use also (3.29) and (3.32) in (3.28) to obtain

$$\dim[\ker(\phi_t)] = \sum_{i=1}^{k} m(i) - (n - k)t + \sum_{i:t \geq m^\perp(i)} (t - m^\perp(i)). \qquad (3.33)$$

Using the equality $\sum_{i=1}^{k} m(i) = \sum_{i=1}^{n-k} m^\perp(i)$ proved in theorem 2.43, we transform the right hand side of (3.33) into

$$\sum_{i=1}^{n-k} (m^\perp(i) - t) - \sum_{i:t \geq m^\perp(i)} (m^\perp(i) - t),$$

and we obtain finally

$$\dim[\ker(\phi_t)] = \sum_{i:t < m^\perp(i)} (m^\perp(i) - t). \qquad (3.34)$$

This formula thus relates the dimension of the $F$-space of $t$-zero runs in $E(G)$ to the degrees $m^\perp(i)$ of the minimal encoder $G^\perp$.

Let us apply this result to the code $C$ generated by the matrix $G$ given in (3.9). A minimal encoder $G^\perp$ of $C^\perp$ is given by

$$G^\perp = \begin{bmatrix} D & 0 & 1 & 1+D & 1 & 1 \\ 1+D & D & D & 1 & 1 & 1+D \\ 1 & 1 & 1+D & 0 & D & 1 \end{bmatrix}, \qquad (3.35)$$

and it satisfies $m^\perp(1) = m^\perp(2) = m^\perp(3) = 1$. As a result, for all $t \geq 1$, the right hand side of (3.34) is zero. Thus, as one can verify on figure 3.2, the $F$-space of the $t$-zero runs of $G$ contains only the zero $(t+1)$-tuple.

## 3.7   Comments

The goal of this chapter was to give a survey of several results on convolutional codes and not to give an encyclopaedic presentation of the code constructions and of the decoding methods known to date. Several references have been mentioned and other related references are [18-20, 22, 52, 54, 64, 88]. The information-theoretic approach to convolutional codes is outside the scope of this book. References [41-42, 113, 115] are concerned with this approach.

## 3.8   Appendix : A conjecture on the symbol minimum distance of $(2,1)$ binary codes

As mentioned in section 3.1, it is not known whether (3.6) is true for the important classes $\mathcal{C}(2,1,m)$ of $(2,1)$ convolutional codes over $F = GF(2)$. It is the goal of this appendix to sketch lines along which (3.6) could perhaps be proved for these codes. In passing we state two conjectures having their own interest. Were these two conjectures to be true, then (3.6) would be true for the classes $\mathcal{C}(2,1,m)$.

As an introduction to our discussion we first apply the classical Gilbert-Varshamov argument [71] to an arbitrary set $\mathcal{B}$ of binary linear $(n,k)$ block codes. Since any $C \in \mathcal{B}$ is a linear code, $sd(C)$ is nothing but the minimal symbol weight $sw(v)$ of all nonzero vectors $v$ in $C$. The question is now whether it is possible to find an integer $d$ such that one can guarantee that at least one code $C \in \mathcal{B}$ satisfies $sd(C) \geq d$. The answer is yes, provided something is known about the number of codes $C \in \mathcal{B}$ that contain an arbitrary nonzero element $v$ of $F^n$. Assume for example that $\mathcal{B}$ has the property that any nonzero $v \in F^n$ is a codeword of at most $M$ codes $C$ of $\mathcal{B}$. In this case, at most $M \sum_{w=1}^{d-1} \binom{n}{w}$ codes $C$ of $\mathcal{B}$ contain a nonzero codeword of symbol weight $\leq d - 1$. This proves the existence of at least one code $C \in \mathcal{B}$ satisfying $sd(C) \geq d$, with $d$ the largest integer for which one has $\sum_{w=1}^{d-1} \binom{n}{w} < |\mathcal{B}|/M$. For example, if $\mathcal{B}$ is the set of *all* binary linear $(n, k)$ block codes, one has $\mathcal{B} = (2^n - 1)(2^n - 2) \cdots (2^n - 2^k)/(2^k - 1)(2^k - 2) \cdots (2^k - 2^{k-1})$ and $M = (2^k - 1)|\mathcal{B}|/(2^n - 1)$.

Let us try to apply this argument to the class $\mathcal{C}_0(m) \subseteq \mathcal{C}(2, 1, m)$ of binary convolutional codes specified by an encoder $G$ having the form

$$G = [g_1, g_2]; \ g_i \in F[D], \ \text{del } g_i = 0, \ \deg g_i = m, \ i = 1, 2, \qquad (3.36)$$

and being noncatastrophic.

Let $\alpha(m)$ denote the fraction of encoders $G$ that satisfy (3.36) and are noncatastrophic. It was shown by Rosenberg [104-105] that $\lim_{m \to \infty} \alpha(m)$ equals $1/3$. On the other hand, if $G$ is a noncatastrophic encoder, then for sufficiently large $m$ its minimum distance $sd[E(G)]$ is achieved by a polynomial information sequence $a = \sum_{i=0}^{\ell} a_i D^i$ with $a_i \in F$ and $a_0 = a_\ell = 1$, of degree $\ell \leq m^2$ and such that $v = aG$ is a simple sequence with respect to $G$. That this must be the case results from the following remarks.

**(i)** A code sequence $v$ that contains as subsequences at least two nonzero simple sequences satisfies $sw(v) \geq 2sd[E(G)]$.

**(ii)** It follows from [4] and [40] that, if $G$ is a noncatastrophic encoder, then a simple sequence $v = \sum_{j=0}^{m+\ell} v_j$ with $v_0 \neq 0$ and $v_{m+l} \neq 0$, in $E(G)$, cannot contain subsequences of $m$ (or more) consecutive words $v_i$ with $0 \leq i \leq m + \ell$, that are zero.

**(iii)** It is known (see [26]) that, for sufficiently large $m$, no $C \in \mathcal{C}(2, 1, m)$ satisfies $sd(C) > m + 1$.

Putting these remarks together we obtain the announced result.

Now denote by $\mathcal{G}(m)$ the set of all noncatastrophic $(2, 1)$ encoders $G$ satisfying (3.36) and by $\mathcal{A}(\ell)$ the set of polynomials $a = 1 + \sum_{i=1}^{\ell-1} a_i D^i + D^\ell$

over $F$. We note that all encoders of $\mathcal{G}(m)$ are minimal (see problem 2.2) and that no two of them generate the same code $C$. Hence, to enumerate the encoders $G \in \mathcal{G}(m)$ is equivalent to enumerating the codes $C \in \mathcal{C}_0(m)$ and we have $|\mathcal{G}(m)| = |\mathcal{C}_0(m)| = \alpha(m)\, 2^{2m-2}$, $|\mathcal{A}(\ell)| = 2^{\ell-1}$.

To obtain a lower bound on the best minimum symbol distance $sd(C)$ that is achievable by a code $C \in \mathcal{C}_0(m)$, we could try to obtain an upper bound $M$ on the number of codes $C \in \mathcal{C}_0(m)$ containing a given sequence $v = (v^1, v^2)$, with del $v^i = 0$, deg $v^i = m + \ell$, $i = 1, 2$. Unfortunately, this simple argument cannot work. Even if $M = 1$ were true, no conclusion would follow from the counting argument because to obtain a conclusive result it would yet be necessary to take into account the fact that most pairs $v = (v^1, v^2)$ are in none of the codes of $\mathcal{C}_0(m)$: for large $\ell$ and $m$, the probability is indeed low that $v^1$ and $v^2$ have a common factor $a$ of prescribed degree $\ell$.

Thus we have to use another method. Let us argue as follows. Given $a \in \mathcal{A}(\ell)$, consider the set $a\mathcal{A}(m)$ and define $B_a(m, w)$ to be the number of nonzero polynomials $v \in a\mathcal{A}(m)$ that have at most $w$ nonzero coefficients:

$$B_a(m, w) := |\{v \in a\mathcal{A}(m) \mid sw(v) \leq w\}| . \qquad (3.37)$$

Should we know the numbers $B_a(m, w)$ for all nonzero polynomials $a$ of each degree $\ell \leq m^2$, we could mimic the classical Gilbert-Varshamov argument as follows. Denote first by $N_a(m, w)$ the number of encoders $G$ in $\mathcal{G}(m)$ satisfying $sw(aG) \leq w$ for some $w \leq m$. This number is obviously upper bounded by

$$N_a(m, w) \leq \sum_{i=1}^{w-1} B_a(m, w - i)\, B_a(m, i). \qquad (3.38)$$

The number $M(\ell, m, w)$ of encoders $G \in \mathcal{G}(m)$ for which at least one polynomial $a \in \mathcal{A}(\ell)$ satisfies $sw(aG) \leq w$ is thus be upper bounded by

$$M(\ell, m, w) \leq \sum_{a \in \mathcal{A}(\ell)} \left[ \sum_{i=1}^{w-1} B_a(m, w - i) B_a(m, i) \right] , \qquad (3.39)$$

and, since only the values $\ell \leq m^2$ have to be considered, the total number $M(m, w)$ of encoders $G \in \mathcal{G}(m)$ for which one has $sd[E(G)] \leq w$ satisfies

$$M(m, w) \leq (m^2 + 1) \max_{0 \leq \ell \leq m^2} M(\ell, m, w). \qquad (3.40)$$

If we could prove $M(m, w) < |\mathcal{C}_0(m)| (= \alpha(m) 2^{2m-2})$, this would imply the existence of at least one encoder $G$ in $\mathcal{G}(m)$ satisfying $sd[E(G)] \geq w + 1$. This discussion makes obvious why any information on the numbers $B_a(m, w)$ is useful for obtaining a lower bound on the largest $sd[E(G)]$ achievable by some $G$ in $\mathcal{G}(m)$.

Our goal is now to find sufficient conditions, stated here as conjectures, on the numbers $B_a(m, w)$, such that (3.6) would be true for fixed binary $(2, 1, m)$ convolutional codes. Let us reverse the order of summation in (3.39). This leads to

$$M(\ell, m, w) \leq \sum_{i=1}^{w-1} J(\ell, m, w, i),$$

with $J(\ell, m, w, i) := \sum_{a \in \mathcal{A}(\ell)} B_a(m, w - i) B_a(m, i)$.

Our first conjecture is then as follows.

**Conjecture 3.6 :** At least for sufficiently large $m$, and for $w \leq m$, $\ell \leq m^2$, the maximum of $J(\ell, m, w, i)$ with respect to $i$ is reached for $i$ equal (or at least "close") to $w/2$.

The truth of this conjecture would imply that (3.39) can be rewritten as

$$M(\ell, m, w) \leq (w - 1) \sum_{a \in \mathcal{A}(\ell)} B_a^2(m, w/2). \qquad (3.41)$$

Now defining the mean value

$$\mu(\ell, m, w/2) := 2^{-(\ell-1)} \sum_{a \in \mathcal{A}(\ell)} B_a(m, w/2), \qquad (3.42)$$

and the variance

$$\sigma^2(\ell, m, w/2) := 2^{-(\ell-1)} \sum_{a \in \mathcal{A}(\ell)} [B_a(m, w/2) - \mu(\ell, m, w/2)]^2 , \qquad (3.43)$$

we can write

$$\sum_{a \in \mathcal{A}(\ell)} B_a^2(m, w/2) = 2^{\ell-1} \mu^2(\ell, m, w/2) \left[ 1 + \frac{\sigma^2(\ell, m, w/2)}{\mu^2(\ell, m, w/2)} \right] . \qquad (3.44)$$

We then borrow from [95] the following estimation of $\mu(\ell, m, w/2)$:

$$\mu(\ell, m, w/2) = \left[ \binom{m+\ell}{w/2} / 2^{\ell-1} \right] 2^{m \, \epsilon_2(m,\ell)}, \qquad (3.45)$$

where $\lim_{m \to \infty} \epsilon_2(m, \lfloor \lambda m \rfloor)$ is zero for fixed $\lambda > 0$, and we rewrite (3.44) as

$$\sum_{a \in \mathcal{A}(\ell)} B_a^2(m, w/2) = \frac{\binom{m+\ell}{w/2}^2}{2^{\ell-1}} \left[ 1 + \frac{\sigma^2(\ell, m, w/2)}{\mu^2(\ell, m, w/2)} \right] 2^{m \, \epsilon_2(m,\ell)} . \qquad (3.46)$$

Using (3.46) and (3.41) in (3.40) we obtain

$$M(m, w) \leq (m^2 + 1)(w - 1) \max_{0 \leq \ell \leq m^2} \frac{\binom{m+\ell}{w/2}^2}{2^{\ell-1}} \left[ 1 + \rho^2 \right] 2^{m \, \epsilon_2(m,\ell)}, \qquad (3.47)$$

where $\rho = \rho(\ell, m, w/2)$ denotes $\sigma(\ell, m, w/2)/\mu(\ell, m, w/2)$.

Thus if the right member of (3.47), denoted here by $Q(m, w)$, is $\leq \alpha(m) 2^{2m-2}$, it follows from conjecture 3.6 that at least one encoder $G \in \mathcal{G}(m)$ satisfies $sd[E(G)] \geq w$. Choose $\lambda \geq 0$, $\omega \in [0, 1]$, $\ell = \lfloor \lambda m \rfloor$ and $w = \lfloor \omega m \rfloor$, and let $m$ be arbitrarily large. Denote

$$\limsup_{m \to \infty} m^{-1} \log[1 + \rho^2(\lfloor \lambda m \rfloor, m, \lfloor \omega m/2 \rfloor)]$$

by $\tau(\omega, \lambda)$. Using Stirling's approximation and the property

$$\lim_{m \to \infty} \alpha(m) = 1/3$$

obtained in [104] we see that, for large $m$, the bound

$$Q(m, w) \leq \alpha(m) \, 2^{2m-2}$$

is equivalent to

$$\max_{\lambda} \{2(1 + \lambda) \, \mathcal{H} \left[ \frac{\omega}{2(1 + \lambda)} \right] - (\lambda + 2) \log 2 + \tau(\omega, \lambda)\} \leq 0, \qquad (3.48)$$

where $\mathcal{H}$ denotes the entropy function defined in natural logarithms. Denote

$$2(1 + \lambda) \, \mathcal{H} \left[ \frac{\omega}{2(1 + \lambda)} \right] - (\lambda + 2) \log 2$$

by $F(\omega, \lambda)$. For $m$ large enough and for any $\epsilon > 0$, the truth of the conjecture 3.6 implies the existence of at least one encoder $G \in \mathcal{G}(m)$ that satisfies $sd[E(G)] \geq (\omega - \epsilon)m$, for all $\omega$ such that $F(\omega, \lambda) + \tau(\omega, \lambda) \leq 0$ is true for all $\lambda \geq 0$. The function $F(\omega, \lambda)$ has a nice analytical form but we lack an expression of $\tau(\omega, \lambda)$. Therefore, we make the following conjecture.

**Conjecture 3.7 :** The largest value of $\omega$ such that the maximum in $\lambda$ of $F(\omega, \lambda) + \tau(\omega, \lambda)$ is nonpositive, is the same as the one for which the quantity $\max_{\lambda} F(\omega, \lambda)$ is nonpositive.

By nature $\tau(\omega, \lambda)$ is nonnegative. The reason to make this conjecture is our feeling that for fixed $\lambda$, $\tau(\omega, \lambda)$ is zero except maybe for "small" values of $\omega$. For these small values of $\omega$, we think that the negative quantity $F(\omega, \lambda)$ satisfies $F(\omega, \lambda) + \tau(\omega, \lambda) < 0$, all $\lambda \geq 0$.

On the basis of conjecture 3.7 we search for the largest $\omega$ such that $\max_{\lambda} F(\omega, \lambda)$ is nonpositive for all $\lambda$, i.e., we solve the system

$$F(\omega, \lambda) = 0, \; \partial F(\omega, \lambda)/\partial \lambda = 0. \qquad (3.49)$$

Making explicit the second equation of (3.49) we obtain

$$2\mathcal{H}[\omega/2(1+\lambda)] - [\omega/(1+\lambda)] \log \left[\frac{2(1-\lambda)-\omega}{\omega}\right] - \log 2 = 0, \quad (3.50)$$

which is equivalent to

$$\log \frac{2(1+\lambda)^2}{[2(1+\lambda)-\omega]^2} = 0. \quad (3.51)$$

On the other hand, equating the expressions of $\mathcal{H}[\omega/2(1+\lambda)]$ in the two equations of (3.49), we obtain

$$\frac{2+\lambda}{1+\lambda} \log 2 = \frac{\omega}{1+\lambda} \log \left[\frac{2(1+\lambda)-\omega}{\omega}\right] + \log 2,$$

which is equivalent to

$$\omega \log_2 \left[\frac{2(1+\lambda)-\omega}{\omega}\right] = 1. \quad (3.52)$$

Then using in (3.52) the equality $1+\lambda = \omega/(2-\sqrt{2})$ derived from (3.51) we obtain

$$\omega = 1/\log_2(1+\sqrt{2}), \quad (3.53)$$

which is exactly the right hand side of (3.6) with $n = 2$ and $R = 1/2$. The value (3.53) is $\omega = .78644$. Using (3.53) in (3.51) we obtain

$$\lambda = [(2-\sqrt{2})\log_2(1+\sqrt{2})]^{-1} - 1.$$

A possible interpretation of this $\lambda$, the value of which is .34254, would be the value of $\ell/m$ such that $sd[E(G)]$ is most often achieved by an information sequence $a$ of degree "close" to $\ell$ for large $m$.

## 3.9    Appendix : Sketch of the bound obtained by Zigangirov

Let $\mathcal{C}(n, k, m)$ be the class of all binary convolutional codes generated by a $k \times n$ convolutional encoder $G$ the entries of which have degree $\leq m$, and at least one of which has degree equal to $m$. As mentioned in section 3.8, many elements of $\mathcal{F}^2$ are in none of the codes of $\mathcal{C}(2, 1, m)$ for fixed $m$. More generally, for fixed $k$ and $n$, many elements of $\mathcal{F}^n$ are in none of the codes of $\mathcal{C}(n, k, m)$ for fixed $m$. For reasons discussed briefly in section 3.8, this leads to difficulties when one tries to obtain a lower bound on the quantity $\underline{sd}(n, k, m)$ introduced in section 3.1. Recently, Zigangirov [118] has apparently succeeded to bypass these difficulties. Here follows a sketch of his argument.

Zigangirov considers a $k \times n$ convolutional encoder over $F = GF(2)$ of the form $G = \sum_{j=0}^{m} G_j D^j$, and an information sequence $a = \sum_{i=0}^{\infty} a_i D^i$ with $a_i \in F^k$ and $a_0 \neq 0$, that produces an encoded sequence $v = aG$ in $\mathcal{F}^n$. He then chooses an integer $t$ between $m+1$ and $k(m+1)$ and considers the "truncated" sequence $v^* := aG$ modulo $D^t$ of the form $v^* = \sum_{i=0}^{t-1} v_i^* D^i$ with $v_i^* \in F^n$. To develop his argument he represents the "truncated mapping" $a \mapsto v^*$ in the following matrix form. He associates with each of the $k$ components $a^j \in \mathcal{F}$ of the information $a$ written as a $k$-tuple $(a^1, \ldots, a^k)$ over $\mathcal{F}$, a $t \times (m + 1)$ matrix $A^j$. The first column of $A^j$ is the transpose of the row $t$-tuple $(a_0^j, a_1^j, \ldots, a_{t-1}^j)$ representing the first $t$ coefficients of the component $a^j$ of $a$. The other columns are obtained by shifting down iteratively the first column and putting zeros in the first places of the resulting $t$-tuples. Thus, if we denote the transpose of a vector $a$ by $a^T$, the second column of $A^j$ is $(0, a_0^j, \ldots, a_{t-2}^j)^T$, the third column is $(0, 0, a_0^j, \ldots, a_{t-3}^j)^T$, and so on. With the $k$-tuple $a = (a^1, \ldots, a^k)$ over $\mathcal{F}$ is then associated the $t \times k(m + 1)$ matrix $A^* = (A^1, \ldots, A^k)$. Zigangirov also associates with the encoder $G$, a matrix over $F$ constructed as follows. He represents the $(i, j)$ entry $g_{i,j}(D) = \sum_{r=0}^{m} (g_{i,j})_r D^r$ of

$G$ by the row vector $(g_{i,j})^* = [(g_{i,j})_0, \ldots, (g_{i,j})_m]$, $(g_{i,j})_r \in F$, and he represents the $j^{\text{th}}$ column $[g_{1,j}(D), \ldots, g_{k,j}(D)]$ of $G$ by the row vector $g_j^* = [(g_{1,j})^*, \ldots, (g_{k,j})^*]$. Thus this row vector is obtained by juxtaposition of $k$ rows $(g_{i,j})^*$, and its length is equal to $(m+1)k$. Zigangirov uses then these row $(m+1)k$-tuples to construct the $(m+1)k \times n$ matrix $G^*$ given by $G^* = \left[(g_1^*)^T, \ldots, (g_n^*)^T\right]$. It should now be clear that the matrix $V^* = A^*G^*$ is a representation of the truncated sequence $v^*$ introduced above. Indeed if the $j^{\text{th}}$ column $(v^*)^j$ of $V^*$ is written as $[(v^*)_0^j, \ldots, (v^*)_{t-1}^j]^T$, the polynomial $(v^*)^j(D) = \sum_{j=0}^{t-1}(v^*)_i^j D^i$ over $F$ is obviously the $j^{\text{th}}$ component of the row $n$-tuple $v^*$ over $F[D]$.

To obtain a lower bound on the quantity $\underline{sd}(n, k, m)$ introduced in section 3.1 (or on the quantity $\lim_{m \to \infty} \underline{sd}(n, k, m)/(m+1)$) one uses then the following usual elimination rule. To check if one can guarantee $\underline{sd}(n, k, m) \geq w$, one picks at random an information $k$-tuple $a$ of delay zero and one eliminates all encoders $G$ such that the corresponding matrix $V^* = A^*G^*$ (where $A^*$ corresponds to $a$ and $G^*$ to $G$) has less than $w$ entries equal to 1. Then one iterates this elimination rule for all informations $a$ of delay zero and verifies that there still remain noneliminated encoders $G$. If such encoders do exist, this means that $\underline{sd}(n, k, m)$ is $\geq w$.

To make this counting feasible, Zigangirov investigates the rank repartition of the matrices $A^*$. For given $k$ and $t$ (and whatever $n$ may be), there are $2^{kt}$ such matrices (or more precisely $(2^k - 1)2^{k(t-1)}$ if one assumes, as he does, that the initial word $a_0$ of $a$ is nonzero). If one knew the rank distribution of these matrices $A^*$, i.e., the number $N(r, t)$ of such matrices having $t$ rows and rank equal to $r$, one could reason as follows.

Consider such a matrix $A^*$ of rank $r$ and let $I$ be a set of $r$ rows of $A^*$ that achieve its rank (see page 19). One has then $\text{rk}[(A^*)^I] = r$. In this case when for given $j$, $g_j^*$ goes through the set of all $2^{k(m+1)}$ possible $k(m+1)$-tuples, then $(A^*)^I(g_j^*)^T$ goes through the set of the $2^r$ possible $r$-tuples, and it achieves any specified $r$-tuple exactly $2^{k(m+1)-r}$ times. On the same way, one sees that when $G^*$ goes through the set of all $2^{nk(m+1)}$

possible $k(m + 1) \times n$ matrices over $F$, then $(A^*)^I G^*$ goes through the set of the $2^{rn}$ possible $r \times n$ matrices, and it achieves any specified matrix $(V^*)^I$ exactly $(2^{k(m+1)-r})^n$ times. Since $(V^*)^I$ has $nr$ entries, the number of matrices $G^*$ such that $(A^*)^I G^*$ contains exactly $w$ nonzero entries is given by $\binom{nr}{w} 2^{nk(m+1)-nr}$ and the number of cancellations of matrices $G^*$ (with respect to symbol weight $w$) due to the matrices $A^*$ having $t$ rows and rank $r$ is thus upper-bounded by $N(r, t) 2^{nk(m+1)-nr} \sum_{j \leq w-1} \binom{nr}{j}$.

Summing for all $r \leq t$, one obtains that the number of eliminated $(n, k, m)$ encoders is upper-bounded by $T(w, m) = T_1(w, m) + T_2(w, m)$ where

$$T_1(w, m) = (t - 1) \max_{r \leq t-1} N(r, t) 2^{nk(m+1)-nr} \sum_{j \leq w-1} \binom{nr}{j}$$

takes into account the ranks $r$ at most equal to $t - 1$, while

$$T_2(w, m) = N(t, t) 2^{nk(m+1)-nt} \sum_{j \leq w-1} \binom{nt}{j}$$

takes into account the rank $r = t$. The countings above are pessimistic in the sense that in general the number of nonzero entries of $V^* = A^* G^*$ is larger than the number of nonzero entries of $(V^*)^I = (A^*)^I G^*$ with $I$ achieving the rank of $A^*$. However this underestimation does not prevent one from obtaining the desired result.

If $T(w, m)$ is smaller than the number $2^{nk(m+1)}$ of $(n, k, m)$ encoders, at least one of these encoders satisfies $sd[E(G)] \geq w$. To find the largest $w$ such that $T(w, m) < 2^{nk(m+1)}$, we need an estimation of the numbers $N(r, t)$. This is the most difficult part in the derivation of the bound. The estimation given in [118] is very short, and it relies on some Russian publications of Zigangirov without any accessible English translation. However that may be, the following estimations are presented [118]:

$$N(r, t) \leq 2^{kr-k(m+1)+t^2/(m+1)+m+1+k} \text{ for } r < t; \quad N(t, t) \leq 2^{kt}. \quad (3.54)$$

One can upper-bound $T(w, m)$ by $2 \max_{i=1,2} T_i(w, m)$. Then using (3.54), one finds that $2\,T_i(m) < 2^{nk(m+1)}$, $i = 1, 2$, is implied by the pair of inequalities

$$(t - 1)w \max_{r \leq t-1} \binom{nr}{w} 2^{[-r(n-k)-k(m+1)+\frac{t^2}{(m+1)}+(m+1)+k]} < 1, \quad (3.55)$$

$$w \binom{nt}{w} 2^{t(k-n)} < 1. \quad (3.56)$$

Choose $\tau > 1$, $1 \leq \rho < \tau$ and $\omega \in [0, 1/2]$, define $t = \lfloor \tau(m + 1) \rfloor$, $r = \lfloor \rho(m+1) \rfloor$ and $w = \lfloor \omega n(m+1) \rfloor$, and use $R = k/n$. Using the Stirling approximation, one sees that for $m$ going to infinity, (3.55) and (3.56) are equivalent to $E_i \leq 0$, $i = 1, 2$ with

$$
\begin{aligned}
E_1 &= \max_{\rho < \tau} \mathcal{H}_2(\frac{\omega}{\rho}) - (1 - R + \frac{R}{\rho}) + (\frac{1 + \tau^2}{n\rho}), \\
E_2 &= \mathcal{H}_2(\frac{\omega}{\tau}) - (1 - R).
\end{aligned}
$$

The inequality $E_2 \leq 0$ is satisfied for all $\omega \in [0, 1/2]$ if one chooses $\tau = [2\mathcal{H}^{-1}(1 - R)]^{-1}$. Assume then that $n$ is "very" large. In this case $E_1 < 0$ can be approximated by

$$\max_{\rho < \tau} \mathcal{H}_2(\frac{\omega}{\rho}) - (1 - R + \frac{R}{\rho}) \leq 0. \quad (3.57)$$

Deriving with respect to $\rho$, one finds that the maximum with respect to $\rho$ is obtained for $\rho$ satisfying

$$(\frac{R}{\omega} \log 2 - \log \frac{\rho - \omega}{\omega})(\frac{\omega}{\rho^2}) = 0,$$

where the logarithms are natural. This value of $\rho$ is $\rho = \omega(1 + 2^{R/\omega})$ and using it in the left hand side of (3.57) one solves in $\omega$ to obtain

$$\omega \leq -R/\log_2(2^{1-R} - 1). \quad (3.58)$$

In other words, any $\omega = w/n(m+1)$ satisfying (3.58) is "achievable" for very large $m$, if $n$ itself is sufficiently large to make $(1 + \tau^2)/n$ negligible. This maximum value of $\omega$ is easily seen to agree with the bound (3.6) obtained by Costello [26] for time-varying codes. One has yet to consider the possibility that the "best" $(n, k, m)$ encoders be catastrophic. That this makes no difficulties follows from [26, p.360].

## PROBLEMS

**3.1** Let $C$ be an $(n, k)$ convolutional code over $F$ and let $C^*$ be an $(n, k-1)$ convolutional code over $F$ satisfying $C^* \subset C$. Let $G^*$ be a basic encoder of $C^*$. Prove that it is possible to add one row to $G^*$ to obtain a *basic* encoder $G$ of $C$.

> Hint : Let $G_b$ be a basic encoder of $C$. Write $G^* = TG_b$ where $T$ is a basic $(k-1) \times k$ encoder. Denote by $t_i$ the determinant of the $(k-1) \times (k-1)$ matrix obtained by suppression of the $i^{\text{th}}$ column of $T$. Use Euclid's algorithm to find polynomials $r_i$ satisfying $\sum_i r_i t_i = 1$. Append $r = (r_1, ..., r_k)$ as the $k^{\text{th}}$ row to $T$ to obtain a $k \times k$ matrix denoted by $T^+$. Then $G = T^+ G_b$ satisfies the required properties.

**3.2** Extend the preceding statement to the case where $C^*$ is an $(n, k-s)$ convolutional code satisfying $C^* \subset C$.

**3.3** Let $v = (v_1, ..., v_n)$ be a polynomial sequence of a convolutional code $C$. Prove that $v$ can be used as a row of a basic encoder of $C$ if and only if the g.c.d. of $\{v_1, ..., v_n\}$ is an element of $F$.

**3.4** Prove that the set of simple sequences is the same for all minimal encoders of a given code.

**3.5** Develop a syndrome implementation of the stack decoder.

**3.6** Give a proof of the estimation (3.45) mentioned in section 3.8.

**3.7** Let $G = G_0 + DG_1$ be a $k \times n$ minimal encoder over $F$ with all its rows of degree exactly 1, let $C$ be $E(G)$ and let $C^\perp$ be the dual of $C$. Prove that the only state transition in $\Sigma(G^\perp)$ producing the zero $n$-tuple over $F$ is the loop around the zero state.

# Chapter 4

# Convolutional codes with automorphisms

It is evident that the number of block codes of length $n$ over a finite field $F$ grows rapidly with $n$, so that for large $n$ it becomes unfeasible to find the best code of length $n$ for a specific application. In place of attempting to find the best code, we may try using a procedure that generates a small subset $S$ of codes of length $n$ over $F$. If this subset is small enough, it may be possible to find the best code in $S$ with the hope that it is practically as good as the best code of length $n$. The most popular subset $S$ considered to date is the set of linear cyclic block codes. A glance in the tables of contents of books such as [71] or [67] will make this statement evident. To evaluate the error correcting capability of cyclic codes one uses their property of being orthogonal to a Vandermonde matrix [71]. This property leads to the celebrated *BCH*-bound on the minimum distance of a cyclic code [12-13, 71]. More general codes are defined to be orthogonal to a modified Vandermonde matrix. These codes include shortened cyclic codes [7] and Goppa codes [46]. They form the class of the subfield subcodes of the modified Reed-Solomon codes [29, 51].

For convolutional codes, no comparable results are available. For this reason it would be attractive to discover a restrictive (but yet flexible enough) algebraic structure in which reasonably good codes could be easily found, even if no analog of the $BCH$-bound would be available. Related to this remark is the following natural question: Is it possible to define convolutional codes that could be viewed as a generalization of cyclic block codes? The answer is yes, and this chapter is a first step towards such a generalization.

Before looking at this generalization we make some further comments about block codes. The class of cyclic block codes is a subclass of the class of block codes with nontrivial *automorphisms*. What is an automorphism of a block code? Let $C_0$ be a block code of length $n$ over $F$, the words $v_i$ of which are represented by row $n$-tuples over $F$. Given a nonsingular $n \times n$ matrix $A$ over $F$, consider the block code $C_0 A = \{v_i A \mid v_i \in C_0\}$. If $C_0 A$ coincide with $C_0$ we say that $A$ is an automorphism of $C_0$. Obviously, $A^{-1}$ is then also an automorphism of $C_0$, and if $A_1$ and $A_2$ are two automorphisms of $C_0$, then $A = A_1 A_2$ is also an automorphism of $C_0$. Hence the set of all automorphisms of $C_0$ is a group denoted by $\overline{\mathrm{Aut}}(C_0)$, which is a subgroup of the group $GL(n, F)$ of all $n \times n$ nonsingular matrices over $F$. By nature $\overline{\mathrm{Aut}}(C_0)$ is a finite group, since it is a subgroup of the finite group $GL(n, F)$. Most often one is interested in finding the automorphisms $A$ of a code $C_0$ that are in a certain subgroup $K$ of $GL(n, F)$. In that respect, two important subgroups $K$ of $GL(n, F)$ are the monomial group $M_n$ and the symmetric group $S_n$. These groups were defined in subsection 1.1.3. We use the notation $\overline{\mathrm{Aut}}_K(C_0)$ to denote the intersection $\overline{\mathrm{Aut}}(C_0) \cap K$. Clearly $\overline{\mathrm{Aut}}(C_0)$ is itself a group.

The present chapter is devoted to the introduction of the concept of automorphism of a convolutional code. In section 4.1 we introduce and discuss the *sliding groups*, which are an important tool in the description of the automorphism group of a convolutional code. In section 4.2 we give a definition of the automorphism group of a convolutional code and we present a method for computing it. Section 4.3 is devoted to the consideration of some technical properties of these automorphism groups.

Some elementary knowledge of graph theory is necessary to read the next chapters. Some references are [5, 49, 73].

# 4.1    Sliding sets and associated graphs

In this section we introduce successively the general sliding sets, the sliding groups and the systematic sliding groups.

## 4.1.1    General sliding sets

Let $K$ be any nonempty finite set and, for $m \geq 1$, let $K^{m+1}$ be the set of ordered $(m+1)$-tuples over $K$, i.e.,

$$K^{m+1} = \{x = (x^{(0)}, \cdots, x^{(m)}) \mid x^{(i)} \in K,\ 0 \leq i \leq m\}. \qquad (4.1)$$

**Definition 4.1 :** A nonempty subset $\Sigma$ of $K^{m+1}$ is said to be a *sliding set of span* $m$ if for all $x = (x^{(0)}, \cdots, x^{(m)})$ in $\Sigma$ there exists at least one element $y$ and one element $z$ in $\Sigma$ that satisfy

$$y^{(i+1)} = x^{(i)} ;\ \ 0 \leq i \leq m-1 , \qquad (4.2)$$

$$z^{(i-1)} = x^{(i)} ;\ \ 1 \leq i \leq m . \qquad (4.3)$$

Any $y \in \Sigma$ satisfying (4.2) is called a *predecessor* of $x$ in $\Sigma$ and any $z \in \Sigma$ satisfying (4.3) is called a *successor* of $x$ in $\Sigma$.

We denote by $r(x)$ the number of predecessors $y$ of $x$ in $\Sigma$ and by $t(x)$ the number of successors $z$ of $x$ in $\Sigma$. For example the set $K^{m+1}$ of all $(m+1)$-tuples over $K$ is a sliding set of span $m$ with $r(x) = t(x) = |K|$ for all $x \in K^{m+1}$.

**Definition 4.2 :** Given a finite set $K$, the *projection* of index $i$ of a subset $\Sigma$ of $K^{m+1}$ is defined to be the set of elements $a$ in $K$ such that there exists at least one $x$ in $\Sigma$ satisfying $x^{(i)} = a$ .

We denote this projection by $\Sigma^{(i)}$. If $\Sigma$ is a sliding set, all projections $\Sigma^{(i)}$ coincide. Thus one has $\Sigma^{(i)} = \Sigma^{(0)}$ for $0 \leq i \leq m$.

With any sliding set $\Sigma$ of span $m$ we associate a directed graph (or *digraph*) denoted by $\Gamma(\Sigma)$ and constructed as follows. We first associate with any $x = (x^{(0)}, \cdots, x^{(m)}) \in K^{m+1}$ the elements $\bar{x}$ and $\underline{x}$ of $K^m$ defined by $\bar{x} := (x^{(1)}, \cdots, x^{(m)})$ and by $\underline{x} := (x^{(0)}, \cdots, x^{(m-1)})$. We then define the sets $\overline{\Sigma} := \{\bar{x} \mid x \in \Sigma\}$ and $\underline{\Sigma} := \{\underline{x} \mid x \in \Sigma\}$. Obviously, for any sliding set $\Sigma$, the two sets $\overline{\Sigma}$ and $\underline{\Sigma}$ coincide. The number of vertices in the digraph $\Gamma(\Sigma)$ is chosen to be $|\underline{\Sigma}|$ and each of its vertices receives the name of a different element $\underline{x}$ of $\underline{\Sigma}$. An arc is then directed from the vertex $y$ to the vertex $\underline{z}$ if there exists some $x$ in $\Sigma$ satisfying $\underline{x} = y$ and $\bar{x} = \underline{z}$. Since $\Sigma$ is a sliding set, there exists for any vertex $\underline{x}$ of $\Gamma(\Sigma)$ at least one arc reaching $\underline{x}$ and one arc arising from $\underline{x}$.

Let us illustrate these concepts by an example. For $K = \{a, b, c, d\}$, let $\Sigma$ be the subset $\{abc, abd, bca, bdb, cab, dbc, ddd\}$ of $K^3$. Obviously this set $\Sigma$ is a sliding set. The values of $r(x)$ and $t(x)$ for $x$ in $\Sigma$ are given in table 4.1. The set $\underline{\Sigma}$ is given by $\underline{\Sigma} = \{ab, bc, bd, ca, db, dd\}$, and the graph $\Gamma(\Sigma)$ is represented in figure 4.1.

**Table 4.1 :** Example of a sliding set.

| $x$ | $r(x)$ | $t(x)$ |
|-----|--------|--------|
| $abc$ | 1 | 1 |
| $abd$ | 1 | 1 |
| $bca$ | 2 | 1 |
| $bdb$ | 1 | 1 |
| $cab$ | 1 | 2 |
| $dbc$ | 1 | 1 |
| $ddd$ | 1 | 1 |

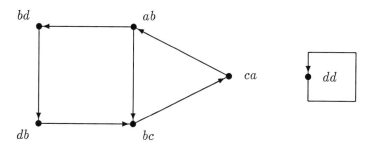

**Figure 4.1** : The graph $\Gamma(\Sigma)$.

Let us recall some concepts of graph theory. More information can
be found for example in [5, 49, 73]. In a digraph, the *in degree* $id(z)$ of
a vertex $z$ is the number of arcs having $z$ as terminal vertex. Similarly
the *out degree* $od(z)$ of $z$ is the number of arcs having $z$ as initial vertex.
A digraph is said to be *pseudosymmetric* if for all its vertices $z$ one has
$od(z) = id(z)$. A pseudosymmetric digraph $\Gamma$ is called *regular* if $od(z)$ is
constant for all vertices $z$ of $\Gamma$. A *path* $b$ of length $t$ in $\Gamma$ is a $t$-tuple of arcs
$b_i$, with $1 \leq i \leq t$, such that, for $i = 1, 2, \cdots, t - 1$, the terminal vertex of
$b_i$ and the initial vertex of $b_{i+1}$ coincide. A path in a digraph is called a
*closed path* of length $t$ if the terminal vertex of its last arc coincides with
the initial vertex of its first arc. An *Eulerian trail* in a finite digraph $\Gamma$ is a
closed path in which each arc of $\Gamma$ occurs exactly once. It is known that a
digraph $\Gamma$ admits an Eulerian trail if and only if it is connected (i.e., if there
exists a path from each vertex to any other vertex) and pseudosymmetric
[73].

Let us associate *labels* with the arcs of the digraph $\Gamma$. With any path
of length $t$ is then associated a $t$-tuple of labels. We call such a $t$-tuple a
*walk* of length $t$. If distinct arcs of a graph have the same label, it is in
general possible that a given walk of length $t$ can be accomplished along
different paths of length $t$.

Given a finite set $K$, again let $\Sigma$ be a sliding subset of $K^{m+1}$ and let $\Gamma(\Sigma)$ be the digraph associated with $\Sigma$. Label the arc of $\Gamma(\Sigma)$ having $\underline{x} = (x^{(0)}, \cdots, x^{(m-1)})$ as initial vertex by the element $x^{(0)}$ of $K$ so that, for any positive integer $t$, a walk of length $t$ in $\Gamma(\Sigma)$ is an element of $K^t$. We call this labelling the *canonical* labelling of the graph $\Gamma(\Sigma)$. In the sequel, all labellings we consider are of this type. We then have the following obvious result.

**Corollary 4.3 :** The $(m+1)$-tuple $x = (x^{(0)}, \cdots, x^{(m)})$ in $K^{m+1}$ is a walk of length $m+1$ in $\Gamma(\Sigma)$ if and only if $x$ is an element of $\Sigma$.

**Definition 4.4 :** An *infinite path* in a digraph $\Gamma$ is a mapping $b : \mathbb{Z} \to \{\text{arcs of } \Gamma\} : i \mapsto b^{(i)}$ such that, for all $i \in \mathbb{Z}$, the terminal vertex of $b^{(i)}$ coincides with the initial vertex of $b^{(i+1)}$.

Using the canonical labelling introduced above, we associate with each infinite path $b$ in $\Gamma(\Sigma)$ the *eternal walk* $\xi$ defined by $\xi : \mathbb{Z} \to K : i \mapsto \xi^{(i)}$ where $\xi^{(i)}$ is the label of the arc $b^{(i)}$ of $b$. The set of these eternal walks is a subset of the set $K^{\mathbb{Z}}$ of all mappings of $\mathbb{Z}$ into $K$.

### 4.1.2  Sliding groups

Let $K$ be a finite multiplicative group the identity of which is denoted by 1. In this case the set $K^{m+1}$ of all $(m+1)$-tuples $x = (x^{(0)}, \cdots, x^{(m)})$ over $K$ is also a group for the multiplication $xy$ defined by

$$(xy)^{(i)} = x^{(i)} y^{(i)}; \ x, y \in K^{m+1}, \ 0 \leq i \leq m. \tag{4.4}$$

**Definition 4.5 :** A sliding set $\Sigma \subseteq K^{m+1}$ is called a *sliding group of span* $m$ if it is a group for the multiplication (4.4).

For any subset $T$ of $\{0, 1, \cdots, m\}$ and for any $\Sigma \subseteq K^{m+1}$, we define $\Sigma(T)$ to be the set of all $x$ in $\Sigma$ that satisfy $x^{(i)} = 1$ for all $i \in T$. If $\Sigma$

is a group, any $x$ in $\Sigma(T)$ satisfies $y^{-1}xy \in \Sigma(T)$ for all $y \in \Sigma$. As a consequence, $\Sigma(T)$ is a normal subgroup of $\Sigma$.

**Theorem 4.6 :** Given a sliding group $\Sigma$, there exists a positive integer $u(\Sigma)$ such that $r(x) = t(x) = u(\Sigma)$ is true for all $x \in \Sigma$.

**Proof :** Since $\Sigma$ is a group, $r(x)$ is equal to $|\Sigma(1, 2, \cdots, m)|$ and $t(x)$ is equal to $|\Sigma(0, 1, \cdots, m-1)|$ for all $x \in \Sigma$. On the other hand, the number of cosets of $\Sigma(1, 2, \cdots, m)$ in $\Sigma$ is $|\overline{\Sigma}|$, and the number of cosets of $\Sigma(0, 1, \cdots, m-1)$ in $\Sigma$ is $|\underline{\Sigma}|$. It follows that for all $x \in \Sigma$ we have $r(x) = |\Sigma|/|\overline{\Sigma}|$ and $t(x) = |\Sigma|/|\underline{\Sigma}|$. From $|\overline{\Sigma}| = |\underline{\Sigma}|$ it follows that the two quantities $r(x)$ and $t(x)$ are equal to some $u(\Sigma)$ depending only on $\Sigma$. This proves $r(x) = t(x) = u(\Sigma)$, all $x \in \Sigma$. $\square$

The following corollary is an obvious consequence of theorem 4.6.

**Corollary 4.7 :** If $\Sigma$ is a sliding subgroup of $K^{m+1}$, then $\Gamma(\Sigma)$ is a regular digraph in which all vertices have degree $u(\Sigma)$.

**Theorem 4.8 :** For any sliding subgroup $\Sigma$ of $K^{m+1}$, the set $\Omega(\Sigma)$ of all eternal walks associated with $\Gamma(\Sigma)$ by the labelling decribed before corollary 4.3 is a group for the multiplication $\xi\eta$ defined by

$$(\xi\eta)^{(i)} = \xi^{(i)}\eta^{(i)}; \; i \in \mathbb{Z}, \; \xi, \eta \in \Omega(\Sigma). \tag{4.5}$$

**Proof :** Given $\lambda \in K^{\mathbb{Z}}$, let $\lambda_i$ be the element $(\lambda^{(i)}, \cdots, \lambda^{(i+m)})$ of $K^{m+1}$. We prove that $\Omega(\Sigma)$ enjoys the properties of a group. First we prove that for $\xi$, $\eta$ in $\Omega(\Sigma)$, $\zeta = \xi\eta$ is also in $\Omega(\Sigma)$. Indeed since $\Sigma$ is a group, $\zeta_i$ is in $\Sigma$ for all $i \in \mathbb{Z}$. Each $\zeta_i$ specifies an arc $(\underline{\zeta_i}, \overline{\zeta_i})$ in $\Gamma(\Sigma)$ and, since, for all $i$, one has $\overline{\zeta_i} = \underline{\zeta_{i+1}}$, the sequence of the arcs $(\underline{\zeta_i}, \overline{\zeta_i})$, $i \in \mathbb{Z}$, is an infinite path in $\Gamma(\Sigma)$. Hence the sequence $\zeta$ of the elements $\zeta^{(i)}$ of $K$ is in $\Omega(\Sigma)$. Next, the associativity is evident. There exists an identity element. For, since $1^{m+1}$ is in $\Sigma$, the arc $(1^m, 1^m)$ is in $\Gamma(\Sigma)$ and $1^{\mathbb{Z}}$ is in $\Omega(\Sigma)$. Finally, each element $\xi \in \Omega(\Sigma)$ has an inverse. Define $r$ to be the period of $\Sigma^{(0)}$. Clearly $\xi^{r-1}$ belongs to $\Omega(\Sigma)$ and satisfies $\xi\xi^{r-1} = 1^{\mathbb{Z}}$. $\square$

**Theorem 4.9 :** Given a sliding group $\Sigma$, the group $\Omega(\Sigma)$ is finite if and only if $u(\Sigma)$ is equal to 1.

**Proof :** If $u(\Sigma) = 1$, then $\Gamma(\Sigma)$ is a set of disjoint cycles $\Gamma_i(\Sigma)$. In this case the number of different infinite paths in $\Gamma(\Sigma)$ is equal to the (finite) number of arcs in $\Gamma(\Sigma)$ and it is an upper bound on $|\Omega(\Sigma)|$. Conversely, if one has $u(\Sigma) \geq 2$, there must exist three different vertices $a = (a^{(0)}, \cdots, a^{(m-1)})$, $b = (b^{(0)}, \cdots, b^{(m-1)})$ and $c = (c^{(0)}, \cdots, c^{(m-1)})$ in $\Gamma(\Sigma)$ such that $(a, b)$ and $(a, c)$ are arcs of $\Gamma(\Sigma)$. Thus we have $a^{(i)} = b^{(i-1)} = c^{(i-1)}$, $1 \leq i \leq m - 1$, and $b^{(m-1)} \neq c^{(m-1)}$, so that at least two different Eulerian trails start from $a$ one having $(a, b)$ as initial arc and the other one having $(a, c)$ as initial arc. Since $b^{(m-1)}$ is not equal to $c^{(m-1)}$, the walks $w(b)$ and $w(c)$ associated with these two Eulerian trails are different, so that the set of all mappings

$$w \; : \; \mathbb{Z} \to \{w(b), w(c)\} \; : \; j \mapsto w^{(j)}$$

is clearly infinite. Any such mapping describes a different eternal walk which is obtained by "concatenation" of the walks $w^{(j)}$. $\square$

### 4.1.3 Systematic sliding groups

Let $K$ be a finite multiplicative group and let 1 be the identity of $K$.

**Definition 4.10 :** A subgroup $\Sigma$ of $K^{m+1}$ is called *systematic* if $1^{m+1}$ is the only element $x$ of $\Sigma$ for which $x^{(i)} = 1$ is satisfied for at least one $i$, $0 \leq i \leq m$.

Systematic sliding groups play an important role in the study of the automorphisms of convolutional codes and we now investigate some of their properties.

**Theorem 4.11 :** If $\Sigma$ is a systematic sliding group, the mappings

$$\pi(j) \; : \; \Sigma \to \Sigma^{(j)} \; : \; x \mapsto x^{\pi(j)} := x^{(j)}; \; 0 \leq j \leq m,$$

are group isomorphisms.

**Proof :** Since $\Sigma$ is a sliding set, all sets $\Sigma^{(j)} = \Sigma^{\pi(j)}$ with $0 \le j \le m$, are identical. If $x_1$ and $x_2$ in $\Sigma$ satisfy $x_1^{(j)} = x_2^{(j)}$ for some $j$ with $0 \le j \le m$, then $x_1^{-1}x_2$ is $1^{m+1}$ since $\Sigma$ is a systematic group. This implies

$$|\Sigma| = |\Sigma^{\pi(j)}|; \quad 0 \le j \le m. \tag{4.6}$$

Since $\pi(j)$ satisfies $(x_1 x_2)^{\pi(j)} = x_1^{\pi(j)} x_2^{\pi(j)}$, it is a group homomorphism. From (4.6), this group homomorphism is an isomorphism. $\square$

From the isomorphisms $\pi(j)$, we define the mappings

$$\beta(i,j) := (\pi(i))^{-1}\pi(j)$$

of $\Sigma^{(i)}$ to $\Sigma^{(j)}$. These mappings are isomorphisms from the group $\Sigma^{(i)}$ to the group $\Sigma^{(j)}$ and since $\Sigma^{(i)}$ coincides with $\Sigma^{(0)}$ for all $i$, they can be also considered as automorphisms of $\Sigma^{(0)}$. Now define $\alpha_0$ to be the automorphism $\beta(0,1)$ of $\Sigma^{(0)}$.

**Theorem 4.12 :** If $\Sigma$ is a systematic sliding subgroup of $K^{m+1}$, the automorphisms $\beta(i,j)$ of $\Sigma^{(0)}$ satisfy $\beta(i,j) = \alpha_0^{j-i}$ for $0 \le i, j \le m$.
**Proof :** By the sliding property of $\Sigma$, one has $\beta(i, i+1) = \alpha_0$ for $0 \le i \le m-1$. Suppose now that $j \ge i+1$. From $\beta(i,j) = \beta(i,i+1)\beta(i+1,i+2)\cdots\beta(j-1,j)$, we obtain

$$\beta(i,j) = \alpha_0^{j-i}. \tag{4.7}$$

Since $\beta(j,i) = (\beta(i,j))^{-1}$, (4.7) remains true for $j \le i$. $\square$

**Theorem 4.13 :** If $\Sigma$ is a systematic sliding group, $u(\Sigma)$ is equal to 1.
**Proof :** Clearly one has $r(1^{m+1}) = 1$. The proof then follows from theorem 4.6. $\square$

As a consequence, the graph $\Gamma(\Sigma)$ associated with a systematic sliding group $\Sigma$ is a union of disjoint cycles. Moreover, it follows from theorem 4.12 that if $\Sigma$ is a systematic group and if $\xi^{(i)}$ and $\xi^{(i+1)}$ are the labels associated with two consecutive arcs of a path $\xi$ in $\Gamma(\Sigma)$, these labels satisfy $\xi^{(i+1)} = (\xi^{(i)})^{\alpha_0}$ . This remark leads to the following theorem.

**Theorem 4.14 :** Let $\Sigma$ be any systematic sliding subgroup of $K^{m+1}$ and let $\Omega(\Sigma)$ be the group of eternal walks in $\Gamma(\Sigma)$ induced by the canonical labelling. Any $\xi \in \Omega(\Sigma)$ satisfies

$$\xi^{(i)} = (\xi^{(0)})^{\alpha_0^i} \; ; \; \text{all } i \in \mathbb{Z} \, ,$$

where $\alpha_0$ is an automorphism of the group $\Sigma^{(0)}$.

## 4.2   Automorphisms of convolutional codes

In this section we introduce the concept of automorphism group of a convolutional code, we show how this group can be computed and we give some of its properties.

### 4.2.1   Definition and general properties of the automorphisms of a convolutional code

A first possibility is to define an automorphism of an $(n, k)$ convolutional code $C$ over $F$ to be a nonsingular $n \times n$ matrix $A$ over $F$ satisfying

$$v \in C \Rightarrow vA \in C, \tag{4.8}$$

where $v$ is represented as a row $n$-tuple over $\mathcal{F}$. For reasons that will become apparent later, this definition is too restrictive. Hence we suggest a more general and more useful definition. Given a finite set $K$, denote by $K^{\mathbb{Z}}$ the set of all mappings $x$

$$x \; : \; \mathbb{Z} \rightarrow K \; : \; i \mapsto x^{(i)} \, . \tag{4.9}$$

If $K$ is a multiplicative group this set $K^{\mathbb{Z}}$ is also a group for the multiplication

$$(xy)^{(i)} = x^{(i)} y^{(i)} \; ; \; x, y \in K^{\mathbb{Z}}, \; i \in \mathbb{Z} \, . \tag{4.10}$$

Assume now that $K$ is a subgroup of the group $GL(n, F)$ of all $n \times n$ nonsingular matrices over $F$. In this case we can define the action of an element $x \in K^{\mathbb{Z}}$ on the set $\mathcal{F}^n$ of Laurent series over $F^n$ by

$$x \in K^{\mathbb{Z}} \; : \; \mathcal{F}^n \to \mathcal{F}^n \; : \; v = \sum_{i=r}^{\infty} v_i D^i \mapsto vx = \sum_{i=r}^{\infty} v_i x^{(i)} D^i . \qquad (4.11)$$

In (4.11), $v_i x^{(i)}$ denotes the element of $F^n$ obtained when the row $n$-tuple $v_i$ over $F$ is postmultiplied by the $n \times n$ matrix $x^{(i)}$ over $F$, and $r$ is some integer at most equal to the delay of $v$.

With $K$ a subgroup of $GL(n, F)$ we have the following definition.

**Definition 4.15 :** Let $C$ be any subset of $\mathcal{F}^n$. The element $x \in K^{\mathbb{Z}}$ is called an *automorphism* of $C$ with respect to $K$ (or $K$-automorphism) if it satisfies $v \in C \; \Rightarrow \; vx \in C$.

This definition implies

$$C \supseteq Cx, \qquad (4.12)$$

for any automorphism $x$ of $C$ and hence

$$C \, x^{r-1} \supseteq C \, x^r \; ; \; \text{all } r \geq 1 . \qquad (4.13)$$

As it is a finite group, $K$ has a finite period. If $r$ is chosen to be the period of $K$, then $x^r = 1^{\mathbb{Z}}$ holds true for all $x \in K^{\mathbb{Z}}$ and (4.13) yields

$$Cx^{r-1} \supseteq C . \qquad (4.14)$$

From (4.12), (4.13) and (4.14), it follows that $x$ is an automorphism of $C$ if and only if

$$Cx = C \qquad (4.15)$$

holds true.

Before studying some properties of the automorphisms of a convolutional code, we introduce other definitions and we give a theorem about them. In (4.11) we have defined the permutation action of $K^Z$ on $\mathcal{F}^n$. A similar permutation action can also be defined for any monomial $D^s$ with $s \in Z$,

$$D^s \; : \; \mathcal{F}^n \to \mathcal{F}^n \; : \; v \mapsto vD^s \; ,$$

and thus for any composition $\xi = D^{s_1} x_1 D^{s_2} x_2 \cdots x_t D^{s_{t+1}}$ of a finite number of elements of $K^Z$ and of powers of $D$. Given $v \in \mathcal{F}^n$, the element $v^* := v\xi$ of $\mathcal{F}^n$ is obtained by computing successively $v_1 = vD^{s_1}$, $v_2 = v_1 x_1$, $v_3 = v_2 D^{s_2}$, $\cdots$, $v_{2t} = v_{2t-1} x_t$, $v^* = v_{2t} D^{s_{t+1}}$. A subset of these compositions is of particular interest. This subset is the set of all compositions $D^{-s} x D^s$, with $x \in K^Z$ and $s \in Z$, of the three permutations $D^{-s}$, $x$ and $D^s$ acting on $\mathcal{F}^n$. Such a composition is denoted by $x^{D^s}$. Using (4.11) we obtain

$$v \, x^{D^s} = \sum_{i=r}^{\infty} v_i x^{(i-s)} D^i \tag{4.16}$$

for any $v = \sum_{i=r}^{\infty} v_i D^i \in \mathcal{F}^n$. It follows from (4.16) that the permutation $x^{D^s}$ of $\mathcal{F}^n$ is nothing but the permutation $y \in K^Z$ that satisfies $y^{(i)} = x^{(i-s)}$ for all $i \in Z$. Moreover, since one has

$$(xy)^{D^s} = x^{D^s} y^{D^s}, \; (x^{D^s})^{D^{-s}} = x \; ; \; \text{all } x \in K^Z \; ,$$

the mapping $x \mapsto x^{D^s}$ is for all $s \in Z$ a group automorphism of $K^Z$.

For a moment, let again $K$ be an arbitrary finite set. For any $x \in K^Z$, we may yet give sense to the writing $x^{D^s}$ by defining $(x^{D^s})^{(i)} := x^{(i-s)}$, $i \in Z$. In particular, the case where $K$ is an abstract group (not explicitly represented as a subgroup of $GL(n, F)$) will be considered at several places in the sequel. This more general use of $D$ occurs in the following definitions.

**Definitions 4.16 :** A subset $H$ of $K^Z$ is said to be *D-normal* if it satisfies $H = H^D(:= D^{-1}HD)$. It is called *D-central* if it satisfies $x = x^D$ for all $x \in H$.

Any *D*-normal subset $H$ of $K^Z$ satisfies $H^{D^r} = H$, all $r \in Z$. However, the condition $x \in H \Rightarrow x^D \in H$ is not sufficient to make $H$ a *D*-normal subset of $K^{\mathbb{Z}}$. Indeed for $a, b \in K$, $a \neq b$, define the elements of $H = \{x_i \in K^{\mathbb{Z}} \mid \text{all } i \geq 0\}$ by $x_i^{(j)} = a$ for $j \geq i$ and by $x_i^{(j)} = b$ for $j < i$. Any $x \in H$ satisfies $x^D \in H$, but since no $x$ in $H$ satisfies $x^D = x_0$ it follows that $H^D$ is a proper subset of $H$. A necessary and sufficient condition to make $H$ a $D$-normal subset of $K^{\mathbb{Z}}$ is

$$x \in H \Rightarrow x^{D^s} \in H \, ; \quad s = +1, -1 \, . \tag{4.17}$$

**Definitions 4.17 :** Any $x \in K^{\mathbb{Z}}$ is called *repetitive* if one has $x^{D^t} = x$ for some nonzero integer $t$. The smallest $t \geq 1$ having this property is called the *repetition length* of $x$. Any set $H \subseteq K^{\mathbb{Z}}$ is called *repetitive* if there exists some integer $T \geq 1$ such that one has $x^{D^T} = x$ for all $x \in H$. The smallest $T$ having this property is called the *repetition length* of $H$.

Any subset $H$ of $K^{\mathbb{Z}}$ having repetition length equal to 1 is obviously $D$-central. If $H$ is repetitive, any $x \in H$ is repetitive and the repetition length of $H$ is the least common multiple of the repetition lengths of its elements. In general, the converse property is not true. For example the set of all repetitive elements of $K^{\mathbb{Z}}$ is not repetitive. However, we have the following theorem.

**Theorem 4.18 :** Any repetitive subset $H$ of $K^{\mathbb{Z}}$ contains a finite number of elements. Conversely, any finite $D$-normal subset $H$ of $K^{\mathbb{Z}}$ is repetitive.
**Proof :** If one has $x^{D^T} = x$ for all $x \in H$, then there exists for any element $(\xi^{(0)}, \cdots, \xi^{(T-1)})$ of $K^T$ at most one $x \in H$ such that $x^{(i)} = \xi^{(i)}$, $0 \leq i \leq T - 1$, and, as a consequence, $|H|$ is at most equal to $|K|^T$. Conversely, if $H$ is $D$-normal, one has

$$x \in H \Rightarrow x^{D^i} \in H \, ; \quad \text{all } i \in \mathbb{Z} \, .$$

Therefore, if $H$ is finite there must exist, for any $x \in H$, some integers $i$ and $j$, $i \neq j$, that satisfy $x^{D^i} = x^{D^j}$. This implies $x^{D^{i-j}} = x$, which shows that $x$ has repetition length $\mid i - j \mid$. Defining then $T$ to be the g.c.d. of the repetition lengths of all $x \in H$, we obtain $x^{D^T} = x$, all $x \in H$, which makes obvious that $H$ is repetitive. $\square$

Let us now go back to the study of the automorphisms of a convolutional code $C$. In the sequel $K$ is again a subgroup of the group $GL(n, F)$. We state two important theorems.

**Theorem 4.19 :** The set of all $x \in K^Z$ that are automorphisms of $C$ is a group.
**Proof :** Easy and omitted. $\square$

We may thus call the set of $x \in K^Z$ that are automorphisms of $C$ the automorphism group of $C$ (with respect to $K$). We denote it by $\mathrm{Aut}(C)$ or by $\mathrm{Aut}_K(C)$ when the mention of $K$ is necessary.

**Theorem 4.20 :** The group $\mathrm{Aut}(C)$ is $D$-normal, i.e., $[\mathrm{Aut}(C)]^D$ coincides with $\mathrm{Aut}(C)$.
**Proof :** It follows from theorem 1.11 that the convolutional code $C$, being an $\mathcal{F}$-space, satisfies $CD^s = C$, all $s \in Z$. It also follows from (4.15) that for any $x \in \mathrm{Aut}(C)$ it satisfies $Cx = C$. This leads to

$$CD^{-s}xD^s = C \, ; \text{ all } s \in Z, \text{ all } x \in \mathrm{Aut}(C) \, ,$$

which implies

$$x \in \mathrm{Aut}(C) \Rightarrow x^{D^s} \in \mathrm{Aut}(C) \, ; \; s = +1, -1 \, .$$

The remark made before (4.17) then implies that $\mathrm{Aut}(C)$ is a $D$-normal group. $\square$

Generalizing definition 4.2 to any subset $H$ of $K^Z$, we define $H^{(i)}$, *the projection of index i of $H$*, by

$$H^{(i)} := \{x^{(i)} \mid x \in H\}.$$

If $H$ is a group, $H^{(i)}$ is a homomorphic image of $H$; one has $(h_1 h_2)^{(i)} = h_1^{(i)} h_2^{(i)}$ for all $h_1, h_2 \in H$. If $H$ is $D$-normal all projections $H^{(i)}$ are identical; one has $H^{(i)} = H^{(0)}$, all $i \in \mathbb{Z}$.

**Corollary 4.21 :** If $C$ is a convolutional code, $(\text{Aut}(C))^{(i)}$ is equal to $(\text{Aut}(C))^{(0)}$ for all $i \in \mathbb{Z}$.

**Proof :** A direct consequence of theorem 4.20. □

Consider now a block code $C_0$ defined to be the $F$-row space of an $F$-matrix $G$, i.e., $C_0 = E_0(G)$, and define the (nonproper) convolutional code $C$ to be the Laurent extension of $C_0$, i.e., $C = E(G)$. A sequence $v = \sum_{i=r}^{\infty} v_i D^i$ is then in $C$ if and only if all its words $v_i$ are in the block code $C_0$. Assume now that $\overline{\text{Aut}}(C_0)$, the automorphism group of the block code $C_0$, contains at least two elements. In this case, the set $(\overline{\text{Aut}}(C_0))^{\mathbb{Z}}$ of all mappings $x : \mathbb{Z} \to \overline{\text{Aut}}(C_0) : i \mapsto x^{(i)}$ is obviously an infinite group. Moreover, for $v \in C$, any $x \in (\overline{\text{Aut}}(C_0))^{\mathbb{Z}}$ satisfies $vx = \sum_{i=r}^{\infty} v_i x^{(i)} D^i$ with $v_i x^{(i)} \in C_0$. It follows that $vx$ is a sequence of $C$, so that the group $\text{Aut}(C)$ is infinite because it contains the infinite subgroup $(\overline{\text{Aut}}(C_0))^{\mathbb{Z}}$. The question arises now whether there are many proper convolutional codes $C$ that have an infinite automorphism group $\text{Aut}_K(C)$. As it will become clear later, these codes are rather exceptional when the order of $K$ is small. In the next subsection we give a method for computing $\text{Aut}_K(C)$, and illustrate this method by computing the automorphism group of a (9,2) convolutional code over GF(2). It turns out that this (9,2) code, which is *not* the Laurent extension of a block code, has an infinite automorphism group. That this is an exceptional case will be explained in chapter 5, where conditions are obtained that guarantee that $\text{Aut}_K(C)$ is a finite group. Here we shall only state the following corollary.

**Corollary 4.22 :** The group $\text{Aut}(C)$ is finite if and only if it is repetitive.

**Proof :** This follows from theorem 4.18 since theorem 4.20 shows that $\text{Aut}(C)$ is $D$-normal. □

Let $H$ be a subset of $\mathrm{Aut}(C)$ and let $H^*$ be the smallest subgroup of $K^{\mathbb{Z}}$ that contains $H^{D^r}$ for all $r \in \mathbb{Z}$, i.e., $H^*$ is the set of all elements $h^*$ of $K^{\mathbb{Z}}$ that can be written as

$$h^* = \Pi_{i=1}^{u} h_i^{D^{s(i)}} \; ; \; h_i \in H \,, \quad s(i) \in \mathbb{Z}, \tag{4.18}$$

for some positive integer $u$.

**Corollary 4.23 :** $H^*$ is a $D$-normal subgroup of $\mathrm{Aut}(C)$.

**Proof :** To prove that $H^*$ is a group we check that it satisfies the axioms given in chapter 1. In particular, in the right hand side of $(h^*)^{-1} = (h_u^{D^{s(u)}})^{-1}(h_{u-1}^{D^{s(u-1)}})^{-1} \cdots (h_1^{D^{s(1)}})^{-1}$, all factors $(h_i^{D^{s(i)}})^{-1}$ are in $H^*$, so that $(h^*)^{-1}$ is itself in $H^*$. Moreover, with $h^*$ as given by (4.18), $(h^*)^{D^r} = \Pi_{i=1}^{u} h_i^{D^{r+s(i)}}$ is an element of $H^*$ for all $r \in \mathbb{Z}$. Hence $H^*$ is $D$-normal by the remark leading to (4.17). $\square$

## 4.2.2 Computation of the automorphism group of a convolutional code

The computation of the automorphism group $\mathrm{Aut}_K(C)$ of a convolutional code $C$ over $F$, with respect to some subgroup $K$ of $GL(n, F)$, is based on two theorems. For $m \geq i \geq 0$, define $C_{i,m}$ to be the $F$-subspace of $F^n$ generated by the coefficients of $D^i$ in the sequences of the set $L_m(C)$ defined in subsection 2.2.1. We shall first establish a connection between $\mathrm{Aut}_K(C)$ and $\overline{\mathrm{Aut}}_K(C_{i,m})$, which is the automorphism group of the block code $C_{i,m}$ with respect to $K$.

**Theorem 4.24 :** Let $C$ be a convolutional code and let $i$ and $m$ be integers satisfying $m \geq i \geq 0$. In this case one has

$$(\mathrm{Aut}_K(C))^{(0)} \subseteq \overline{\mathrm{Aut}}_K(C_{i,m}). \tag{4.19}$$

**Proof :** Any $x \in \mathrm{Aut}_K(C)$ permutes the elements of $L_m(C)$. It follows that one has $x \in \mathrm{Aut}_K(C) \Rightarrow x^{(i)} \in \overline{\mathrm{Aut}}_K(C_{i,m})$, which implies

$(\mathrm{Aut}_K(C))^{(i)} \subseteq \overline{\mathrm{Aut}}_K(C_{i,m})$. Together with corollary 4.21, this implies (4.19). $\square$

Let now $x^* = (x^{(0)}, \cdots, x^{(i)}, \cdots, x^{(m)})$ be an element of $K^{m+1}$. We let act $x^*$ on the set of polynomials of degree $\leq m$ over $F^n$ by defining, for any $v = \sum_{i=0}^{m} v_i D^i$, $v_i \in F^n$,

$$v \circ x^* := \sum_{i=0}^{m} v_i x^{(i)} D^i.$$

Given a convolutional code $C$ and the corresponding set $L_m(C)$, the set of $x^* \in K^{m+1}$ that satisfy $v \in L_m(C) \Rightarrow v \circ x^* \in L_m(C)$ is obviously a group for the multiplication $x^* y^*$ defined by

$$x^* y^* = (x^{(0)} y^{(0)}, \cdots, x^{(i)} y^{(i)}, \cdots, x^{(m)} y^{(m)}).$$

We denote this group by $\mathrm{Aut}_K^*[L_m(C)]$. The second theorem of this subsection relates $\mathrm{Aut}_K(C)$ to $\mathrm{Aut}_K^*[L_m(C)]$.

**Theorem 4.25 :** Suppose that the convolutional code $C$ satisfies

$$E[L_m(C)] = C, \tag{4.20}$$

for some integer $m$. In this case, $x \in K^{\mathbb{Z}}$ is in $\mathrm{Aut}_K(C)$ if and only if for all $i \in \mathbb{Z}$ the element $x_i^* = (x^{(i)}, \cdots, x^{(i+m)})$ of $K^{m+1}$ is in $\mathrm{Aut}_K^*[L_m(C)]$.
**Proof :** Any $x \in \mathrm{Aut}_K(C)$ satisfies

$$v \in L_m(C) \Rightarrow v D^i x D^{-i} = v x^{D^{-i}} \in L_m(C); \text{ all } i \in \mathbb{Z},$$

so that, for all $i \in \mathbb{Z}$, $x_i^*$ is in $\mathrm{Aut}_K^*[L_m(C)]$. Conversely, let $x \in K^{\mathbb{Z}}$ be such that, for all $i \in \mathbb{Z}$, $x_i^*$ is in $\mathrm{Aut}^*[L_m(C)]$. We prove that, in this case, $x$ is an element of $\mathrm{Aut}_K(C)$. Choose first a set of $k$ polynomials $g_j$, $1 \leq j \leq k$, of $L_m(C)$ as a basis of the $\mathcal{F}$-space $C$. Any $v \in C$ can be written as

$$v = \sum_{j=1}^{k} g_j a_j; \ a_j = \sum_{i=r}^{\infty} (a_j)_i D^i, \ (a_j)_i \in F. \tag{4.21}$$

Defining the element $\phi_i$ of $L_m(C)$ to be $\phi_i = \sum_{j=1}^{k} g_j(a_j)_i$, we develop (4.21) as $v = \sum_{i=r}^{\infty} \phi_i D^i$. Postmultiplying by $x$, we obtain

$$vx = \sum_{i=r}^{\infty} \phi_i(D^i x D^{-i})D^i = \sum_{i=r}^{\infty} (\phi_i \circ x_i^*)D^i$$

where, for all $i$, the polynomial $\phi_i \circ x_i^*$ is in $L_m(C)$, since $x_i^*$ is an element of $\text{Aut}^*[L_m(C)]$. Moreover, for $i = r, r+1, \cdots$, the sequences $(\phi_i \circ x_i^*)D^i$ form a progressive collection. Hence, by theorem 1.10, $vx$ is in $C = E[L_m(C)]$ for all $v \in C$, which implies $x \in \text{Aut}_K(C)$. $\square$

On the basis of these theorems, it follows that the first part of the computation of $\text{Aut}_K(C)$ is to find those $(m+1)$-tuples $x_i^* = (x^{(i)}, \cdots, x^{(i+m)})$ in $K^{m+1}$ that can match the elements $x$ of $\text{Aut}_K(C)$. To find these elements $x_i^*$ of $K^{m+1}$, one can use the following algorithm.

**Algorithm A4.1.**

**(i)** For some pairs $(m, i)$ with $m \geq i \geq 0$, compute the group $\overline{\text{Aut}}_K(C_{i,m})$. Define the group $\mathcal{K}$ to be the intersection of these groups $\overline{\text{Aut}}_K(C_{i,m})$.

**(ii)** By theorem 4.24, $(\text{Aut}_K(C))^{(0)}$ is a subgroup of $\mathcal{K}$. Choose an integer $m$ satisfying (4.20) and list all elements of $\mathcal{K}^{m+1}$.

**(iii)** Cancel in this list all elements that are not in $\text{Aut}_K^*[L_m(C)]$.

**(iv)** Cancel the elements whose $m$ last (or first) components do not appear as the $m$ first (or last) components of an element of the list.

**(v)** Repeat step (iv) as long as cancellations occur.

**(vi)** Denote by $\Sigma$ the set of elements that belong to the list after the five preceding steps.

The purpose of the first three steps of the algorithm is to list the elements of $\text{Aut}_K^*[L_m(C)]$. In the following steps one deletes from this list all elements that cannot appear as "substrings" $x_i^* = (x^{(i)}, \cdots, x^{(i+m)})$ of some $x \in \mathrm{Aut}_K(C)$, because one cannot extend them in both directions to obtain an element $x \in K^Z$ satisfying $x_i^* \in \mathrm{Aut}_K^*[L_m(C)]$ for all $i \in Z$. We give now an example of how to apply steps (iv) and (v) of the algorithm A4.1. Suppose that a code $C$ satisfies $C = E[L_2(C)]$ and that $B := \mathrm{Aut}_K^*[L_2(C)]$ is given by

$$B = \{(a,b,c),(b,c,d),(c,d,e),(d,e,c),(e,c,d),(f,f,f)\},$$

where $a, b, c, d, e$ and $f$ are different elements of $K$. Since $B$ does not contain any triple of the form $(g, a, b)$ for some $g \in K$, no $x \in K^Z$ can simultaneously satisfy $(x^{(i)}, x^{(i+1)}, x^{(i+2)}) = (a, b, c)$ and $x^{(i-1)}, x^{(i)}, x^{(i+1)}) \in B$ for some $i \in Z$. For this reason the triple $(a, b, c)$ is removed from the list of triples that can be substrings of the elements $x$ of $\mathrm{Aut}_K(C)$. The new set

$$B = \{(b,c,d),(c,d,e),(d,e,c),(e,c,d),(f,f,f)\}$$

does not contain a triple of the form $(g, b, c)$, $g \in K$. For this reason the triple $(b, c, d)$ is also removed from $B$.

Obviously, the iteration of step (iv) does not lead to any further removal. The set $\Sigma$ that is produced in this case is

$$\Sigma = \{(c,d,e),(d,e,c),(e,c,d),(f,f,f)\}.$$

Going back to the general case we prove the following theorem.

**Theorem 4.26 :** The set $\Sigma$ produced by the algorithm mentioned above is a sliding subgroup of $\mathrm{Aut}_K^*[L_m(C)]$ and it contains as subsets all sliding subsets of $\mathrm{Aut}_K^*[L_m(C)]$.

**Proof :** We first prove that $\Sigma$ is a sliding set. Indeed, if $\Sigma$ is not a sliding set there exists $x^* \in \Sigma$ that does not satisfy the properties required in definition 4.1. This is impossible because all these $x^*$ were removed from $\Sigma$ by the iteration of step (iv) of the algorithm A4.1.

We then prove that a sliding subset $\Sigma^*$ of $\mathrm{Aut}_K^*[L_m(C)]$ is contained in $\Sigma$. Indeed, no $x^*$ in such a subset can be removed by step (iv) of the algorithm A4.1.

Finally, we prove that $\Sigma$ is a group. Define $\Sigma^*$ to be the group generated by $\Sigma$, i.e., the set of all finite products

$$x^* = x_1^* x_2^* \cdots x_r^*; \quad x_i^* \in \Sigma. \tag{4.22}$$

Obviously one has $\Sigma \subseteq \Sigma^*$. To prove $\Sigma^* \subseteq \Sigma$, we show that $\Sigma^*$ is a sliding subset of $\mathrm{Aut}_K^*[L_m(C)]$. The property $\Sigma^* \subseteq \Sigma$ then follows from the previous step. Since $\Sigma$ is a subset of the group $\mathrm{Aut}_K^*[L_m(C)]$, so is $\Sigma^*$. To prove that $\Sigma^*$ is sliding we remark that, since $\Sigma$ is sliding, there exists, for any $x_i^*$ appearing in (4.22), at least one element $y_i^*$ and one element $z_i^*$ in $\Sigma$ that satisfy $\underline{x}_i^* = \bar{y}_i^*$, $\bar{x}_i^* = \underline{z}_i^*$. Since $\Sigma^*$ is a group, $y^* = y_1^* y_2^* \cdots y_r^*$ and $z^* = z_1^* z_2^* \cdots z_r^*$ are in $\Sigma^*$ and they satisfy $\underline{x}^* = \bar{y}^*$, $\bar{x}^* = \underline{z}^*$. Since this is true for any $x^* \in \Sigma^*$, the group $\Sigma^*$ is a sliding set. $\square$

As it is done in section 4.1, we associate with the sliding group $\Sigma$ the directed graph $\Gamma(\Sigma)$ having as vertices the elements $\underline{x}^* \in K^m$ for which $x^* = (x^{(0)}, \cdots, x^{(m)})$ is in $\Sigma$, and as arcs the ordered pairs $(\underline{x}^*, \bar{x}^*)$ with $x^* \in \Sigma$. Labelling all arcs $(\underline{x}^*, \bar{x}^*)$ of $\Gamma(\Sigma)$ by the first component $x^{(0)}$ of $x^*$, we obtain the group $\Omega(\Sigma)$ of all eternal walks in $\Gamma(\Sigma)$ that are induced by this labelling (see theorem 4.8.) We can now give the following characterization of $\mathrm{Aut}_K(C)$.

**Theorem 4.27 :** The automorphism group $\mathrm{Aut}_K(C)$ coincides with the group $\Omega(\Sigma)$ of eternal walks in the digraph $\Gamma(\Sigma)$.
**Proof :** Any $x \in \Omega(\Sigma)$ is such that $x_i^* = (x^{(i)}, \cdots, x^{(i+m)})$ is an element of $\mathrm{Aut}_K^*[L_m(C)]$. From theorem 4.25, this implies $x \in \Omega(\Sigma) \Rightarrow x \in \mathrm{Aut}_K(C)$. Conversely, it follows from theorem 4.25 that any $x \in \mathrm{Aut}_K(C)$ satisfies $x_i^* \in \mathrm{Aut}_K^*[L_m(C)]$, all $i \in \mathbb{Z}$. Since this is the only restriction that $x$ must satisfy to be in $\Omega(\Sigma)$ we obtain $x \in \mathrm{Aut}_K(C) \Rightarrow x \in \Omega(\Sigma)$.
$\square$

It is now time to present some examples; they will be chosen in the class of binary codes, $F = GF(2)$. In this case $\mathcal{F}$ will denote the set of

Laurent series over $GF(2)$. Let $n$ be the length of the convolutional code $C$ and choose the group $K$, with respect to which $\mathrm{Aut}_K(C)$ is computed, to be the symmetric group $S_n$ of order $n! = n(n-1)\cdots 3.2$ in its natural action as permutation group on the $n$ coordinates of $F^n$. The matrix representation of $K$ then consists of all $n \times n$ permutation matrices, thus having a unique 1 in each row and each column and zeros elsewhere. Another way to represent an element $\pi$ of $K = S_n$ (as we shall do at several places) is to write $\pi$ as a product of cycles. Here is an example of these two representations, where $n$ is chosen to be 9 and any $v \in F^n$ is represented as a row 9-tuple $v = (v_0, \cdots, v_8)$ over $F$. Consider the three following permutation matrices.

$$
L = \begin{bmatrix}
\cdot & 1 & \cdot & \cdot & \cdot & \cdot & \cdot & \cdot & \cdot \\
\cdot & \cdot & 1 & \cdot & \cdot & \cdot & \cdot & \cdot & \cdot \\
1 & \cdot & \cdot & \cdot & \cdot & \cdot & \cdot & \cdot & \cdot \\
\cdot & \cdot & \cdot & \cdot & 1 & \cdot & \cdot & \cdot & \cdot \\
\cdot & \cdot & \cdot & \cdot & \cdot & 1 & \cdot & \cdot & \cdot \\
\cdot & \cdot & \cdot & 1 & \cdot & \cdot & \cdot & \cdot & \cdot \\
\cdot & \cdot & \cdot & \cdot & \cdot & \cdot & \cdot & 1 & \cdot \\
\cdot & \cdot & \cdot & \cdot & \cdot & \cdot & \cdot & \cdot & 1 \\
\cdot & \cdot & \cdot & \cdot & \cdot & \cdot & 1 & \cdot & \cdot
\end{bmatrix},
$$

$$
M = \begin{bmatrix}
\cdot & \cdot & \cdot & 1 & \cdot & \cdot & \cdot & \cdot & \cdot \\
\cdot & \cdot & \cdot & \cdot & 1 & \cdot & \cdot & \cdot & \cdot \\
\cdot & \cdot & \cdot & \cdot & \cdot & 1 & \cdot & \cdot & \cdot \\
\cdot & \cdot & \cdot & \cdot & \cdot & \cdot & 1 & \cdot & \cdot \\
\cdot & \cdot & \cdot & \cdot & \cdot & \cdot & \cdot & 1 & \cdot \\
\cdot & \cdot & \cdot & \cdot & \cdot & \cdot & \cdot & \cdot & 1 \\
1 & \cdot & \cdot & \cdot & \cdot & \cdot & \cdot & \cdot & \cdot \\
\cdot & 1 & \cdot & \cdot & \cdot & \cdot & \cdot & \cdot & \cdot \\
\cdot & \cdot & 1 & \cdot & \cdot & \cdot & \cdot & \cdot & \cdot
\end{bmatrix},
$$

$$N = \begin{bmatrix} 1 & . & . & . & . & . & . & . & . \\ . & . & 1 & . & . & . & . & . & . \\ . & 1 & . & . & . & . & . & . & . \\ . & . & . & . & . & 1 & . & . & . \\ . & . & . & . & . & . & . & 1 & . \\ . & . & . & . & . & . & 1 & . & . \\ . & . & . & 1 & . & . & . & . & . \\ . & . & . & . & . & 1 & . & . & . \\ . & . & . & 1 & . & . & . & . & . \end{bmatrix} ,$$

where for reasons of typographical clarity the zeros are represented by dots. The action of these three matrices on $v = (v_0, \cdots, v_8) \in F^9$ is given by

$$vL = (v_2, v_0, v_1, v_5, v_3, v_4, v_8, v_6, v_7),$$

$$vM = (v_6, v_7, v_8, v_0, v_1, v_2, v_3, v_4, v_5),$$

$$vN = (v_0, v_2, v_1, v_6, v_8, v_7, v_3, v_5, v_4).$$

To represent these permutations by product of cycles, we identify the entries $v_i$, $0 \le i \le 8$, of $v$ by their indices $i$. The representation of $M$ by a product of cycles is given by

$$\mu = (0, 3, 6)(1, 4, 7)(2, 5, 8).$$

The meaning of $\mu$ is that, for any $v \in F^9$, it moves $v_0$ to coordinate 3, $v_3$ to coordinate 6, $v_6$ to coordinate 0, $v_1$ to coordinate 4, and so on. In the same way, the coordinate permutations carried out by $L$ and $N$ are represented respectively by

$$\lambda = (0, 1, 2)(3, 4, 5)(6, 7, 8) ,$$

$$\nu = (0)(1, 2)(3, 6)(4, 8)(5, 7) .$$

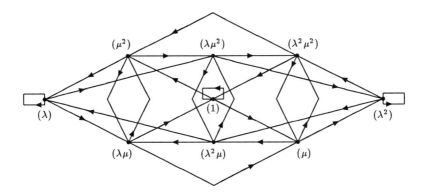

**Figure 4.2** : The component $\Gamma_1$ of the graph $\Gamma(\Sigma)$.

Cycles of length 1, such as $(0)$ in $\nu$, are often omitted. Thus one writes

$$\nu = (1,2)(3,6)(4,8)(5,7).$$

In general, if $w$ is the $n$-tuple obtained from the application of the permutation $\pi$ to the coordinates of the $n$-tuple $v$, we write $w = v\pi$, whatever the representation of $\pi$ may be.

With these remarks in mind we consider the $(9,2)$ code $C$ over $GF(2)$ defined to be the $\mathcal{F}$-row space of

$$G = \begin{bmatrix} 0 & 1+D & 1+D & 1 & D & 1+D & 1 & 1+D & D \\ 1+D & 0 & 1+D & 1+D & 1 & D & D & 1 & 1+D \end{bmatrix},$$
$$(4.23)$$

and for this code $C$ we carry out the six steps of the algorithm A4.1.

**(i)** Since $G$ is a minimal encoder, it is easy to compute the set $L_1(C)$, which is nothing but the $F$-row space of $G$. The subgroup $\mathcal{K} := \overline{\text{Aut}}_K(C_{0,1}) \cap \overline{\text{Aut}}_K(C_{1,1})$ of $K = S_9$ has order 18. It is the group generated by the three permutations $\lambda, \mu$ and $\nu$ that we have considered above. These permutations satisfy

$$\lambda^3 = \mu^3 = \nu^2 = 1,$$

$$\lambda\mu = \mu\lambda, \ \nu\lambda = \lambda^2\nu, \ \nu\mu = \mu^2\nu ,$$

where 1 denotes the identity permutation.

**(ii)** Obviously, $C$ is equal to $E(L_1(C))$ and the list $\mathcal{K}^2$ contains $18^2 = 324$ elements.

**(iii)** Only 54 of these elements are in $\mathrm{Aut}_K^*[L_1(C)]$.

**(iv-v)** Since $\mathrm{Aut}_K^*[L_1(C)]$ is a sliding set, no further cancellation is necessary.

**(vi)** Thus the sliding group $\Sigma$ contains 54 elements.

The graph $\Gamma(\Sigma)$ associated with $\Sigma$ contains two connected components, denoted by $\Gamma_1$ and $\Gamma_2$. The first component $\Gamma_1$ is represented in figure 4.2. The second component $\Gamma_2$ is identical to $\Gamma_1$ except for the labelling of its vertices; if $\xi$ is the label of a vertex of $\Gamma_1$, the corresponding vertex of $\Gamma_2$ is labelled by $\nu\xi$. The group $\mathrm{Aut}_K(C)$ is the set $\Omega(\Sigma)$ of all eternal walks in $\Gamma(\Sigma)$. Since $u(\Sigma)$ is equal to 3 it follows from theorem 4.9 that $\Omega(\Sigma)$ is an infinite group.

Consider now a second example. Let $C$ be the (7,3) convolutional code over $GF(2)$ defined to be the $\mathcal{F}$-row space of $G := G_0 + DG_1 + D^2G_2$ where the $3 \times 7$ matrices $G_i$ are given by

$$G_0 = \begin{bmatrix} 1 & 1 & 1 & . & 1 & . & . \\ . & 1 & 1 & 1 & . & 1 & . \\ . & . & 1 & 1 & 1 & . & 1 \end{bmatrix}, \ G_1 = \begin{bmatrix} 1 & . & . & 1 & . & 1 & 1 \\ . & . & 1 & . & 1 & 1 & 1 \\ . & 1 & . & 1 & 1 & 1 & . \end{bmatrix},$$

$$G_2 = \begin{bmatrix} . & 1 & 1 & 1 & . & 1 & . \\ . & . & 1 & 1 & 1 & . & 1 \\ 1 & . & . & 1 & 1 & 1 & . \end{bmatrix}.$$

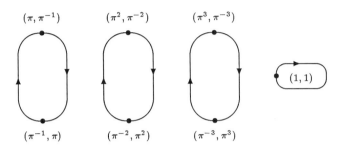

**Figure 4.3 :** The graph $\Gamma(\Sigma)$ of the $(7,3)$ code described in subsection 4.2.2.

Since the g.c.d. of the $3 \times 3$ minors of $G$ is 1, it follows from corollary 2.36 that $G$ is a basic encoder, and since $\text{rk}(G_2)$ is equal to 3 it follows from lemma 2.37 that $G$ is a minimal encoder. It is then easy to obtain the elements of the $F$-space $L_2[E(G)]$ that are needed to perform algorithm A4.1. Using this algorithm with $K = S_7$ we obtain a sliding group $\Sigma \subseteq K^3$ that contains 7 elements. To describe $\Sigma$, we represent any $v \in F^7$ by $v = (v_0, v_1, \cdots, v_6)$ and we denote by $\pi$ the cyclic permutation $(0, 1, 2, 3, 4, 5, 6)$. We thus obtain

$$\Sigma = \{(\pi^i, \pi^{-i}, \pi^i) \mid 0 \leq i \leq 6\}.$$

The graph $\Gamma(\Sigma)$ associated with this sliding set $\Sigma$ is represented in figure 4.3. From $\mu(\Sigma) = 1$, it follows that the group $\text{Aut}_K(C) = \Omega(\Sigma)$ of all eternal walks in $\Gamma(\Sigma)$ is a finite group of order $|\Omega(\Sigma)| = 7$.

## 4.3   Some other properties of $\text{Aut}_K(C)$

In this section we give some technical properties of the automorphism groups of convolutional codes. First we state two results about certain subgroups of $\text{Aut}_K(C)$.

**Corollary 4.29 :** Let $C$ be a convolutional code over $F$ satisfying $C =$

$E[L_m(C)]$ and let $H = H^D$ be a $D$-normal subgroup of $\mathrm{Aut}_K(C)$. Define $\Sigma(H)$ to be the set of $(m+1)$-tuples $(x^{(i)}, \cdots, x^{(i+m)})$ that appear as "substrings" in any $x \in H$, and define $\overline{H}$ to be the set $\Omega[\Sigma(H)]$ of all eternal walks in $\Gamma[\Sigma(H)]$. In this case $\overline{H}$ is a subgroup of $\mathrm{Aut}_K(C)$.

**Proof :** The proof is an easy consequence of theorem 4.25. $\square$

**Theorem 4.30 :** Let $C$ be a convolutional code over $F$ satisfying $C = E[L_m(C)]$ and let $H = H^D$ be a $D$-normal subgroup of $\mathrm{Aut}_K(C)$. In this case there exists a subgroup $\mathcal{H} = \mathcal{H}^D$ of $\mathrm{Aut}_K(C)$ enjoying the three properties

**(i)** $\mathcal{H}$ is repetitive, hence finite.

**(ii)** $\mathcal{H}^{(0)} = H^{(0)}$.

**(iii)** If one denotes by $\Sigma(H)$ (resp. by $\Sigma(\mathcal{H})$) the set of $(m+1)$-tuples $(x^{(i)}, \cdots, x^{(i+m)})$ that appear as "substrings" of any $x \in H$ (resp. $x \in \mathcal{H}$), then $\Sigma(H)$ is equal to $\Sigma(\mathcal{H})$. This implies $\Omega[\Sigma(H)] = \Omega[\Sigma(\mathcal{H})]$.

**Proof :** From $H = H^D$ it follows that $\Sigma(H)$ is a sliding group and that $\Gamma[\Sigma(H)]$ is a regular digraph. Suppose that $\Gamma[\Sigma(H)]$ contains $R$ connected components $\Gamma_r$, $1 \leq r \leq R$. All these components are regular digraphs. Denote by $\ell(r)$ the number of arcs in $\Gamma_r$. Being a regular digraph, $\Gamma_r$ admits an Eulerian trail. Let $a_r = (a_r^{(0)}, \cdots, a_r^{\ell(r)-1}) \in K^{\ell(r)}$ be the sequence of labels that is associated with the sequence of arcs of such an Eulerian trail. Associate with $a_r$ the element $x_r \in K^{\mathbb{Z}}$ specified by $x_r^{(j)} = a_r^{(i)}$, for $j = i \bmod \ell(r)$, and denote by $\mathcal{H}$ the group generated by all $x_r^{D^s}$ with $1 \leq r \leq R$ and $s \in \mathbb{Z}$. Obviously, $\mathcal{H}$ is repetitive (the repetition length is the l.c.m. of the $R$ numbers $\ell(r)$) and hence finite. It is $D$-normal and, since any element of $H^{(0)}$ appears in at least one $x_r$, one has $\mathcal{H}^{(0)} = H^{(0)}$. To prove (iii) we note first that any $x = (x^{(0)}, \cdots, x^{(m)}) \in \Sigma(H)$ specifies one arc $(\underline{x}, \overline{x})$ in $\Gamma[\Sigma(H)]$ and that, conversely, with any arc in $\Gamma[\Sigma(H)]$ there is associated one element of $\Sigma(H)$. On the other hand, the group $\Sigma(\mathcal{H})$ is generated by the elements of $K^{m+1}$ that are walks of length $m+1$ in the Eulerian trails used to define $\mathcal{H}$. Since these trails are Eulerian, the elements in question constitute precisely the set $\Sigma(H)$. $\square$

The second question considered in this section is the following. What can be said about the automorphism groups of two different codes when one is deduced from the other one by a "simple operation"? First we consider a pair $(C, \hat{C})$ of reciprocal codes and, in connection with the concept of reciprocal code, we introduce the concept of reciprocal group $\hat{H}$ of a subgroup $H$ of $K^{\mathbb{Z}}$. With any $x \in K^{\mathbb{Z}}$ we associate the reciprocal $\hat{x} \in K^{\mathbb{Z}}$ of $x$ defined by $\hat{x}^{(i)} := x^{(-i)}$ , and with any subset $H$ of $K^{\mathbb{Z}}$ we associate its reciprocal set $\hat{H}$ defined by $\hat{H} := \{\hat{x} \mid x \in H\}$. It is clear that $H$ is a group isomorphic to $H$. On the basis of theorem 4.25 the following statement is quite obvious.

**Theorem 4.31 :** When $C$ and $\hat{C}$ are reciprocal codes, one has $\text{Aut}(\hat{C}) = \widehat{\text{Aut}}(C)$.

Consider now a pair $(C, C^{\perp})$ of dual convolutional codes. To relate $\text{Aut}(C)$ to $\text{Aut}(C^{\perp})$ we need some definitions. Let $K$ be a subgroup of $GL(n, F)$, i.e., a group of nonsingular $n \times n$ matrices over $F$. Given $x \in K$, we denote by $x^T$ the transpose of the matrix $x$. Then we extend this notation to $K^{\mathbb{Z}}$. Given any $x \in K^{\mathbb{Z}}$, we denote by $x^T$ the mapping $x^T : \mathbb{Z} \to K : i \mapsto (x^{(i)})^T$ , and we call it the transpose of $x$. We denote then by $\tilde{x}$ the reciprocal of $x^T$ which can be written as $\tilde{x} = (\hat{x})^T$. Finally, for any subset $H$ of $K^{\mathbb{Z}}$ we define $H^T = \{x^T \mid x \in H\}$ , $\tilde{H} = \{\tilde{x} \mid x \in H\}$ .

**Theorem 4.32 :** The groups $\text{Aut}(C)$ and $\text{Aut}(C^{\perp})$ satisfy

$$\text{Aut}(C^{\perp}) = \widetilde{\text{Aut}}(C)$$

**Proof :** We shall prove that for any $x \in \text{Aut}(C)$ one has

$$w \in C^{\perp} \Rightarrow w\tilde{x} \in C^{\perp}, \tag{4.24}$$

which implies $\text{Aut}(C^{\perp}) \supseteq \widetilde{\text{Aut}}(C)$. Since $(C^{\perp})^{\perp}$ is equal to $C$, we can then interchange the role of $C^{\perp}$ and $C$ to obtain $\text{Aut}(C) \supseteq \widetilde{\text{Aut}}(C^{\perp})$ and, since

$\widetilde{\mathrm{Aut}}(C) = \mathrm{Aut}(C)$, the theorem will be proved. Let us thus prove (4.24). Any $w \in C^{\perp}$ satisfies

$$(vx^{D^s})w^T = 0\,; \text{ all } v \in C\,,\ s \in \mathbb{Z}\,,\ x \in \mathrm{Aut}(C)\,.$$

This identity can be written as

$$\Big(\sum_i v_i x^{(i-s)} D^i\Big)\Big(\sum_j w^T_{\ j} D^j\Big) = 0$$

or equivalently as

$$\sum_r \Big\{\sum_{i+j=r} v_i [w_j (x^{(i-s)})^T]^T\Big\} D^r = 0. \qquad (4.25)$$

In particular, for $r = s$, (4.25) implies

$$\sum_r \Big\{\sum_i v_i [w_{r-i}(x^{(i-r)})^T]^T\Big\} D^r = 0\,.$$

Setting $j = r - i$ we obtain

$$\Big(\sum_i v_i D^i\Big)\Big(\sum_j (w_j (x^{(-j)})^T)^T D^j\Big) = 0.$$

Since this is true for all $v \in C$, it follows that

$$w\tilde{x} = \sum_j w_j (x^{(-j)})^T D^j$$

is in $C^{\perp}$ for all $w \in C^{\perp}$. $\square$

## 4.4 Comments

There are at least two reasons to study convolutional codes having nontrivial automorphisms. One is that this study uses attractive mathematical techniques. Another is that it furnishes powerful tools for constructing very good codes for certain applications. While the first reason can be viewed as being academic, the second one is undoubtedly of some practical importance. From this point of view, one could question the significance of section 4.2, which does not lead as such to any specific code construction. It seems, however, important to first study several theoretical properties of the automorphisms of convolutional codes. The reader will find later, in chapters 10 and 11 for example, that he has made a good use of his time when reading the first chapters of this book.

This fourth chapter is mainly based on [31] where the concept of automorphism of a convolutional code was intoduced. Other references will be given in the following chapters.

## PROBLEMS

**4.1** Let $K$ be a finite group and let $H$ be the set of all repetitive elements of $K^{\mathbb{Z}}$. Prove that $H$ is a group.

**4.2** Replace the $(7,3)$ convolutional encoder $G = G_0 + DG_1 + D^2 G_2$ considered in subsection 4.2.2 by $G^* = G_0 + DG_1 + D^2 G_0$. Find $\text{Aut}_K[E(G^*)]$ for $K = S_7$.

**4.3** Let $G(D)$ be a convolutional encoder over $F$ and define $C := E[G(D)]$ and $C^* := E[G(D^r)]$. Characterize $\text{Aut}_K(C^*)$ in terms of $\text{Aut}_K(C)$.

# Chapter 5

# When is $\mathrm{Aut}_K(C)$ an infinite group?

Let $C$ be an $(n, k)$ convolutional code over the finite field $F$ and let $K$ be a subgroup of the group $GL(n, F)$ of all $n \times n$ nonsingular matrices over $F$. In this chapter we give partial solutions to the following problem: to find necessary and sufficient conditions on $C$ and $K$ for $\mathrm{Aut}_K(C)$ to be an infinite group.

This chapter contains four sections. In section 5.1, we prove first that if a convolutional code $C$ satisfies a certain condition depending on $K$, then $\mathrm{Aut}_K(C)$ is an infinite group. Conversely, we prove a necessary solution satisfied by a convolutional code $C$ having an infinite automorphism group $\mathrm{Aut}_K(C)$ and a technical property described below. In section 5.2, we define the class of dense codes and we show that if a dense code $C$ does not satisfy the necessary condition of section 5.1, then the form of any $x \in \mathrm{Aut}_K(C)$ is as given in theorem 4.14. In section 5.3 we try to fill the gap between the necessary and the sufficient condition of section 5.1 by obtaining another necessary condition. In fact we show that if a dense code $C$ has an infinite automorphism group $\mathrm{Aut}_K(C)$, then $(\mathrm{Aut}_K(C))^{(0)}$ has a normal series of subgroups that enjoys some specific properties. Section 5.4 is an appendix that gives the properties of some subgroup of the automorphism group of a block code. The references for this chapter are [92, 93].

# 5.1   General conditions for $\mathrm{Aut}_K(C)$ to be an infinite group

Let $K$ be a subgroup of the group $GL(n, F)$. We shall say that $x \in K$ stabilizes $v \in F^n$ if one has $vx = v$. Consider then the set of all $x \in K$ that stabilize some $v \in F^n$. We call this set the *stabilizer* of $v$ in $K$. This stabilizer is a group that we denote by $\overline{\mathrm{Stab}}_K(v)$. Similarly, let $V$ be any subset of $F^n$ and consider the set of all $x \in K$ that stabilize all $v \in V$. We call this set the stabilizer of $V$ in $K$ and we denote it by $\overline{\mathrm{Stab}}_K(V)$. It can be written as $\overline{\mathrm{Stab}}_K(V) = \bigcap_{v \in V} \overline{\mathrm{Stab}}_K(v)$, and it is obviously a subgroup of the automorphism group $\overline{\mathrm{Aut}}_K(V)$ of the block code $V$.

Consider an element $x \in K^{\mathbb{Z}}$ and an element $v \in \mathcal{F}^n$. We say that $x \in K^{\mathbb{Z}}$ stabilizes $v \in \mathcal{F}^n$ if one has $vx = v$. The set of all $x \in K^{\mathbb{Z}}$ that stabilize some $v \in \mathcal{F}^n$ is a group. We call it the stabilizer of $v$ with respect to $K$, and we denote it by $\mathrm{Stab}_K(v)$. Let $V$ be any subset of $\mathcal{F}^n$ and consider the set of all $x \in K^{\mathbb{Z}}$ that stabilize all $v \in V$. We call this set the stabilizer of $V$ with respect to $K$ and we denote it by $\mathrm{Stab}_K(V)$. It can be written as $\mathrm{Stab}_K(V) = \bigcap_{v \in V} \mathrm{Stab}_K(v)$ and it is obviously a subgroup of the group $\mathrm{Aut}_K(V)$ of all $x \in K^{\mathbb{Z}}$ that satisfy $v \in V \Rightarrow vx \in V$.

Let $C$ be an $(n, k)$ convolutional code over the field $F$, and let $G = \sum_{j=0}^m G_j D^j$ be a $k \times n$ encoder of $C$. By nature the group $\mathrm{Stab}_K(C)$ is a subgroup of the automorphism group $\mathrm{Aut}_K(C)$, which implies that $|\mathrm{Stab}_K(C)| = \infty$ is a sufficient condition to have $|\mathrm{Aut}_K(C)| = \infty$. This simple remark is used to obtain a sufficient condition for $\mathrm{Aut}_K(C)$ to be an infinite group. Associate indeed with $C$ the block code $B(C)$ defined to be the $F$-space generated by the rows of the $m + 1$ matrices $G_j$, $0 \leq j \leq m$. The block code $B (= B(C))$ is the set of elements of $F^n$ that occur as words in the sequences of the convolutional code $C$. We have the following theorem.

**Theorem 5.1 :** If the convolutional code $C$ is such that $\overline{\text{Stab}}_K(B)$ has order $\geq 2$, the group $\text{Aut}_K(C)$ is an infinite group.

**Proof :** $\text{Stab}_K(C)$ is nothing but $\{\overline{\text{Stab}}_K(B)\}^\mathbb{Z}$, so that $|\overline{\text{Stab}}_K(B)| \geq 2$ implies $|\text{Stab}_K(C)| = \infty$. The theorem follows from $\text{Aut}_K(C) \supseteq \text{Stab}_K(C)$.

$\square$

This theorem gives a sufficient condition for $\text{Aut}_K(C)$ to be an infinite group. We obtain now a necessary condition for $\text{Aut}_K(C)$ to be an infinite group. Assume first that $G = \sum_{i=0}^m G_i D^i$ is a minimal $k \times n$ convolutional encoder over $F$ that enjoys the following property.

**Property 5.2 :** For $1 \leq j \leq k$, the degrees $m(j)$ of the rows of $G$ all have the same value $m \geq 1$. Equivalently one has

$$\text{rk}(G_0) = \text{rk}(G_m) = k. \tag{5.1}$$

It follows from corollary 2.15 that if property 5.2 is true for one minimal encoder $G$ of the convolutional code $C$ then it is also true for all minimal encoders of $C$. To use this property we associate, besides $B$, two other block codes with $C$. They are denoted by $B^+$ and $B^-$ and are defined as follows. The block code $B^+$ is the $F$-space generated by the rows of the $m$ matrices $G_1, G_2, \cdots, G_m$ and the block code $B^-$ is the $F$-space generated by the rows of the $m$ matrices $G_0, G_1, \cdots, G_{m-1}$. It is easy to verify that if the minimal encoder $G$ satisfies property 5.2, then the block codes $B^+$ and $B^-$ are the same for all minimal encoders of $C = E(G)$.

**Theorem 5.3 :** If the minimal encoders $G$ of $C$ satisfy property 5.2 and if $\text{Aut}_K(C)$ is an infinite group, then the groups $\overline{\text{Stab}}_K(B^+)$ and $\overline{\text{Stab}}_K(B^-)$ have order at least 2.

**Proof :** Let $\Sigma$ be the largest sliding subgroup of the group $\text{Aut}_K^*[L_m(C)]$ defined before theorem 4.25. If $\text{Aut}_K(C)$ is an infinite group, it follows from theorem 4.9 that $\Sigma$ contains at least one element $s_1 = (1^m, h_1)$ satisfying $h_1 \neq 1$. Since $\Sigma$ is a sliding set, it contains for all $j \leq m$ at least one element of the form $s_j = (1^{m+1-j}, h_1, \cdots, h_j)$ with $h_1 \neq 1$. Since $m$ is the smallest degree of the nonzero polynomial sequences of $C$, any $g = \sum_{i=0}^m g_i D^i$ in $E_0(G) = L_m(C)$ has to satisfy $g - (g \circ s_j) = 0$ for $1 \leq j \leq m$ with the operation $\circ$ as defined after theorem 4.24. Indeed the coefficient of $D^0$ in $g - (g \circ s_j)$ is zero; this implies that if $g - (g \circ s_j)$ is nonzero, then $D^{-1}[g - (g \circ s_j)]$ is a polynomial of degree $\leq m - 1$ in $C$. Hence we obtain

$$g_{m+1-j} h_1 = g_{m+1-j}; \ 1 \leq j \leq m, \text{ all } g \in E_0(G). \tag{5.2}$$

As a result $h_1$ belongs to $\overline{\text{Stab}}_K[E_0(G_j)]$ for $1 \leq j \leq m$, so that $h_1$ is in $\overline{\text{Stab}}_K(B^+)$. Hence the group $\overline{\text{Stab}}_K(B^+)$ contains at least two elements, namely 1 and $h_1$. A similar proof holds for the group $\overline{\text{Stab}}_K(B^-)$. $\square$

Let us remark that if one has $B = B^+ = B^-$, and if $C$ satisfies property 5.2, then the sufficient condition of theorem 5.1 coincides with the necessary condition of theorem 5.3.

As a first application of this theorem we consider the code $C = E(G)$ over $F = GF(2)$ where $G$ is given by (4.23). Writing $G = G_0 + G_1 D$, we have $B^+ = E_0(G_1)$, $B^- = E_0(G_0)$ and $B^+ \cap B^- = \{0\}$. In this example $B^+$ and $B^-$ are proper subsets of $B$. We choose $K$ to be the symmetric group $S_9$ of all $9 \times 9$ matrices over $F$ having a unique 1 in each row and in each column and we use the notations of chapter 4. Then we see that $\overline{\text{Stab}}_K(B^-)$ contains at least 1, $\mu\lambda$ and $\mu^2\lambda^2$ while $\overline{\text{Stab}}_K(B^+)$ contains at least 1, $\mu$ and $\mu^2$. Thus the group $\text{Aut}_K(C)$ can be an infinite group since it satisfies the necessary condition of theorem 5.3. However, since $\overline{\text{Stab}}_K(B)$ contains only the identity, theorem 5.1 cannot be used to prove that $\text{Aut}_K(C)$ is an infinite group.

As a second application we consider the (7,3) code $C = E(G)$ over $F = GF(2)$ where $G$ is the matrix $G = G_0 + G_1 D + G_2 D^2$ specified at the end of subsection 4.2.2. In this case $B^+$ is the $F$-space of $\begin{pmatrix} G_1 \\ G_2 \end{pmatrix}$, $B^-$ is the $F$-space of $\begin{pmatrix} G_0 \\ G_1 \end{pmatrix}$ and $B = B^+ = B^-$ is the set of all 7-tuples over $F$ containing an even number of ones. Let $K$ be the symmetric group $S_7$ of all $7 \times 7$ matrices over $F$ having a unique 1 in each row and each column. Since the stabilizer $\overline{\mathrm{Stab}}_{S_7}(B)$ contains only the identity, it follows from theorem 5.3 that $\mathrm{Aut}_{S_7}(C)$ is a finite group (see also subsection 4.2.2). Now let $K$ be the group $GL(7,F)$ of all nonsingular $7 \times 7$ matrices over $F = GF(2)$. It is proved in appendix 5.4 that the group $\overline{\mathrm{Stab}}_K(B)$ has the following structure. Let $v$ be a 7-tuple over $F$ that contains an even number of ones, let $P(v)$ be the $7 \times 7$ matrix having all its rows equal to $v$, and define $P^*(v) := I_7 - P(v)$. It follows from appendix 5.4 that the group $\overline{\mathrm{Stab}}_K(B)$ is nothing but the set of the 64 matrices $P^*(v)$ associated with the 7-tuples $v$ containing an even number of ones. Thus the group $\mathrm{Aut}_{GL(7,F)}(C)$, which contains the infinite group $[\overline{\mathrm{Stab}}_K(B)]^{\mathbb{Z}}$ as a subgroup, is an infinite group. This illustrates the influence of the group $K$ over the order of $\mathrm{Aut}_K(C)$.

Let us extend theorem 5.3 to codes the minimal encoders of which do not satisfy property 5.2. Consider first the following example. Assume that an ordered minimal encoder $G$ over $F$ contains rows of two different degrees, for example $m_1 = 2$ and $m_2 = 4$. Write it as $G = \begin{pmatrix} \Gamma_1 \\ \Gamma_2 \end{pmatrix}$ where the submatrix $\Gamma_r = \sum_{j=0}^{m_r} \Gamma_{r,j} D^j$ contains the rows of $G$ having degree $m_r$. If $\mathrm{Aut}_K[E(G)]$ is an infinite group, the sliding subgroup $\Sigma$ of $K^5$ that is associated with it contains at least four elements $s_j = (1^{5-j} h_1, \cdots, h_j)$, $1 \le j \le 4$, with $h_1 \ne 1$. The shortest nonzero sequences of $C = E(G)$ have length 3. As in the proof of theorem 5.3, this implies that any $g \in E_0(\Gamma_1)$ satisfies

$$g - [g \circ (1, 1, h_1)] = 0, \quad g - [g \circ (1, h_1, h_2)] = 0,$$

so that $h_1$ belongs to $\overline{\mathrm{Stab}}_K[E_0(\Gamma_{1,j})]$ for $j = 1, 2$. Let now $g$ be any sequence of $E_0(\Gamma_2)$. Since any nonzero sequence of $C$ has length $\ge 3$ we have $g - (g \circ s_1) = 0$, $g - (g \circ s_2) = 0$, which implies $h_1 \in \overline{\mathrm{Stab}}_K[E_0(\Gamma_{2,j})]$, for $j = 3, 4$. It follows that $\mathrm{Aut}_K(C)$ cannot be an infinite group unless $|\overline{\mathrm{Stab}}_K(B_2^+)| \geq 2$ holds, where $B_2^+$ is the sum of the $F$-row spaces of the matrices $\Gamma_{1,1}, \Gamma_{1,2}, \Gamma_{2,3}$ and $\Gamma_{2,4}$. A similar argument shows that $\mathrm{Aut}_K(C)$ cannot be an infinite group unless $|\overline{\mathrm{Stab}}_K(B_2^-)| \geq 2$ holds, where $B_2^-$ is the sum of the $F$-row spaces of the matrices $\Gamma_{1,0}, \Gamma_{1,1}, \Gamma_{2,0}$ and $\Gamma_{2,1}$. This is an illustration of the following general statement.

**Theorem 5.4 :** Let $G = \begin{pmatrix} \Gamma_1 \\ \vdots \\ \Gamma_R \end{pmatrix}$ be an ordered minimal encoder of an

$(n, k)$ convolutional code $C$ over $F$ where $\Gamma_r = \sum_{j=0}^{m_r} \Gamma_{r,j} D^j$ denotes the submatrix of $G$ containing all its rows of degree $m_r$ with $1 \leq r \leq R$ and $m_r < m_{r+1}$. Define $B_{m_1}^+$ to be the sum of the $F$-row spaces of the $F$-matrices $\Gamma_{r,m_r-j}$ for $j = 0, 1, \cdots, m_1 - 1$, all $r$, and define $B_{m_1}^-$ to be the sum of the $F$-row spaces of the $F$-matrices $\Gamma_{r,j}$ for $j = 0, 1, \cdots, m_1 - 1$, all $r$. If the group $\mathrm{Aut}_K[E(G)]$ is an infinite group, the two groups $\overline{\mathrm{Stab}}_K(B_{m_1}^+)$ and $\overline{\mathrm{Stab}}_K(B_{m_1}^-)$ have order $\geq 2$.

**Proof :** The proof is a simple generalization of the analysis of the particular case treated above. We omit the details. $\square$

**Corollary 5.5 :** Let $C$ be a convolutional code of length $n$ over $F$, let $B$ be the block code of the words of $C$, and let $K$ be a subgroup of $GL(n, F)$. If $B$ equals $F^n$, then $\mathrm{Stab}_K(C)$ contains only $\{1^Z\}$.

**Proof :** Let $K$ be $GL(n, F)$. It follows from appendix 5.4 that $\overline{\mathrm{Stab}}_K(F^n)$ contains only the identity. Assume that some component $x^{(i)}$ of $x \in \mathrm{Stab}_K(C)$ is not 1. Then it follows from $B = F^n$ that there exists a code sequence $v = \sum_{j=r}^{\infty} v_j D^j$, $r \in Z$, such that one of its words, $v_s$ for example, satisfies $v_s x^{(i)} \neq v_s$. In this case $v D^{i-s} x$ is not equal to $v D^{i-s}$, which precludes $x$ from being in $\mathrm{Stab}_K(C)$. $\square$

## 5.2 Automorphisms of dense codes

In section 5.1 we were concerned with conditions to be satisfied by a convolutional code that has an infinite automorphism group. In this section we show that, in some cases where this group is finite, it has a very precise form. The class of codes to which the results of this section apply is the class of dense codes.

**Definition 5.6 :** An $(n, k)$ convolutional code $C$ is called *dense* if its complexity $\mu(C)$ is $\geq 1$ and if its minimal encoders $G = \sum_{j=0}^{m} G_j D^j$ satisfy $\mathrm{rk}(G_j) = k, \quad 0 \leq j \leq m$.

The property to be a dense code is somewhat stronger than property 5.2 and we conclude from theorem 5.3 that if at least one of the groups $\overline{\mathrm{Stab}}_K(B^+)$ and $\overline{\mathrm{Stab}}_K(B^-)$ associated with a dense code $C$ has order 1, then $\mathrm{Aut}_K(C)$ is a finite group. In this case the following statements make its structure more apparent.

**Theorem 5.7 :** If a dense code $C$ of span $m$ is such that at least one of its associated groups $\overline{\mathrm{Stab}}_K(B^+)$ and $\overline{\mathrm{Stab}}_K(B^-)$ has order 1, then the largest sliding subgroup $\Sigma$ of $\mathrm{Aut}_K^*[L_m(C)]$ is systematic.

**Proof :** We prove that if $\overline{\mathrm{Stab}}_K(B^+)$ has order 1 then, for $0 \leq i \leq m$, the only $s \in \Sigma$ satisfying $s^{(i)} = 1$ is $1^{m+1}$. If $\overline{\mathrm{Stab}}_K(B^-)$ has order 1, the proof is similar. Let $s$ be an element of $\Sigma$. We prove first that, under the hypotheses of the theorem, $s^{(i)} = 1$ implies $s^{(j)} = 1$ for all $j \geq i$. To prove this it is sufficient to prove that, for $0 \leq i \leq m - 1$, $s^{(i)} = 1$ implies $s^{(i+1)} = 1$. We denote $s^{(i+1)}$ by $h$. Since $\Sigma$ is a sliding set containing $s$, it contains, for all $j$ with $0 \leq j \leq m - 1$, an element $s_j$ satisfying $s_j^{(j)} = 1$, $s_j^{(j+1)} = h$. Since $C$ is a dense code, any $g = \sum_{j=0}^{m} g_j D^j$ in $E_0(G)$ is specified as soon as any of its words $g_j$ is specified. Moreover, any polynomial sequence of $C$ that has degree $m$ is also in $E_0(G)$. As a consequence, the two polynomials $g$ and $g \circ s_j$ are in $E_0(G)$ and, since they have the same coefficient of $D^j$, they coincide. In particular this implies

$g_{j+1}h = g_{j+1}$ for $0 \leq j \leq m-1$ and for all $g \in E_0(G)$, or equivalently $h \in \overline{\mathrm{Stab}}_K(B^+)$. Since $\overline{\mathrm{Stab}}_K(B^+)$ was assumed to contain only 1, we have $h = 1$.

It remains to prove that $s^{(i)} = 1$ implies $s^{(j)} = 1$ for all $j \leq i$. To prove this it is sufficient to prove that, for $1 \leq i \leq m$, $s^{(i)} = 1$ implies $s^{(i-1)} = 1$. Let $s$ be any element of $\Sigma$ satisfying $s^{(i)} = 1$ and denote $s^{(i-1)}$ by $h$. Since $\Sigma$ is a sliding set it contains an $(m+1)$-tuple $\hat{s}$ having the form $(h, 1, \hat{s}^{(2)}, \cdots, \hat{s}^{(m)})$. By the first part of the proof, $s^{(i)}$ is 1 for $i \geq 2$ so that $s^*$ is equal to $(h, 1^m)$. If $h$ is not 1, then the group $\mathrm{Aut}_K(C) = \Omega(\Sigma)$ of eternal walks in $\Gamma(\Sigma)$ is an infinite group because the quantity $u(\Sigma)$ considered in theorem 4.4 is $\geq 2$. This is a contradiction because $|\overline{\mathrm{Stab}}_K(B^+)| = 1$ implies by theorem 5.3 that $\mathrm{Aut}_K(C)$ is a finite group. $\square$

**Corollary 5.8 :** If $C$ is a dense code of span $m \geq 1$ and if at least one of the groups $\overline{\mathrm{Stab}}_K(B^+)$ and $\overline{\mathrm{Stab}}_K(B^-)$ has order 1, there exists some automorphism $\alpha$ of $(\mathrm{Aut}_K(C))^{(0)}$ satisfying

$$x^{(i)} = (x^{(0)})^{\alpha^i} ; \text{ all } i \in \mathbb{Z}, \text{ all } x \in \mathrm{Aut}_K(C). \tag{5.3}$$

**Proof :** From theorem 5.7, the largest sliding subgroup $\Sigma$ of $\mathrm{Aut}_K^*[L_m(C)]$ is systematic. The proof follows from theorem 4.14. $\square$

A subgroup $H$ of $K^{\mathbb{Z}}$ will be called $\alpha$-*constant*, with respect to a certain automorphism $\alpha$ of $H^{(0)}$, when it satisfies $x^{(i)} = (x^{(0)})^{\alpha^i}$ for all $x \in H$ and all $i \in \mathbb{Z}$. By nature any $\alpha$-constant group is $D$-normal. At first sight, one may think that $\alpha$-constant groups are very particular automorphism groups for convolutional codes. However, corollary 5.8 indicates that this form is not as peculiar as it may seem to be, at least when the group $K$ is chosen to be a reasonably small subgroup of $GL(n, F)$. In particular, if $K$ is the monomial group mentioned in subsection 1.1.3 and if $C_0$ is a block code over $F$ with no zero coordinate, the property $|\overline{\mathrm{Stab}}_K(C_0)| \geq 2$ implies that two coordinates of $C_0$ are equal within a nonzero constant factor of

$F$. (This point is mentioned in appendix 5.4.) We say in this case that $C_0$ is $F$-*repeated*. It follows that, when $K$ is chosen to be the monomial group, $\alpha$-constant automorphism groups $\mathrm{Aut}_K(C)$ are the rule for dense codes in so far as the block codes $B^+$ and $B^-$ associated with $C$ are not $F$-repeated.

## 5.3  Other conditions on $(\mathrm{Aut}_K(C))^{(0)}$ when $\mathrm{Aut}_K(C)$ is infinite

For a dense convolutional code $C$, the results obtained in section 5.1 may be insufficient to solve the problem of deciding whether $\mathrm{Aut}_K(C)$ is an infinite group when $B^+$ and $B^-$ are strict subsets of $B$. For this reason we devote some efforts to obtaining other necessary conditions to be satisfied when $\mathrm{Aut}_K(C)$ is an infinite group. These new conditions turn on the structure of the largest sliding subgroup $\Sigma$ of $\mathrm{Aut}_K^*[L_m(C)]$. In particular, we shall show that, if $\mathrm{Aut}_K(C)$ is an infinite group, then the structure of $\Sigma^{(0)} = (\mathrm{Aut}_K(C))^{(0)}$ is related to the span $m$ of $C$. Our first goal is to obtain information on the subgroups $\Sigma(0, 1, \cdots, i)$ of $\Sigma$ that were defined in subsection 4.1.2. In general, a predecessor $s_{i+1}^*$ of $s_i = (1^i, h_0, \cdots, h_{m-i})$ has the form $s_{i+1}^* = (h_{-1}, 1^i, h_0, \cdots, h_{m-i-1})$ and there may exist no such predecessor $s_{i+1}^*$ with $h_{-1} = 1$. However, when $C$ is a dense code we have the following lemma.

**Lemma 5.9 :** Let $C$ be a dense convolutional code generated by the minimal encoder $G = \sum_{j=0}^m G_j D^j$, let $\Sigma$ be the largest sliding subgroup of $\mathrm{Aut}_K^*[L_m(C)]$ and suppose that, for some integer $i \geq 0$, the $(m+1)$-tuple $s_i := (1^i, h_0, \cdots, h_{m-i})$ is in $\Sigma$. In this case, $s_{i+1} := (1^{i+1}, h_0, \cdots, h_{m-i-1})$ is also in $\Sigma$.

**Proof :** By hypothesis, $\Sigma$ contains $s_i$ and, since it is a multiplicative group, it contains also the multiplicative identity $1^{m+1}$. Hence, if $s_{i+j} = (1^{i+j}, h_0, h_1, \cdots, h_{m-i-j})$ is in $\mathrm{Aut}_K^*[L_m(C)]$, for $j = 1, 2, \cdots, m - i$, the iteration of step (iv) of algorithm A4.1 will not delete any of these $s_{i+j}$. Thus it is sufficient to prove that $\mathrm{Aut}^*_K[L_m(C)]$ contains $s_{i+j}$ for $j = 1, 2, \cdots, m-i$. This is done as follows. Since $C$ is a dense code, there exists for $0 \le i \le m$ at most one polynomial $v = \sum_{j=0}^m v_j D^j$ in $E_0(G)$ that has a prescribed coefficient $v_i$ of $D^i$. Therefore, any $s \in K^{m+1}$ satisfying $s^{(i)} = 1$ for some $i$ is in $\mathrm{Aut}^*_K[L_m(C)]$ if and only if it satisfies $v \circ s = v$ for all $v$ in $L_m(C) = E_0(G)$. Remark now that, since $\Sigma$ is a sliding set, for all $j \le m-i$ it contains at least one element $s^*_{i+j} = (h_{-j}, \cdots, h_{-1}, 1^i, h_0, \cdots, h_{m-i-j})$ that satisfies

$$v \in E_0(G) \Rightarrow v \circ s^*_{i+j} = v.$$

This implies

$$v \in E_0(G) \Rightarrow v \circ s_{i+j} = v,$$

which makes clear that $s_{i+j}$ is in $\mathrm{Aut}^*_K[L_m(C)]$. $\square$

**Lemma 5.10 :** If $C$ is a dense code, then, for all $i$ satisfying $0 \le i \le m$, the subgroup $\Sigma(0, 1, \cdots, i)$ of $\Sigma$ has order $(u(\Sigma))^{m-i}$.

**Proof :** For $i = m$ the property is trivial. From theorem 4.4 we have

$$| \Sigma(0, 1, \cdots, m-1) | = u(\Sigma), \qquad (5.3)$$

which is the announced property for $i = m - 1$. Let us show that if the property is true for some $i \ge 1$, it is also true for $i - 1$. Any $s_{i+1} = (1^{i+1}, h_0, \cdots, h_{m-i-1})$ in $\Sigma(0, 1, \cdots, i)$ has $u(\Sigma)$ successors in $\Sigma(0, 1, \cdots, i-1)$ and the sets of successors of two different elements of $\Sigma(0, 1, \cdots, i)$ are disjoint. Hence we have

$$|\Sigma(0, 1, \cdots, i-1)| \ge u(\Sigma)|\Sigma(0, 1, \cdots, i)|,$$

where the strict inequality is possible only if $\Sigma$ contains elements such as

$$\bar{s}_{i+1} = (h_{-1}, 1^i, h_0, \cdots, h_{m-i-1}); \ h_{-1} \ne 1$$

without containing

$$s_{i+1} = (1^{i+1}, h_0, \cdots, h_{m-i-1}).$$

We show that this situation is impossible. Indeed, by the sliding property $\Sigma$ contains the predecessor $s_i = (1^i, h_0, \cdots, h_{m-i})$ of $\bar{s}_{i+1}$, which implies by lemma 5.9 that $s_{i+1}$ is also in $\Sigma$. Hence we have

$$|\Sigma(0, 1, \cdots, i - 1)| = u(\Sigma)|\Sigma(0, 1, \cdots, i)| \; ; \; 1 \leq i \leq m, \qquad (5.4)$$

which gives the announced result by use of (5.3). $\square$

**Lemma 5.11 :** Let $C$ be a convolutional code over $F$ that satisfies

$$|\overline{\mathrm{Stab}}_K(B)| = 1, \; |\overline{\mathrm{Stab}}_K(B^+)| \geq 2, \; |\overline{\mathrm{Stab}}_K(B^-)| \geq 2,$$

and is generated by the minimal encoder $G = \sum_{j=0}^m G_j D^j$. Let $\Sigma$ be the largest sliding subgroup of $\mathrm{Aut}_K^*[L_m(C)]$. Then no two different elements $s_1$ and $s_2$ of $\Sigma$ satisfy simultaneously $s_1^{(0)} = s_2^{(0)}$, $s_1^{(m)} = s_2^{(m)}$.

**Proof :** Define $s := s_1 s_2^{-1}$. Since $\Sigma$ is a group, the statement of the lemma is equivalent to saying that $s \in \Sigma$ and $s^{(0)} = s^{(m)} = 1$ imply $s = 1^{m+1}$. To prove $s = 1^{m+1}$, assume that $s^{(j)}$ is not 1 for some $j$ in $[1, m-1]$. Since $s^{(0)}$ is 1 and since $C$ is a dense code, $s^{(j)}$ must leave all words of $E_0(G_i)$ invariant for $i \geq j$ (see the proof of lemma 5.9). Similarly, since $s^{(m)}$ is 1, $s^{(j)}$ must also leave the words of $E_0(G_i)$ invariant for $i \geq j$. It follows that $s^{(j)}$ is in $\overline{\mathrm{Stab}}_K(B)$. If $s^{(j)}$ is not 1, $|\overline{\mathrm{Stab}}_K(B)| \geq 2$ holds, which is a contradiction. $\square$

Lemmas 5.10 and 5.11 imply that, for all $i$, $(\Sigma(0, 1, \cdots, i))^{(m)}$ is a subgroup of order $(u(\Sigma))^{m-i}$ of $(\mathrm{Aut}_K(C))^{(0)}$ and, since $\Sigma$ is a sliding group, $(\Sigma(0, 1, \cdots, i))^{(j)}$ is, for $j \geq i$, a subgroup of order $(u(\Sigma))^{j-i}$ of $(\mathrm{Aut}_K(C))^{(0)}$, which depends only on $j - i$ but not on the specific values of $j$ and $i$. We denote this group by $H_{m-j+i}$.

**Theorem 5.12 :** For $1 \leq i \leq j \leq m$, the group $H_{m-i}$ is a normal subgroup of order $(u(\Sigma))^{j-i}$ of $H_{m-j}$ and of $(\mathrm{Aut}_K(C))^{(0)}$.

**Proof :** To prove $H_{m-i} \triangleleft H_{m-j}$ we remark that, for any $s \in \Sigma(0, 1, \cdots, m-j)$ and for any $i \leq j$, the left coset $s\Sigma(0, 1, \cdots, m-i)$ is identical to the right coset $(\Sigma(0, 1, \cdots m - i))s$. The proof of $H_{m-i} \lhd (\text{Aut}_K(C))^{(0)}$ is similar. The statement on the order of $H_{m-i}$ follows from the remarks above. $\square$

**Theorem 5.13 :** Let $K$ be any subgroup of $GL(n, F)$. Define $m$ to be the largest integer such there exists a normal series $H_0 \rhd H_1 \rhd \cdots \rhd H_{m-1} \rhd H_m = \{1\}$ having the following properties.

**(i)** All $H_j$ are normal subgroups of a given subgroup $H$ of $K$.

**(ii)** All indices $[H_{j-1} : H_j]$, $1 \le j \le m$, are equal to $|H_{m-1}|$.

Then any $(n, k)$ dense convolutional code $C$ over $F$ such that $\overline{\text{Stab}}_K(B)$ has order 1 and $\text{Aut}_K(C)$ is an infinite group, has a span $< m$.

**Proof :** This is a direct consequence of lemmas 5.9 to 5.11 and of theorem 5.12. $\square$

Let us give an example of application of this theorem. Write the matrix $G$ given by (4.23) as $G = G_0 + DG_1$ and define a new matrix $G^* = G + D^2G_0$. Consider then the codes $C = E(G)$ and $C^* = E(G^*)$ and choose $K$ to be the group of order 18 generated by the 3 matrices $L$, $M$ and $N$ given in subsection 4.2.2. The group $\text{Aut}_K(C)$ is known to be infinite. Let us check that this is in agreement with the conditions of theorem 5.13. Define indeed $H_0$ to be the group of order 9 generated by $L$ and $M$, and $H_1$ to be the group of order 3 generated by $L$. We have

$$H_0 \rhd H_1 \rhd H_2 = \{1\}; \quad K \rhd H_i, \text{ for } i = 0, 1, 2;$$

$$[H_0 : H_1] = [H_1 : H_2] = 3.$$

Since the span $\text{sp}(C)$ is equal to 1 (which is $< 2$), $\text{Aut}_K(C)$ may be an infinite group. On the other hand, the group $\text{Aut}_K(C^*)$ has to be finite. The span of $E(G^*)$ is indeed equal to 2 and $K$ does not contain 4 subgroups $H_j$, $j = 0, \cdots, 3$, satisfying the conditions of theorem 5.13.

## 5.4   Appendix : The stabilizer of a subspace of $F^n$ in $GL(n, F)$

In this appendix we characterize the group $\overline{\mathrm{Stab}}_K(B)$ when $B$ is a $k$-dimensional $F$-subspace of $F^n$ and $K$ is the general linear group $GL(n, F)$. We begin with the very special case where $B$ is the $F$-row space of the $k \times n$ matrix $G_0 = \begin{pmatrix} I_k & 0_k^{n-k} \end{pmatrix}$ with $0_i^j$ the $i \times j$ zero matrix. Then we show how to obtain a similar result in the general case and we give some examples. We conclude this appendix by making some remarks on $\overline{\mathrm{Stab}}_K(B)$ when $K$ is the monomial group $M_n$ of all $n \times n$ matrix with one nonzero element in each row and each column.

Consider first the case where one has $B = E_0(G_0)$ with $G_0 = \begin{pmatrix} I_k & 0_k^{n-k} \end{pmatrix}$. The group $\overline{\mathrm{Stab}}_K[E_0(G_0)]$ is then the set of nonsingular $n \times n$ matrices $P_0$ over $F$ such that $G_0 P_0$ is equal to $G_0$.

**Lemma 5.14 :** The group $\overline{\mathrm{Stab}}_K[E_0(G_0)]$ is the set of $n \times n$ matrices $P_0$ having the form

$$P_0 = \begin{pmatrix} I_k & 0_k^{n-k} \\ M & X \end{pmatrix} \tag{5.5}$$

where $X$ is any nonsingular $(n - k) \times (n - k)$ matrix over $F$ and $M$ is an arbitrary $(n - k) \times k$ matrix over $F$.

**Proof :** Obviously, when $P_0$ has the form (5.5), one has $G_0 P_0 = G_0$. Conversely, $G_0 P_0 = G_0$ implies that the $k$ first rows of $P_0$ have the form $\begin{pmatrix} I_k & 0_k^{n-k} \end{pmatrix}$ and, since $P_0$ has to be a nonsingular matrix, $X$ is also nonsingular. $\square$

**Lemma 5.15 :** The order of the group $\overline{\mathrm{Stab}}_K[E_0(G_0)]$ is equal to

$$q^{k(n-k)} \prod_{i=0}^{n-k-1} (q^{n-k} - q^i)$$

where $q = |F|$.

**Proof :** In (5.5) the matrix $M$ is unrestricted so that there are $q^{k(n-k)}$ possible choices for it. On the other hand, the matrix $X$ has to be non-singular. Since the number of $(n-k) \times (n-k)$ nonsingular matrices over $F$ is $\prod_{i=0}^{n-k-1}(q^{n-k} - q^i)$, the total number of nonsingular matrices having the form (5.5) is as given in the statement of the lemma. $\square$

Let us now consider the more general case where $B$ is the $F$-row space of an $F$-matrix $G = (G_1 G_2)$ with $G_1$ a $k \times k$ nonsingular matrix and $G_2$ an arbitrary $k \times (n-k)$ matrix. The next theorem gives a characterization of the group $\overline{\mathrm{Stab}}_K[E_0(G)]$, which is the set of $n \times n$ nonsingular matrices $P$ over $F$ satisfying $GP = G$.

**Theorem 5.16 :** Let $G = (G_1 G_2)$ be a $k \times n$ matrix over $F$, with $G_1$ a $k \times k$ nonsingular matrix over $F$, and define $\Gamma$ to be the $n \times n$ $F$-matrix

$$\Gamma := \begin{pmatrix} G_1 & G_2 \\ 0_{n-k}^k & I_{n-k} \end{pmatrix}. \tag{5.6}$$

The group $\overline{\mathrm{Stab}}_K[E_0(G)]$ is the set of matrices $P = \Gamma^{-1} P_0 \Gamma$, where $P_0$ has the form (5.5).

**Proof :** $G_0$ is equal to $G\Gamma^{-1}$. For some $P_0$ having the form (5.5) define $P := \Gamma^{-1} P_0 \Gamma$ and compute

$$GP = (G\Gamma^{-1})P_0\Gamma = (G_0 P_0)\Gamma = G_0\Gamma = G,$$

which makes clear that $P$ is an element of $\overline{\mathrm{Stab}}_K[E_0(G)]$. Conversely, if $GP$ is equal to $G$, one has $(G\Gamma^{-1})(\Gamma P\Gamma^{-1}) = G\Gamma^{-1}$ and, from $G\Gamma^{-1} = G_0$, it follows that $\Gamma P\Gamma^{-1}$ belongs to $\overline{\mathrm{Stab}}_K(E_0(G_0))$. Hence the matrix $P_0 = \Gamma P\Gamma^{-1}$ has the same form (5.5), which proves the theorem. $\square$

In the case where $G = (G_1 G_2)$ has rank $k$ but $G_1$ has not, the generalization is as follows. Let $\pi$ be an $n \times n$ permutation matrix such that $G$ is equal to $G^* \pi$, with $G^*$ a $k \times n$ matrix the first $k$ columns of which form a matrix of rank $k$. From theorem (5.16), it follows that $\overline{\mathrm{Stab}}_K(E_0(G^*))$ is the set of matrices $P^* = (\Gamma^*)^{-1} P_0 \Gamma^*$ where $P_0$ is any matrix of the form (5.5) and where $\Gamma^*$ is the $n \times n$ matrix having $G^*$ as its first $k$ rows and $\left( 0^k_{n-k} I_{n-k} \right)$ as its last $n - k$ rows. The group $\overline{\mathrm{Stab}}_K(E_0(G))$ is then easily seen to be $(\Gamma^* \pi)^{-1} \overline{\mathrm{Stab}}_K[E_0(G_0)](\Gamma^* \pi)$.

Let us consider some examples. Choose $F = GF(2)$, $n = 4$ and

$$
G = \begin{pmatrix} 1 & . & . & 1 \\ . & 1 & . & 1 \\ . & . & 1 & 1 \end{pmatrix} .
$$

The matrix $\Gamma$ of (5.6) is then given by

$$
\Gamma = \begin{pmatrix} 1 & . & . & 1 \\ . & 1 & . & 1 \\ . & . & 1 & 1 \\ . & . & . & 1 \end{pmatrix}
$$

and it satisfies $\Gamma^{-1} = \Gamma$. The matrices $P_0$ mentioned in lemma 5.14 have the form

$$
P_0 = \begin{pmatrix} 1 & . & . & . \\ . & 1 & . & . \\ . & . & 1 & . \\ m_1 & m_2 & m_3 & 1 \end{pmatrix} , \qquad m_i \in GF(2) .
$$

Thus the group $\overline{\mathrm{Stab}}_K[E_0(G)]$ contains eight matrices $P = \Gamma^{-1} P_0 \Gamma$, one for each value of the binary triple $\mathbf{m} = (m_1, m_2, m_3)$. The general form of these matrices $P$ is

$$
P(\mathbf{m}) = \begin{pmatrix} 1 + m_1 & m_2 & m_2 & m_1 + m_2 + m_3 \\ m_1 & 1 + m_2 & m_3 & m_1 + m_2 + m_3 \\ m_1 & m_2 & 1 + m_3 & m_1 + m_2 + m_3 \\ m_1 & m_2 & m_3 & 1 + m_1 + m_2 + m_3 \end{pmatrix} .
$$

More generally, if $G$ is the matrix $(I_k \ U)$ where $U$ denotes the all-one column $k$-tuple, then $\overline{\text{Stab}}_K[E_0(G)]$ contains the $2^k$ matrices $P(\mathbf{m}) = I_{k+1} - X(\mathbf{m})$ where $\mathbf{m}$ is any binary $(k+1)$-tuple of *even* symbol weight and $X(\mathbf{m})$ is the $(k+1) \times (k+1)$ matrix having all its rows equal to $\mathbf{m}$.

Going back to the general case, we see that when $K$ is the group $GL(n, F)$ and when the $F$-dimension of the linear block code $B$ over $F$ is $\leq n - 1$, one always has $|\overline{\text{Stab}}_K(B)| \geq 2$. Only when $\dim_F(B)$ is equal to $n$ is the order of $\overline{\text{Stab}}_K(B)$ equal to 1.

For some subgroups $K$ of $GL(n, F)$, it is yet possible to characterize the $F$-spaces $B$ that satisfy $|\overline{\text{Stab}}_K(B)| \geq 2$. For $K = S_n$, one has $|\overline{\text{Stab}}_K(B)| \geq 2$ if and only if two coordinates of $B$ are equal. For $K = M_n$ (and $|F| \geq 3$), one has $|\overline{\text{Stab}}_K(B)| \geq 2$ if and only if $B$ has two coordinates that are equal within a nonzero factor of $F$.

## PROBLEM

**5.1** Let $F$ be $GF(3)$ and number the entries of $F^8$ by the integers $0, 1, ..., 6, 7$. Let $K$ be the subgroup of $S_8$ generated by

$$\lambda = (0, 1)(2, 3)(4, 5)(6, 7),$$

$$\mu = (0, 2)(1, 3)(4, 6)(5, 7),$$

$$\nu = (0, 4)(1, 5)(2, 6)(3, 7).$$

Consider the three following encoders

$$G_1 = (2 + 2D \ \ 1 + 2D \ \ 2 + D \ \ 1 + D \ \ 2 + 2D \ \ 1 + 2D \ \ 2 + D \ \ 1 + D),$$

$$G_2 = (2 + 2D \ \ 2 + D \ \ 1 + 2D \ \ 1 + D \ \ 1 + D \ \ 1 + 2D \ \ 2 + D \ \ 2 + 2D),$$

$$G_3 = \begin{pmatrix} G_1 \\ G_2 \end{pmatrix}.$$

Denote the code $E(G_i)$ by $C_i$. For $i = 1, 2, 3$, compute the group $\text{Aut}_K(C_i)$ and verify that it satisfies the theorems proved in this chapter.

# Chapter 6

# Further properties of groups, rings and modules

In this chapter we go deeper into the description of some mathematical structures that are used in the sequel. In section 6.1 we give more details on the group structure introduced in chapter 1. In particular the normalizer and the centralizer of a group are defined and some of their properties are mentioned. Permutation groups acting on $X^n$, the set of all $n$-tuples over a set $X$, are then considered. Among these permutation groups are the right regular representations of abstract groups. These right regular representations are often used in the sequel and we characterize their normalizers and their centralizers. In section 6.2 the definition is given of a module over a ring and some structural properties of rings and modules are described. Section 6.3 is devoted to an illustration by a simple example of some concepts introduced in the preceding sections.

## 6.1 Further properties of groups

The goal of this section is to introduce some properties of groups that are useful in representing convolutional codes having nontrivial automorphisms. In subsection 6.1.1 we define the centralizer and the normalizer of a group and we give two lemmas. In subsection 6.1.2 we associate with any finite abstract group $\mathcal{H}$ a permutation group acting on $\mathcal{H}$. This group is denoted by $R(\mathcal{H})$ and is called the right regular representation of $\mathcal{H}$. We shall explain here how to obtain the centralizer and the normalizer of $R(\mathcal{H})$ in the symmetric group $S(\mathcal{H})$ of all permutations of the elements of $\mathcal{H}$.

## 6.1.1    Centralizers and normalizers

Let $K$ be a group and let $H$ be any subgroup of $K$.

**Definition 6.1 :** The set of all $k \in K$ that satisfy $k^{-1}hk = h$ for all $h \in H$ is called the *centralizer* of $H$ in $K$ and it is denoted by $C_K(H)$.

**Definition 6.2 :** The set of all $k \in K$ that satisfy $k^{-1}Hk = H$ is called the *normalizer* of $H$ in $K$ and it is denoted by $N_K(H)$.

Of course, if one has $K \triangleright H$, then $N_K(H)$ is equal to $K$. It is easy to verify that the sets $C_K(H)$ and $N_K(H)$ are subgroups of $K$ and that $C_K(H)$ is a subgroup of $N_K(H)$. We prove two lemmas about these groups.

**Lemma 6.3 :** Let $n_1$ and $n_2$ be two elements of $N_K(H)$ satisfying

$$n_1^{-1}hn_1 = n_2^{-1}hn_2 \; ; \; \text{all } h \in H \; . \tag{6.1}$$

In this case, $n_1 n_2^{-1}$ is in $C_K(H)$.
**Proof :** Write (6.1) as $(n_1 n_2^{-1})^{-1} h(n_1 n_2^{-1}) = h \; ; \; \text{all } h \in H. \; \square$

**Lemma 6.4 :** The group $N_K(H)$ is a subgroup of $N_K[C_K(H)]$.
**Proof :** We have to prove that for any $\omega \in C_K(H)$ and any $n \in N_K(H)$, $n^{-1}\omega n$ is an element of $C_K(H)$, i.e., we have to prove that

$$(n^{-1}\omega n)^{-1} h(n^{-1}\omega n) = h$$

is true for all $h \in H$. This is equivalent to

$$n^{-1}(\omega^{-1}(nhn^{-1})\omega)n = h \; ; \; \text{all } h \in H \; . \tag{6.2}$$

Since $n$ is in $N_K(H)$, $nhn^{-1}$ is an element of $H$, and since $\omega$ is an element of $C_K(H)$, one has $\omega^{-1}(nhn^{-1})\omega = nhn^{-1}$. This makes (6.2) self-evident.
□

## 6.1.2 The regular representation of a group

Up to now we have used the notation $v = (v_0, \cdots, v_{n-1})$ to represent $n$-tuples over a field $F$, thus giving to the entries $v_i$ of $v$ an integer label $i$ between 0 and $n - 1$. Instead of using integers as labels, one may find it useful to label the entries of $v$ by the elements $h_i$, $i = 0, 1, \cdots, n - 1$, of an abstract group $\mathcal{H}$ of order $n$. Thus we write

$$v = [v(h_0), v(h_1), \cdots, v(h_{n-1})]; \; v(h_i) \in F \; . \tag{6.3}$$

In this case, any $v \in F^n$ can be identified with a formal sum

$$v = \sum_{h \in \mathcal{H}} hv(h) \; ; \; v(h) \in F \; , \tag{6.4}$$

which is an element of the group algebra $A = F\mathcal{H}$. The representation (6.4) of $F^n$ leads to an economical representation of the action of a *permutation* group of order $n$, isomorphic to $\mathcal{H}$, and acting in a specific manner on the entries $v(h)$ of any $v \in F^n$. Associate with any $h^* \in \mathcal{H}$ the coordinate permutation $r(h^*)$ defined by

$$r(h^*) : v \mapsto vh^* = \sum_{h \in \mathcal{H}} hh^* v(h) \; . \tag{6.5}$$

In (6.5), any entry $v(h)$ of $v$ is moved from the position indexed by $h$ to the position indexed by $hh^*$. The set of the $n$ permutations $r(h^*)$, $h^* \in \mathcal{H}$, is a group isomorphic to $\mathcal{H}$ for the multiplication

$$r(h_1)r(h_2) = r(h_1h_2); \; h_1, h_2 \in \mathcal{H} \; . \tag{6.6}$$

This group acts on the entries $v(h_i)$ of $v$ according to (6.5). It is called the *right regular representation* of the (abstract) group $\mathcal{H}$ and is denoted by $R(\mathcal{H})$. The action of the group $R(\mathcal{H})$ on $F^n$ is of course representable by a group of $n \times n$ permutation matrices, but the representation given in (6.5), which uses the right multiplication of the elements $v \in A$ by the elements $h^* \in \mathcal{H}$, is more compact. We shall often make use of the latter representation in the sequel.

The *left regular representation* of $\mathcal{H}$, denoted by $L(\mathcal{H})$, is defined in a similar manner. It is the set of permutations $\ell(h^*)$, $h^* \in \mathcal{H}$, acting as

$$\ell(h^*) : v \mapsto h^*v = \sum_{h \in \mathcal{H}} h^*hv(h) \, , \tag{6.7}$$

and it is a group for the multiplication $\ell(h_1)\ell(h_2) = \ell(h_1h_2)$. Of course, if $\mathcal{H}$ is an Abelian group, then the permutation groups $R(\mathcal{H})$ and $L(\mathcal{H})$ coincide.

These permutation groups, when acting on $F^n$ as in (6.5) or in (6.7), have received much attention in block coding theory. The cyclic codes, which remain invariant under the regular representation of a cyclic group, are an important topic of this theory [87]. Some classes of block codes that remain invariant under the regular representation of an Abelian group, have also received some attention [8-9, 28, 70]. As explained below, the regular representations of general groups can be given an equally important role in the theory of convolutional codes.

The regular representations $R(\mathcal{H})$ and $L(\mathcal{H})$ are subgroups of order $n$ of $S(\mathcal{H})$, the symmetric group of order $n!$ and degree $n = |\mathcal{H}|$, in its natural action on the $n$ elements of $\mathcal{H}$. In the sequel we use at several places the normalizer $N_{S(\mathcal{H})}[R(\mathcal{H})]$ of $R(\mathcal{H})$ in $S(\mathcal{H})$. Thus we need a precise characterization of this normalizer. Let us denote by $\mathrm{Aut}(\mathcal{H})$ the set of all automorphisms of the group $\mathcal{H}$ and let us use the exponential notation to represent the action of an element $\alpha$ of $\mathrm{Aut}(\mathcal{H})$

$$\alpha : \mathcal{H} \to \mathcal{H} \; : \; h \mapsto h^\alpha \, . \tag{6.8}$$

The set $\text{Aut}(\mathcal{H})$ is a subgroup of $S(\mathcal{H})$ called the automorphism group of $\mathcal{H}$. The set of $\alpha \in \text{Aut}(\mathcal{H})$ that satisfy $h \mapsto h^\alpha = x^{-1}hx$ for some $x \in \mathcal{H}$ is a subgroup of $\text{Aut}(\mathcal{H})$ that is called the group of *inner* automorphisms of $\mathcal{H}$. If no such $x \in \mathcal{H}$ exists, $\alpha$ is called an *outer* automorphism of $\mathcal{H}$. We let now act $\text{Aut}(\mathcal{H})$ not only on the group $\mathcal{H}$ but also on the permutation group $R(\mathcal{H})$ isomorphic to $\mathcal{H}$ by defining

$$[r(h)]^\alpha := r(h^\alpha) ; \quad \alpha \in \text{Aut}(\mathcal{H}) . \tag{6.9}$$

Using (6.9) in (6.6) we have

$$[r(h_1 h_2)]^\alpha = r[(h_1 h_2)^\alpha] = r(h_1^\alpha h_2^\alpha) = r(h_1^\alpha)r(h_2^\alpha).$$

This makes $\text{Aut}(\mathcal{H})$ act as the automorphism group of $R(\mathcal{H})$. For $h_1, h_2 \in \mathcal{H}$, $\alpha \in \text{Aut}(\mathcal{H})$, one has

$$[h_1 r(h_2)]^\alpha = (h_1 h_2)^\alpha = h_1^\alpha h_2^\alpha = h_1^\alpha r(h_2^\alpha) = h_1^\alpha [r(h_2)]^\alpha,$$

which shows that (6.8) and (6.9) are compatible.

For a finite group $\mathcal{H}$, consider then the set of all pairs $(r, \alpha)$ with $r \in R(\mathcal{H})$ and $\alpha \in \text{Aut}(\mathcal{H})$, endowed with the multiplication

$$(r, \alpha)(s, \beta) = (rs^{\alpha^{-1}}, \alpha\beta); \ r, s \in R(\mathcal{H}), \ \alpha, \beta \in \text{Aut}(\mathcal{H}), \tag{6.10}$$

where $\alpha^{-1}$ is the inverse of $\alpha \in \text{Aut}(\mathcal{H})$ and where $s^{\alpha^{-1}} \in R(\mathcal{H})$ is defined according to (6.9). The set of all pairs $(r, \alpha)$ with $r \in R(\mathcal{H})$ and $\alpha \in \text{Aut}(\mathcal{H})$, is called the *holomorph* [48] of the group $\mathcal{H}$ and it is denoted by $\text{Hol}(\mathcal{H})$.

**Theorem 6.5 :** The holomorph $\text{Hol}(\mathcal{H})$ of the group $\mathcal{H}$ is a group for the multiplication (6.10).

**Proof :** $\text{Hol}(\mathcal{H})$ satisfies the axioms of a group (see subsection 1.1.1).

**(i)** Closure: in (6.10), $rs^{\alpha^{-1}}$ is an element of $R(\mathcal{H})$ and $\alpha\beta$ is an element of $\text{Aut}(\mathcal{H})$.

**(ii)** Associativity: the element $[(r_1, \alpha_1)(r_2, \alpha_2)](r_3, \alpha_3)$ and the element $(r_1, \alpha_1)[(r_2, \alpha_2)(r_3, \alpha_3)]$ are both equal to $(r_1 r_2^{\alpha_1^{-1}} r_3^{(\alpha_1 \alpha_2)^{-1}}, \alpha_1 \alpha_2 \alpha_3)$.

**(iii)** The identity in $\mathrm{Hol}(\mathcal{H})$ is $(1_R, 1_A)$ will $1_R$ the identity of $R(\mathcal{H})$ and $1_A$ the identity of $\mathrm{Aut}(\mathcal{H})$.

**(iv)** The inverse $((r^\alpha)^{-1}, \alpha^{-1})$ of $(r, \alpha)$ is an element of $\mathrm{Hol}(\mathcal{H})$. $\square$

The group $\mathrm{Hol}(\mathcal{H})$ is called the *semi-direct* product of $R(\mathcal{H})$ and $\mathrm{Aut}(\mathcal{H})$ [48]. We let it act as a set of permutations of $\mathcal{H}$ as follows

$$(r, \alpha) : \mathcal{H} \to \mathcal{H} \; : \; h \mapsto (hr)^\alpha \; . \tag{6.11}$$

That (6.11) defines a permutation of $\mathcal{H}$ results from the fact that when $h$ takes all possible values in $\mathcal{H}$ so does $(hr)^\alpha$. To prove that

$$[h(r, \alpha)](s, \beta) = h[(r, \alpha)(s, \beta)] \; ; \; \text{all } (r, \alpha), (s, \beta) \in \mathrm{Hol}(\mathcal{H}) \; , \tag{6.12}$$

is true for all $h \in \mathcal{H}$, we note that, since $\alpha$ and $\beta$ are in $\mathrm{Aut}(\mathcal{H})$, both sides of (6.12) are equal to $(hr)^{\alpha\beta} s^\beta$. Hence the permutation action (6.11) is compatible with the group structure of $\mathrm{Hol}(\mathcal{H})$, and this makes $\mathrm{Hol}(\mathcal{H})$ in its action (6.11) a subgroup of $S(\mathcal{H})$.

Denote now by $S_1(\mathcal{H})$ the subgroup of $S(\mathcal{H})$ preserving the identity of $\mathcal{H}$. Since all automorphisms of $\mathcal{H}$ preserve the identity of $\mathcal{H}$, the group $\mathrm{Aut}(\mathcal{H})$ is a subgroup of $S_1(\mathcal{H})$ and the set $\{(r, \alpha) \mid r \in R(\mathcal{H}), \alpha \in S_1(\mathcal{H})\}$ contains $\mathrm{Hol}(\mathcal{H})$ as a subset. Generalizing (6.11), we let this more general set act on $\mathcal{H}$ as

$$(r, \alpha) \in (R(\mathcal{H}), S_1(\mathcal{H})) \; : \; \mathcal{H} \to \mathcal{H} \; : \; h \mapsto (hr)^\alpha. \tag{6.13}$$

Obviously, any such pair $(r, \alpha)$ represents a different element of $S(\mathcal{H})$. On the other hand, there are $|\mathcal{H}| \, |S_1(\mathcal{H})| = |S(\mathcal{H})|$ such pairs. As a consequence, any element of $S(\mathcal{H})$ can be represented by a unique pair $(r, \alpha) \in (R(\mathcal{H}), S_1(\mathcal{H}))$. We use this representation of $S(\mathcal{H})$ to prove the following theorem.

**Theorem 6.6** : The normalizer $N_{S(\mathcal{H})}[R(\mathcal{H})]$ of $R(\mathcal{H})$ in $S(\mathcal{H})$ is the holomorph $\text{Hol}(\mathcal{H})$ of the group $\mathcal{H}$.

**Proof** : Let us remark that any $(s, \alpha) \in S(\mathcal{H})$ can be written in a unique way as $(s, \alpha) = (s, 1)(1, \alpha)$, where 1 denotes the identity in $S_1(\mathcal{H})$ or in $\mathcal{H}$, and that $(s, 1)^{-1} = (s^{-1}, 1)$ and $(1, \alpha)^{-1} = (1, \alpha^{-1})$ hold. By theorem 6.5, $\text{Hol}(\mathcal{H})$ is a group. It follows that to prove the theorem we have to show that all pairs $(s, 1)$ with $s \in R(\mathcal{H})$, are in $N_{S(\mathcal{H})}[R(\mathcal{H})]$ and that the pairs $(1, \alpha)$ with $\alpha \in S_1(\mathcal{H})$ are in $N_{S(\mathcal{H})}[R(\mathcal{H})]$ if and only if $\alpha$ is an element of $\text{Aut}(C)$.

That $(s, 1)$ is in $N_{S(\mathcal{H})}[R(\mathcal{H})]$ follows from the fact that it is an inner automorphism of $R(\mathcal{H})$. One has

$$h[(s, 1)^{-1} r_1(s, 1)][(s, 1)^{-1} r_2(s, 1)] = h[(s, 1)^{-1}(r_1 r_2)(s, 1)]$$

for all $h \in \mathcal{H}$ and all $s, r_1, r_2 \in R(\mathcal{H})$, where all square brackets are in $R(\mathcal{H})$ and where $(s, 1)^{-1} r_1(s, 1)$ is equal to $(s, 1)^{-1} r_2(s, 1)$ if and only if $r_1 = r_2$.

Now consider the pair $(1, \alpha)$ with $\alpha \in S_1(\mathcal{H})$. We have to prove that

$$(1, \alpha^{-1}) R(\mathcal{H})(1, \alpha) = R(\mathcal{H})$$

is true if and only if $\alpha$ is in $\text{Aut}(\mathcal{H})$. If $\alpha$ is in $\text{Aut}(\mathcal{H})$, $h(1, \alpha^{-1}) r(1, \alpha) = [(h^{\alpha^{-1}}) r]^\alpha$ is equal to $h r^\alpha$ for all $h \in \mathcal{H}$ and all $r \in R(\mathcal{H})$, which shows that $(1, \alpha)$ is in $N_{S(\mathcal{H})}[R(\mathcal{H})]$. Conversely, if $(1, \alpha)$ is in $N_{S(\mathcal{H})}[R(\mathcal{H})]$, then $h(1, \alpha^{-1}) r(1, \alpha)$ can be written as $h r^\alpha$ with $r \mapsto r^\alpha$ a permutation of $R(\mathcal{H})$. Moreover, writing $h[(1, \alpha^{-1}) r_1(1, \alpha)][(1, \alpha^{-1}) r_2(1, \alpha)] = h(1, \alpha^{-1}) r_1 r_2(1, \alpha)$ as

$$h r_1^\alpha r_2^\alpha = h(r_1 r_2)^\alpha$$

makes it obvious that $\alpha$ is in $\text{Aut}(\mathcal{H})$. $\square$

Another representation of $S(\mathcal{H})$ is the set of pairs $(s, \beta)$ with $s \in L(\mathcal{H})$ and $\beta \in S_1(\mathcal{H})$, that act [48] on $\mathcal{H}$ as

$$(s, \beta) : \mathcal{H} \to \mathcal{H} \; : \; h \mapsto h(s, \beta) = (sh)^\beta. \tag{6.14}$$

The subset $\mathrm{Hol}(\mathcal{H})$ of $S(\mathcal{H})$ is then the set of such pairs $(s,\beta)$, where $\beta$ is an element of $\mathrm{Aut}(\mathcal{H})$. It is a group for the multiplication

$$(r,\alpha)(s,\beta) = (s^{\alpha^{-1}}r, \alpha\beta), \tag{6.15}$$

which is compatible with the action (6.14), since one has

$$h[(r,\alpha)(s,\beta)] = [h(r,\alpha)](s,\beta).$$

Moreover, any element $(s,\beta)$ of $\mathrm{Hol}(\mathcal{H}) = N_{S(\mathcal{H})}[R(H)]$ has a unique decomposition as a product $(s,1)(1,\beta)$. This second representation of $\mathrm{Hol}(\mathcal{H})$ is used to prove the following theorem.

**Theorem 6.7 :** The centralizer $C_{S(\mathcal{H})}[R(\mathcal{H})]$ of $R(\mathcal{H})$ in $S(\mathcal{H})$ is the left regular representation $L(\mathcal{H})$ of $\mathcal{H}$.

**Proof :** Since $C_{S(\mathcal{H})}[R(\mathcal{H})]$ is a subgroup of $N_{S(\mathcal{H})}[R(\mathcal{H})]$, any element $(s,\beta)$ of $S(\mathcal{H})$ is in $C_{S(\mathcal{H})}[R(\mathcal{H})]$ only if $\beta$ is an element of $\mathrm{Aut}(\mathcal{H})$. Thus we have to find the pairs $(s,\beta)$ with $s \in L(\mathcal{H})$ and $\beta \in \mathrm{Aut}(\mathcal{H})$, that satisfy

$$h(s,\beta)^{-1}r(s,\beta) = hr \; ; \;\; \text{all } h \in \mathcal{H}, \text{ all } r \in R(\mathcal{H}),$$

for the action (6.14). We use the decomposition of $(s,\beta)$ as $(s,1)(1,\beta)$. From (6.14), one has

$$h(s,1)^{-1}r(s,1) = s(s^{-1}hr) = hr \, ; \text{ all } h \in \mathcal{H}, \text{ all } r \in R(\mathcal{H}),$$

which makes clear that any $(s,1)$ in $\mathrm{Hol}(\mathcal{H})$ is in $C_{S(\mathcal{H})}[R(\mathcal{H})]$. Now consider the pairs $(1,\beta)$, $\beta \in \mathrm{Aut}(\mathcal{H})$. Since $\beta$ is an element of $\mathrm{Aut}(\mathcal{H})$, the expression $h(1,\beta)^{-1}r(1,\beta) = [(h^{\beta^{-1}})r]^\beta$ is equal to $hr^\beta$. This makes obvious that $(1,\beta)$ is in $C_{S(\mathcal{H})}[R(\mathcal{H})]$ if and only if $\beta$ is the identity.

As a consequence, $C_{S(\mathcal{H})}[R(\mathcal{H})]$ is the set of pairs $(s,1)$ acting as in (6.14), i.e., it is the left regular representation $L(\mathcal{H})$ of $\mathcal{H}$. $\square$

Let us illustrate these concepts by a simple example. We choose $\mathcal{H}$ to be the group of order 6 with two generators $\lambda$ and $\mu$ satisfying

$$\lambda^3 = \mu^2 = 1, \; \mu\lambda = \lambda^2\mu \, .$$

The elements of $\mathcal{H}$ are the 6 monomials $\mu^i\lambda^j$, $i = 0, 1$, $j = 0, 1, 2$. Consider now the right regular representation $R(\mathcal{H})$ of $\mathcal{H}$ acting on $F^6$ when represented as in (6.4). For ease of representation, we use two different labellings of the 6 coordinates permuted by $R(\mathcal{H})$. The first labels are the elements of $\mathcal{H}$ and the second labels are the integers from 0 up to 5. The correspondence between these two labellings is given in table 6.1. The second labelling is introduced here only because it saves space, which is important in table 6.4.

**Table 6.1** : The two labellings of the coordinates of $F^6$.

| $1^{st}$ labelling : | 1 | $\lambda$ | $\lambda^2$ | $\mu$ | $\mu\lambda$ | $\mu\lambda^2$ |
|---|---|---|---|---|---|---|
| $2^{nd}$ labelling : | 0 | 1 | 2 | 3 | 4 | 5 |

The action of $r(\mu^k\lambda^\ell) \in R(\mathcal{H})$ on the content $v(\mu^i\lambda^j)$ of the coordinate labelled by $\mu^i\lambda^j$ is to move it to the coordinate labelled by $\mu^i\lambda^j[r(\mu^k\lambda^\ell)]$, which is $\mu^{i+k}\lambda^{\ell+j}$ for $k = 0$ and $\mu^{i+k}\lambda^{\ell-j}$ for $k = 1$. Using the two labellings of table 6.1, we represent these permutation actions in table 6.2 by products of cycles.

**Table 6.2** : $R(\mathcal{H})$ as a permutation group on $\mathcal{H}$.

| $h \in \mathcal{H}$ | $r(h)$ $1^{st}$ labeling | $2^{nd}$ labeling |
|---|---|---|
| 1 | $(1)(\lambda)(\lambda^2)(\mu)(\mu\lambda)(\mu\lambda^2)$ | $(0)(1)(2)(3)(4)(5)$ |
| $\lambda$ | $(1, \lambda, \lambda^2)(\mu, \mu\lambda, \mu\lambda^2)$ | $(0, 1, 2)(3, 4, 5)$ |
| $\lambda^2$ | $(1, \lambda^2, \lambda)(\mu, \mu\lambda^2, \mu\lambda)$ | $(0, 2, 1)(3, 5, 4)$ |
| $\mu$ | $(1, \mu)(\lambda, \mu\lambda^2)(\lambda^2, \mu\lambda)$ | $(0, 3)(1, 5)(2, 4)$ |
| $\mu\lambda$ | $(1, \mu\lambda)(\lambda, \mu)(\lambda^2, \mu\lambda^2)$ | $(0, 4)(1, 3)(2, 5)$ |
| $\mu\lambda^2$ | $(1, \mu\lambda^2)(\lambda, \mu\lambda)(\lambda^2, \mu)$ | $(0, 5)(1, 4)(2, 3)$ |

Consider now the action of Aut($\mathcal{H}$) on $\mathcal{H}$. We can specify its elements by giving their action on a pair $(\lambda, \mu)$ of generators of $\mathcal{H}$. It turns out that Aut($\mathcal{H}$) has order 6. Each of its elements is induced by one of the following 6 actions:

$$(\lambda, \mu) \mapsto (\lambda^i, \mu\lambda^j); \ 1 \leq i \leq 2, \ 0 \leq j \leq 2. \qquad (6.16)$$

This results from the fact that the automorphisms of a group have to preserve the cycle structure of this group. Thus any automorphism of $\mathcal{H}$ has to map $\lambda$ on an element of order 3 (i.e., $\lambda$ or $\lambda^2$) and $\mu$ on an element of order 2 (i.e., $\mu$, $\mu\lambda$ or $\mu\lambda^2$). These 6 possible mappings $\alpha$ are then easily shown to be in Aut($\mathcal{H}$) since they satisfy $(h_1 h_2)^\alpha = h_1^\alpha h_2^\alpha$, all $h_1, h_2 \in \mathcal{H}$. The action (6.16) of Aut($\mathcal{H}$) is given in the first column of table 6.3. In the two last columns of this table, the permutation actions of Aut($\mathcal{H}$) on $\mathcal{H}$ are given by use of the two labellings of table 6.1.

Table 6.3 : The action of Aut($\mathcal{H}$) as a permutation group on $\mathcal{H}$.

| $(\lambda, \mu) \mapsto$ | Action on the elements of $\mathcal{H}$ | |
| | $1^{\text{st}}$ labelling | $2^{\text{nd}}$ labelling |
| --- | --- | --- |
| $(\lambda, \mu)$ | $(1)(\lambda)(\lambda^2)(\mu)(\mu\lambda)(\mu\lambda^2)$ | $(0)(1)(2)(3)(4)(5)$ |
| $(\lambda, \mu\lambda)$ | $(1)(\lambda)(\lambda^2)(\mu, \mu\lambda, \mu\lambda^2)$ | $(0)(1)(2), (3, 4, 5)$ |
| $(\lambda, \mu\lambda^2)$ | $(1)(\lambda)(\lambda^2)(\mu, \mu\lambda^2, \mu\lambda)$ | $(0)(1)(2)(3, 5, 4)$ |
| $(\lambda^2, \mu)$ | $(1)(\lambda, \lambda^2)(\mu)(\mu\lambda, \mu\lambda^2)$ | $(0)(1, 2)(3)(4, 5)$ |
| $(\lambda^2, \mu\lambda)$ | $(1)(\lambda, \lambda^2)(\mu)(\mu\lambda)(\mu\lambda^2)$ | $(0)(1, 2)(3, 4)(5)$ |
| $(\lambda^2, \mu\lambda^2)$ | $(1)(\lambda, \lambda^2)(\mu, \mu\lambda^2)(\mu\lambda)$ | $(0)(1, 2)(3, 5)(4)$ |

Using tables 6.2 and 6.3, we can construct the normalizer Hol($\mathcal{H}$) of $R(\mathcal{H})$ in $S(\mathcal{H})$. This normalizer consists of all pairs $(r, \alpha)$ with $r \in R(\mathcal{H})$ and $\alpha \in$ Aut($\mathcal{H}$), acting on $\mathcal{H}$ as in (6.11). To represent the action of the elements of Hol($\mathcal{H}$) on $\mathcal{H}$, we use only the second labelling of $\mathcal{H}$. This representation is given in table 6.4. In the permutations of this table, we omit all cycles of length 1. As for the centralizer of $R(\mathcal{H})$ in $S(\mathcal{H})$, which is nothing but the left regular representation $L(\mathcal{H})$, it is given in table 6.5.

**Table 6.4** : The normalizer of $R(\mathcal{H})$ in $S(\mathcal{H})$.

| $(\lambda,\mu) \mapsto$ ╲ $r(h)$ | $r(1)$ | $r(\lambda)$ | $r(\lambda^2)$ |
|---|---|---|---|
| $(\lambda,\mu)$ | identity | $(0,1,2)(3,4,5)$ | $(0,2,1)(3,5,4)$ |
| $(\lambda,\mu\lambda)$ | $(3,4,5)$ | $(0,1,2)(3,5,4)$ | $(0,2,1)$ |
| $(\lambda,\mu\lambda^2)$ | $(3,5,4)$ | $(0,1,2)$ | $(0,2,1)(3,4,5)$ |
| $(\lambda^2,\mu)$ | $(1,2)(4,5)$ | $(0,2)(3,5)$ | $(0,1)(3,4)$ |
| $(\lambda^2,\mu\lambda)$ | $(1,2)(3,4)$ | $(0,2)(4,5)$ | $(0,1)(3,5)$ |
| $(\lambda^2,\mu\lambda^2)$ | $(1,2)(3,5)$ | $(0,2)(3,4)$ | $(0,1)(4,5)$ |

| $(\lambda,\mu) \mapsto$ ╲ $r(h)$ | $r(\mu)$ | $r(\mu\lambda)$ | $r(\mu\lambda^2)$ |
|---|---|---|---|
| $(\lambda,\mu)$ | $(0,3)(1,5)(2,4)$ | $(0,4)(1,3)(2,5)$ | $(0,5)(1,4)(2,3)$ |
| $(\lambda,\mu\lambda)$ | $(0,4,2,5,1,3)$ | $(0,5,2,3,1,4)$ | $(0,3,2,4,1,5)$ |
| $(\lambda,\mu\lambda^2)$ | $(0,5,1,4,2,3)$ | $(0,3,1,5,2,4)$ | $(0,4,1,3,2,5)$ |
| $(\lambda^2,\mu)$ | $(0,3)(1,4)(2,5)$ | $(0,5,1,3,2,4)$ | $(0,4,2,3,1,5)$ |
| $(\lambda^2,\mu\lambda)$ | $(0,4,1,5,2,3)$ | $(0,3,2,5,1,4)$ | $(0,5)(1,3)(2,4)$ |
| $(\lambda^2,\mu\lambda^2)$ | $(0,5,2,4,1,3)$ | $(0,4)(1,5)(2,3)$ | $(0,3,1,4,2,5)$ |

**Table 6.5** : The centralizer $L(\mathcal{H})$ of $R(\mathcal{H})$ in $S(\mathcal{H})$.

| $h \in \mathcal{H}$ | $L(h)$ 1st labelling | 2nd labelling |
|---|---|---|
| $1$ | $(1)(\lambda)(\lambda^2)(\mu)(\mu\lambda)(\mu\lambda^2)$ | $(0)(1)(2)(3)(4)(5)$ |
| $\lambda$ | $(1,\lambda,\lambda^2)(\mu,\mu\lambda^2,\mu\lambda)$ | $(0,1,2)(3,5,4)$ |
| $\lambda^2$ | $(1,\lambda^2,\lambda)(\mu,\mu\lambda,\mu\lambda^2)$ | $(0,2,1)(3,4,5)$ |
| $\mu$ | $(1,\mu)(\lambda,\mu\lambda)(\lambda^2,\mu\lambda^2)$ | $(0,3)(1,4)(2,5)$ |
| $\mu\lambda$ | $(1,\mu\lambda)(\lambda,\mu\lambda^2)(\lambda^2,\mu)$ | $(0,4)(1,5)(2,3)$ |
| $\mu\lambda^2$ | $(1,\mu\lambda^2)(\lambda,\mu)(\lambda^2,\mu\lambda)$ | $(0,5)(1,3)(2,4)$ |

Similar tables can be obtained for any group $\mathcal{H}$ for which $\text{Aut}(\mathcal{H})$ is available. Let us mention two particular cases.

(i) If $\mathcal{H}$ is the cyclic group of order $n$ having $x$ as generator : $x^n = 1$, then $\text{Aut}(\mathcal{H})$ is the set of permutations of $\mathcal{H}$ induced by $x \mapsto x^r$, where $r$ is prime with respect to $n$.

(ii) If $\mathcal{H}$ is the Abelian group of order $p^2$ with $x$ and $y$ as generators : $x^p = y^p = 1$, then $\text{Aut}(\mathcal{H})$ is the set of permutations of $\mathcal{H}$ induced by $x \mapsto x^{b_{11}} y^{b_{12}}$ , $y \mapsto x^{b_{21}} y^{b_{22}}$, such that the $2 \times 2$ matrix of the $b_{ij}$ has a nonzero determinant modulo $p$.

## 6.2   Rings and Modules

This section states, without proof, some properties of modules and rings. In subsection 6.2.1 we give the definition of a module and we state some properties of this structure. In subsection 6.2.2 we give some properties of rings. These statements are used in particular in the next chapter to state and to prove some structure theorems for convolutional codes having a prescribed automorphism group. A basic reference containing proofs of the results stated here (and much more) is the book of C.W. Curtis and I. Reiner [27]. The reader will find there most of the explanations he might desire about the subjects sketched below. Throughout this section $R$ denotes a ring with a multiplicative identity 1.

### 6.2.1   Modules and their properties

**Definition 6.8 :** An additive Abelian group $M$ is called a right $R$-module if, for all $r \in R$ and all $m \in M$, a product $mr \in M$ is defined that satisfies

(i) $(m_1 + m_2)r = m_1 r + m_2 r$,

(ii) $m(r_1 + r_2) = mr_1 + mr_2$,

**(iii)** $m(r_1 r_2) = (m r_1) r_2,$

**(iv)** $m1 = m,$

for all $r, r_1, r_2 \in R$ and all $m, m_1, m_2 \in M$.

The definition of a left $R$-module is of course quite similar. An additive subgroup $M_1$ of $M$ is called a *right submodule* of $M$ if $m \in M_1$ implies $mr \in M_1$ for all $r \in R$.

**Definition 6.9 :** A module $M$ that does not contain any nonzero proper submodule is called *irreducible*.

If $M_1$ and $M_2$ are submodules of the right $R$-module $M$, the sum $\mathcal{M}$ of $M_1$ and $M_2$ is defined by

$$\mathcal{M} := \{ m_1 + m_2 \mid m_1 \in M_1, \ m_2 \in M_2 \} . \tag{6.17}$$

The sum $\mathcal{M}$ of $M_1$ and $M_2$ is a submodule of $M$ and it is the smallest submodule of $M$ that contains both $M_1$ and $M_2$. The definition (6.17) is then extended to the sum $\mathcal{M} = M_1 + M_2 + \cdots + M_k$ of $k$ submodules $M_i$ of $M$ by

$$\mathcal{M} := \{ m_1 + m_2 + \cdots + m_k \mid m_i \in M_i, \ 1 \le i \le k \} . \tag{6.18}$$

If one has

$$(m_1 + m_2 + \cdots + m_k = 0, \ m_i \in M_i) \Rightarrow (m_i = 0 \text{ for all } i) \tag{6.19}$$

one says that the module $\mathcal{M}$ is the *direct sum* of the modules $M_i$, which one denotes by

$$\mathcal{M} = M_1 \oplus M_2 \oplus \cdots \oplus M_k. \tag{6.20}$$

Any submodule $M_i$ is then called a *direct summand* of $\mathcal{M}$. In this case, any $m \in \mathcal{M}$ can be expressed in a unique way as

$$m = m_1 + m_2 + \cdots + m_k; \quad m_i \in M_i. \tag{6.21}$$

Indeed, given any expression $m = m_1' + m_2' + \cdots + m_k'$ with $m_i' \in M_i$, one obtains $\sum_{i=1}^{r}(m_i - m_i') = 0$, and from (6.19) this implies $m_i = m_i'$ for all $i$.

Let $M$ be a right $R$-module and let

$$M = M_1 \supset M_2 \supset M_3 \supset \cdots \qquad (6.22)$$

be a chain of nested submodules $M_i$ of $M$. The module $M$ is said to satisfy the *descending chain condition* (or DCC) if no chain (6.22) can contain an infinite number of modules $M_i$. Let now

$$M \supset \cdots \supset M_3 \supset M_2 \supset M_1 \qquad (6.23)$$

be another chain of nested submodules $M_i$ of $M$. The module $M$ is said to satisfy the *ascending chain condition* (or ACC) if no chain like (6.23) can contain an infinite number of modules.

Many properties of right $R$-modules are proved under the hypothesis that $R$ is a ring with minimum condition, the definition of which is given now.

**Definition 6.10 :** A ring is called a ring with right (resp. left) *minimum* condition if any chain of right (resp. left) ideals $R = I_1 \supset I_2 \supset I_3 \supset \cdots$ has a finite length.

A subset $\{m_1, m_2, \cdots\}$ of a right $R$-module $M$ is called a set of *generators* of $M$ if every element $m$ of $M$ can be expressed as $m = \sum_i m_i r_i$, with a finite number of nonzero $r_i \in R$. The right $R$-module $M$ is said to be finitely generated if it has a finite set of generators. In an irreducible right $R$-module $M$, any nonzero element generates $M$ as an $R$-module.

A right $R$-module $M$ is said to be *indecomposable* if it contains at least one nonzero element and if it is impossible to express $M$ as a direct sum of two nonzero submodules. The importance of indecomposable right $R$-modules follows from the following two theorems proved in [27].

**Theorem 6.11** : If the submodules of the right $R$-module $M$ satisfy the DCC, then $M$ can be expressed as a direct sum of a finite number of indecomposable modules.

**Theorem 6.12** : Let $M$ be a right $R$-module satisfying the DCC and the ACC, and let

$$M = M_1 \oplus M_2 \oplus \cdots \oplus M_h = N_1 \oplus N_2 \oplus \cdots \oplus N_k$$

be two decompositions of $M$ into direct sums of nonzero indecomposable submodules. Then one has $h = k$ and there exists a permutation $(j_1, \cdots, j_h)$ of $(1, \cdots, h)$ such that $M_r$ is isomorphic to $N_{j_r}$ with $1 \leq r \leq h$.

This last theorem, known as the Krull-Schmidt theorem, is proved in section 14 of [27].

**Definition 6.13** : A right $R$-module $M$ is said to be *completely reducible* if every submodule $M_1$ of $M$ is a direct summand of $M$, i.e., if there exists a submodule $M_2$ of $M$ such that $M = M_1 \oplus M_2$.

One can prove that any submodule of a completely reducible module is completely reducible, so that if $M$ is a completely reducible right $R$-module, it can be expressed as a direct sum of irreducible submodules.

The following theorem is a version of a fundamental result due to Maschke. A proof is given in [27].

**Theorem 6.14** : Let $G$ be a finite group, let $F$ be a field of characteristic $p$ and let $A = FG$ be the group algebra of $G$ over $F$. If $|G|$ is relatively prime with $p$, then every right $A$-module is completely reducible.

Let us introduce a concept that plays a central role in the following chapter.

**Definition 6.15** : Let $R$ be a ring with minimum condition and let $M$ be a right $R$-module. The *socle* of $M$ is the sum of all irreducible submodules of $M$.

If $M$ is a finitely generated right $R$-module, the socle $S$ of $M$ is the unique maximal completely reducible submodule of $M$ [27].

### 6.2.2   Further properties of rings

A ring $R$ can be seen as a right module over itself. Thus all properties of $R$-modules mentioned in the previous paragraph have an equivalent as properties of the ring $R$ itself. The following definitions and properties are worth mentioning.

**Definitions 6.16 :** An element $n \in R$ is *nilpotent* if there exists some positive integer $m$ such that $n^m = 0$. An element $e \in R$ is *idempotent* if it is nonzero and if it satisfies $e^2 = e$. The idempotents $e_1$ and $e_2$ are called *orthogonal* if $e_1 e_2 = e_2 e_1 = 0$. An idempotent $e$ is called *primitive* if it is impossible to express it as the sum of two orthogonal idempotents.

Let $I$ be a right ideal of $R$, and denote by $I^m$ the set of all products $r_1 r_2 \cdots r_m$ of $m$ elements $r_i$ of $I$. The ideal $I$ is called *nilpotent* if, for some positive integer $m$, all elements of $I^m$ are zero.

If $I_1, I_2, \cdots, I_k$ are right ideals in a ring $R$, the sum $I_1 + I_2 + \cdots + I_k$ is defined by

$$I_1 + I_2 + \cdots + I_k = \{r_1 + r_2 + \cdots + r_k \mid r_i \in I_i,\, 1 \leq i \leq k\}. \qquad (6.24)$$

This sum is said to be direct, and written then as $I_1 \oplus I_2 \oplus \cdots \oplus I_k$, if $r_1 + r_2 + \cdots r_k = 0$ implies $r_i = 0$ for all $i$.

The following theorems [27] elucidate some structural properties of rings.

**Theorem 6.17 :** In a ring $R$ with minimum condition, every nonnilpotent ideal contains an idempotent element.

**Theorem 6.18 :** In a ring $R$ with minimum condition, the sum of all nilpotent right ideals of $R$ is a two-sided nilpotent ideal $N$ which contains every nilpotent left ideal of $R$.

This two-sided ideal $N$ is called the *radical* of $R$, denoted by rad $R$. We remark in passing that when $R$ is a ring with minimum condition, it follows from exercise 25.4 in [27] that the socle $S$ of a right $R$-module $M$ is the annihilator of the radical $N$ of $R$, i.e., the set of $m \in M$ such that $mn = 0$ is satisfied by all $n \in N$. If rad $R$ contains only 0, then $R$ is called a *semi-simple* ring. If the ring $R$ is not semi-simple, its radical $N$ is not a direct summand of $R$.

Finite group algebras were defined in chapter 1. They are examples of rings that will be extensively used in the sequel. It follows from Maschke's theorem [27] that the group algebra $A = FH$ is a semi-simple ring if and only if $|F|$ and $|H|$ are relatively prime.

An ideal $I$ in the ring $R$ is said to be *indecomposable* if it cannot be written as a direct sum of two nontrivial subideals. Any ring $R$ with minimum condition can be written as a direct sum of a finite number of indecomposable right ideals $I_i$ generated by primitive idempotents $e_i$. Thus in this case one has

$$R = I_1 \oplus I_2 \oplus \cdots \oplus I_k ; \quad I_i = e_i R , \quad 1 \le i \le k .$$

An ideal $I$ in the ring $R$ is said to be *minimal* if it does not contain any nontrivial subideal. A minimal ideal is indecomposable but the converse is generally not true. However, in a semi-simple ring, any indecomposable ideal is minimal. If $R$ is a semi-simple ring with minimum condition, it can be written as a direct sum of a finite number of minimal right ideals $I_i$ generated by idempotents $e_i$. In this case these idempotents are called *minimal*. If $e$ is an idempotent element of a semi-simple ring $R$ with minimum condition, then $e$ is a minimal idempotent if and only if $eRe$ is a *skewfield* i.e., a ring in which the nonzero elements form a group (not necessarily commutative) for the multiplication. Since all finite skewfields are fields [48], the skewfield $eRe$ is a field for any finite ring $R$ and $eRe$ then admits a primitive element.

When a ring $R$ is considered as a right module over itself, the irreducible submodules of this module are nothing but the minimal ideals in $R$. The *right* (resp. *left*) *socle* of $R$ is then defined to be the sum of all minimal right (resp. left) ideals of $R$.

**Definition 6.19** : For any subset $R^*$ of a ring $R$, the *left annihilator* $\ell(R^*)$ of $R^*$ is defined by

$$\ell(R^*) := \{a \in R \mid aR^* = 0\} \,,$$

and the *right annihilator* $r(R^*)$ of $R^*$ is defined by

$$r(R^*) := \{a \in R \mid R^*a = 0\} \,.$$

Let now $N$ be the radical of a ring $R$ that satisfies both the left and right minimum condition.

**Theorem 6.20** : The right socle of $R$ is $\ell(N)$ and the left socle of $R$ is $r(N)$.

This theorem is stated as lemma 58.3 in [27].

A ring $R$ satisfying the right minimum condition is called a *quasi-Frobenius* ring if it satisfies

$$\ell[r(J)] = J \,, \quad r[\ell(I)] = I \,, \tag{6.25}$$

for every left ideal $J$ and every right ideal $I$ in $R$.

**Theorem 6.21** : All finite group algebras are quasi-Frobenius rings.

This theorem is proposed as exercise 58.2.d in [27]. It permits us to use (6.25) in all finite group algebras.

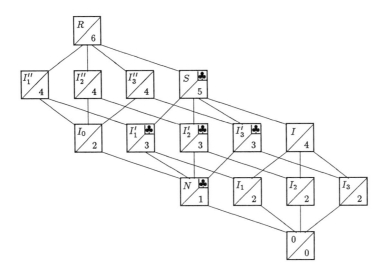

**Figure 6.1 :** The ideals in the algebra of the group $\mathcal{H}$ over $GF(2)$.

## 6.3    An example of the structure of ideals

To illustrate several concepts introduced in section 6.2, we now give the complete structure of the ideals in a specific non-semi-simple ring $R$ by means of the corresponding Hasse diagram [107]. Let $\mathcal{H}$ be the group of order 6 considered in section 6.1, with generators $\lambda$ and $\mu$ satisfying $\lambda^3 = \mu^2 = 1$, $\lambda\mu = \mu\lambda^2$. Let $F$ be $GF(2)$ and define $R$ to be the group algebra $F\mathcal{H}$. The Hasse diagram of $R$ is represented in figure 6.1. In any box of this figure is given the name ($I_2''$ for example) of the ideal represented by the box, and an integer between 0 and 6 that is the dimension of the ideal when considered as a vector space over $F$. The trivial ideal containing only zero is denoted by 0. The ring $R$ is not semi-simple. It has a nontrivial radical $N = nR = Rn$, generated by $n = (1 + \mu)(1 + \lambda + \lambda^2)$, which is a minimal ideal having dimension 1 as a vector space over $F$. Beside $N$, the ring $R$ contains three minimal nonnilpotent right ideals denoted by $I_1, I_2$ and $I_3$ and generated respectively by the idempotents

$$e_1 = 1 + \lambda^2 + \mu\lambda + \mu\lambda^2 \,,$$

$$e_2 = 1 + \lambda + \mu\lambda + \mu\lambda^2 \,,$$

$$e_3 = 1 + \lambda^2 + \mu + \mu\lambda^2 \,.$$

The three ideals $I_i'$ are the direct sums $N \oplus I_i$ for $i = 1, 2, 3$. The ideal $I$ is given by any of the direct sums $I_1 \oplus I_2$, $I_1 \oplus I_3$ or $I_2 \oplus I_3$, and it satisfies $I = eR$ where $e = \lambda + \lambda^2$ is idempotent. The ideal $I_0$ is the indecomposable right ideal generated by the idempotent $e_0 = 1 + \lambda + \lambda^2$. The ideals $I_i''$ are the direct sums $I_0 \oplus I_i$ for $i = 1, 2, 3$. They are generated by the idempotents $e_i'' = e_i + e_0$. The ideal $S$ is the socle of $R$. It can be written either as $N \oplus I_1 \oplus I_2$, or $N \oplus I_1 \oplus I_3$ or $N \oplus I_2 \oplus I_3$. In figure 6.1, the five boxes marked with ♣ represent ideals with no idempotent generator.

## PROBLEMS

**6.1** Let $H$ be the Abelian group of order 8 generated by the elements $x$, $y$ and $z$ that satisfy $x^2 = y^2 = z^2 = 1$, and let $F$ be $GF(3)$. Prove that, in the algebra $A = FH$, the element $e(a_1, a_2, a_3, a_4) = a_1(a_2 + x)(a_3 + y)(a_4 + z)$, $a_i \in \{1, 2\}$, is idempotent if and only if the number of $a_i$ that are equal to 2 is odd.

**6.2** Prove that if $e(a_1, a_2, a_3, a_4)$ is idempotent, it generates a minimal ideal in $A$ and that this ideal has dimension 1 when it is considered as a vector space over $GF(3)$.

**6.3** Prove that $A$ is the direct sum of the 8 ideals $e(a_1, a_2, a_3, a_4)A$ for which the number of $a_i$ that are equal to 2 is odd.

**6.4** Let $H$ be finite Abelian group and let $F$ be a finite field such that $|F|$ is relatively prime with $|H|$. In this case there is a unique decomposition of $A$

as a direct sum of minimal ideals. Moreover, each minimal ideal contains a unique idempotent.

Hint: see [28].

# Chapter 7

# Structure and decomposition of $H$-codes

By theorem 4.20, we know that, for any convolutional code $C$, the group $\mathrm{Aut}_K(C)$ is a $D$-normal subgroup of $K^{\mathbf{Z}}$. In this chapter we try to answer the question: What can be said about a convolutional code $C$ such that $\mathrm{Aut}_K(C)$ contains an arbitrary $D$-normal subgroup $H$? In section 7.1 we elucidate the general structure of these codes. In section 7.2 we give the definition of normal sequences, and we prove some properties of codes "generated" by such sequences. In section 7.3 we show that, under a reasonable hypothesis, we can construct a minimal encoder containing only normal sequences and mirroring the structure of the codes it generates. Section 7.3 can be considered as being of central importance in the theory of convolutional codes with automorphisms.

## 7.1    General structure of $H$-codes

Let $K$ be a subgroup of $GL(n, F)$, the group of all $n \times n$ nonsingular matrices over the finite field $F$, and let $H$ be a $D$-normal subgroup of $K^{\mathbf{Z}}$.

**Definition 7.1 :** An $(n, k)$ convolutional code $C$ over the field $F$ is called an *H-code* if its automorphism group $\mathrm{Aut}_K(C)$ contains $H$ as a subgroup.

In this section we prove that any *H*-code $C$ has the structure of a module over a well-defined algebra.

Let us first recall formulas (4.10) and (4.11) that define the multiplication in $K^Z$ and the action of $K^Z$ on $\mathcal{F}^n$. Given a $D$-normal subgroup $H$ of $K^Z$, let us denote by $A$ the group algebra $FH$ of $H$ over the finite field $F$. Any $a \in A$ can be written as

$$a = \sum_{x \in H} x a(x) ; \quad a(x) \in F ,$$

where the number of nonzero $a(x)$ is finite. The addition and the multiplication in $A$ were defined in subsection 1.1.3.

The projection of index $i$ of a subgroup $H$ of $K^Z$ was defined in subsection 4.2.1, and we now extend this definition to any element $a$ of $A = FH$. For any $i \in Z$, the *projection* $a^{(i)}$ *of index* $i$ of an element $a = \sum_{x \in H} x a(x)$ of $A$ is defined by

$$a^{(i)} := \sum_{x \in H} x^{(i)} a(x),$$

and it is an element of the group algebra $A^{(i)} := FH^{(i)}$. Since $H$ is a $D$-normal group, one has $H^{(i)} = H^{(0)}$ and also $A^{(i)} = A^{(0)}$ for all $i \in Z$.

Let us now introduce several *actions* of the algebras $A^{(0)}$ and $A$. First we let act $A^{(0)}$ on $F^n$ as follows. For $v \in F^n$ and $a^{(i)} \in A^{(0)}$, we define

$$v a^{(i)} := \sum_{x \in H} v x^{(i)} a(x) \tag{7.1}$$

where $v x^{(i)}$ is the element of $F^n$ obtained when the row $n$-tuple $v$ is post-multiplied by the element $x^{(i)}$ of $GL(n, F)$. As the reader may verify, definition (7.1) endows $F^n$ with the structure of an $A^{(0)}$-module. Then we let the algebra $A$ act on $F^n$ by defining, for any $a = (\cdots, a^{(-1)}, a^{(0)}, a^{(1)}, \cdots)$ in $A$, the action

$$a : F^n \to F^n : v \mapsto va := va^{(0)} , \tag{7.2}$$

where $va^{(0)}$ is the element of $F^n$ that is obtained as in (7.1). This action makes $F^n$ a right $A$-module. Third, we define the action of $A$ on the set $\mathcal{F}^n$ of Laurent series over $F^n$. This action is given by

$$a \in A : \mathcal{F}^n \to \mathcal{F}^n : v = \sum_{i=r}^{\infty} v_i D^i \mapsto va = \sum_{i=r}^{\infty} v_i a^{(i)} D^i . \qquad (7.3)$$

Here also the meaning of $v_i a^{(i)}$ is as defined in (7.1). This action makes $\mathcal{F}^n$ a right $A$-module. In particular one has $(va_1)a_2 = v(a_1 a_2)$ for all $v \in \mathcal{F}^n$ and all $a_1, a_2 \in A$, so that axiom (iii) of definition 6.8 is satisfied.

For the sake of conciseness let us now denote by $\mathcal{A}$ the Laurent extension $A((D))$ of $A = FH$,

$$\mathcal{A} := \{ a = \sum_{j=s}^{\infty} a_j D^j \mid a_j \in A, \ s \in \mathbb{Z} \}. \qquad (7.4)$$

The last action we consider here is the action of $\mathcal{A}$ on $\mathcal{F}^n$. With $v_i \in F^n$ and $a_j \in A$, it is defined as

$$a = \sum_{j=s}^{\infty} a_j D^j \ : \ \mathcal{F}^n \to \mathcal{F}^n \ : \ v = \sum_{i=r}^{\infty} v_i D^i \mapsto va = \sum_{j=s}^{\infty} (va_j) D^j , \qquad (7.5)$$

where, according to (7.3), the sequence $va_j$ can be developed as $\sum_i v_i a_j^{(i)} D^i$ with $v_i \in F^n$ and $a_j^{(i)} \in A^{(i)}$. The set $\mathcal{A}$ is a group for the addition

$$a + b = \sum_{i=s}^{\infty} (a_i + b_i) D^i ; \ a, b \in \mathcal{A}, \qquad (7.6)$$

where $a_i + b_i$ denotes addition in $A$ and where $s$ has to be chosen not larger than the minimum of del$(a)$ and del$(b)$. To define a multiplication in $\mathcal{A}$ we need to generalize a notation of section 4.2. Given an element $a = \sum_{x \in H} xa(x) \in A = FH$ with $a(x) \in F$, we denote by $a^{D^s}$ the expression $\sum_{x \in H} x^{D^s} a(x)$. Since $H$ is assumed to be a $D$-normal group, $a^{D^s}$ is also an element of $A = FH$. We define then the multiplication of $a = \sum_{i=r}^{\infty} a_i D^i$ and $b = \sum_{j=s}^{\infty} b_j D^j$ in $A$ by

$$ab = \sum_{ij} a_i b_j^{D^{-i}} D^{i+j}. \tag{7.7}$$

The operations (7.6) and (7.7) give the set $A$ the structure of an algebra. We verify, for example, that the multiplication (7.7) is associative. This is implied by

$$aD^i(bD^jcD^k) = (aD^ibD^j)cD^k ; \quad a, b, c \in A, \ i, j, k \in \mathbb{Z},$$

which follows from the fact that both sides of this equation are equal to $ab^{D^{-i}}c^{D^{-(i+j)}}D^{i+j+k}$. Let us remark that $A$ is an algebra over the field $F$ but not over the field $\mathcal{F}$. For $a, b \in A$, the equality $(fa)b = a(fb)$ is indeed satisfied for $f \in F$ but not necessarily for $f \in \mathcal{F}$ since one has, for example, $(Da)b = a^{D^{-1}}b^{D^{-1}}D$ and $a(Db) = ab^{D^{-1}}D$.

When $A$ acts on $\mathcal{F}^n$ in agreement with (7.5) it satisfies

$$v(ab) = (va)b , \ v \in \mathcal{F}^n ; \ a, b \in A. \tag{7.8}$$

To prove (7.8) we remark that with $v_i \in F^n$ and $a_j, b_k \in A$, one has

$$v_iD^i(a_jD^jb_kD^k) = (v_iD^ia_jD^j)b_kD^k , \tag{7.9}$$

since both sides of (7.9) are equal to $v_ia_j^{D^{-i}}b_k^{D^{-(i+j)}}D^{i+j+k}$. This compatibility between the multiplication (7.7) in the algebra $A$ and the action (7.5) of $A$ on $\mathcal{F}^n$ endows $\mathcal{F}^n$ with the structure of a right $A$-module. In particular, axiom (iii) of definition 6.8 is satisfied.

Obviously, any $A$-submodule $M$ of the $A$-module $\mathcal{F}^n$ satisfies the axioms of a vector space over the field $\mathcal{F}$. As a consequence it follows from some remarks made in subsection 1.1.3 that, in any descending chain of modules $\mathcal{F}^n = M_0 \supset M_1 \supset M_2 \supset \cdots$, the $\mathcal{F}$-dimension of $M_{i+1}$ is strictly smaller than the $\mathcal{F}$-dimension of $M_i$. Therefore, the length of such a chain is $\leq n$. A similar property is true for ascending chains of $\mathcal{A}$-submodules of $\mathcal{F}^n$. This shows that the $\mathcal{A}$-module $\mathcal{F}^n$ satisfies both the DCC and the ACC.

For any $D$-normal subgroup $H$ of $K^{\mathbb{Z}}$, we define then an $H$-set to be any finite subset $\mathcal{V}$ of $\mathcal{F}^n$ that remains invariant under $H$. This property can be expressed by $\mathcal{V}H = \mathcal{V}$. If the $H$-set $\mathcal{V}$ is an $F$-space, i.e., if $\mathcal{V}$ coincides with $E_0(\mathcal{V})$, then $\mathcal{V}A$ coincides with $\mathcal{V}$ for $A = FH$.

**Lemma 7.2 :** If $\mathcal{V}$ is an $H$-set, $E(\mathcal{V})$ is an $\mathcal{A}$-submodule of $\mathcal{F}^n$.
**Proof :** It is sufficient to prove that, for any $v$ in $E(\mathcal{V})$, any $f = \sum_{i=r}^{\infty} f_i D^i$ in $\mathcal{F}^n$ and any $a = \sum_{j=s}^{\infty} a_j D^j$ in $\mathcal{A}$, the sequence $vfa$ is in $E(\mathcal{V})$. Since $H$ is $D$-normal, $a \in A$ implies $a^{D^i} \in A$ for all $i \in \mathbb{Z}$, and, as a consequence, $b = fa$ is in $\mathcal{A}$. Write now $b = \sum_{k=r+s}^{\infty} b_k D^k$ with $b_k \in A$. Since $\mathcal{V}$ is an $H$-set, it follows that for any $v \in \mathcal{V}$ and for any $b_k \in A$, the element $w_k := vb_k$ of $\mathcal{F}^n$ is in $E_0(\mathcal{V})$. Thus $vfa$ can be written as

$$ vb = \sum_{k=r+s}^{\infty} w_k \, D^k , \tag{7.10} $$

with all $w_k D^k$ in $E_0(\mathcal{V})$. Since the collection of sequences $w_k D^k$ with $k = r + s$, $r + s + 1, \cdots$, is progressive, it follows from theorem 1.10 that $vfa = vb$ is in $E[E_0(\mathcal{V})] = E(\mathcal{V})$. $\square$

**Theorem 7.3 :** A convolutional code $C$ of span $m$ is an $H$-code if and only if it is an $\mathcal{A}$-submodule of $\mathcal{F}^n$, i.e., if and only if $C\mathcal{A}$ is equal to $C$.
**Proof :** To prove the *if* statement we note that, since $H$ is a subset of $\mathcal{A}$ containing the identity, $C\mathcal{A} = C$ implies $CH = C$. To prove the *only if* statement we remark that $\mathcal{V} = L_m(C)$ is an $H$-set that generates $C$ as an $\mathcal{F}$-space and we apply lemma 7.2. $\square$

We conclude this section by giving a property of the block codes $C_{i,m}$ that are associated with a convolutional $H$-code $C$. These codes were defined in subsection 4.2.2.

**Corollary 7.4 :** If $C$ is a convolutional $H$-code over $F$ with $H$ a $D$-normal subgroup of $K^Z$, then the block codes $C_{i,m}$ are $A$-submodules of $F^n$ for $A = FH$.

**Proof :** Since $H$ is $D$-normal, one has $(CA)_{i,m} \supseteq C_{i,m}A \supseteq C_{i,m}$. Now $CA = C$ implies $(CA)_{i,m} = C_{i,m}$ so that one has $C_{i,m}A = C_{i,m}$. $\square$

As a particular case, the block code $C^0 := C_{0,\infty}$ of the initial words of $C$ is an $A$-module.

# 7.2 Normal sequences and generated modules

The decomposition of convolutional $H$-codes that is proposed in section 7.3 will make frequent use of the $H$-*normal sequences*. Here we define these sequences and investigate some properties of the modules they generate.

**Definition 7.5 :** Given a $D$-normal subgroup $H = H^D$ of $K^Z$, a nonzero sequence $v = \sum_{i=0}^{\infty} v_i D^i$, $v_i \in F^n$, is called $H$-*normal* if it satisfies

$$v_0 a = 0 \Rightarrow va = 0; \quad \text{all } a \in A = FH .$$

It is an interesting problem to find the general form of all sequences that are $H$-normal for a given $D$-normal group $H$. In chapter 9, we solve it in a useful particular case, but the general problem remains open.

Let us now investigate some properties of modules generated by $H$-normal sequences. In the following statements, $A$ always denotes the group algebra $FH$.

**Theorem 7.6 :** Let $v = \sum_{j=0}^{\infty} v_j D^j$, $v_j \in F^n$, be an $H$-normal sequence, and let $C = v\mathcal{A}$ be the right $\mathcal{A}$-module generated by $v$. Let $C^0$ be the set of the initial words of $C$. Then one has $C^0 = v_0 A$.

**Proof :** Let $va$ be any element of the right $\mathcal{A}$-module generated by $v$, and write $a$ as $a = \sum_{j=r}^{\infty} a_j D^j$, $a_j \in A$. Let $s$ be the smallest integer for which $va_s$ is nonzero. Since $v$ is $H$-normal, it follows that $v_0 a_s$ is also nonzero. Clearly, $v_0 a_s$ is the nonzero initial word of $va$. Since $v_0 a_s$ belongs to $v_0 A$, this proves $C^0 \subseteq v_0 A$. Conversely, for any $a \in A$ the element $v_0 a$ of $v_0 A$ is obviously an initial word of $va$, which implies $C^0 \supseteq v_0 A$. □

**Theorem 7.7 :** The $H$-code $C = v\mathcal{A}$ generated by the $H$-normal sequence $v$ is an irreducible right $\mathcal{A}$-module if and only if $C^0 = v_0 A$ is an irreducible right $A$-module.

**Proof :** We suppose that $C^0 = v_0 A$ is an irreducible $A$-module and we prove that $C = v\mathcal{A}$ is an irreducible $\mathcal{A}$-module. If $C$ is not an irreducible right $\mathcal{A}$-module, let $C'$ be an irreducible right $\mathcal{A}$-submodule of $C$. By corollary 7.4, $(C')^0$ is an $A$-submodule of $F^n$, and $C \supseteq C'$ implies that all initial words of $C'$ are initial words of $C$. Now, since $C^0 = v_0 A$ is an irreducible $A$-module and since $C'$ is nonzero, one has $C^0 = (C')^0$. As a consequence of corollary 2.20, the $\mathcal{F}$-dimensions of $C$ and $C'$ are equal. From $C \supseteq C'$ one obtains $C = C'$, which shows that $C$ is an irreducible $\mathcal{A}$-module.

Conversely, let us suppose that $v\mathcal{A}$ is an irreducible module. We then prove that $v_0 A$ is also an irreducible module. Since $v\mathcal{A}$ is irreducible one has

$$vb \neq 0 \;\Rightarrow\; vb\mathcal{A} = v\mathcal{A} ; \quad \text{all } b \in \mathcal{A} . \tag{7.11}$$

Defining $C_b := vb\mathcal{A}$, we can write (7.11) as

$$C_b \neq \{0\} \;\Rightarrow\; C_b = C . \tag{7.12}$$

We remark that if $C_b$ is nonzero, then $vb$ and $v$ are both $H$-normal sequences. In this case, by theorem 7.6, the sets of initial words in $C_b$ and $C$ are given respectively by $v_0 b A$ and $v_0 A$, and it follows from (7.12) that $v_0 b A$ equals $v_0 A$ for all $b$ such that $v_0 b$ is nonzero. This proves that any nonzero element $v_0 b$ of $v_0 A$ generates $v_0 A$ as an $A$-module or equivalently that $v_0 A$ is an irreducible $A$-module (see subsection 6.2.1). □

**Corollary 7.8 :** The $A$-module $vA$ generated by an $H$-normal sequence $v = \sum_{i=0}^{\infty} v_i D^i$ is irreducible if and only if $v_0 A$ is an irreducible $A$-module.

**Proof :** Assume first that $vA$ is an irreducible $A$-module but that $v_0 A$ is not. In this case there would exist $b \in A$ such that $v_0 b$ is nonzero and $v_0 bA$ is a proper submodule of $v_0 A$. As a consequence, no $a \in A$ satisfying $v_0 ba = v_0$ would exist. However, since $vA$ is an irreducible $A$-module and since $vb$ is nonzero, there exists some $a \in A$ satisfying $vba = v$, whence $v_0 ba = v_0$, which leads to a contradiction.

Conversely, if $v_0 A$ is irreducible, then for all $a \in A$ such that $v_0 a$ is nonzero there exists $b \in B$ that satisfies $v_0 ab = v_0$. Since $v$ is normal, $v(ab - 1^Z)$ is zero (with $1^Z$ the identity of $H$) so that one has $vab = v$. This implies that, for all $a$ such that $va$ is nonzero, $vaA$ equals $vA$. Equivalently, $vA$ is an irreducible $A$-module. $\square$

**Theorem 7.9 :** Let $v_1, \cdots, v_r$ be $H$-normal sequences represented by $v_j = \sum_{i=0}^{\infty} (v_j)_i D^i$ with $(v_j)_i \in F^n$ and $1 \leq j \leq r$, and assume that the sum of the $A$-modules $(v_j)_0 A$, for $1 \leq j \leq r$, is direct. In this case the sum of the $\mathcal{A}$-modules $v_j \mathcal{A}$ is also direct.

**Proof :** Define $v = \sum_{j=1}^{r} v_j a_j$ with $a_j \in \mathcal{A}$. We have to show that $v$ cannot be zero if at least one $v_j a_j$ is nonzero. Write $a_j = \sum_{i=s}^{\infty} (a_j)_i D^i$, $(a_j)_i \in A$, and let $t$ be the smallest integer for which $v_j (a_j)_t$ is nonzero for at least one $j$. Since the sequences $v_j$ are $H$-normal, $(v_j)_0 (a_j)_t$ is nonzero as soon as $v_j (a_j)_t$ is nonzero, while the contributions $(v_j)_i (a_j)_{t-i}$, for $1 \leq j \leq r$ and $i \geq 1$, to the coefficients of $D^t$ in $v$ are zero. Since the sum of the modules $(v_j)_0 A$ is direct and since $(v_j)_0 (a_j)_t$ is nonzero for at least one $j$, it follows that the coefficient of $D^t$ in $v$ is nonzero. $\square$

## 7.3 Canonical minimal encoders for $H$-codes

By theorem 7.3 we know that an $H$-code $C$ over the finite field $F$ is an $\mathcal{A}$-submodule of $\mathcal{F}^n$. It is the goal of this section to make explicit the fact that it is often possible to construct a minimal encoder of $C$ that mirrors this $\mathcal{A}$-module structure.

Let $H$ be a $D$-normal subgroup of $K^{\mathbb{Z}}$, with $K$ a subgroup of the group $GL(n, F)$ of all $n \times n$ nonsingular matrices over the finite field $F$. While the group $H$ and the algebra $A = FH$ may be infinite, the projection $H^{(0)}$ of $H$ and the group algebra $A^{(0)} = FH^{(0)}$ are finite. For this simple reason, the ring $A^{(0)}$ satisfies the right and left minimum conditions of definition 6.10.

When $A^{(0)}$ acts on $F^n$ according to equation (7.1), it gives $F^n$ the structure of an $A^{(0)}$-module. We denote by $S$ the socle of this $A^{(0)}$-module, i.e., the sum of all irreducible $A^{(0)}$-submodules of $F^n$. Since the ring $A^{(0)}$ satisfies both the left and right minimum condition, it follows from subsection 6.2.2 that this socle $S$ is the annihilator of the radical of $A^{(0)}$. When $A^{(0)}$ is a semi-simple algebra, rad $A^{(0)}$ reduces to $\{0\}$ and the socle of the $A^{(0)}$-module $F^n$ is $F^n$ itself. When $A^{(0)}$ is not semi-simple, the socle $S$ of the $A^{(0)}$-module $F^n$ is the unique maximal completely reducible submodule of $F^n$ (see subsection 6.2.1). In any cases $S$ can be expressed as a direct sum $S = S_1 \oplus S_2 \oplus \cdots \oplus S_u$ of at most $n$ irreducible $A^{(0)}$-submodules $S_i$.

Considering then $F^n$ as being an $A$-module instead of an $A^{(0)}$-module, we see that $S_i$ is an irreducible $A$-submodule of $F^n$ if and only if it is an irreducible $A^{(0)}$-submodule of $F^n$. This follows from the fact that in (7.2), $A$ acts on $F^n$ only by means of its projection $A^{(0)}$. The socle of $F^n$ viewed as an $A$-module is thus nothing but the socle $S$ of $F^n$ viewed as an $A^{(0)}$-module.

Let us now denote by $\mathcal{S}$ the Laurent extension $S((D))$ of $S$, i.e.,

$$\mathcal{S} = \left\{ s = \sum_{i=r}^{\infty} s_i D^i \,\middle|\, s_i \in S, \ r \in \mathbb{Z} \right\}.$$

In section 7.1, it was shown that $\mathcal{F}^n$ can be endowed with the structure of a right $\mathcal{A}$-module. It turns out that the subset $\mathcal{S}$ of $\mathcal{F}^n$ is an $\mathcal{A}$-submodule of $\mathcal{F}^n$. Indeed, given $s \in \mathcal{S}$ and $a = \sum_{j=r}^{\infty} a_j D^j \in \mathcal{A}$, the coefficient of any

$D^i$ in $sa$ is a finite sum $\sum_j s_{i-j}a_j$ all terms of which are in the submodule $S$ of $F^n$.

**Lemma 7.10 :** Let $G$ be a $k \times n$ encoder of an $(n, k)$ convolutional $H$-code $C$ over $F$. All words of any row of $G$ are in $S$ if and only if $C$ is an $\mathcal{A}$-submodule of $S$.

**Proof :** Easy and omitted. $\square$

**Definition 7.11 :** Any convolutional $H$-code is called a *locally reducible* convolutional code (with respect to $\mathcal{A}$) if it is an $\mathcal{A}$-submodule of $S$.

All convolutional $H$-codes considered in the sequel are assumed to be locally reducible with respect to the Laurent extension $\mathcal{A}$ of $A = FH$. This is the restriction implied by the word *often* in the second sentence of this section.

Let $C$ be an $(n, k)$ convolutional $H$-code over the field $F$ and let $G$ be an ordered minimal encoder of $C$. Let us assume that $G$ contains $k_1$ rows of degree $m_1$, $k_2$ rows of degree $m_2, \cdots, k_R$ rows of degree $m_R$, with $m_1 < m_2 < \cdots < m_R$, $\sum_{r=1}^{R} k_r = k$ and $k_r > 0$, all $r$. Since $G$ is a minimal encoder, one has $\sum_{r=1}^{R} k_r m_r = \mu(C)$. Such a minimal encoder of $C$ can be obtained independently of the particular structure of $C$ (see section 2.2). When $C$ is an $H$-code and thus, by theorem 7.3, an $\mathcal{A}$-submodule of $\mathcal{F}^n$, it would be nice to select a minimal encoder $G$ that mirrors these algebraic properties. We shall prove in this section that such a minimal encoder does exist, at least when $C$ is an $\mathcal{A}$-submodule of $S$. More precisely we shall show that a locally reducible convolutional code $C$ admits a decomposition $C = \mathcal{S}_1 \oplus \mathcal{S}_2 \oplus \cdots$ as a sum of irreducible $\mathcal{A}$-submodules $\mathcal{S}_i$ of $S$, such that at least one *minimal* encoder $G$ of $C$ has the property that each of these direct summands $\mathcal{S}_i$ is generated as an $\mathcal{F}$-space by a subset of the rows of $G$. The following theorem is a first step in this direction.

**Theorem 7.12 :** The set $S$ is a completely reducible right $\mathcal{A}$-module, in the sense that it can be written as a direct sum of irreducible right $\mathcal{A}$-modules.

**Proof :** Decompose $S$, the socle of $F^n$ viewed as an $A^{(0)}$-module, as $S = S_1 \oplus S_2 \oplus \cdots \oplus S_u$ where all $S_i$ are irreducible $A^{(0)}$-modules satisfying $S_i = v_i A^{(0)}$ for an arbitrary nonzero $v_i \in S_i$. Denote the Laurent extension $S_i((D))$ of $S_i$ by $\mathcal{S}_i$. Obviously $\mathcal{S}$ is the sum of the $\mathcal{A}$-modules $\mathcal{S}_i$. These modules are irreducible by theorem 7.7, and their sum is direct by theorem 7.9. □

Before going further let us make a general remark. There is no field $F^*$ such that an $(n, k)$ convolutional $H$-code $C$ is at the same time a *finite* dimensional vector space over $F^*$ and a module over an $F^*$-algebra. The field over which $C$ is a finite dimensional vector space is $\mathcal{F}$ and the algebras over which $C$ is a module are $A$ and $\mathcal{A}$. However these two algebras are $F$-algebras, not $\mathcal{F}$-algebras. In particular, as mentioned after (7.7), $\mathcal{A}$ does not satisfy the axiom (ii) of an algebra given in section 1.1.3, if the field element $f$ is in $\mathcal{F}$ but not in $F$. This remark is relatively important because in their book Curtis and Reiner [27 p.47] consider only modules over $F^*$-algebra that are finite dimensional vector spaces over $F^*$. Therefore, some caution is necessary in the application of the statements of [27] in the present context. However, this point will not present a problem in this section. All modifications of the encoders that we use here are based on the possibility of decomposing $S$ as a sum of irreducible $A$-modules (not on the decomposition of $\mathcal{S}$ as a sum of irreducible $\mathcal{A}$-modules) and, fortunately, the subset $S$ of $F^n$ is a finite dimensional vector space over $F$ *and* a module over the $F$-algebra $A$.

Let us now go back to the construction of a minimal encoder that should mirror the $\mathcal{A}$-module structure of an $H$-code $C$.

**Lemma 7.13 :** If $C$ is an $H$-code, then $L_m(C)$ is an $A$-module for all $m$.

**Proof :** $L_m(C)$ is an $F$-space that remains invariant under $H$. □

Now write the ordered minimal encoder $G$ of the $H$-code $C$ considered after definition 7.11 as

$$
G = \begin{bmatrix} \Gamma'_1 \\ \Gamma'_2 \\ \vdots \\ \Gamma'_R \end{bmatrix}.
\tag{7.13}
$$

In (7.13), $\Gamma'_r$ denotes the submatrix of $G$ containing all its rows of degree $m_r$. As a consequence it can be written as $\Gamma'_r = \sum_{i=0}^{m_r} \Gamma'_{r,i} D^i$, where $\Gamma'_{r,i}$ is a $k_r \times n$ matrix over $F$. Since $G$ is a minimal encoder it enjoys the predictable span property and as a consequence the $F$-space $L_{m_1}[E(G)]$ is nothing but $E_0(\Gamma'_1)$.

The next theorem may be seen as giving the initial condition to be used in an algorithm producing a canonical encoder.

**Theorem 7.14 :** All elements of $E_0(\Gamma'_1)$ are $H$-normal sequences.

**Proof :** Since $G$ is a minimal encoder and since $m_1$ is the lowest degree of its rows, $C = E(G)$ does not contain any nonzero polynomial sequence of degree $\leq m_1 - 1$. Let $v = \sum_{i=0}^{m_1} v_i D^i$, with $v_i \in F^n$, be a nonzero element of $E_0(\Gamma'_1)$. Since $C$ is an $H$-code, $va$ is in $C$ for all $a \in A$. If $v$ is not $H$-normal, i.e., if one has $v_0 a = 0$ for some $a \in A$, while $va$ is nonzero, then $vaD^{-1}$ is a nonzero polynomial in $C$ of degree $\leq m_1 - 1$. Hence the contradiction. $\square$

By theorem 2.27, $\Gamma'_1$ is a minimal encoder and, by theorem 2.19, $\Gamma'_{1,0}$ generates the block code $C_{0,m_1}$ as an $F$-space. Since $C$ is assumed to be locally reducible, it follows from lemma 7.10 that all its words are in the socle $S$ of $F^n$ viewed as an $A^{(0)}$-module or an $A$-module. In particular, $C_{0,m_1}$ is an $A$-module (corollary 7.4) and this module is completely reducible. Since $A$-submodules are $F$-subspaces, there exists a $k_1 \times k_1$ nonsingular matrix $T_1$ over $F$ that satisfies

$$
T_1 \Gamma'_{1,0} =
\begin{bmatrix}
G_0^1 \\
\vdots \\
G_0^s \\
\vdots \\
G_0^{f(1)}
\end{bmatrix}
, \tag{7.14}
$$

where, for $1 \le s \le f(1)$, all $F$-spaces $E_0(G_0^s)$ are irreducible $A$-modules, the sum of which is direct and equal to $C_{0,m_1}$. We use this matrix $T_1$ to construct from $\Gamma'_1$ the equivalent encoder $\Gamma_1 = \sum_{j=0}^{m_1} \Gamma_{1,j} D^j$ given by $\Gamma_1 = T_1 \Gamma'_1$. We write this subencoder $\Gamma_1$ as

$$
\Gamma_1 =
\begin{bmatrix}
G^1 \\
\vdots \\
G^s \\
\vdots \\
G^{f(1)}
\end{bmatrix}
, \tag{7.15}
$$

where the $G^s$ are polynomial matrices of formal degree $m_1$; thus $G^s = \sum_{j=0}^{m_1} G_j^s D^j$.

Consider now $L_{m_2}(C)$. Since a minimal encoder has the predictable span property, any polynomial in $L_{m_2}(C)$ is the sum of two polymomials: the first one is in $E_0(\Gamma'_2)$ and the second one is in $E_{m_2-m_1}(\Gamma_1)$. By theorem 2.27, the matrix $\begin{bmatrix} \Gamma_1 \\ \Gamma'_2 \end{bmatrix}$ is a minimal encoder and, by theorem 2.19 and corollary 7.4, the $F$-row space of $\begin{bmatrix} \Gamma_{1,0} \\ \Gamma'_{2,0} \end{bmatrix}$ is the $A$-module $C_{0,m_2}$. Let us now remark that $C_{0,m_1}$ is an $A$-submodule of $C_{0,m_2}$ and that $C_{0,m_2}$ is itself an $A$-submodule of the socle $S$ of the $A$-module $F^n$. According to definition 6.13 and to the comments made after it, $C_{0,m_1}$ is direct summand of $C_{0,m_2}$. Thus one has

$$
C_{0,m_2} = C_{0,m_1} \oplus C_2 ,
$$

where $C_2$ itself can be written as a direct sum of irreducible $A$-modules. As a consequence there exists a $(k_1 + k_2) \times (k_1 + k_2)$ nonsingular matrix $T_2$ with the following characteristics. First, it has the form

$$T_2 = \begin{bmatrix} I_{k_1} & 0 \\ X & Y \end{bmatrix}$$

where $Y$ is a $k_2 \times k_2$ nonsingular matrix, $0$ is the $k_1 \times k_2$ zero matrix and $X$ is a $k_2 \times k_1$ matrix. Second, it satisfies

$$T_2 \begin{bmatrix} \Gamma_{1,0} \\ \Gamma'_{2,0} \end{bmatrix} = \begin{bmatrix} \Gamma_{1,0} \\ \Gamma_{2,0} \end{bmatrix}$$

where $\Gamma_{2,0}$ has a form similar to the form (7.14) of $\Gamma_{1,0}$. Thus we can write

$$\begin{bmatrix} \Gamma_{1,0} \\ \Gamma_{2,0} \end{bmatrix} = \begin{bmatrix} G_0^1 \\ \vdots \\ G_0^{f(1)} \\ G_0^{1+f(1)} \\ \vdots \\ G_0^{f(2)} \end{bmatrix},$$

where the sum of the irreducible $A$-modules $E_0(G_0^s)$ is direct, and the rank of $\begin{bmatrix} \Gamma_{1,0} \\ \Gamma_{2,0} \end{bmatrix}$ is $k_1 + k_2$.

Then define $\Gamma_2$ by

$$\begin{bmatrix} \Gamma_1 \\ \Gamma_2 \end{bmatrix} := T_2 \begin{bmatrix} \Gamma_1 \\ \Gamma'_2 \end{bmatrix}.$$

Like the matrix $\Gamma_1$ given in (7.15), $\Gamma_2$ is a juxtaposition of a certain number of submatrices $G^s = \sum_{j=0}^{m_2} G_j^s D^j$.

For $r \geq 3$, this treatment can be extended to the other submatrices $\Gamma'_r$ of the minimal encoder $G$ given by (7.13). We can successively replace each of these matrices $\Gamma_r'$ by a new matrix $\Gamma_r$. The rows of this new matrix have a degree that does not exceed the degree $m_r$ of the rows of $\Gamma_r'$, and the $k_r \times n$ matrix $\Gamma_{r,0}$ over $F$ has a form similar to (7.14). All $F$-matrices $G_0^s$ with $1 + f(r-1) \leq s \leq f(r)$, generate $F$-spaces that are irreducible $A$-submodules of $F^n$, and the sum of all these submodules is direct. Continuing in this way up to $r = R$, we obtain a new encoder denoted by $G$ that has the form

$$G = \begin{bmatrix} G^1 \\ \vdots \\ G^{f(1)} \\ G^{1+f(1)} \\ \vdots \\ G^s \\ \vdots \end{bmatrix}. \tag{7.16}$$

Another way to represent $G$ is

$$G = \begin{bmatrix} \Gamma_1 \\ \Gamma_2 \\ \vdots \\ \Gamma_R \end{bmatrix}. \tag{7.17}$$

By construction, the rows of $\Gamma_r$ have degree at most $m_r$. The degree of these rows is actually *equal* to $m_r$ because the initial matrix given by (7.13) was already a minimal encoder, thus satisfying $\sum_r k_r m_r = \mu[E(G)]$.

The encoder $G$ of (7.16) or (7.17) is not yet the minimal encoder that should mirror the $A$-module structure of $C$ and we shall modify it further to give it the required form. This is done as follows. We know from theorem 7.14 that the rows of the submatrix $\Gamma_1$ of $G$ are already $H$-normal. Hence all rows of $G$ are $H$-normal if $G$ is equal to $\Gamma_1$. If $G$ has the form (7.17) with $R \geq 2$, we proceed as follows. In the matrices $G^u$ appearing in (7.16), the $F$-matrices $G_0^u$ are such that for all $u$ they generate an irreducible $A$-module. Thus we can represent this module as $g_0^u A$ for any nonzero $n$-tuple $g_0^u$ in $E_0(G_0^u)$. Denote then by $U(r)$, $1 \leq r \leq R$, the set of integers $u$ such that the rows of the matrix $G^u$ have degree $m_r$ and, for $r \geq 2$, let $g = \sum_{j=0}^{m_r} g_j D^j$ be any row of $\Gamma_r$. Since $C$ is locally reducible all words $g_j$ of $g$ are in the socle $S$ of $F^n$ viewed as an $A$-module, and we can express the coefficient $g_1$ of $D$ in $g$ as

$$g_1 = \sum_{u \in U(1)} g_0^u a_u^{[1]} + g_1^*, \tag{7.18}$$

where $g_0^u$ is any generator of the $A$-module $E_0(G_0^u)$, $a_u^{[1]}$ is some element of $A$ and $g_1^*$ has zero components in the irreducible $A$-modules $g_0^u A = E(G_0^u)$, $u \in U(1)$. We then define

$$g^{[1]} = g - \left( \sum_{u \in U(1)} g^u a_u^{[1]} \right) D, \tag{7.19}$$

where $g^u$ is the unique element of $E_0(\Gamma_1)$ having $g_0^u$ as initial word. If $m_r$ is equal to $1 + m_1$, then $g$ is simply replaced by $g^{[1]}$ in $G$. If $m_r$ is larger than $1 + m_1$, we further modify $g^{[1]}$ as follows. We write $g^{[1]} = \sum_{j=0}^{m_r} g_j^{[1]} D^j$ and we express $g_2^{[1]}$ as

$$g_2^{[1]} = \sum_{u \in U(1)} g_0^u a_u^{[2]} + g_2^*, \tag{7.20}$$

where $g_2^*$ has zero components in the irreducible $A$-modules $g_0^u A$, $u \in U(1)$. We define then

$$g^{[2]} = g^{[1]} - ( \sum_{u \in U(1)} g^u a_u^{[2]}) D^2 . \tag{7.21}$$

If $m_r$ is equal to $2 + m_1$, $g$ is replaced by $g^{[2]}$ in $G$. Otherwise we continue this procedure up to obtaining, for $t = m_r - m_1$, the new sequence

$$g^{[t]} = g^{[t-1]} - \left( \sum_{u \in U(1)} g^u a_u^{[t]} \right) D^t . \tag{7.22}$$

The row $g$ of $G$ is then replaced by $g^{[t]}$. We call this computation of $g^{[t]}$ from $g$ a partial normalizing process. We achieve this process on all rows $g$ of $G$ that are not in $\Gamma_1$.

To simplify the notation we still denote the obtained matrix by $G$. If we write $G$ as $\sum_{j=0}^{m_R} G_j D^j$, the new matrix $G$ has the same coefficient $G_0$ of $D^0$ as the original one. Thus we can still represent it as in (7.16) if the emphasis is put on the irreducible module structure of the spaces $E_0(G_0^s)$, or as in (7.17) if we insist on the different constraint lengths $m_1, m_2 \cdots, m_R$.

Let us first show that this new matrix $G$ is still a minimal encoder of the code $C$ generated by the original minimal encoder $G$. Since $C$ is an $H$-code and since the original encoder $G$ is a minimal encoder, any sum $\sum_{u \in U(1)} g^u a_u^{[i]}$, with $1 \leq i \leq t$, appearing in the right side of (7.19), (7.21) or (7.22) is indeed a sequence in $E_0(\Gamma_1)$ and, since $g$ is not in $E_0(\Gamma_1)$, the replacement of $g$ by $g^{[i]}$ in $G$ with $1 \leq i \leq t$, is obviously a nonsingular transformation. The new $G$ thus generates the same $\mathcal{F}$-space as the old one. Moreover the condition $t + m_1 = m_r$ guarantees deg $g^{[t]} \leq$ deg $g$. Since the original encoder $G$ was minimal, thus satisfying $M(G) = \mu(C)$, the parameter $M(G)$ of the new encoder cannot be less than that of the original encoder, and the polynomial $g^{[t]}$ given by (7.21) satisfies deg $g^{[t]} =$ deg $g$.

It follows from theorem 7.14 that, in the original encoder $G$, the sequences of $E_0(\Gamma_1)$ were already $H$-normal. Hence, as $T_1$ is a nonsingular $F$-matrix, the $k_1$ first rows of the new matrix $G$ are $H$-normal. We now prove that, in the new encoder $G$, the $k_2$ rows of $\Gamma_2$ are also $H$-normal sequences.

**Theorem 7.15 :** In the new encoder $G$ all sequences in $E_0(\Gamma_2)$ are $H$-normal.

**Proof :** Suppose that the sequence $g = \sum_{j=0}^{m_2} g_j D^j$ in $E_0(\Gamma_2)$ is not $H$-normal. In this case there exists a nonzero $a \in A$ such that $g_0 a$ is zero and $ga$ is nonzero. Denote the sequence $g a D^{-\text{del}(ga)}$ by $\gamma = \sum_{j=0}^{m} \gamma_j D^j$, where

$\gamma_0$ and $\gamma_m$ are nonzero. By construction $m$ is less than $m_2$, and since no nonzero polynomial sequence of $C$ has degree less than $m_1$, $m$ is $\geq m_1$. Therefore, since $G$ is a minimal encoder and $m$ is less than $m_2$, the element $\gamma$ belongs to $E(\Gamma_1)$ so that $\gamma_0$ belongs to $E_0(\Gamma_{1,0})$. As a consequence, $\gamma_0$ cn be expressed as

$$\gamma_0 = \sum_{u \in U_1} g_0^u \, a_u^{[0]}; \ a_u^{[0]} \in A, \qquad (7.23)$$

where at least one $g_0^u \, a_u^{[0]}$ is nonzero. Since the coefficient $\gamma_0$ of $D^{\mathrm{del}(ga)}$ in $ga$ has nonzero components in the irreducible modules $g_0^u A$ with $u \in U(1)$, then a fortiori $g_{\mathrm{del}(ga)}$, the coefficient of $D^{\mathrm{del}(ga)}$ in $g$, has also nonzero components in the irreducible modules $g_0^u A$ with $u \in U(1)$. Now this is impossible because these components were cancelled in the partial normalizing process described above. Hence the contradiction that proves the theorem. $\square$

If the matrix $G$ in (7.17) contains only 2 submatrices $\Gamma_r$, the matrix $G$ obtained by the transformations above is already the announced encoder whose properties are described below. If $R$ is $\geq 3$, the procedure is continued as follows. Let $g = \sum_{j=0}^{m_r} g_j D^j$ be a row of the submatrix $\Gamma_r$ of $G$ with $r \geq 3$. Since $C$ is locally reducible, all words $g_j$ of $g$ are in the socle $S$ of $F^n$ viewed as an $A$-module and we can express $g_1$ as

$$g_1 = \sum_{u \in U(2)} g_0^u a_u^{[1]} + g_1^*, \qquad (7.24)$$

where $g_0^u$ is any generator of the $A$-module $E_0(G_0^s)$, $a_u^{[1]}$ is some element of $A$ and $g_1^*$ has zero components in the irreducible $A$-modules $g_0^u A = E_0(G_0^u)$, $u \in U(1) \cup U(2)$. Of course these $a_u^{[1]}$ and $g_1^*$ have nothing to do with the ones used in (7.18). Define

$$g^{[1]} = g - \left( \sum_{u \in U(2)} g^u a_u^{[1]} \right) D, \qquad (7.25)$$

where $g^u$ is the element of $E_0(\Gamma_2)$ having $g_0^u$ as initial word. Since $C$ is an
$H$-code, $g^{[1]}$ is still a code sequence. If $m_r$ is equal to $1 + m_2$, then $g$ is
replaced by $g^{[1]}$ in $G$. Otherwise the procedure is continued as in the partial
normalizing process of $\Gamma_2$, which means that we write $g^{[1]} = \sum_{j=0}^{m_r} g_j^{[1]} D^j$
and we express $g_2^{[1]}$ as

$$g_2^{[1]} = \sum_{u \in U(2)} g_0^u \, a_u^{[2]} + g_2^* \,, \tag{7.26}$$

where $g_2^*$ has zero components in the irreducible $A$-modules $g_0^u A$ with $u \in
U(2)$. We define

$$g^{[2]} = g^{[1]} - \left( \sum_{u \in U(2)} g^u \, a_u^{[2]} \right) D^2 \,, \tag{7.27}$$

and continue in this way up to obtaining, for $t = m_r - m_2$, a sequence $g^{[t]}$
of the form (7.22), but with $U(1)$ replaced by $U(2)$. The row $g$ of $G$ is then
replaced by $g^{[t]}$. For $i = 1, 2, \cdots, m_r - m_2$, the elements $g_i^*$ of $F^n$ that are
produced in this way have zero components in the irreducible modules $g_0^u A$,
$u \in U(2)$, but they have also zero components in the irreducible modules
$g_0^u A$, $u \in U(1)$. The reader will indeed check that, after the normalizing
process of $\Gamma_2$, any row $g = \sum_{j=0}^{m_r} g_j D^j$ of the submatrix $\Gamma_r$ of $G$ is such
that the word $g_j$ may have nonzero components in $g_0^u A$, $u \in U(1)$, only for
$j \geq m_r - m_1 + 1$.

This partial normalizing process is based on the irreducible modules
$E_0(G_0^u)$ with $u \in U(2)$, and it is performed for all rows $g$ of the matrices
$\Gamma_3, \Gamma_4, \cdots, \Gamma_R$. We still denote the obtained matrix by $G$ and write it again
as in (7.16) or (7.17). Following the same argument as the one given before
theorem 7.15, we prove easily that the new encoder $G$ is still a minimal
convolutional encoder. As in the proof of theorem 7.15, we can also prove
that all sequences of $E_0(\Gamma_3)$ are now $H$-normal like the sequences of $E_0(\Gamma_1)$
and $E_0(\Gamma_2)$. We iterate this procedure for $r = 4, 5, \cdots, R$, up to obtaining

a minimal encoder $G$ having all its rows that are $H$-normal sequences. Since the matrices $G_0^u$ were not modified during this process, all spaces $E_0(G_0^u)$, $u = 1, 2, \cdots, f(R)$, remain irreducible $A$-modules.

The encoder $G$ obtained at the end of this procedure is the announced encoder that will be proved to mirror the structure of $C$. We shall call it a *canonical* encoder. We can yet represent it as in (7.16) and, in this case, we call its submatrices $G^s$ the *canonical* subencoders of $G$.

**Theorem 7.16 :** Let $G^u$ be a canonical subencoder of the canonical encoder $G$ for the $H$-code $C = E(G)$. In this case $E_0(G^u)$ is an irreducible $A$-module and $E(G^u)$ is an irreducible $\mathcal{A}$-module.

**Proof :** First we prove that $E_0(G^u)$ is an irreducible $A$-module. To prove this statement we shall prove that, for any nonzero $f$ and $g$ in $E_0(G^u)$, there exists $a \in A$ such that $g = fa$. We suppose that the canonical subencoder $G^u$ of $G$ is a submatrix of $\Gamma_r$ for some integer $r$ in $[1, R]$; thus we can write $f = \sum_{j=0}^{m_r} f_j D^j$, $g = \sum_{j=0}^{m_r} g_j D^j$. By construction $E_0(G_0^u)$ is an irreducible $A$-module so that there exists $a \in A$ such that $g_0$ is equal to $f_0 a$. We prove that $h^* := g - fa$ is zero. If it is nonzero, let us define the polynomial $h := h^* D^{-\text{del } h^*}$ and let us write it as $h = \sum_{j=0}^{m} h_j D^j$ with $h_0 \neq 0$, $h_m \neq 0$ and $m < m_r$. This sequence $h$ is in $L_m(C)$. Since $G$ is a minimal encoder it has the predictable span property. This implies $h_0 \in E_0[G_0(m)]$, where $G(m) = \sum_{j=0}^{m} G_j(m) D^j$ is the submatrix of $G$ containing its rows of degree $\leq m$. Let us show that $h_0$ has zero components in the irreducible $A$-modules $E_0(G_0^s)$ when $G^s$ is a canonical submatrix of $G(m)$. To do that, we have to remember the normalizing process leading to an encoder $G$ all rows of which are $H$-normal sequences. The word $h_0$ of $h$ is indeed the coefficient

$$g_{\text{del } h^*} - [f_{\text{del } h^*} D^{\text{del } h^*} a D^{-\text{del } h^*}]$$

of $D^{\text{del } h^*}$ in $g - fa$. On the other hand, the normalizing process is such that $g_{\text{del } h^*}$ and $f_{\text{del } h^*}$ have zero components in the $A$-modules $E_0(G_0^s)$, with $G^s$ a canonical submatrix of $G(m)$. Therefore $h_0$ is zero, since it has zero components in all $A$-modules $E_0(G_0^s)$ for which $G^s$ is a submatrix of $G(m)$. Hence the contradiction, proving that $h^*$ is zero.

To prove that $E(G^s)$ is an irreducible $A$-module we remark that $E_0(G^s)$ is an $H$-set, i.e., a finite subset of $\mathcal{F}^n$ that remains invariant under $H$. Hence, $E(G^s)$ is an $A$-module by lemma 7.2. Obviously, since $E_0(G^s)$ is an irreducible $A$-module, the $A$-module $E(G^s)$ is generated by any row of $G^s$. This $A$-module is irreducible by theorem 7.7. $\square$

Thus we have seen that, in any canonical encoder $G$ of an $H$-code $C$, any canonical subencoder $G^s$ can be specified by giving one nonzero (and $H$-normal) element of $E_0(G^s)$. We shall say that any $H$-normal sequence $g$ is $H$-irreducible when $gA$ is an irreducible $A$-module. In this case, we call $gA$ an irreducible $H$-code.

The following statements give information on the $F$-matrices $G_j^u$ in the canonical subencoders $G^u = \sum_{j=0}^{m_r} G_j^u D^j$ of $\Gamma_r$ with $1 \leq r \leq R$.

**Theorem 7.17 :** Let $\kappa_u$ be the number of rows of $G^u$. The rank $\rho_u(j)$ of a nonzero $F$-matrix $G_j^u$ is equal to $\kappa_u$.

**Proof :** Suppose that one has $1 \leq \rho_u(j) \leq \kappa_u - 1$. Then there exists in $E_0(G^u)$ a nonzero $g = \sum_{i=0}^{m_r} g_i D^i$ with $g_j \neq 0$ and a nonzero $f = \sum_{i=0}^{m_r} f_i D^i$ with $f_j = 0$. Since, by theorem 7.16, $E_0(G^u)$ is an irreducible $A$-module, there exists $a \in A$ such that $g - fa$ is zero, which is impossible if one has $g_j \neq 0$ and $f_j = 0$. Hence the contradiction. $\square$

**Corollary 7.18 :** Let $g = \sum_{i=0}^{m_r} g_i D^i$ be a row of a $\kappa_s \times n$ canonical submatrix $G^s$ of the canonical encoder $G$ of the $H$-code $C$. If $g_j$ is nonzero and satisfies $g_j D^j a = 0$, then $ga$ is zero.

**Proof :** If $g_j$ is nonzero, then by theorem 7.17 the rank of $G_j^s$ equals $\kappa_s$. Since $ga$ can be written as $\sum_{i=0}^{m_i}(\alpha \; G_i^s) D^i$ for some $\alpha \in F^{\kappa_s}$, we have $\alpha \, G_j^s = 0$. This implies $\alpha = 0$, whence $ga = 0$. $\square$

Now consider a convolutional code $C$ of length $n$ over $F$ and its automorphism group $\text{Aut}_K(C)$ where $K$ is a given subgroup of $GL(n, F)$. Suppose that there exist two different $D$-normal subgroups $H_1$ and $H_2$ of $\text{Aut}_K(C)$ that satisfy $H_1^{(0)} = H_2^{(0)}$. Consider then two normalizing processes for a minimal encoder $G$ of $C$, the first one on the basis of the property $C = CH_1$ and the second one on the basis of $C = CH_2$.

**Corollary 7.19 :** If $H_1^{(0)}$ coincides with $H_2^{(0)}$, both normalizing processes can lead to the same set of canonical submatrices $G^s$.

**Sketch of the proof :** Since $H_1^{(0)} = H_2^{(0)}$, equations such as (7.20), (7.21), (7.25) or (7.27) give identical results on the basis of $A := FH_1$ and $A := FH_2$. We omit the details. $\square$

Let us quote the following corollaries. Their proofs are elementary and omitted.

**Corollary 7.20 :** Let $C$ be a convolutional $H$-code over $F$ and let $G$ be a canonical encoder of $C$. Let $G^s = \sum_{i=0}^{m_r} G_i^s D^i$ be a canonical subencoder of $G$ such that $G_j^s$ is nonzero. In this case $E_0(G_j^s)$ is an irreducible $A$-module, with $A = FH$.

**Corollary 7.21 :** Assume that, for a given positive integer $k$, there is exactly one irreducible $A$-submodule $B$ of $F^n$ satisfying $\dim_F(B) = k$. In this case there exists only one $H$-code of dimension $k$ over $\mathcal{F}$, namely the improper convolutional code $B((D))$.

**Corollary 7.22 :** Let $g = g(D)$ be an $H$-normal sequence of degree $m$ such that $gA$ is an irreducible $A$-module, and denote $D^m g(D^{-1})$ by $\hat{g}(D)$. With $\hat{H}$, the reciprocal group of $H$ introduced in section 4.3, define $\hat{A} := F\hat{H}$ and $\hat{\mathcal{A}} := \hat{A}((D))$. The sequence $\hat{g}$ is $\hat{H}$-normal and the convolutional code $\hat{C} = \hat{g}\hat{\mathcal{A}}$ is an irreducible $\hat{\mathcal{A}}$-module, which is the reciprocal (see section 2.4) of the convolutional code $C = g\mathcal{A}$.

Let us conclude this section by giving some complementary results about building encoders from a set of $H$-normal sequences. Assume first that the polynomial $H$-normal sequence $g$ generates an irreducible $\mathcal{A}$-module $g\mathcal{A}$ and denote by $\mathcal{G}(g)$ the set of all bases of $g\mathcal{A}$ viewed as an $F$-space.

**Theorem 7.23 :** If an element $G$ of $\mathcal{G}(g)$ is a catastrophic encoder, then all elements of $\mathcal{G}(g)$ are catastrophic encoders. If one element of $\mathcal{G}$ is noncatastrophic, all elements of $\mathcal{G}(g)$ are minimal encoders.

**Proof :** Let $k$ denote the $\mathcal{F}$-dimension of $g\mathcal{A}$. Given $G \in \mathcal{G}(g)$ there exists, for any $G' \in \mathcal{G}(g)$, a $k \times k$ $F$-matrix $A'$ satisfying $G' = A'G$. If $G$ is catastrophic, i.e., if there exists $a \in \mathcal{F}^k$ satisfying $\ell(a) = \infty$ and $\ell(aG) < \infty$, then, with $a' = a(A')^{-1}$, one has obviously $\ell(a') = \infty$ and $\ell(a'G') < \infty$. $\square$

We remark that if the elements of $\mathcal{G}(g)$ are noncatastrophic, then they are minimal by theorem 7.17 and lemma 2.37.

**Theorem 7.24 :** Let $g^1, \cdots, g^r$ be polynomial $H$-normal sequences such that the $g^i\mathcal{A}$ are irreducible $\mathcal{A}$-modules the sum of which is direct. Then define

$$G = \begin{bmatrix} G^1 \\ \vdots \\ G^r \end{bmatrix},$$

with $G^i$ an arbitrary matrix of $\mathcal{G}(g^i)$. In this case the catastrophic character of $G$ depends on the set $\{g^1, \cdots, g^r\}$ but not on the particular bases $G^i$ that are chosen for the $F$-spaces $g^i A$.

**Proof :** Easy and omitted. $\square$

These two theorems permit one to speak of the catastrophic or non-catastrophic property of a set of $H$-normal sequences, independently of the basis $G^i$ of the $F$-space $g^i A$ that is used as a submatrix of $G$.

**Corollary 7.25 :** Let $g$ and $\hat{g}$ be as in Corollary 7.22, and $\mathcal{G}(g)$ be as defined before theorem 7.23. The elements $\hat{G}$ of $\mathcal{G}(\hat{g})$ are catastrophic encoders, if and only if the elements $G$ of $\mathcal{G}(g)$ are catastrophic encoders.

## 7.4   Comments

The main point of this chapter is the normalizing algorithm of section 7.3 leading to a canonical encoder $G$ satisfying theorem 7.16. As a result, to any convolutional $H$-code $C$ that is an $\mathcal{A}$-submodule of $\mathcal{S}$, there corresponds at least one set of $H$-irreducible polynomial sequences $g^s$, with $1 \leq s \leq f$, such that, by choosing a basis $G^s$ for the $F$-space $g^s A$ and by collecting these $f$ bases $G^s$ into an encoder $G$, we obtain a minimal encoder of the $H$-code $C$. The natural question is now whether the converse statement is true. If we choose $f$ $H$-irreducible sequences $g^s$ and if we construct $f$ bases $G^s$ for the $F$-spaces $g^s A$, do we obtain a minimal encoder by collecting together these $f$ bases $G^s$? Theorems 7.23 and 7.24 are first results in this direction. However, to answer this question several problems have yet to be solved. The first one is to know when the sum $\sum_s g^s A$ of the $\mathcal{A}$-modules is direct. In the solution of this problem, theorem 7.9 may be of great help. The second problem is to know when $G$ is a minimal encoder. This problem will be solved in chapter 9 in a case where the group $H$ has some specified properties.

The material presented in this chapter was developed at three successive levels of generality in [90], [30] and [31]. Roos [103] has shown that, when $H^{(0)}$ contains a cyclic subgroup with some additional properties, the normalizing process described above can be simplified.

PROBLEMS

**7.1** Let $G$ be a canonical encoder of an $H$-code $C$ and let $\Gamma_i$ be the submatrix of $G$ containing its rows of degree $m_i$ with $1 \leq i \leq R$. Prove that, for $m_s < m_r$ and $j \leq m_r - m_s$, the word $g_j^r$ of the sequence $g^r = \sum_{j=0}^{m_r} g_j^r D^j$

in $E_0[\Gamma_r]$ has zero components in the $A$-module $g_0^s A$ for $A = FH$.

**7.2** Try to extend the approach of [97] to the general case considered in this chapter. Show that such an extension needs a characterization of the right annihilator of the irreducible modules in the socle of $F^n$ viewed as an $A$-module.

# Chapter 8

# Equivalences between convolutional codes

The choice of a convolutional code for a specific application may be a difficult task. To make this task easier it would be nice to have tools to decide whether two different codes have the same performances in a specific context. The tools developed in this chapter give a partial solution to this problem and they permit one to find large classes of codes having for example the same symbol weight enumerator for their minimal encoders (see problem 3.4).

To make things clearer, we consider first a linear *block* code $C$ of length $n$ and dimension $k$ over the finite field $F$. Let $K$ be a subgroup of the group $GL(n, F)$ and, for $\phi \in K$, denote by $C\phi$ the block code obtained from $C$ if one lets act $\phi$ on the words $v$ of $C$, i.e.,

$$C\phi = \{v\phi \mid v \in C\} .$$

In the special case where one has $C\phi = C$, then, by definition, $\phi$ is an automorphism of the block code $C$.

When two block codes $C_1$ and $C_2$ satisfy $C_1\phi = C_2$ with $\phi \in K$, we say that $C_1$ and $C_2$ are $K$-equivalent block codes and we denote this property by $C_1 \overset{K}{=} C_2$. The choice of the group $K$ in which we search for an element $\phi$ satisfying $C_1\phi = C_2$, is of course an important feature of this relation $\overset{K}{=}$. If the group $K$ is too large, the $K$-equivalences will not be very meaningful. For example, with $K = GL(n, F)$ *all* linear $(n, k)$ block codes over $F$ are equivalent as can be proved by using some of the statements of section 5.4.

A useful equivalence is the one that preserves the parameters of the code that are meaningful for a specific application. If we choose the minimum symbol distance as a criterion, $K$ should be the monomial group $M_n$, and if we choose the complete composition enumerator [71] as a criterion, $K$ should be the symmetric group $S_n$.

The automorphism group $\overline{\mathrm{Aut}}_K(C\phi)$ of the block code $C\phi$ is related to the group $\overline{\mathrm{Aut}}_K(C)$, since from $C\,\overline{\mathrm{Aut}}_K(C) = C$ and $C\phi\,\overline{\mathrm{Aut}}_K(C\phi) = C\phi$ one readily obtains

$$\overline{\mathrm{Aut}}_K(C\phi) = \phi^{-1}\,\overline{\mathrm{Aut}}_K(C)\phi\,. \tag{8.1}$$

When a block code $C$ satisfies $CH = C$ for some subgroup $H$ of $K$, we may be interested in enumerating the block codes $C_i$ $(i = 1, 2, \cdots)$ that satisfy $C_i \overset{K}{=} C$ and $C_iH = C_i$. In this case, the elements $\phi_i$ of $K$ that satisfy $C\phi_i = C_i$ also have to satisfy $C\phi_iH = C\phi_i$, which is equivalent to the group inclusion property

$$\phi_i\, H\, \phi_i^{-1} \subseteq \overline{\mathrm{Aut}}_K(C)\,. \tag{8.2}$$

If $H$ coincides with $\overline{\mathrm{Aut}}_K(C)$, this condition becomes

$$\phi_i\, H\, \phi_i^{-1} = H\,, \tag{8.3}$$

which shows that the $\phi_i$ have to satisfy

$$\phi_i \in N_K(H)\,. \tag{8.4}$$

As an example, let $H$ be the cyclic group of order $n$ in its natural permutation action on the coordinates of $F^n$. A generator $x$ of $H$ satisfies

$x^n = 1$ and $x^m \neq 1$ for $0 < m < n$. To describe a linear block code $C$ over $F$ that remains invariant under $H$, we represent any $n$-tuple $(v_0, v_1, \cdots, v_{n-1})$ over $F$ by the polynomial $v(x) = \sum_{i=0}^{n-1} v_i x^i$. The block code $C$ can then be defined to be the set of polynomials of formal degree $n - 1$ that are multiples of some polynomial divisor $g(x)$ of $x^n - 1$ [87]. For $e$ prime with respect to $n$, we define $\phi(e)$ in $K = S_n$ to be the permutation of $F^n$ induced by

$$\phi(e) : F^n \rightarrow F^n : v(x) \mapsto v(x^e)$$

where $v(x^e)$ is computed using the relation $x^n = 1$. The code $C\phi(e)$ is then given by

$$C\phi(e) = \{v(x^e) \mid v(x) \in C\},$$

and it satisfies $C\phi(e)H = C\phi(e)$. Indeed, from

$$v(x)\phi(e)x^r[\phi(e)]^{-1} = [v(x^e)x^r][\phi(e)]^{-1} = v(x)x^{r/e}$$

(with $r/e$ the division modulo $n$), one sees that $\phi(e)$ is an element of $N_{S_n}(H)$.

This chapter is devoted to a generalization of these ideas to convolutional codes. The main questions we have to answer are the following ones.

**a)** How do we define equivalences between convolutional codes?

**b)** Which equivalences preserve the property that a code remain invariant under some subgroup of $K^{\mathbb{Z}}$?

In section 8.1, we define the $K^{\mathbb{Z}}$-equivalences between convolutional codes and we give some of their properties. In section 8.2, we obtain the equations to be satisfied by the $K^{\mathbb{Z}}$-equivalences that preserve some part of the automorphism group of a convolutional code. How to solve these equations is discussed in section 8.3.

## 8.1 Properties of the $K^Z$-equivalences between convolutional codes

We have discussed above the notion of $K$-equivalence between block codes. To generalize this notion to convolutional codes, we consider an arbitrary element $\phi \; : \; Z \to K \; : \; i \mapsto \phi^{(i)}$ of $K^Z$ and we let it act on $\mathcal{F}^n$ as in (4.11). This element $\phi$ of $K^Z$ transforms any convolutional code $C$ into the set $C\phi = \{v\phi \mid v \in C\}$. In this context the following questions are quite natural.

(i) When is $C\phi$ a convolutional code?

(ii) If $C\phi$ is a convolutional code, how can we derive $\mathrm{Aut}_K(C\phi)$ from $\mathrm{Aut}_K(C)$ ?

(iii) If $C\phi$ is a convolutional code, how can we obtain a canonical encoder of $C\phi$ from a canonical encoder of $C$ ?

Let us introduce a definition.

**Definition 8.1 :** Let $K$ be a subgroup of $GL(n, F)$ and let $C$ be a convolutional code over $F$. We call $\phi \in K^Z$ a *convolutional $K^Z$-equivalence* of $C$ if $C\phi$ is also a convolutional code.

The convolutional codes $C$ and $C\phi$ are called *$K^Z$-equivalent* codes, which we denote by $C \overset{K^Z}{=} C\phi$. The following theorem gives a general characterization of the convolutional $K^Z$-equivalences of a given convolutional code $C$.

**Theorem 8.2 :** Let $C$ be a convolutional code over $F$. Any $\phi \in K^Z$ is a convolutional $K^Z$-equivalence of $C$ if and only if the element $\phi^{D^{-1}}\phi^{-1} = D\phi D^{-1}\phi^{-1}$ of $K^Z$, which satisfies

$$(D\phi D^{-1}\phi^{-1})^{(i)} = \phi^{(i+1)}(\phi^{(i)})^{-1},$$

belongs to $\mathrm{Aut}_K(C)$.

**Proof :** We prove first the *if* condition, i.e., we prove that if $D\phi D^{-1}\phi^{-1}$ is in $\text{Aut}_K(C)$ then $C\phi$ is an $\mathcal{F}$-space that is generated by polynomial sequences. Obviously $C\phi$ is an $F$-space that contains any sum $\sum_{i=0}^{\infty} w_i$, with $w_i \in C\phi$, such that the $w_i$ form a progressive collection. As a consequence it follows from theorem 1.11 that $C\phi$ is an $\mathcal{F}$-space if and only if $C\phi D$ is equal to $C\phi$. By use of $CD = C$, this is equivalent to $CD\phi D^{-1}\phi^{-1} = C$, which is true by hypothesis. It remains to be shown that $C\phi$ is generated as an $\mathcal{F}$-space by polynomial sequences. To show this we prove that if $m$ is the span of $C$, then $C\phi$ coincides with $E[L_m(C\phi)]$. Consider any sequence $w$ in $C\phi$ and express the sequence $v := w\phi^{-1}$ of $C$ as

$$v = \sum_{i=r}^{\infty} v_i D^i \, ; \, v_i \in L_m(C). \tag{8.5}$$

Such an expression is always possible since $m$ is the span of $C$. From $CD = C$ and from the property $C\phi D = C\phi$ that we have proved above, it follows that $w_i := v_i D^i \phi D^{-i}$ is in $L_m(C\phi)$. Therefore, from (8.5) we write $w$ in $C\phi$ as $w = \sum_{i=r}^{\infty} w_i D^i$ with $w_i \in L_m(C\phi)$, which means by theorem 1.10 that $C\phi$ is a subset of $E[L_m(C\phi)]$. Conversely it is obvious that $C\phi$ contains $L_m(C\phi)$ as a subset and, since $C\phi$ is an $\mathcal{F}$-space, it follows that $C\phi$ also contains $E[L_m(C\phi)]$ as a subset. As a consequence we have $C\phi = E[L_m(C\phi)]$, which means that $C\phi$ is generated by polynomial sequences.

We prove now the *only if* condition, i.e., we prove that if $C$ and $C\phi$ are convolutional codes, then $D\phi D^{-1}\phi^{-1}$ is in $\text{Aut}_K(C)$. Indeed, starting from $CD = C$ and $C\phi D = C\phi$, we obtain directly $CD\phi D^{-1}\phi^{-1} = C$ . $\square$

To discuss the statement of theorem 8.2, we define

$$x := D\phi D^{-1}\phi^{-1}, \tag{8.6}$$

which is an element of $K^{\mathbb{Z}}$. Usually $x$ is called the *commutator* of $D$ and $\phi$. Writing (8.6) as $x\phi = \phi^{D^{-1}}$, we obtain $x^{(i)}\phi^{(i)} = \phi^{(i+1)}$ for all $i \in \mathbb{Z}$, which implies

$$\phi^{(i+r)} = x^{(i+r-1)}x^{(i+r-2)}\cdots x^{(i)}\phi^{(i)}\,;\ i \in \mathbb{Z},\ r \geq 1\,. \tag{8.7}$$

For $i = 0$, we obtain from (8.7)

$$\phi^{(r)} = x^{(r-1)}x^{(r-2)}\cdots x^{(0)}\phi^{(0)}\,;\ r \geq 1\,, \tag{8.8}$$

and for $i = -r$ we obtain

$$\phi^{(-r)} = (x^{(-r)})^{-1}(x^{(1-r)})^{-1}\cdots(x^{(-1)})^{-1}\phi^{(0)}\,;\ r \geq 1\,. \tag{8.9}$$

Equations (8.8) and (8.9) are used to make more explicit the conditions of theorem 8.2 characterizing a convolutional $K^{\mathbb{Z}}$-equivalence $\phi$ of a convolutional code $C$. The results of the discussion above can indeed be summarized as follows.

**Property 8.3 :** The element $\phi$ of $K^{\mathbb{Z}}$ is a convolutional $K^{\mathbb{Z}}$-equivalence of the convolutional code $C$ if and only if there exist $\phi^{(0)} \in K$ and $x \in \mathrm{Aut}_K(C)$ such that $\phi$ satisfies (8.8) and (8.9). Thus, any convolutional $K^{\mathbb{Z}}$-equivalence $\phi$ of $C$ can be written as

$$\phi = \phi(\phi^{(0)}, x)\,;\ \phi^{(0)} \in K,\ x \in \mathrm{Aut}_K(C)\,. \tag{8.10}$$

This answers question (i) above. Consider now question (ii). Suppose that $\phi$ is a convolutional $K^{\mathbb{Z}}$-equivalence of the convolutional code $C$. Obviously $C\phi(\phi^{-1}x\phi)$ equals $C\phi$ for any $x \in \mathrm{Aut}_K(C)$ and $C(\phi y\phi^{-1})$ equals $C$ for any $y \in \mathrm{Aut}_K(C\phi)$. As a result we have

$$\mathrm{Aut}_K(C\phi) = \phi^{-1}\mathrm{Aut}_K(C)\phi\,, \tag{8.11}$$

which is the convolutional analog of (8.1) and answers question (ii).

In connection with this same question (ii), let $H$ be a $D$-normal subgroup of $\mathrm{Aut}_K(C)$. Given a convolutional $K^{\mathbb{Z}}$-equivalence $\phi = \phi(\phi^{(0)}, x)$ of $C$, it is clear from (8.10) that $H^\phi := \phi^{-1}H\phi$ is a subgroup of $\mathrm{Aut}_K(C\phi)$.

The following theorem solves the problem of deciding whether $H^\phi$ is also a $D$-normal group (thus satisfying $H^{\phi D} = H^\phi$).

**Theorem 8.4 :** For some $x \in \mathrm{Aut}_K(C)$, let $\phi = \phi(\phi^{(0)}, x)$ be a convolutional $K^{\mathbb{Z}}$-equivalence of the convolutional code $C$ and let $H$ be a $D$-normal subgroup of $\mathrm{Aut}_K(C)$. In this case $H^\phi$ is $D$-normal if and only if one has

$$x \in N_{\mathrm{Aut}_K(C)}(H) . \tag{8.12}$$

**Proof :** Since $H$ equals $H^D$, the statement $H^{\phi D} = H^\phi$ is equivalent to $H^{D\phi D^{-1}\phi^{-1}} = H$, i.e., by (8.6), to $H^x = H$ (with $H^x := x^{-1}Hx$) . $\square$

Let us now consider the question (iii) stated above. We have the following theorem.

**Theorem 8.5 :** Let $C$ be an $(n, k)$ convolutional code over the field $F$, let $G$ be a minimal encoder of $C$ and let $\phi$ be a convolutional $K^{\mathbb{Z}}$-equivalence of $C$. Denote the $i^{\mathrm{th}}$ row of $G$ by $g_i$. In this case the $k \times n$ encoder $G\phi$ having $g_i\phi$ as $i^{\mathrm{th}}$ row is a minimal encoder of $C\phi$.

**Proof :** Since $\phi$ is a convolutional $K^{\mathbb{Z}}$-equivalence of $C$, the image $C\phi$ is a convolutional code, and it contains at least $k$ elements that are linearly independent over $\mathcal{F}$, namely the $k$ rows of $G\phi$. For this reason, the $\mathcal{F}$-dimension $k_\phi$ of $C\phi$ is not less than $k$. Conversely the multiplicative inverse $\phi^{-1}$ of $\phi$ is a convolutional $K^{\mathbb{Z}}$-equivalence of $C\phi$, and reversing the argument above we have $k \geq k_\phi$. Hence $k$ equals $k_\phi$, and $G\phi$ generates $C\phi$ as an $\mathcal{F}$-space.

Let us now prove that $G\phi$ is a minimal encoder. If it is not minimal let $\overline{G}$ be a minimal encoder of $C\phi$. From the first part of this proof, the encoder $\overline{G}\phi^{-1}$ generates $C$ as an $\mathcal{F}$-space. Since the sum $M$ of the degrees of its rows satisfies $M = \mu(C\phi) < \mu(C)$, this leads to the contradiction $M < \mu(C)$. Hence $G\phi$ is a minimal encoder. $\square$

Similarly, one can prove that if $G$ is a catastrophic encoder of $C$, then $G\phi$ is a catastrophic encoder of $C\phi$ (see problem 8.1).

The last theorem of this section is concerned with the action of a convolutional $K^{\mathbb{Z}}$-equivalence on the $H$-normal sequences of an $H$-code $C$.

**Theorem 8.6 :** Let $K$ be a subgroup of $GL(n, F)$ and let $H$ be a $D$-normal subgroup of $K^{\mathbb{Z}}$. Let $g$ be an $H$-normal sequence that generates the irreducible $\mathcal{A}$-module $C = g\mathcal{A}$ with $\mathcal{A} = A((D))$ and $A = FH$, and let $\phi$ be a convolutional $K^{\mathbb{Z}}$-equivalence of $C$ satisfying $D\phi D^{-1}\phi^{-1} \in N_{\mathrm{Aut}_K(C)}(H)$. In this case $g\phi$ is an $H^\phi$-normal sequence that generates $C\phi$ as an irreducible $A^\phi((D))$-module where $A^\phi = FH^\phi$. More generally let $C$ be the direct sum $\sum_{i=1}^r g_i\mathcal{A}$ of the irreducible $\mathcal{A}$-modules $C_i = g_i\mathcal{A}$ generated by the $H$-normal sequences $g_i$. If $D\phi D^{-1}\phi^{-1}$ is in $N_{\mathrm{Aut}_K(C)}(H)$, then $C\phi$ is the direct sum $\sum_{i=1}^r (g_i\phi) A^\phi((D))$ where $g_i\phi$ is $H^\phi$-normal and generates the irreducible $A^\phi((D))$-module $C_i\phi$.

**Proof :** It uses simple verification. We omit the details. □

**Corollary 8.7 :** Let $G$ be a canonical encoder of the convolutional $H$-code $C$ and let $\phi$ be a convolutional $K^{\mathbb{Z}}$-equivalence of $C$ that satisfies $D\phi D^{-1}\phi^{-1} \in N_{\mathrm{Aut}_K(C)}(H)$. In this case $G\phi$ is a canonical encoder of the $H^\phi$-code $C\phi$.

**Proof :** From theorem 8.5 we know that $G\phi$ is a minimal encoder of $C\phi$, and from theorem 8.6 we know that all its rows are $H^\phi$- normal. The proof that if $G^s$ is a canonical subencoder of $G$ then $G^s\phi$ generates ( as an $\mathcal{F}$-space) an irreducible $A^\phi((D))$-module is easy and omitted. □

## 8.2 Convolutional $K^{\mathbb{Z}}$-equivalences preserving automorphisms

How can we enumerate the $(n, k)$ convolutional codes over $F = GF(q)$ that are equivalent for some performance criterion? The main tool we use for this purpose is $K^{\mathbb{Z}}$-equivalence. Of course the group $K$ with respect to which $K^{\mathbb{Z}}$-equivalences are computed is an essential feature in that respect. To be meaningful it should be in agreement with the performance criterion we use to evaluate the codes.

To evaluate the $(n, k)$ convolutional code $C$, let us use as a first criterion the composition enumerator $\eta^G(z_\infty, z_0, \cdots, z_{q-1})$ where $G$ is any minimal encoder of $C$ (see problem 3.4). It should be clear that if we choose $K$ to be the symmetric group $S_n$ of all $n \times n$ matrices over $\{0, 1\}$ having a unique 1 in each row and in each column, then the property $C_1 \overset{K^z}{=} C_2$ will imply that the composition enumerators associated with the minimal encoders $G_1$ and $G_2$ of $C_1$ and $C_2$ are identical.

Next, if the criterion of goodness we use for $C = E(G)$ with $G$ a minimal encoder is the symbol weight enumerator $\eta^G(x)$ or the minimum symbol distance $sd(C)$, we can choose $K$ to be the monomial group $M_n$ of all $n \times n$ matrices over $F$ with a unique nonzero element in each row and in each column. The equivalence $C_1 \overset{K^z}{=} C_2$ will then imply that these two codes have the same symbol weight enumerator.

Finally if the criterion is the word distance enumerator $\eta^G(y)$ or the word minimum distance $wd(C)$, we can choose $K$ to be the group $GL(n, F)$ of all nonsingular $n \times n$ matrices over $F$.

After having discussed which groups $K$ could be used to compute meaningful $K^z$-equivalences, we investigate which of these convolutional $K^z$-equivalences preserve the automorphism group (or some part of it) of a given convolutional code. Let $H$ be a $D$-normal subgroup of $K^z$ and let $\mathcal{C}^1(H)$ be the set of all convolutional $H$-codes $C$ over $F$. The first problem we consider is to find all codes in $\mathcal{C}^1(H)$ that are $K^z$-equivalent to a given $C \in \mathcal{C}^1(H)$. To find these codes we have to find the set of all $\phi \in K^z$ that satisfy

$$D\phi D^{-1}\phi^{-1} \in \mathrm{Aut}_K(C), \qquad (8.13)$$

$$C\phi H = C\phi. \qquad (8.14)$$

The first condition guarantees that $C\phi$ is a convolutional code and the second one guarantees that this convolutional code remains invariant under $H$. It follows from the preceding section that the solutions $\phi$ to (8.13) have the form

$$\phi = \phi(\phi^{(0)}, x) \, ; \; \phi^{(0)} \in K, \; x \in \mathrm{Aut}_K(C), \qquad (8.15)$$

where the dependence of $\phi$ on its arguments $\phi^{(0)}$ and $x$ is given by (8.8) and (8.9). As for the condition (8.14), it is equivalent to $C\phi H\phi^{-1} = C$, which means

$$\phi H \phi^{-1} \subseteq \mathrm{Aut}_K(C). \qquad (8.16)$$

Thus the solutions to the system ((8.13),(8.14)) are exactly the elements of $K^{\mathbf{Z}}$ having the form (8.15) and satisfying (8.16). Hence, to list all appropriate $\phi \in K^{\mathbf{Z}}$, we should know the full automorphism group $\mathrm{Aut}_K(C)$ of $C$. For at least two reasons this is not a very nice situation. The first reason is that, for given $H$, it is easier to list the $H$-codes than to compute their full automorphism group, at least in the special but interesting cases that are treated in the following chapters. The second reason is that we would like to obtain general results on $H$-codes without having to make any further assumption about $\mathrm{Aut}_K(C)$. For these reasons we restrict our search to those $\phi$ that satisfy

$$\phi = \phi(\phi^{(0)}, x) \, ; \; \phi^{(0)} \in K, \; x \in H, \qquad (8.17)$$

$$\phi H \phi^{-1} = H. \qquad (8.18)$$

Any $\phi$ satisfying these two equations also satisfies (8.15) and (8.16) but the converse is not true. As a consequence, if we list all elements $\phi$ of $K^{\mathbf{Z}}$ that satisfy (8.17) and (8.18) we do not necessarly obtain all $\phi$ in $K^{\mathbf{Z}}$ that satisfy (8.15) and (8.16). However, this does not seem to have significant consequences in practice. For many $H$-codes $C$ considered in the following chapters, the group $H$ will indeed be the full automorphism group (with respect to the given $K$). In this case, the system (8.17),(8.18) is equivalent to the system (8.15),(8.16).

When $C_1$ and $C_2$ are two $H$-codes satisfying $C_1\phi = C_2$ for some $\phi \in K^{\mathbf{Z}}$ satisfying (8.17) and (8.18), we call this $\phi$ a convolutional $K^{\mathbf{Z}}$-equivalence (of the *first kind*) with respect to $H$ of the convolutional code $C_1$.

The second problem can be stated as follows. With the $D$-normal subgroup $H$ of $K^Z$, let us associate the set $\mathcal{P}(H)$ of all $D$-normal subgroups $H'$ of $K^Z$ having the form

$$H' = \phi^{-1} H \phi \, ; \; \phi \in K^Z \, , \tag{8.19}$$

and satisfying

$$(H')^{(0)} = H^{(0)} \, . \tag{8.20}$$

Let us then define $\mathcal{C}^2(H)$ to be the set of all convolutional codes $C$ that remain invariant under at least one group $H'$ in $\mathcal{P}(H)$. Obviously $\mathcal{C}^2(H)$ contains as subsets all sets $\mathcal{C}^1(H')$ such that $H'$ is a $D$-normal group satisfying (8.19) and (8.20). Given $C$ in $\mathcal{C}^1(H)$, the problem is now to find all codes in $\mathcal{C}^2(H)$ that are equivalent to $C$.

However, for the same two reasons as those mentioned above, the elements $x$ used to construct the convolutional $K^Z$-equivalence $\phi = \phi(\phi^{(0)}, x)$ of $C$ will be chosen in $H$ rather than in the full group $\mathrm{Aut}_K(C)$. The resulting elements $\phi$ of $K^Z$ will then be called convolutional $K^Z$-equivalences of the *second kind* (with respect to $H$) of the convolutional code $C_1$.

The next section is devoted to identifying the equivalences of these two types in more explicit terms.

## 8.3 Determination of the convolutional $K^Z$-equivalences

Let us first explain how to find the convolutional $K^Z$-equivalences of the second kind, for a given $H$-code $C$. These are the elements $\phi$ of $K^Z$ that satisfy equation (8.17) (or more explicitly the pair of equations (8.8) and (8.9), and have the property that the group $H' := \phi^{-1} H \phi$ satisfies (8.20) together with $D$-normality

$$(H')^D = H' . \tag{8.21}$$

By theorem 8.4, $H' = H^\phi$ is a $D$-normal group if and only if the element $x \in K^Z$ used to construct $\phi$ by (8.10) is in the normalizer $N_{\mathrm{Aut}_K(C)}(H)$ of $H$ in $\mathrm{Aut}_K(C)$. Since in (8.17) we require that $x$ be in the subgroup $H$ of $N_{\mathrm{Aut}_K(C)}(H)$, the group $H' = \phi^{-1}H\phi$ is automatically $D$-normal and (8.21) is satisfied. Consider now equation (8.20). By definition, it is equivalent to

$$H^{(0)} = (\phi^{(0)})^{-1} H^{(0)} \phi^{(0)}, \tag{8.22}$$

which means that $\phi^{(0)}$ is in the normalizer $N_K(H^{(0)})$ of $H^{(0)}$ in $K$. As a consequence the three statements (8.17), (8.20) and (8.21) are satisfied if and only if $\phi^{(0)}$ is in the normalizer $N_K(H^{(0)})$ of $H^{(0)}$ in $K$. Hence, if $C$ is a convolutional $H$-code, the elements $\phi \in K^Z$ that are $K^Z$-equivalences of the second kind of $C$ are given by equations (8.8) and (8.9) where $\phi^{(0)}$ is any element of $N_K(H^{(0)})$ and $x$ is any element of $H$.

In contrast with this remarkably simple result the enumeration of the convolutional $K^Z$-equivalences of the first kind is a complicated matter. We shall only consider the case where $H$ is an $\alpha$-constant subgroup of $K^Z$ (see section 5.2) for which the automorphism $\alpha$ of $H^{(0)}$ is representable by

$$\alpha : H^{(0)} \rightarrow H^{(0)} : x^{(0)} \mapsto (x^{(0)})^\alpha = \alpha_0^{-1}x^{(0)}\alpha_0, \tag{8.23}$$

for some $\alpha_0 \in N_K(H^{(0)})$ with $K$ a given subgroup of $GL(n, F)$. The requirement that $H$ be $\alpha$-constant is justified by the remark, made at the end of section 5.2, that it is reasonable to expect that the automorphism groups of convolutional codes are often $\alpha$-constant. However, the requirement that $\alpha$ be representable as in (8.23), with $\alpha_0$ an element of $K$, may be a restrictive requirement.

To link the $\alpha$-constant property of $\mathrm{Aut}_K(C)$ to the structure of the $D$-normal subgroups $H$ of $\mathrm{Aut}_K(C)$, we need the following lemma.

**Lemma 8.8 :** Any $D$-normal subgroup $H$ of an $\alpha$-constant $D$-normal subgroup $\overline{H}$ of $K^Z$ is $\alpha$-constant.

**Proof :** Since $\overline{\overline{H}}$ is $\alpha$-constant, any $x \in \overline{\overline{H}}$ satisfies

$$x^{(i)} = (x^{(0)})^{\alpha^i} ; \; i \in \mathbb{Z}, \tag{8.24}$$

with $\alpha$ an automorphism of $\overline{H}^{(0)}$. In particular all $x$ in the subgroup $H$ of $\overline{H}$ satisfy (8.24). Hence, to prove that $H$ is $\alpha$-constant, we have only to prove that the restriction to $H^{(0)}$ of an automorphism $\alpha$ of $\overline{H}^{(0)}$ is also an automorphism of $H^{(0)}$ when $H$ is a $D$-normal subgroup of $\overline{H}$. This is done as follows. For any subgroup $H$ of $\overline{H}$ we have

$$H^{(1)} = (H^{(0)})^\alpha . \tag{8.25}$$

On the other hand, since we assume that $H$ is $D$-normal we have

$$H^{(i)} = H^{(0)} ; \text{ all } i \in \mathbb{Z}. \tag{8.26}$$

From (8.25) and (8.26) we obtain $H^{(0)} = (H^{(0)})^\alpha$, which shows that $\alpha$ is an automorphism of $H^{(0)}$. $\square$

It follows from lemma 8.8 that, when $\mathrm{Aut}_K(C)$ is an $\alpha$-constant group, all $D$-normal subgroups $H$ of $\mathrm{Aut}_K(C)$ are also $\alpha$-constant. Let $H$ be such an $\alpha$-constant $D$-normal subgroup of $K^\mathbb{Z}$, with $\alpha$ satisfying (8.23). The convolutional $K^\mathbb{Z}$-equivalences of the first kind of the $H$-codes are those $\phi \in K^\mathbb{Z}$ that satisfy (8.17) and (8.18). By putting (8.23) in any $\phi$ of the form (8.17) we obtain

$$\phi^{(r)} = \alpha_0^{-r}(x^{(0)}\alpha_0)^r \phi^{(0)}, \quad \text{all } r \in \mathbb{Z} . \tag{8.27}$$

Consider now equation (8.18), meaning that $\phi$ is an element of $N_{K^\mathbb{Z}}(H)$. When $H$ is $\alpha$-constant with $\alpha$ satisfying (8.23), a useful characterization of $N_{K^\mathbb{Z}}(H)$ is given by the following theorem.

**Theorem 8.9 :** When $H$ is a $D$-normal $\alpha$-constant subgroup of $K^\mathbb{Z}$, with $\alpha$ satisfying (8.23), then $N_{K^\mathbb{Z}}(H)$ is the set of $\phi \in K^\mathbb{Z}$ satisfying the conditions

$$\phi^{(0)} \in N_K(H^{(0)}), \tag{8.28}$$

$$\phi^{(i)} = \alpha_0^{-i}\phi^{(0)}\omega_i\alpha_0^i\,;\ \omega_i \in C_K(H^{(0)}), \tag{8.29}$$

for all $i \in \mathbb{Z}$, with $C_K(H^{(0)})$ the centralizer of $H^{(0)}$ in $K$.

**Proof :** Assume first that (8.28) and (8.29) are true. For all $i \in \mathbb{Z}$ and all $x \in H$, one has

$$(\phi^{-1}x\phi)^{(i)} = \alpha_0^{-i}\omega_i^{-1}(\phi^{(0)})^{-1}(\alpha_0^i x^{(i)}\alpha_0^{-i})\phi^{(0)}\omega_i\alpha_0^i\,.$$

Using (5.3), (8.23), (8.28) and $\omega_i \in C_K(H^{(0)})$, we obtain

$$(\phi^{-1}x\phi)^{(i)} = \alpha_0^{-i}[(\phi^{(0)})^{-1}x^{(0)}\phi^{(0)}]\,\alpha_0^i\,, \tag{8.30}$$

where the bracket $y^{(0)} := [(\phi^{(0)})^{-1}x^{(0)}\phi^{(0)}]$ belongs to $H^{(0)}$. Since $H$ is $\alpha$-constant with $\alpha$ satisfying (8.23), there exists $y \in H$ such that $y^{(i)}$ equals $\alpha_0^{-i}y^{(0)}\alpha_0^i$ for all $i \in \mathbb{Z}$. Hence equation (8.30) implies that $\phi^{-1}x\phi = y$ is in $H$ for all $x \in H$, so that $\phi$ is in $N_{K^{\mathbb{Z}}}(H)$.

Assume conversely that $\phi$ is an element of $N_{K^{\mathbb{Z}}}(H)$ or, equivalently, that for all $x \in H$, the element $y := \phi^{-1}x\phi$ of $K^{\mathbb{Z}}$ belongs to $H$. Condition (8.28) is then automatically satisfied. Since $H$ is $\alpha$-constant with $\alpha$ satisfying (8.23), this means that, for all $x \in H$, there exists $y \in H$ satisfying

$$(\phi^{(i)})^{-1}(\alpha_0^{-i}x^{(0)}\alpha_0^i)\phi^{(i)} = \alpha_0^{-i}y^{(0)}\alpha_0^i\,;\ \text{all } i \in \mathbb{Z}\,. \tag{8.31}$$

We write (8.31) as

$$(\alpha_0^i\phi^{(i)}\alpha_0^{-i})^{-1}x^{(0)}(\alpha_0^i\phi^{(i)}\alpha_0^{-i}) = y^{(0)}\,;\ \text{all } i \in \mathbb{Z}\,. \tag{8.32}$$

Defining then

$$\overline{\phi}^{(i)} := \alpha_0^i\phi^{(i)}\alpha_0^{-i}\,, \tag{8.33}$$

we write (8.32) as

$$(\overline{\phi}^{(i)})^{-1}x^{(0)}(\overline{\phi}^{(i)}) = y^{(0)}\,;\ \text{all } i \in \mathbb{Z}\,.$$

This means that all $\phi$ are in $N_K(H^{(0)})$ and implies in particular (8.28). As a consequence of lemma 6.3, we have then $\overline{\phi}^{(i)} = \phi^{(0)}\omega_i$ for some $\omega_i \in C_K(H^{(0)})$. In view of (8.33) this implies (8.29). □

It follows from theorem 8.9 and from the discussion preceding it that, when $H$ is an $\alpha$-constant group and when $\alpha$ satisfies (8.23), then the system (8.17),(8.18) is equivalent to the system (8.27),(8.28),(8.29). To obtain the solutions of this last system, we express $\omega_i$ by use of (8.27) and (8.29) in the form

$$\omega_i = (\phi^{(0)})^{-1}(x^{(0)}\alpha_0)^i\phi^{(0)}\alpha_0^{-i} . \tag{8.34}$$

For $x^{(0)} \in H^{(0)}$ and for $\phi^{(0)} \in N_K(H^{(0)})$, (8.34) specifies an element $\omega(\phi^{(0)}, x^{(0)}) = (\cdots, \omega_{-1}, \omega_0, \omega_1, \cdots, \omega_i, \cdots)$ of $[GL(n, F)]^{\mathbb{Z}}$ that satisfies $\omega_0 = 1$. Only those $\omega$ that are in the subgroup $[C_K(H^{(0)})]^{\mathbb{Z}}$ of $K^{\mathbb{Z}}$ are admissible for use in (8.29). The following theorem shows that the enumeration of these $\omega$ is easier than it seems to be.

**Theorem 8.10 :** Any $\omega(\phi^{(0)}, x^{(0)})$ specified by (8.34) is an element of $[C_K(H^{(0)})]^{\mathbb{Z}}$ if and only if $\omega_1$ is in $C_K(H^{(0)})$.
**Proof :** The *only if* part is trivial. Let us prove the *if* part. From (8.34) we obtain $\omega_i = (\omega_1\alpha_0)^i\alpha_0^{-i}$ for all $i$, which is equivalent to

$$\omega_i = \prod_{s=0}^{i-1} (\alpha_0^s\omega_1\alpha_0^{-s}) , \quad \omega_{-i} = \prod_{s=1}^{i} (\alpha_0^{-s}\omega_1\alpha_0^s) ; \quad i \geq 1. \tag{8.35}$$

Since $\alpha_0$ normalizes $H^{(0)}$, it follows from lemma 6.4 that it also normalizes $C_K(H^{(0)})$. Therefore all factors in the right hand sides of (8.35) are in $C_K(H^{(0)})$ as soon as $\omega_1$ is in $C_K(H^{(0)})$. □

The two last theorems above lead to the following algorithm to compute all convolutional $K^{\mathbb{Z}}$-equivalences of the first kind of a convolutional $H$-code $C$, with $H$ an $\alpha$-constant group.

**Algorithm A8.1**

**(i)** Calculate $N_K(H^{(0)})$ and $C_K(H^{(0)})$ .

**(ii)** Obtain the solutions $\phi^{(0)} \in N_K(H^{(0)})$, $x^{(0)} \in H^{(0)}$, $\omega_1 \in C_K(H^{(0)})$ of

$$\omega_1 = (\phi^{(0)})^{-1} x^{(0)} \alpha_0 \phi^{(0)} \alpha_0^{-1} \ .$$

**(iii)** Obtain from (8.27) the convolutional $K^Z$-equivalences $\phi$ that are associated with these solutions.

## 8.4   Comments

The results of this chapter first appeared in [93] and [94]. In chapters 10 and 11, several examples will be given of the use of convolutional $K^Z$-equivalences for enumerating and analyzing nonequivalent codes. The techniques discussed in this chapter often make it feasible to enumerate all $K^Z$-inequivalent $H$-codes having specified parameters.

### PROBLEM

**8.1** Let $G$ be a catastrophic encoder of a convolutional code $C$ and let $\phi$ be a $K^Z$-equivalence of $C$. Prove that $G\phi$ is a catastrophic encoder of $C\phi$.

# Chapter 9

# Semiregular convolutional codes

Let $K$ be a subgroup of $GL(n, F)$ and let $H$ be a $D$-normal subgroup of $K^{\mathbb{Z}}$. Suppose that all elements $x$ of $H$ satisfy $x^{(i)} = (x^{(0)})^{\alpha^i}$, all $i \in \mathbb{Z}$, for some automorphism $\alpha$ of $H^{(0)}$. In chapter 5, the groups $H$ having this property were called $\alpha$-constant and it was argued that when $K$ is chosen to be the monomial group $M_n$ of degree $n$ over the finite field $F$ and when $C$ is a convolutional code of length $n$ over $F$, then the automorphism group $\mathrm{Aut}_K(C)$ is often an $\alpha$-constant subgroup of $K^{\mathbb{Z}}$. In this chapter, we consider a class of $\alpha$-constant subgroups of $K^{\mathbb{Z}}$, and we analyze the properties of the codes that remain invariant under these groups. The action of these groups on $\mathcal{F}^n$ will be called a generalized semiregular action and the codes that remain invariant under these groups will be called semiregular convolutional codes.

This chapter contains five sections. In section 9.1 we introduce the notion of a semiregular convolutional code. In section 9.2 we give the form of the normal sequences of these codes. In section 9.3 we consider the problem to verify if the encoders of semiregular convolutional codes are minimal. In section 9.4 we investigate some properties of the convolutional

$K^{\mathbb{Z}}$-equivalences between regular convolutional codes. Some comments are made in section 9.5.

## 9.1  Definition of semiregular convolutional codes

Let $F$ be a finite field and let $\mathcal{F}$ be the field of Laurent series over $F$. In the preceding chapters, the set $\mathcal{F}^n$ of $n$-tuples over $\mathcal{F}$ was endowed with the structure of a module over the algebra $\mathcal{A}$, which is the Laurent extension of some group algebra $A = FH$ with $H$ a $D$-normal subgroup of $K^{\mathbb{Z}}$ for a given subgroup $K$ of $GL(n, F)$. In this section we consider a special case of this structure, which will lead to several practical constructions of convolutional codes given in the next chapter.

We introduce this special case as follows. Let $\mathcal{H}^{(0)}$ be a multiplicative group of order $n$ and let $\alpha$ be an automorphism of $\mathcal{H}^{(0)}$. With the pair $(\mathcal{H}^{(0)}, \alpha)$ we associate the subset $\mathcal{H}$ of $(\mathcal{H}^{(0)})^{\mathbb{Z}}$ defined by

$$\mathcal{H} = \{ h \in (\mathcal{H}^{(0)})^{\mathbb{Z}} \mid h^{(i)} = (h^{(0)})^{\alpha^i}; \text{ all } i \in \mathbb{Z}, \text{ all } h^{(0)} \in \mathcal{H}^{(0)} \}. \qquad (9.1)$$

Since $\alpha$ is an automorphism of $\mathcal{H}^{(0)}$, this set $\mathcal{H}$ is a multiplicative subgroup of $(\mathcal{H}^{(0)})^{\mathbb{Z}}$. We shall use the notation $\mathcal{H} =< \mathcal{H}^{(0)}, \alpha >$ for the group (9.1).

To describe the properties of such a group $\mathcal{H} =< \mathcal{H}^{(0)}, \alpha >$, we make use of the same notations introduced in the preceding chapter for arbitrary subgroups of $[GL(n, F)]^{\mathbb{Z}}$. In particular, given $h \in \mathcal{H}$, the elements $h^D$ and $h^{D^{-1}}$ of $(\mathcal{H}^{(0)})^{\mathbb{Z}}$ are defined by

$$(h^D)^{(i)} = h^{(i-1)}, \ (h^{D^{-1}})^{(i)} = h^{(i+1)}; \text{ all } i \in \mathbb{Z} .$$

Since $\alpha$ is an automorphism of $\mathcal{H}^{(0)}$, the group $\mathcal{H}^D = \{ h^D \mid h \in \mathcal{H} \}$ coincides with $\mathcal{H}$ so that it is natural to call it an *(abstract) D-normal group*. Note that the well-defined mappings $\beta(i, j) : h^{(i)} \mapsto h^{(j)}$, $h \in \mathcal{H}$, are automorphisms of $\mathcal{H}^{(0)}$, for all $i, j \in \mathbb{Z}$.

With the group $\mathcal{H}$ given by (9.1), let us now associate a certain subgroup of $K^\mathbb{Z}$ with $K$, the symmetric group of order $n$ and degree $n$ in its natural action on $F^n$. To do that we use the elements $h_i$, $0 \leq i \leq n-1$, of the $D$-normal group $\mathcal{H} = <\mathcal{H}^{(0)}, \alpha>$ of order $n$ as labels of the $n$ entries of the elements $v$ of $F^n$. Thus we write

$$v = [v(h_0), \cdots, v(h_{n-1})] \; ; \; v(h_i) \in F \text{ for all } i. \tag{9.2}$$

This permits us to represent any $v \in F^n$ as a formal sum

$$v = \sum_{h \in \mathcal{H}} h \, v(h) , \tag{9.3}$$

which is an element of the group algebra $A = F\mathcal{H}$. As noted in subsection 6.1.2 (see (6.5)), the writing (9.3) leads to an economical representation of a permutation group isomorphic to $\mathcal{H}$ and acting on the entries $v(h_i)$ of $v$.

Let us extend the notation (9.3) to the elements of $\mathcal{F}^n$ considered as Laurent series over $F^n$. Any $v \in \mathcal{F}^n$ can be written as $v = \sum_{i=r}^{\infty} v_i D^i$ with $v_i$ in $A$. In this representation, each $n$-tuple $v_i$ is identified, via (9.3), to an element of $A = F\mathcal{H}$. As a consequence, any $v \in \mathcal{F}^n$ is identified with an element of $\mathcal{A} = A((D))$.

This notation is useful for giving an economical representation of a permutation group of order $n$ isomorphic to $\mathcal{H}$ and acting on the entries $v_i(h)$ of all words $v_i$ of any $v \in \mathcal{F}^n$. With any $\overline{h} \in \mathcal{H}$, we can indeed associate the element $r(\overline{h})$ of $K^\mathbb{Z}$. The action of $r(\overline{h})$ on $\mathcal{F}^n$ is given by

$$r(\overline{h}) : v = \sum_{i=r}^{\infty} v_i D^i \mapsto v\overline{h} = \sum_{i=r}^{\infty} v_i \, \overline{h}^{D^{-i}} D^i . \tag{9.4}$$

In (9.4) the entry $v_i(h)$ of $v_i$ is moved from the position indexed by $h$ to the position indexed by $h \, \overline{h}^{D^{-i}}$. As a consequence, the set $\{r(\overline{h}) \mid \overline{h} \in \mathcal{H}\}$ acts as a set of permutations on any set $F^n D^i$, for any $i \in \mathbb{Z}$, but this action may be different for different values of $i$. The set $\{r(\overline{h}) \mid \overline{h} \in \mathcal{H}\}$ is a group isomorphic to $\mathcal{H}$. We call it the *generalized right regular representation* of

$\mathcal{H}$ and we denote it by $GR(\mathcal{H})$.[3] The actions of the $n$ elements $r(\overline{h})$ of $GR(\mathcal{H})$ are of course representable by elements of a $D$-normal subgroup of $K^{\mathbb{Z}}$ where $K$ is the set of all $n \times n$ permutation matrices. However the representation (9.4) that makes use of the multiplication by elements of $\mathcal{H}$ is often preferable.

**Definition 9.1 :** Let $K$ be the symmetric group $S_n$ in its natural action on the $n$ coordinates of $F^n$. A *regular convolutional $\mathcal{H}$-code* $C$ of length $n$ over $F$ is a convolutional code whose automorphism group $\mathrm{Aut}_K(C)$ contains as a subgroup the generalized right regular representation $GR(\mathcal{H})$ of some $D$-normal group $\mathcal{H} = < \mathcal{H}^{(0)}, \alpha >$ of order $n$.

The next theorem specifies the structure of these regular $\mathcal{H}$-codes.

**Theorem 9.2 :** Let $\mathcal{H}$ be the group $< \mathcal{H}^{(0)}, \alpha >$, with $\alpha$ an automorphism of the group $\mathcal{H}^{(0)}$ of order $n$, and let $\mathcal{A}$ be the algebra $A((D))$ with $A = F\mathcal{H}$. A convolutional code $C$ over $F$ is a regular $\mathcal{H}$-code if and only if it is a right ideal in $\mathcal{A}$, generated as an $\mathcal{F}$-space by a set of finite length sequences.

**Sketch of the proof :** Any right ideal in $\mathcal{A}$ remains invariant under the group $\mathcal{H}$. Moreover, when considered as an $\mathcal{F}$-space, any right ideal in $\mathcal{A}$ generated by a set of finite length sequences, admits a basis of polynomials over $F^n$. By definition, such an ideal is a regular convolutional $\mathcal{H}$-code. Conversely any regular convolutional $\mathcal{H}$-code is an ideal in $\mathcal{A}$. Indeed, for any $v \in C$ and any $a \in \mathcal{A}$, the $\mathcal{H}$-code property and the $\mathcal{F}$-space property imply that $va$ is also in $C$. $\square$

Consider the group $\mathcal{H} = < \mathcal{H}^{(0)}, \alpha >$, with $\alpha$ an automorphism of the finite group $\mathcal{H}^{(0)}$ of order $n$. On the basis of theorem 9.2, we choose to represent $\mathcal{F}^n$ by $\mathcal{A}$, and we represent the regular $\mathcal{H}$-codes as ideals in $\mathcal{A}$. It is easy to verify that in this representation, the irreducible $GR(\mathcal{H})$-codes are nothing but the minimal ideals in $\mathcal{A}$.

---

[3] A generalized left regular representation $GL(\mathcal{H})$ can be defined in a similar way.

We consider now the set $\mathcal{A}^t$ of $t$-tuples over $\mathcal{A}$ and, for any $v = (v^1, \cdots, v^t)$ in $\mathcal{A}^t$ and any $a$ in $\mathcal{A}$, we define the multiplication

$$va = (v^1 a, \cdots, v^t a) . \tag{9.5}$$

This multiplication is in agreement with definition 6.8, so that it endows $\mathcal{A}^t$ with the structure of a right $\mathcal{A}$-module. Since theorem 9.2 gives a necessary and sufficient condition for a code to be a regular $\mathcal{H}$-code, we can generalize the concept of regular $\mathcal{H}$-code by weakening the condition of this theorem.

**Definition 9.3 :** Assume that $\mathcal{H} = < \mathcal{H}^{(0)}, \alpha >$ is a group of order $n_0$. A *semiregular convolutional $\mathcal{H}$-code $C$* of length $n = n_0 t$ is defined to be a right $\mathcal{A}$-submodule of $\mathcal{A}^t$ that is generated by finite length sequences.

To represent an element $v$ of $\mathcal{F}^n$ as an element $(v^1, \cdots, v^t)$ of $\mathcal{A}^t$ (and in particular $v \in F^n$ as an element of $A^t$) is justified by the possibility of representing in this case the action of some permutation group isomorphic to $\mathcal{H}$ by a simple multiplication. We call this permutation group, considered as a subgroup of $K^{\mathbb{Z}}$, with $K$ the symmetric group of degree $n$, a *generalized right semiregular representation* of the group $\mathcal{H}$, and we denote it by $GR^{[t]}(\mathcal{H})$. The reader will convince himself that the use of the multiplication by elements of $\mathcal{H}$ to denote the action of $H = GR^{[t]}(\mathcal{H})$ preserves the structural properties of $\mathcal{F}^n$ and $F^n$. In particular, any irreducible module generated by $v \in F^n$ over the algebra $FH$ becomes an irreducible module over $A = F\mathcal{H}$, generated by the representation $(v^1, \cdots, v^t)$ of $v$ as an element of $A^t$. Thus the socle of $F^n$ viewed as an $FH$-module becomes the socle of $A^t$ viewed as an $A$-module.

It turns out that the concepts of regular and semiregular codes are very useful when one tries to construct specific convolutional codes. In particular the problem of enumerating these codes has a nice and practical solution. Indeed it follows from the results of chapter 7 that the enumeration of the convolutional $H$-codes, with $H$ a $D$-normal subgroup of $K^{\mathbb{Z}}$, is not far from being solved if we have an algorithm for enumerating the $H$-normal sequences. In the next section, the form of the $H$-normal sequences will be made explicit when $H$ is a generalized right semiregular representation $GR^{[t]}(\mathcal{H})$ of some group $\mathcal{H} =< \mathcal{H}^{(0)}, \alpha >$. This often makes the enumeration problem quite tractable. In section 9.3, we shall see that it is often easy to verify whether a well defined encoder that is naturally associated with a $GR^{[t]}(\mathcal{H})$-normal sequence is catastrophic or not. All these features make regular and semiregular $\mathcal{H}$-codes very attractive.

To conclude this section, we show how some codes considered in the preceding chapters can be put in the present setting. First let $C$ be the $(7,3)$ convolutional code over $F = GF(2)$ considered in subsection 4.2.2. To represent it by use of the tools above, we define $\mathcal{H}^{(0)}$ to be the cyclic group of order 7 generated by the element $\xi$ satisfying $\xi^7 = 1$, and we choose $\alpha$ to be the automorphism of $\mathcal{H}^{(0)}$ defined by $(\xi^r)^\alpha = \xi^{-r}$ for $r = 0, 1, \cdots, 6$. The group $\mathcal{H} =< \mathcal{H}^{(0)}, \alpha >$ is nothing but the cyclic group of order 7 represented as a subgroup of $(\mathcal{H}^{(0)})^Z$ and generated by the element $x$ that satisfies $x^{(i)} = \xi$ for even $i$ and $x^{(i)} = \xi^{-1}$ for odd $i$. For $1 \le i \le 7$, we index the $i^{th}$ column of the encoder $G$ of $C$ by $x^{i-1}$, and we represent the three rows of $G$ by

$$g_1 = (1 + x + x^2 + x^4) + (1 + x^3 + x^5 + x^6)D + (x + x^2 + x^3 + x^5)D^2,$$

$$g_2 = (x + x^2 + x^3 + x^5) + (x^2 + x^4 + x^5 + x^6)D + (x^2 + x^3 + x^4 + x^6)D^2,$$

$$g_3 = (x^2 + x^3 + x^4 + x^6) + (x + x^3 + x^4 + x^5)D + (1 + x^3 + x^4 + x^5)D^2.$$

Since $x^{D^r} = x^{(-1)^r}$, we have $g_2 = g_1 x$ and $g_3 = g_1 x^2$, and we can verify that any nonzero $g$ in $E_0(G)$ is equal to $g_1 x^i$ for some $i$ in $[0, 6]$. For example, $g_1 + g_2$ is equal to $g_1 x^3$. Conversely any sequence $g_1 x^i$ is in $E_0(G)$. As a consequence, any $v \in E(G)$ can be written as

$$v = g_1 \sum_{i=r}^{\infty} x^{b(i)} D^i; \quad b(i) \in \{0, 1, \cdots, 6, \infty\},$$

where $x^\infty$ is interpreted as zero. Conversely any such expression, and more generally any expression such as $g_1(\sum_{i=r}^{\infty} a_i D^i)$, $a_i \in F\mathcal{H}$, represents a sequence of $E(G)$. The reader may verify that this gives to $C = E(G)$ the structure of an ideal in the algebra $\mathcal{A} = A((D))$ with $A = F\mathcal{H}$.

A similar treatment is possible for the binary code specified by the encoder $G$ given in (4.23). Let $\mathcal{H}^{(0)}$ be the Abelian group of order 9 defined by the generators $\xi$ and $\eta$ and the rules $\xi^3 = \eta^3 = 1$, $\xi\eta = \eta\xi$. To define $\mathcal{H}$ we use the automorphism $\alpha$ of $\mathcal{H}^{(0)}$ specified by $\xi^\alpha = \xi$, $\eta^\alpha = \eta\xi^2$. The subgroup $\mathcal{H} = <\mathcal{H}^{(0)}, \alpha>$ of $(\mathcal{H}^{(0)})^Z$ has order 9 and it is generated by the elements $x$ and $y$ of $(\mathcal{H}^{(0)})^Z$ that satisfy $x^{(i)} = \xi$ for all $i \in Z$, and $y^{(i)} = \eta$ for $i \equiv 0(3)$, $y^{(i)} = \eta\xi^2$ for $i \equiv 1(3)$, $y^{(i)} = \eta\xi$ for $i \equiv 2(3)$. Indexing then the columns of $G$ by the elements of $\mathcal{H}$ in the order $(1, x, x^2, y, yx, yx^2, y^2, y^2x, y^2x^2)$, we represent the two rows of $G$ by

$$g_1 = (1 + yx + y^2x^2)(x + x^2) + (1 + y + y^2)(x + x^2)D,$$

$$g_2 = (1 + yx + y^2x^2)(1 + x^2) + (1 + y + y^2)(1 + x^2)D.$$

Let us remark that we have, for example, $g_2 = g_1 x$, $g_1 + g_2 = g_1 x^2$, $g_1 y = g_1 x^2$. More generally the space $E_0(G)$ is nothing but the set $g_1 A$ with $A = F\mathcal{H}$ and the space $E(G)$ is nothing but the set $g_1 \mathcal{A}$ with $\mathcal{A} = A((D))$. This gives $E(G)$ the stucture of a minimal ideal in $\mathcal{A}$.

## 9.2 Normal sequences in semiregular convolutional codes

Let $\mathcal{H}$ be $<\mathcal{H}^{(0)}, \alpha>$, with $\mathcal{H}^{(0)}$ a group of order $n_0$ and $\alpha$ an automorphism of $\mathcal{H}^{(0)}$. The action of the automorphism $\alpha$ of $\mathcal{H}^{(0)}$ can be extended as follows. First we consider $\alpha$ as being an automorphism of $\mathcal{H} = <\mathcal{H}^{(0)}, \alpha>$ by defining $h^\alpha$, for all $h \in \mathcal{H}$, to be the element of $\mathcal{H}$ satisfying $(h^\alpha)^{(i)} = (h^{(i)})^\alpha$. Hence we have $(h^\alpha)^D = h$. Then we consider $\alpha$ as being also an automorphism of $A = F\mathcal{H}$ and of $A^t$. Given

$v = \sum_{h \in \mathcal{H}} h\, v(h)$ with $v(h) \in F$, we define $v^{\alpha} := \sum_{h \in \mathcal{H}} h^{\alpha}\, v(h)$ and, given $v = (v^1, \cdots, v^t)$ in $A^t$, we define $v^{\alpha} := [(v^1)^{\alpha}, \cdots, (v^t)^{\alpha}]$. For $v$ in $A^t$, $a$ in $A$ and $s$ in $\mathbb{Z}$, we had $v\, D^s\, a = v\, a^{D^{-s}} D^s$. This last expression can now be written as $v\, a^{\alpha^s} D^s$.

Then choosing $n$ to be a multiple of $n_0$ and writing $n = n_0 t$, we can represent any element $v$ of $\mathcal{F}^n$ as a $t$-tuple over the Laurent extension $\mathcal{A}$ of $A = F\mathcal{H}$. In this case, definition 7.5 becomes the following

**Definition 9.4 :** The element $v = \sum_{j=0}^{\infty} v_j D^j$ (with $v_j$ in $A^t$), of $\mathcal{A}^t$ is called an $\mathcal{H}$-normal sequence if it satisfies

$$v_0 a = 0 \;\Rightarrow\; va = 0 \,; \quad \text{all } a \in A \,. \tag{9.6}$$

When a distinction is necessary, an $\mathcal{H}$-normal sequence will also be called a $GR(\mathcal{H})$-normal sequence or a $GR^{[t]}(\mathcal{H})$-normal sequence. The form of these $\mathcal{H}$-normal sequences is characterized by the next theorem.

**Theorem 9.5 :** Let $\mathcal{H}$ be $< \mathcal{H}^{(0)}, \alpha >$ and let $v = \sum_{j=0}^{\infty} v_j D^j$ be a sequence over $A^t = (F\mathcal{H})^t$, with $v_j = (v_j^1, \cdots, v_j^t)$, $v_j^i \in A$, and $v_0 \neq 0$. In this case, $v$ satisfies (9.6) if and only if, for every $j \geq 0$, the vector $v_j$ satisfies $v_j^T = (B_j v_0^T)^{\alpha^j}$, where $B_j$ is a $t \times t$ matrix over $A$, $v_j^T$ denotes the transpose of $v_j$, and $B_0$ is the identity matrix $I_t$.

**Proof :** Let us first prove that any $v$ having this form satisfies (9.6). From $v\, D^j\, a = v\, a^{\alpha^j} D^j$ we have indeed $(va)^T = \sum_{j=0}^{\infty} [(B_j v_0^T) a]^{\alpha^j} D^j$, which makes it obvious that $v_0 a = 0$ implies $va = 0$.

Assume conversely that $v = \sum_{j=0}^{\infty} v_j D^j$ satisfies (9.6). Since $\alpha$ is an automorphism of $A$, the sequence $v$ can be expressed as $v = \sum_{j=0}^{\infty} \phi_j^{\alpha^j} D^j$ with $\phi_j = [(v_j^1)^{\alpha^{-j}}, \cdots, (v_j^t)^{\alpha^{-j}}]$. In this case we have $va = \sum_{j=0}^{\infty} (\phi_j a)^{\alpha^j} D^j$. Denote now by $U$ the sum of the $t$ left ideals $A v_0^i$ with $1 \leq i \leq t$. The statement $v_0 a = 0$ implies that $a$ is any element of the right annihilator $r(U)$ of $U$ (see section 6.2). Moreover the implication $v_0 a = 0 \Rightarrow \phi_j a = 0$, for all $j$, means that the components $(v_j^i)^{\alpha^{-j}}$, $1 \leq i \leq t$, of $\phi_j$ are arbitrary elements in the left annihilator $\ell[r(U)]$ of $r(U)$. Since $A$ is a finite group algebra, it follows from theorem 6.21 that $\ell[r(U)]$ equals $U$ which means that the components of $\phi_j$ can be written in the form $(v_j^i)^{\alpha^{-j}} = \sum_{k=1}^t b_{j,i}^k v_0^k$. Equivalently, $\phi_j^T$ is representable as $B_j v_0^T$, with $B_j$ the $t \times t$ matrix over $A$ having $b_{j,i}^k$ as $(i,k)$ entry. Thus, $v_j^T = (\phi_j^T)^{\alpha^j}$ can be written as $v_j^T = (B_j v_0^T)^{\alpha^j}$. The choice $B_0 = I_t$ is obviously possible. $\square$

Having obtained the general form of $\mathcal{H}$-normal sequences, we still need the form of $\mathcal{H}$-normal sequences that generate *irreducible* $\mathcal{A}$-submodules of $\mathcal{A}^t$. To obtain this form we write again any element $v$ of $\mathcal{A}^t$ having delay zero as

$$v = \sum_{j=0}^{\infty} \phi_j^{\alpha^j} D^j , \qquad (9.7)$$

where $\phi_j = (\phi_j^1, \cdots, \phi_j^t)$ is an element of $A^t$.

**Theorem 9.6 :** Let $\mathcal{H}$ be $< \mathcal{H}^{(0)}, \alpha >$ and let $v$ be represented as in (9.7). The sequence $v$ is $\mathcal{H}$-normal and it generates an irreducible right $\mathcal{A}$-module if and only if $\phi_0$ is nonzero and all $\phi_j^i$ are in the same left ideal $A\phi_0^i$ in $A$, where $\phi_0^i$ is a nonzero component of $\phi_0$, that generates an irreducible right $A$-module $\phi_0^i A$.

**Proof :** Assume that $\phi_0$ is nonzero and all $\phi_j^i$ are in the same left ideal $A\phi_0^i$ in $A$. The sequence $v$ written as in (9.7) is then obviously $\mathcal{H}$-normal. The proof that it generates an irreducible $\mathcal{A}$-module follows from theorem 7.7 and from the property stated in problem 9.5 that $\phi_0 A$ is an irreducible $A$-module.

Conversely, assume that $v$ is $\mathcal{H}$-normal and $v\mathcal{A}$ is an irreducible right $\mathcal{A}$-module. By theorem 7.7, $\phi_0 A$ is then an irreducible $A$-module. As a consequence, $\phi_0^i \neq 0$ and $\phi_0^i a = 0$ imply $va = 0$ for all $a$ in the group algebra $A$, and hence also $\phi_j^k a = 0$ for all $j$ and all $k$, because otherwise $vaA$ would be a proper submodule of $vA$. Define $U := A\phi_0^i$ for some nonzero $\phi_0^i$. As in the proof of theorem 9.5, the property $\phi_0^i a = 0$ implies $a \in r(U)$. Moreover, since all nonzero $\phi_j^k$ have to satisfy $\phi_j^k a = 0$, they are in $\ell[r(U)]$. Since $A$ is a finite group algebra, it follows from theorem 6.21 that $\ell[r(U)]$ coincides with $U$, which proves that $\phi_j^k$ is in $A\phi_0^i$, for all $j$ and all $k$. $\square$

Let now $H$ be a $D$-normal subgroup of $[GL(n,F)]^{\mathbb{Z}}$, let $A$ be $FH$ and let $\mathcal{A}$ be the Laurent extension $A((D))$ of $A$. In chapter 7, it was proved that any locally reducible convolutional $H$-code is a direct sum of irreducible $\mathcal{A}$-modules. Since all nonzero polynomial sequences of the lowest degree in an irreducible $\mathcal{A}$-module are necessarily $H$-normal, the enumeration of $H$-codes amounts more or less to the enumeration of all sets of $H$-normal sequences that generate irreducible $\mathcal{A}$-modules the sum of which is direct. Further comments on this question are made in section 9.5. When $H$ is a generalized right semiregular representation $GR^{[t]}(\mathcal{H})$ with $\mathcal{H} = <\mathcal{H}^{(0)}, \alpha>$, the preceding theorem solves this enumeration problem. To check the direct sum condition we can use theorem 7.9.

## 9.3   Minimal encoders for regular Abelian codes

Let $K$ be a subgroup of $GL(n,F)$, let $H$ be a $D$-normal subgroup of $K^{\mathbb{Z}}$, and define $A := FH$ and $\mathcal{A} := A((D))$. We suppose that we have a set of $H$-normal sequences

$$v^s = \sum_{j=0}^{m_s} v_j^s \, D^j \, ; \quad v_j^s \in F^n, \quad 1 \leq s \leq u \, ,$$

such that the $\mathcal{A}$-modules $v_0^s A$ are irreducible and their sum is direct. In this case we know from theorems 7.7 and 7.9 that the $\mathcal{A}$-modules $v^s \mathcal{A}$ are also irreducible and that their sum is also direct. With each $v^s$ we associate a basis $G^s$ of the irreducible (see corollary 7.8) $\mathcal{A}$-module $v^s \mathcal{A}$ viewed as an $F$-space and we define $G$ to be the matrix obtained by superposition of all these bases $G^s$, i.e.,

$$
G := \begin{bmatrix} G^1 \\ \vdots \\ G^s \\ \vdots \\ G^u \end{bmatrix}. \tag{9.8}
$$

It follows from the results of chapter 7 that any convolutional $H$-code has a minimal encoder $G$ of the form (9.8). However, the converse is not true. An encoder of the form (9.8) is not necessarily minimal and it may even be catastrophic, as it will appear in this section.

To check that a $k \times n$ encoder $G$ such as (9.8) is minimal, we have to verify that it satisfies conditions (2.8), (2.9) and (2.10). The first two conditions can be verified with relative ease by use of theorem 2.16. The verification of (2.10) is more difficult and it may necessitate computation of the g.c.d. of all $k \times k$ minors of $G$. In the particular case where $C = E(G)$ remains invariant under a generalized right regular representation $GR(\mathcal{H})$, a rather direct verification is possible. To describe this verification we need the following tools.

Let $F$ be a finite field, let $\mathcal{H}^{(0)}$ be a group of order $n$ and let $\alpha$ be an automorphism of $\mathcal{H}^{(0)}$. Define $\mathcal{H} :=< \mathcal{H}^{(0)}, \alpha >$, $A := F\mathcal{H}$ and $\mathcal{A} := A((D))$. We shall need to divide the minimal ideals in $A$ as follows. Picking any minimal right ideal $I$ in $A$, we first construct the set

$$
Q(I) = \{I_r := I^{\alpha^r} \mid r = 0, 1, \cdots\},
$$

where $I^\alpha$ denotes the set $\{a^\alpha \mid a \in I\}$. Taking any minimal right ideal $I'$ in $A$ that is not in $Q(I)$, we list also the set

$$
Q(I') = \{I'_r := (I')^{\alpha^r} \mid r = 0, 1, \cdots\},
$$

and we continue in this way until all minimal ideals in $A$ have been exhausted.

To prove the results of this section we make three hypotheses. We assume first that $\mathcal{H}^{(0)}$ is an *Abelian* group. In this case $\mathcal{H} = <\mathcal{H}^{(0)}, \alpha >$ is also an Abelian group. Next, we assume that the order $n$ of $\mathcal{H}$ and $\mathcal{H}^{(0)}$ is relatively prime with $|F|$, which makes $A = F\mathcal{H}$ a finite semi-simple ring or algebra. In this case it follows from problem 6.4 that there is a *unique* (up to ordering) decomposition $A = I_1 \oplus I_2 \oplus \cdots \oplus I_q$ of $A$ as a direct sum of minimal ideals. In other words any minimal ideal $I$ in $A$ is some $I_i$ occurring in the decomposition above. Moreover each of these minimal ideals is generated by an idempotent: $I_i = e_i A$ with $e_i^2 = e_i$. From these two first hypotheses (and from theorem 9.6) it follows that the polynomial $GR(\mathcal{H})$-normal sequences that generate minimal ideals in $\mathcal{A}$ (or equivalently irreducible $\mathcal{A}$-modules) have the form

$$v = \sum_{i=0}^{m} (v_0 a_i)^{\alpha^i} D^i \, ; \, v_0 a_0 \neq 0 \, , \tag{9.9}$$

where $v_0 A \, (= A v_0)$ is a minimal ideal in $A$ (hence an irreducible $A$-module) and where $v_0 a_i A \neq \{0\}$ implies $v_0 a_i A = v_0 A$. Since all ideals in $A$ contain an idempotent generator, there exists $a$ in $A$ such that $v_0 a_0 a = e$ with $e$ the idempotent generator of the minimal ideal $v_0 A$. Since $v\mathcal{A}$ is also a minimal ideal (in $\mathcal{A}$) and since $va$ is nonzero, $va\mathcal{A}$ is equal to $v\mathcal{A}$, and thus we can replace $v$ by $va$ as a generator of $v\mathcal{A}$. Denoting once more this new sequence by $v$ we see that it has the form

$$v = \sum_{i=0}^{m} (ea_i)^{\alpha^i} D^i \, ; \, e^2 = e \, , \tag{9.10}$$

where $a_0$ is 1, $a_i$ is in $A$ and $eA$ is a minimal ideal in $A$. This minimal ideal $eA$ contains a primitive element $ea$, for some $a$ in $A$. In other words, we have $eA = \{e, \, ea, \, (ea)^2, \cdots \}$. Thus we can write (9.10) as

$$v = \sum_{i=0}^{m} [(ea)^{\phi(i)}]^{\alpha^i} D^i \, ; \, \phi(0) = 0 \, , \, \phi(i) \in \mathbb{N} \cup \{\infty\} \, . \tag{9.11}$$

where $\mathbb{N}$ denotes the set of nonnegative integers, and where we have used the conventions $(ea)^0 = e$ and $(ea)^\infty = 0$. Thus any minimal ideal in $\mathcal{A}$ containing a finite length nonzero sequence also contains an $\mathcal{H}$-normal sequence $v$ of the form (9.11). We shall say in this case that the $\mathcal{H}$-normal sequence $v$ is associated with the idempotent $e$ .

It follows from a remark made after theorem 6.18 that, since $\mathcal{H}$ is an Abelian group, the minimal ideal $eA = Ae = eAe$ in $A$ is isomorphic to a finite field $F^*$. In this isomorphism the idempotent $e$ is mapped on 1 and $ea$ is mapped on a primitive element of $F^*$.

Before explaining how we can verify if an encoder $G$ satisfies (2.10), we have yet to state the third and last hypothesis announced above. We first state this condition in the particular case where the encoder $G$ contains only one canonical subencoder associated with a sequence $v$ of the form (9.11). This condition turns on the idempotent $e$ in (9.11) and it is expressed by

$$e^{\alpha^\ell} = e \quad \Rightarrow \quad (ea)^{\alpha^\ell} = ea , \tag{9.12}$$

where $ea$ is some primitive element of $eA$. It implies that $f^{\alpha^\ell}$ coincides with $f$ for all elements $f$ of $I = eA$. The smallest value of $\ell$ such that $e^{\alpha^\ell}$ equals $e$ we denote it by $\ell_0$.

When we build a $k \times n$ basis $G = \sum_{i=0}^m G_i D^i$ for the irreducible $A$-module $vA$ viewed as an $F$-space, then, for each $i$, either $G_i$ is the zero matrix or it generates $I^{\alpha^i}$ as an $F$-space. In particular the rank of a nonzero $G_i$ is equal to $k$ by theorem 9.17. If, for $t \in \mathbb{Z}$, the $F$-matrices $G_i$ and $G_{i+t\ell_0}$ are nonzero matrices, it follows from the definition of $\ell_0$ that they generate the same $F$-space. (This is not true in general if $\mathcal{H}$ is not Abelian. In this case the form (9.10) of the $\mathcal{H}$-normal sequences is $v = \sum(a_ie)^{\alpha^i} D^i$ with $e^2 = e$, and two different nonzero elements $a_1e$ and $a_2e$ in $Ae$ may be such that $a_1eA$ does not coincide with $a_2eA$.) Conversely if $i - j$ is not divisible by $\ell_0$, $G_i$ and $G_j$ generate row spaces having only the zero vector in common. Moreover, since the decomposition of $A$ as a direct sum of minimal ideals is unique, it follows that if a nonzero word $v_i$

in $E_0(G_i)$ can be expressed as $v_i = v_i^* + v_j$ for some nonzero $v_j$ in $E_0(G_j)$, then $v_i^*$ is in $E_0(G_i)$ and $j - i$ is divisible by $\ell_0$.

Now denote $u \in \mathcal{F}^k$ explicitly by $u(D) = \sum_{i=r}^{\infty} u_i D^i$, with $u_i \in F^k$. As a result of the preceding remarks, $G$ will satisfy the condition $\ell[u(D)] = \infty \Rightarrow \ell[u(D)G] = \infty$ (which is nothing but (2.10)) if and only if it satisfies

$$\ell[u(D^{\ell_0})] = \infty \quad \Rightarrow \quad \ell[u(D^{\ell_0})G] = \infty .  \tag{9.13}$$

The equivalence between (2.10) and (9.13) depends on the property that a nonzero $G_i$ generates $I^{\alpha^i}$ as a row space over $F$, but not on the property that $E(G)$ is an ideal in $\mathcal{A}$. It turns out that, when $C = E(G)$ is a minimal ideal in $\mathcal{A}$, this extra structure leads to a new formulation of (9.13) and to a practical criterion to verify that $G$ satisfies (2.10). Write the right hand side of (9.13) as $\sum_i (u_i G) D^{i\ell_0}$. Since $E_0(G)$ is the right $A$-module $vA$, one has $u_i G = v w_i$ for some $w_i$ in $A$. Hence (9.13) can be rewritten as

$$\ell[w(D^{\ell_0})] = \infty \quad \Rightarrow \quad \ell[v(D)w(D^{\ell_0})] = \infty ,  \tag{9.14}$$

where $v(D)$ is the unique element of $E_0(G)$ having the form (9.11) and where $w(D)$ is any element of $e\mathcal{A}$. We write $w(D^{\ell_0})$ as

$$w(D^{\ell_0}) = \sum_{i=r}^{\infty} (ea)^{\omega(i)} D^{i\ell_0} ; \; \omega(i) \in \mathbb{N} \cup \{\infty\} .$$

In (9.14), $v(D)$ plays the role of $G$ in (9.13) and $w(D^{\ell_0})$ plays the role of $u(D^{\ell_0})$ in (9.13). Since the minimal idempotent $e$ satisfies (9.12), we can rewrite the polynomial $GR(\mathcal{H})$-normal sequence $v(D)$ given in (9.11) as

$$v(D) = \sum_{j=0}^{\ell_0-1} [\bar{v}_j(D^{\ell_0})]^{\alpha^j} D^j,$$

with

$$\bar{v}_j(D^{\ell_0}) = \sum_{i \equiv j(\ell_0)} (ea)^{\phi(i)} D^{i-j}.  \tag{9.15}$$

This leads to

$$v(D)w(D^{\ell_0}) = \sum_{j=0}^{\ell_0-1} [\overline{v}_j(D^{\ell_0})w(D^{\ell_0})]^{\alpha^j} D^j . \qquad (9.16)$$

In (9.15), $\overline{v}_j(D)$ is a polynomial in $D$ over the minimal ideal $I = Ae = eA$ isomorphic to some finite field $F^*$. Moreover (9.12) and (9.16) make it clear that (9.14) is satisfied if and only if the $1 \times \ell_0$ polynomial matrix $\boldsymbol{\Gamma}$ over $F^*$ defined as

$$\boldsymbol{\Gamma} = [\overline{v}_0(D), \cdots, \overline{v}_j(D), \cdots, \overline{v}_{\ell_0-1}(D)] \qquad (9.17)$$

is a noncatastrophic encoder, i.e., if and only if the g.c.d. of the polynomials $\overline{v}_j(D)$ over $F^*$ is an element of $F^*$. We state this result as a theorem.

**Theorem 9.7 :** Let $A = F\mathcal{H}$ satisfy the three conditions above. Let $v$ be an $\mathcal{H}$-normal polynomial over $A$ and let $G$ be a basis of $vA$ viewed as an $F$-space. In this case, the matrix $G$, considered as a basis of the $\mathcal{F}$-space $C = vA$, is noncatastrophic if and only if the associated encoder $\boldsymbol{\Gamma}$ over $F^*$ is noncatastrophic.

We illustrate this theorem by the following example. Let $\mathcal{H}^{(0)}$ be the cyclic group of order 7 consisting of the set of powers of $\xi$ endowed with the relation $\xi^7 = 1$, and let $\alpha$ be the automorphism of $\mathcal{H}^{(0)}$ specified by $(\xi^r)^\alpha = \xi^{-r}$ for $0 \leq r \leq 6$. Define then $\mathcal{H} := < \mathcal{H}^{(0)}, \alpha >$. It is a group isomorphic to $\mathcal{H}^{(0)}$ and it is generated by the element $x$ of $(\mathcal{H}^{(0)})^{\mathbb{Z}}$ that satisfies $x^{(i)} = \xi$ for even $i$ and $x^{(i)} = \xi^{-1}$ for odd $i$. Then choose $F$ to be $GF(2)$. The element $e = 1 + x + x^2 + x^4$ is idempotent in $A = F\mathcal{H}$ and it generates the minimal ideal $I = eA = Ae$, which is isomorphic to $F^* = GF(2^3)$. The pair $(e, \alpha)$ satisfies (9.12) and the corresponding value of $\ell_0$ is 2. Consider now the two $\mathcal{H}$-normal sequences

$$v_1 = e + (ex)^\alpha D + (ex)^{\alpha^2} D^2 + (ex^2)^{\alpha^3} D^3,$$

$$v_2 = e + (ex)^\alpha D + (ex)^{\alpha^2} D^2 + (ex^3)^{\alpha^3} D^3,$$

and denote by $\beta$ the primitive element of $F^* = GF(2^3)$ on which the primitive element $ex$ of $I$ is mapped by an isomorphism between $I$ and $F^*$. Following the steps leading to (9.17) we can associate with $v_1$ and $v_2$ the polynomial matrices $\Gamma_1$ and $\Gamma_2$ over $F^*$ given by $\Gamma_1 = [1 + \beta D, \ \beta + \beta^2 D]$ and $\Gamma_2 = [1 + \beta D, \ \beta + \beta^3 D]$. Obviously the encoder $\Gamma_1$ is catastrophic and the encoder $\Gamma_2$ is not. This proves that any basis $G_1$ of the $F$-space $v_1 A$ is a catastrophic convolutional encoder and that any basis $G_2$ of the $F$-space $v_2 A$ is a noncatastrophic convolutional encoder.

Let us now generalize the discussion above to the case where $C$ is a direct sum $\sum_s v^s A$ of several minimal ideals $v^s A$ with $v^s = \sum_{j=0}^{m_1} v_j^s D^j$ an $\mathcal{H}$-normal sequence. As above, we assume that $\mathcal{H}$ is an Abelian group and that $A = F\mathcal{H}$ is a semisimple algebra. The appropriate extension of the third condition is described below.

For any $v^s$ we construct a basis $G^s$ of the $F$-space $v^s A$ and we obtain $G$ as in (9.8). How can we verify that this encoder $G$ satisfies (2.10)? We proceed as follows. Given any minimal ideal $I$ in $A$ we denote by $\sigma(I)$ the set of integers $s$ for which the ideal $v_0^s A$ is in $Q(I)$ and we denote by $G_I$ the submatrix of $G$ obtained by juxtaposition of the matrices $G^s$ for $s \in \sigma(I)$.

**Lemma 9.8 :** The encoder $G$ satisfies (2.10) if and only if all its subencoders $G_I$ satisfy (2.10).

**Proof :** It follows from problem 6.4 that, when $\mathcal{H}$ is a finite Abelian group and $A = F\mathcal{H}$ is a semi-simple algebra, there is a unique decomposition of $A$ as a direct sum of minimal ideals. This property implies that any nonzero word appearing in the $\mathcal{F}$-row space of $G_I$ cannot appear in the $\mathcal{F}$-row space of $G_J$ for $J \notin Q(I)$. As a consequence the subencoders $G_I$ can be tested independently with respect to (2.10). $\square$

Let us now describe the third condition in the general case where $G$ contains more than one canonical subencoder. Given a nonempty submatrix $G_I$ of $G$ associated with the minimal ideal $I$ in $A$, we denote by $e_I$

the generating idempotent of $I$. Condition (9.12) is now replaced by the assumption that, for all $I$ such that $G_I$ is a nonempty submatrix of $G$, the idempotent $e := e_I$ satisfies (9.12). Due to the isomorphism between all minimal ideals $I^{\alpha^r}$ (for $r = 0, 1, \cdots$) of $Q(I)$, the element $e_I^{\alpha^r}$ will satisfy (9.12) if and only if $e_I$ satisfies (9.12). With each $Q(I)$, and thus with each $G_I$, we associate an integer $\ell_0(I) \geq 1$ which is defined to be the smallest $\ell \geq 1$ such that $e_I^{\alpha^\ell} = e_I$. Of course, for $I \neq J$, it may happen that $\ell_0(I)$ is not equal to $\ell_0(J)$.

Let us denote by $C_I$ the $\mathcal{F}$-row space of $G_I$. Thus one has

$$C_I = \sum_{s \in \sigma(I)} v^s A,$$

where the $v^s$ can be written as

$$v^s = \sum_{i=0}^{m_s} [(ea)^{\phi_s(i)}]^{\alpha^{i+\mu(s)}} D^i ; \quad \phi_s(i) \in \mathbb{N} \cup \{\infty\} . \tag{9.18}$$

In (9.18), $ea$ is a primitive element in $I = eA$, the range of $\mu(s)$ is the set $\{0, 1, \cdots, \ell_0(I) - 1\}$, and $s_1 \neq s_2$ implies $\mu(s_1) \neq \mu(s_2)$. Moreover we have $v^s A = v^s(e^{\alpha^{\mu(s)}} A)$ for all $s$. Let $w^s$ be any element of $e^{\alpha^{\mu(s)}} A$ and let $\mathbf{w}$ be a row $|\sigma(I)|$-tuple of $|\sigma(I)|$ sequences $w^s$ with $s \in \sigma(I)$. Condition (2.10) can be rewritten for the matrix $G_I$ as

$$\ell(\mathbf{w}) = \infty \quad \Rightarrow \quad \ell\left(\sum_{s \in \sigma(I)} v^s w^s\right) = \infty . \tag{9.19}$$

The same reasoning that shows the equivalence of (2.10), (9.13) and (9.14) when $G$ generates a minimal ideal, can now be used to prove for the matrix $G_I$ the equivalence of (2.10), (9.19) and

$$\ell[\mathbf{w}(D^{\ell_0(I)})] = \infty \quad \Rightarrow \quad \ell\left[\sum_{s \in \sigma(I)} v^s(D) D^{\mu(s)} w^s(D^{\ell_0(I)})\right] = \infty . \tag{9.20}$$

We can now expand $v^s(D) D^{\mu(s)}$ as

$$v^s(D) D^{\mu(s)} = \sum_{j=0}^{\ell_0(I)-1} [\bar{v}_j^s(D^{\ell_0(I)})]^{\alpha^j} D^j,$$

with

$$\overline{v}_j^s(D^{\ell_0(I)}) = \sum_{i+\mu(s)\equiv j(\ell_0(I))} (ea)^{\phi_s(i)} D^{i+\mu(s)-j} . \qquad (9.21)$$

The elements $\overline{v}_j^s(D)$ are polynomials in $D$ over the minimal ideal $I = eA = Ae$ that is isomorphic to some finite field $F^*$. Let now $\xi(s)$ be any one-to-one mapping of $\sigma(I)$ to $\{1, 2, \cdots, | \sigma(I) |\}$ and let $\boldsymbol{\Gamma}_I$ be the $| \sigma(I) | \times \ell_0(I)$ polynomial matrix over $F^*$ having $\overline{v}_j^s(D)$ in position $(\xi(s), j)$. Taking into account the isomorphism between the minimal ideals $e^{\alpha^j}A$, for $0 \leq j \leq \ell_0(I) - 1$, and the finite field $F^*$, we see that (9.20) can be rewritten as

$$\ell(\mathbf{w}) = \infty \quad \Rightarrow \quad \ell(\mathbf{w}\boldsymbol{\Gamma}_I) = \infty; \quad \text{all } \mathbf{w} \in [F^*((D))]^k . \qquad (9.22)$$

The conclusion is stated in the following theorem.

**Theorem 9.9 :** The encoder $G_I$ over $F^*$ is noncatastrophic if and only if the corresponding encoder $\boldsymbol{\Gamma}_I$ over $F^*$ is noncatastrophic i.e., if and only if if the g.c.d. of its $|\sigma(I)| \times |\sigma(I)|$ minors is in $F^*$.

We give now an example to illustrate this theorem. Let $\mathcal{H}^{(0)}$ be the elementary Abelian group of order 9, i.e., the set of monomials $\xi^i \eta^j$, $0 \leq i, j \leq 2$, with the relations $\xi^3 = \eta^3 = 1$ and $\xi\eta = \eta\xi$. Let $\alpha$ be the automorphism of $\mathcal{H}^{(0)}$ specified by $\xi^\alpha = \xi$, $\eta^\alpha = \xi\eta$, and define $\mathcal{H} :=< \mathcal{H}^{(0)}, \alpha >$. We denote by $x^i y^j$ the element $z$ of $\mathcal{H}$ that satisfies $z^{(0)} = \xi^i \eta^j$, $0 \leq i, j \leq 2$. For $F = GF(2)$ the algebra $A = F\mathcal{H}$ is semi-simple. Its dimension as an $F$-space is equal to 9, and it contains 4 minimal ideals of dimension 2 and one minimal ideal of dimension 1. One of the ideals of dimension 2 is generated by the idempotent $e = (x + x^2)(1 + y + y^2)$ which satisfies $e^\alpha = (x + x^2)(1 + xy + x^2 y^2)$, $e^{\alpha^2} = (x + x^2)(1 + xy^2 + x^2 y)$ and $e^{\alpha^3} = e$. The pair $(e, \alpha)$ satisfies (9.12) and the corresponding value of $\ell_0$ is 3.

Consider now the two $\mathcal{H}$-normal sequences

$$v_1 = e + e^\alpha D + e^{\alpha^2} D^2 + (ex)^{\alpha^3} D^3 + e^{\alpha^4} D^4,$$

$$v_2 = e^\alpha + (ex)^{\alpha^2} D + (ex^2)^{\alpha^3} D^2 + e^{\alpha^4} D^3 + (ex)^{\alpha^6} D^5.$$

The convolutional code $C = v_1\mathcal{A} \oplus v_2\mathcal{A}$ is a $(9,4)$ binary convolutional code. Let $G_i$ be a $2 \times 9$ basis for $v_i A$ viewed as an $F$-space. To verify that the encoder

$$G = \begin{pmatrix} G_1 \\ G_2 \end{pmatrix}$$

is noncatastrophic, we can compute the g.c.d. of the 126 $4 \times 4$ minors of $G$. A faster method is to apply theorem 9.9. We first check that $G$ equals $G_I$ with $I = eA$. Applying the method above we associate with $G$ the $2 \times 3$ encoder $\boldsymbol{\Gamma}_I$ over $F^* = GF(2^2)$ defined as

$$\boldsymbol{\Gamma}_I = \begin{bmatrix} 1 + \beta D & 1 + D & 1 \\ \beta^2 D + \beta D^2 & 1 + D & \beta \end{bmatrix},$$

where $\beta$ is a primitive element of $F^*$. The three $2 \times 2$ minors of $\boldsymbol{\Gamma}_I$ are $(1 + D)(1 + D + \beta D^2)$, $\beta + \beta D^2$ and $\beta^2 + \beta^2 D$, and their g.c.d. is $1 + D$. As a consequence $\boldsymbol{\Gamma}_I$ and $G$ are both catastrophic.

The method described in this section can also be used to check whether encoders of semiregular codes are catastrophic or not. We omit the details (see problem 9.1).

## 9.4 Convolutional $K^{\mathbb{Z}}$-equivalences for regular codes

Let $\mathcal{H}^{(0)}$ be a finite group of order $n$ and let $\alpha$ be an automorphism of $\mathcal{H}^{(0)}$. Define $\mathcal{H}_\alpha :=< \mathcal{H}^{(0)}, \alpha >$. Then consider a regular convolutional $\mathcal{H}_\alpha$-code $C$ over the finite field $F$. The code $C$ remains invariant under the generalized regular representation $GR(\mathcal{H}_\alpha)$ of the group $\mathcal{H}_\alpha$ or, equivalently, $C$ is an ideal in the algebra $\mathcal{A}_\alpha := A_\alpha((D))$ with $A_\alpha := F\mathcal{H}_\alpha$. Thus the code $C$ is an element of the set $C^2(GR(\mathcal{H}_\alpha))$ of all codes that remain invariant under a $D$-normal group $H$ having the property that $H^{(0)}$ is the right regular representation $R(\mathcal{H}^{(0)})$ of the group $\mathcal{H}^{(0)}$ (see chapter 6).

Now let $K$ be the symmetric group of order $n!$ and degree $n$ in its natural action on $F^n$. We consider the following general question. What can be said about the convolutional codes in $\mathcal{C}^2(GR(\mathcal{H}_\alpha))$ that are $K^{\mathbb{Z}}$-equivalent to a given regular $\mathcal{H}_\alpha$-code $C$? We prove that any element $\phi$ of $K^{\mathbb{Z}}$, which is a convolutional $K^{\mathbb{Z}}$-equivalence of the second kind of $C$ (with respect to $GR(\mathcal{H}_\alpha)$), has the property that $C\phi$ is a regular $\mathcal{H}_\beta$-code for $\mathcal{H}_\beta = <\mathcal{H}^{(0)}, \beta>$, with $\beta$ an automorphism of $\mathcal{H}^{(0)}$. Indeed, since $\phi$ is a convolutional $K^{\mathbb{Z}}$-equivalence of the second kind of the regular $\mathcal{H}_\alpha$-code $C$, it can be expressed as $\phi = \phi(\phi^{(0)}, x)$ for some $\phi^{(0)} \in N_K[R(\mathcal{H}^{(0)})]$ and some $x \in GR(\mathcal{H}_\alpha) \subseteq \mathrm{Aut}_K(C)$. As a consequence $x$ is in the normalizer $N_{\mathrm{Aut}_K(C)}[GR(\mathcal{H}_\alpha)]$ so that, by theorem 8.4, $\phi^{-1}GR(\mathcal{H}_\alpha)\phi$ is a $D$-normal group. Moreover it is isomorphic to the group $GR(\mathcal{H}_\alpha)$. In particular we remark that $1^{\mathbb{Z}}$ is the only element $x$ of $\phi^{-1}GR(\mathcal{H}_\alpha)\phi$ satisfying $x^{(i)} = 1$ for at least one $i \in \mathbb{Z}$. Denote now by $m$ the span of the code $C$ and by $\Sigma$ the sliding subgroup of $K^{m+1}$ that is used to construct $\mathrm{Aut}_K(C\phi)$. It follows from the remark above that $\Sigma$ is a systematic sliding group (see subsection 4.1.3). Applying theorem 4.14, we see that $\phi^{-1}GR(\mathcal{H}_\alpha)\phi$ is nothing but the group $GR(\mathcal{H}_\beta)$ where $\beta$ is some automorphism of $\mathcal{H}^{(0)}$. This proves the following result.

**Theorem 9.10 :** Let $C$ be a regular convolutional $\mathcal{H}_\alpha$-code with $\mathcal{H}_\alpha$ given by $<\mathcal{H}^{(0)}, \alpha>$ and let $\phi$ be a convolutional $K^{\mathbb{Z}}$-equivalence of the second kind of $C$. In this case there exists an automorphism $\beta$ of $\mathcal{H}^{(0)}$ such that $C\phi$ is a regular $\mathcal{H}_\beta$-code for $\mathcal{H}_\beta = <\mathcal{H}^{(0)}, \beta>$.

## 9.5   Comments

The material of this chapter originates from [30, 93]. As mentioned above, when $\mathcal{H} = <\mathcal{H}^{(0)}, \alpha>$ is Abelian and $A = F\mathcal{H}$ is semi-simple, the results of section 9.3 may be used to enumerate all $GR(\mathcal{H}^{(0)})$-codes over $F$ of span at most equal to a given $m$, at least in the case where condition (9.12), or its extended version described later, is satisfied.

The method is as follows. We write $A = e_1 A \oplus e_2 A \oplus \cdots \oplus e_q A$, where the $e_i$ are all minimal idempotents of $A$. Then we enumerate all polynomials $v$ of degree $\leq m$ over $A$ having the form (9.11) with $e$ equal to any of the $q$ minimal idempotents $e_s$ considered above. For each $s$ in $[1, q]$, we choose at most one sequence $v^s$ (of the form (9.11)) associated with the idempotent $e_s$. Assuming that we have chosen $u (\leq q)$ such sequences $v^s$, we construct then an encoder $G$ having the form (9.8). The verification that $G$ is noncatastrophic is made as explained in section 9.3. If $G$ is catastrophic, this means that $E(G)$ can be generated by another encoder $G'$ having the same form but satisfying $M(G') < M(G)$. If it is noncatastrophic and if theorem 2.16 shows that it satisfies (2.8) and (2.9), then it is minimal by theorem 2.24. It is not difficult to prove that two minimal encoders $G_1$ and $G_2$ constructed along the lines above by use of two different sets of $\mathcal{H}$-normal sequences having the form (9.11) are such that $E(G_1)$ does not coincide with $E(G_2)$. Hence, having listed all encoders of span $\leq m$ with the structure above and deleting then all nonminimal encoders, we are left with encoders of distinct codes. Conversely it follows from the results of chapter 7 that, in this way, we have obtained at least one minimal encoder for all $\mathcal{H}$-codes of span $\leq m$ over $F$.

## PROBLEMS

**9.1** Generalize the results of section 9.3 to the encoders of semiregular Abelian codes.

**9.2** Let $F$ be a finite field. Given $\mathcal{H} := < \mathcal{H}^{(0)}, \alpha >$, with $\alpha$ an automorphism of the group $\mathcal{H}^{(0)}$ of order $n$, consider a convolutional code $C$ that is a minimal ideal in $A((D))$ with $A = F\mathcal{H}$ and $(|F|, n) = 1$. Let then $v$ be an $\mathcal{H}$-normal sequence of $C$. Prove that a basis $G$ of the $F$-space $vA$ is a minimal encoder of $C$ if and only if $C$ does not contain any nonzero sequence $w$ satisfying $\ell(w) < \ell(v)$.

**9.3** If the $\mathcal{H}$-normal sequence $v$ of problem 9.2 does not satisfy $\ell(v) \leq \ell(w)$ for all nonzero sequences $w$ of $C$, prove that the encoder $G$ is catastrophic and show how to obtain $a \in A((D))$ that satisfies $\ell(a) = \infty$ and $\ell(av) < \ell(v)$.

Hint : Use the fact that a minimal ideal in $A$ is isomorphic to a field.

**9.4** Under the hypotheses of problem 9.2, express $F^n$ as a direct sum $I_1 \oplus I_2 \oplus \cdots \oplus I_r$ of minimal ideals $I_s$ in $A = F\mathcal{H}$. Prove that, if no two different minimal ideals $I_s$ and $I_t$ have the same dimension as vector spaces over $F$, then no ideal in $A((D))$ is a proper convolutional code.

**9.5** Let $H$ be a finite group. Define $A := FH$ with $F$ a finite field, and consider the element $\phi = (\phi^1, \cdots, \phi^t)$ of $A^t$. Assume that $\phi^1 A$ is a minimal ideal in $A$ ( or equivalently an irreducible $A$-module) and that, for $j \geq 2$, one has $\phi^j = a_j \phi^1$ with $a_j$ in $A$. Prove that $\phi A$ is an irreducible $A$-module.

Hint : If $\phi A$ is not irreducible, there must exist $a \in A$ such that $(\phi a)A$ is an irreducible $A$-module. Moreover $\phi^1 a$ cannot be zero since this would imply $\phi a = 0$, so that $\phi a A$ would be the zero module. However from $\phi^1 a \neq 0$ and from the property of $\phi^1 A$ to be an irreducible (nonzero) module, there exists $b \in A$ satisfying $\phi^1 ab = \phi^1$. Hence $\phi^j ab = \phi^j$ holds true for all $j$, which implies $(\phi a)b = \phi$. This shows that $\phi$ is an element of $\phi a A$, which implies $(\phi a)A \supseteq \phi A$. Combined with $\phi A \subseteq (\phi a)A$, this implies $\phi a A = \phi A$, which shows that $\phi A$ is irreducible.

# Chapter 10

# Construction of codes with a large symbol distance

In this and the following chapter, we show how the tools we have developed can be used to construct convolutional codes having good distance properties. In this chapter we try to discover regular $\mathcal{H}_\alpha$-codes $C$ of short length $n$ having a large symbol distance $sd(C)$. In our search for such codes we shall make use of the convolutional $K^{\mathbb{Z}}$-equivalences that are adapted to this problem. Since the criterion is the minimum symbol distance, we can choose $K$ to be the monomial group $M_n$ or any of its subgroups. When the alphabet $F$ is $GF(2)$, this group $M_n$ coincides with the symmetric group $S_n$ of order $n!$ and degree $n$ in its natural action on $F^n$.

In chapter 9 we associated with each automorphism $\alpha$ of the group $\mathcal{H}^{(0)}$ of order $n$, the subgroup $\mathcal{H}_\alpha :=< \mathcal{H}^{(0)}, \alpha >$ of $(\mathcal{H}^{(0)})^{\mathbb{Z}}$, the group algebra $A_\alpha := F\mathcal{H}_\alpha$ and the Laurent extension $\mathcal{A}_\alpha := A_\alpha((D))$ which is also an algebra. By definition, the number of different algebras $\mathcal{A}_\alpha$ constructed on the basis of $\mathcal{H}^{(0)}$ is equal to $|\mathrm{Aut}(\mathcal{H}^{(0)})|$. When we enumerate the codes that are ideals in these algebras $\mathcal{A}_\alpha$, we would like to take into account the fact that, for different automorphisms $\alpha$ and $\beta$ of $\mathcal{H}^{(0)}$, there may exist $K^{\mathbb{Z}}$-equivalences of the second kind transforming any ideal in $\mathcal{A}_\beta$ into an ideal in $\mathcal{A}_\alpha$, and other $K^{\mathbb{Z}}$-equivalences achieving the converse transformation. In this case, with $K = M_n$, all convolutional codes that are ideals in $\mathcal{A}_\beta$ will have, among other properties, the same minimum symbol distance as some corresponding ideals in $\mathcal{A}_\alpha$. Therefore, within $K^{\mathbb{Z}}$-equivalences, it will thus be sufficient to analyze the ideals in $\mathcal{A}_\alpha$.

The present chapter contains four sections where we successively consider binary codes of length 6, 7, 9 and 10, a fifth section devoted to codes over larger alphabets and a sixth one devoted to long binary codes.

## 10.1   Codes of length 6

In this section we analyze a class of binary convolutional codes having length 6 and dimension 2. Let $\mathcal{H}^{(0)}$ be the dihedral group $D_3$ (of order 6) generated by the elements $\lambda$ and $\mu$ satisfying $\lambda^3 = \mu^2 = (\lambda\mu)^2 = 1$. In subsection 6.1.2 we have described the groups $\mathrm{Aut}(\mathcal{H}^{(0)})$, $R(\mathcal{H}^{(0)})$ and $L(\mathcal{H}^{(0)})$, considered as permutation groups acting on the elements of $\mathcal{H}^{(0)}$. In particular the group $\mathrm{Aut}(\mathcal{H}^{(0)})$ was shown to have order 6. As a consequence there exist six different groups $\mathcal{H}_\alpha =< \mathcal{H}^{(0)}, \alpha >$ and hence six different generalized regular permutation groups $GR(\mathcal{H}_\alpha)$. It follows from theorem 9.2 that a code that remains invariant under $GR(\mathcal{H})$ can be seen as an ideal in the algebra $\mathcal{A}_\alpha := A_\alpha((D))$ with $A_\alpha = F\mathcal{H}_\alpha$. Among these groups $\mathcal{H}_\alpha$ we are particularly interested in the group $\mathcal{H}_1 =< \mathcal{H}^{(0)}, 1 >$ associated with the identity automorphism $\alpha = 1$. This group is

$$\mathcal{H}_1 = \{\nu^{\mathbb{Z}} \mid \nu \in \mathcal{H}^{(0)}\}, \tag{10.1}$$

where $\nu^{\mathbb{Z}}$ denotes the element of $(\mathcal{H}^{(0)})^{\mathbb{Z}}$ having all its components equal to $\nu$.

Let $K$ be $S(\mathcal{H}^{(0)})$, i.e., the symmetric group $S_6$ of order 6! permutating the six elements of $\mathcal{H}^{(0)}$. We represent this action by the multiplicative notation $h^{(0)} \mapsto h^{(0)}\phi^{(0)} \in \mathcal{H}^{(0)}$ for $\phi^{(0)} \in K$. We then let act any element

$\phi$ of $K^{\mathbb{Z}}$ on $(\mathcal{H}^{(0)})^{\mathbb{Z}}$ according to the rule $h \mapsto h\phi$ where $h\phi$ denotes the element of $(\mathcal{H}^{(0)})^{\mathbb{Z}}$ specified by $(h\phi)^{(i)} = h^{(i)}\phi^{(i)}$ for all $i \in \mathbb{Z}$.

If $h$ is in the subgroup $\mathcal{H}_{\alpha} = < \mathcal{H}^{(0)}, \alpha >$ of $(\mathcal{H}^{(0)})^{\mathbb{Z}}$ and if $\phi$ is an element of $K^{\mathbb{Z}}$, then $h\phi$ will generally not be in any of the six groups $\mathcal{H}_{\beta}$ with $\beta$ in $\mathrm{Aut}(\mathcal{H}^{(0)})$. However if $C$ is a regular $\mathcal{H}_{\alpha}$-code, and if $\phi$ is one of its convolutional $K^{\mathbb{Z}}$-equivalences of the second kind with respect to $(GR(\mathcal{H}_{\alpha}))^{(0)} = R(\mathcal{H}^{(0)})$, then it follows from theorem 9.10 that there exists $\beta \in \mathrm{Aut}(\mathcal{H}^{(0)})$ such that $C\phi$ is a regular convolutional $\mathcal{H}_{\beta}$-code. Thus it is interesting to know which are the groups $\mathcal{H}_{\alpha}$ such that any regular $\mathcal{H}_{\alpha}$-code $C$ is transformed into a regular convolutional $\mathcal{H}_1$-code $C\phi_{\alpha}$ by means of some well chosen element $\phi_{\alpha}$ of $K^{\mathbb{Z}}$. The following theorem gives the answer to this question.

**Theorem 10.1 :** For all $\alpha \in \mathrm{Aut}(\mathcal{H}^{(0)})$ there exists $\phi_{\alpha} \in K^{\mathbb{Z}}$ that transforms any convolutional regular $\mathcal{H}_{\alpha}$-code $C$ into a convolutional regular $\mathcal{H}_1$-code $C\phi_{\alpha}$.

**Proof :** Any $\mathcal{H}_{\alpha}$-code $C$ remains invariant under the subgroup $GR(\mathcal{H}_{\alpha})$ of $K^{\mathbb{Z}}$. Hence, for any $\phi_{\alpha}^{(0)} \in N_K(\mathcal{H}^{(0)})$ and any $x \in GR(\mathcal{H}_{\alpha})$, the element $\phi_{\alpha} = \phi_{\alpha}(\phi_{\alpha}^{(0)}, x)$ given by (8.8) and (8.9) transforms $C$ in another convolutional code $C\phi_{\alpha} = C\phi_{\alpha}D$ that is $K^{\mathbb{Z}}$-equivalent to $C$, and has the property that $\mathrm{Aut}_K(C\phi_{\alpha})$ contains $\phi_{\alpha}^{-1}GR(\mathcal{H}_{\alpha})\phi_{\alpha}$ as a subgroup. As a consequence if one has

$$\phi_{\alpha}^{-1}GR(\mathcal{H}_{\alpha})\phi_{\alpha} = GR(\mathcal{H}_1), \qquad (10.2)$$

then $C\phi$ remains invariant by $GR(\mathcal{H}_1)$. Thus to achieve the proof we have only to give, for all $\alpha \in \mathrm{Aut}_K(\mathcal{H}^{(0)})$, an element $\phi_{\alpha} \in K^{\mathbb{Z}}$ that is a convolutional $K^{\mathbb{Z}}$-equivalence of all $\mathcal{H}_{\alpha}$-codes and transforms them into $\mathcal{H}_1$-codes. In other words we have to list six elements $\phi_{\alpha} = \phi_{\alpha}(\phi_{\alpha}^{(0)}, x)$ with $\alpha \in \mathrm{Aut}(\mathcal{H}^{(0)})$ and $x \in GR(\mathcal{H}^{(0)})$ such that $\phi_{\alpha}^{-1}GR(\mathcal{H}_{\alpha})\phi_{\alpha}$ equals $GR(\mathcal{H}_1)$. Here follow these elements $\phi_{\alpha} = \phi_{\alpha}(\phi_{\alpha}^{(0)}, x)$. For all of them, $\phi_{\alpha}^{(0)}$ is the identity.

For $\alpha$ specified by $\lambda^\alpha = \lambda^2$ and $\mu^\alpha = \mu$, the group $\mathcal{H}_\alpha$ contains $\mu^Z$ and we verify that the element $\phi_\alpha = \phi_\alpha[1, r(\mu^Z)]$ of $K^Z$, where $r(h)$ is the element of $GR(\mathcal{H}_\alpha)$ associated with $h \in \mathcal{H}_\alpha$, satisfies

$$\phi_\alpha^{-1} GR(\mathcal{H}_\alpha) \phi_\alpha = GR(\mathcal{H}_1). \tag{10.3}$$

For $\alpha$ specified by $\lambda^\alpha = \lambda$, $\mu^\alpha = \mu\lambda$, the group $\mathcal{H}_\alpha$ contains $\lambda^Z$ and $\phi_\alpha[1, r(\lambda^Z)]$ satisfies (10.3). For $\alpha$ specified by $\lambda^\alpha = \lambda^2$, $\mu^\alpha = \mu\lambda$, the group $\mathcal{H}_\alpha$ contains $(\mu\lambda^2)^Z$ and $\phi_\alpha[1, r((\mu\lambda^2)^Z)]$ satisfies (10.3). For $\alpha$ specified by $\lambda^\alpha = \lambda$, $\mu^\alpha = \mu\lambda^2$, the group $\mathcal{H}_\alpha$ contains $(\lambda^2)^Z$ and $\phi_\alpha[1, r((\lambda^2)^Z)]$ satisfies (10.3). For $\alpha$ specified by $\lambda^\alpha = \lambda^2$, $\mu^\alpha = \mu\lambda^2$, the group $\mathcal{H}_\alpha$ contains $(\mu\lambda)^Z$ and $\phi_\alpha[1, r((\mu\lambda)^Z)]$ satisfies (10.3). $\square$

It follows from theorem 10.1 that any regular $\mathcal{H}_\alpha$-code $C$ can be transformed by means of a suitable $\phi_\alpha \in K^Z$ into another convolutional code $C\phi_\alpha$ that is a regular $\mathcal{H}_1$-code. Using theorem 9.2 we conclude that any convolutional code that is an ideal in $\mathcal{A}_\alpha$ is $K^Z$-equivalent to some ideal in $\mathcal{A}_1$. Since $\phi_\alpha$ is in $K^Z$ and since $K$ acts by permutation on $F^6$, the symbol weight properties of $C$ are preserved under the action of $\phi_\alpha$. For this reason, we can restrict our search for good $\mathcal{H}_\alpha$-codes to the case $\alpha = 1$.

Let us now go back to the structure of $A_1 = F\mathcal{H}_1$, which is of course the same as the structure of $F\mathcal{H}_1^{(0)}$ represented in figure 6.1. (In this figure $\mathcal{H}_1^{(0)}$ was denoted by $\mathcal{H}$.) It appears that $A_1$ contains three minimal right ideals of dimension 2 that are generated respectively by

$$e_1 = 1 + \lambda^2 + \mu\lambda + \mu\lambda^2 \, ,$$

$$e_2 = 1 + \lambda + \mu\lambda + \mu\lambda^2 \, ,$$

$$e_3 = 1 + \lambda^2 + \mu + \mu\lambda^2 \, ,$$

where $\mu^i \lambda^j$ is used in place of $(\mu^i \lambda^j)^Z$ for simplicity. The same convention is used throughout this section. The three elements $e_i$ are idempotent. Note that $e_1\lambda$, $e_2\lambda^2$ and $e_3\lambda$ are also idempotent.

The form of $\mathcal{H}_1$-normal sequences $g$ having $e_k$ as initial word, with $1 \leq k \leq 3$, is given by

$$g = \sum_{j=0}^{m} \lambda^{b(j)} e_k D^j \,;\ b(0) = 0\,,\ b(j) \in \{0, 1, 2, \infty\}\,, \tag{10.4}$$

where $\lambda^\infty$ is used to denote 0. Since $\lambda^b e_k A_1$ is a minimal ideal, the ideals $g A_1$ are minimal, and, since the $F$-dimension of $e_k A_1$ is 2, it follows from theorem 7.6 and corollary 2.20 that the $\mathcal{F}$-dimension of $g A_1$ is also equal to 2. The form (10.4) results from theorem 9.6 and from the fact that, for $1 \leq k \leq 3$, the ideal $A_1 e_k$ is nothing but the set $\{\lambda^b e_k \mid b \in \{0, 1, 2, \infty\}\}$. The sequences of type (10.4) in which $b(0)$ is 1 or 2 do not generate new ideals $g A_1$. Indeed the ideal $\lambda^b e_k A_1$ in $A_1$ coincides, for all $b \in \{0, 1, 2\}$ and all $k \in \{1, 2, 3\}$, with another ideal $e_i A_1$ for some $i \in \{1, 2, 3\}$. As a consequence, any sequence $g'$ of the form (10.4) with $b(0) = 1$ or $b(0) = 2$ has the property that $g' A_1$ (and hence also $g' \mathcal{A}_1$) contains a sequence $g$ of the form (10.4). In passing we remark that the three ideals $\lambda^b e_k A_1$ for fixed $k$ and for $b = 0, 1, 2$ are nothing but the three ideals $e_k A_1$ for $k = 1, 2, 3$.

Going back to (10.4), we classify the $\mathcal{H}_1$-codes generated by $g$ according to which idempotent $e_k$ is used to define $g$, and we denote by $\mathcal{D}_k$ the set of $\mathcal{H}_1$-codes $g \mathcal{A}_1$ such that $e_k$ is the idempotent used in (10.4) to construct $g$.

**Theorem 10.2 :** For $k = 2$ and for $k = 3$, any code in the set $\mathcal{D}_k$, is $K^{\mathbb{Z}}$-equivalent to some code in the set $\mathcal{D}_1$.

**Proof :** It follows from table 6.4 (where $\mathcal{H}^{(0)}$ is denoted by $\mathcal{H}$) that the permutations $\phi_2^{(0)} = (1, \lambda, \lambda^2)$ and $\phi_3^{(0)} = (\mu, \mu\lambda^2, \mu\lambda)$ (denoted there by $(0, 1, 2)$ and $(3, 4, 5)$ respectively) belonging to $K = S(\mathcal{H}^{(0)})$, belong also to $N_K[R(\mathcal{H}^{(0)})]$. Considering then the two convolutional $K^{\mathbb{Z}}$-equivalences $\phi_2 = \phi_2(\phi_2^{(0)}, 1^{\mathbb{Z}})$ and $\phi_3 = \phi_3(\phi_3^{(0)}, 1^{\mathbb{Z}})$, we see that they satisfy

$$\phi_k^{-1} GR(\mathcal{H}_1) \phi_k = GR(\mathcal{H}_1)\,,\ e_k \phi_k = e_1 \,;\ \ k = 2, 3\,. \tag{10.5}$$

Assume that the $\mathcal{H}_1$-normal sequence $g$ given in (10.4) is constructed by means of the idempotent $e_k$ with $k = 2$ or $3$. The first equation of (10.5) says that $(g\mathcal{A}_1)\phi_k$ is yet an $\mathcal{H}_1$-code and the second equation says that this code belongs to $\mathcal{D}_1$. $\square$

Up to now we have more or less reduced the problem of enumerating the convolutional $\mathcal{H}_\alpha$-codes (of dimension 2) for $\alpha \in \text{Aut}(\mathcal{H}^{(0)})$ to the problem of enumerating all $\mathcal{H}_1$-normal sequences

$$g = \sum_{j=0}^{m} \lambda^{b(j)} e_1 D^j \, ; \ \ b(0) = 0, \ b(j) \in \{0, 1, 2, \infty\}, \tag{10.6}$$

where we assume $b(m) \neq \infty$ in such a way that the degree of $g$ be equal to $m$. However some polynomials $g$ of the form (10.6) may be such that the bases of the $F$-space $gA$ are catastrophic convolutional encoders. On the other hand, some distinct codes $C = g\mathcal{A}_1$, with $g$ as given by (10.6), are yet $K^{\mathbf{Z}}$-equivalent. The following theorem contains a result about these equivalences. In the sequel, the $\mathcal{H}_1$-normal sequence $g$ of (10.6) will be specified by the $(m+1)$-tuple $\underline{b} = [b(0), \cdots, b(m)]$.

**Theorem 10.3 :** The $(m+1)$-tuples $\underline{b}$ and $2\underline{b} = [2b(0), \cdots, 2b(m)]$ (with $2b(i)$ computed modulo 3) specify $\mathcal{H}_1$-normal sequences that generate $K^{\mathbf{Z}}$-equivalent codes.
**Proof :** Pick out in table 6.4 the element $\phi^{(0)} = (0, 2)(4, 5)$ of $N_K[R(\mathcal{H}^{(0)})]$. The convolutional $K^{\mathbf{Z}}$-equivalence $\phi(\phi^{(0)}, 1^{\mathbf{Z}})$ satisfies

$$\phi^{-1} GR(\mathcal{H}_1)\phi = GR(\mathcal{H}_1)$$

and, if $g$ is specified by $\underline{b}$, then $g\phi$ is specified by $2\underline{b}$. $\square$

The last type of "equivalence" we consider is *not* a convolutional $K^{\mathbf{Z}}$-equivalence. However, it preserves the minimum symbol distance (but not the distance profile) of the codes to which it is applied. It can be described as follows. With the $\mathcal{H}_1$-normal sequence $g$ written as in (10.6) we associate the sequence

$$\hat{g} = \sum_{j=0}^{m} \lambda^{\hat{b}(j)} \, e_1 \, D^j \,, \tag{10.7}$$

where $\hat{b}(j)$ is equal to $b(m-j)$ holds, and we call $\hat{g}$ the reciprocal sequence of $g$. The sequence $g$ is $\mathcal{H}_1$-normal and $g\mathcal{A}_1$ is a minimal ideal. Moreover, one has $\hat{\mathcal{H}}_1 = \mathcal{H}_1$. As a consequence of corollary 7.22, it follows that $\hat{g}$ is $\mathcal{H}_1$-normal and generates the minimal ideal $\hat{C} = \hat{g}\mathcal{A}_1$, which is the reciprocal code of $C = g\mathcal{A}_1$, and has the same minimum distance as it. Moreover, we know from corollary 7.25 that a basis $\hat{G}$ of the $F$-space $\hat{g}\mathcal{A}_1$ is a catastrophic encoder if and only if a basis $G$ of the $F$-space $g\mathcal{A}_1$ is a catastrophic encoder.

However, if $b(m)$ is nonzero, then $\hat{b}(0)$ is nonzero, which implies that $\hat{C}$ is not in $\mathcal{D}_1$. In this case to send $\hat{C}$ into $\mathcal{D}_1$ we apply to $\hat{C}$ a convolutional $K^{\mathbb{Z}}$-equivalence $\phi$ satisfying $\phi^{-1}GR(\mathcal{H}_1)\phi = GR(\mathcal{H}_1)$ and $\lambda^{\hat{b}(0)}e_1\phi^{(0)} = e_1$. When $\hat{b}(0)$ is equal to 1, we use the $K^{\mathbb{Z}}$-equivalence $\phi[(1,2)(3,5),1^{\mathbb{Z}}]$. Its action on the components $\hat{b}(i)$ of the $(m+1)$-tuple $\underline{\hat{b}}$ specifying $\hat{g}$ is to interchange 0 and 1 and to fix 2 and $\infty$. Similarly, when $\hat{b}(0)$ is equal to 2, we use the $K^{\mathbb{Z}}$-equivalence $\phi[(0,1)(3,4),1^{\mathbb{Z}}]$. Its action on the components $\hat{b}(i)$ of $\underline{\hat{b}}$ is to interchange 0 and 2 and to fix 1 and $\infty$.

Let us now give an example of how to use the $K^{\mathbb{Z}}$-equivalence mentioned in theorem 10.3 and the equivalence by reciprocity that we have just described. Consider the $\mathcal{H}_1$-normal sequence $g = g(\underline{b})$ of degree 3 in $D$ that is specified by the 4-tuple $\underline{b} = [0,1,2,2]$. By application of theorem 10.3 there is a convolutional $K^{\mathbb{Z}}$-equivalence that transforms $g(\underline{b})$ into $g(2\underline{b}) = g([0,2,1,1])$. On the other hand the equivalence by reciprocity transforms $g(\underline{b})$ into $g([2,2,1,0])$ and $g(2\underline{b})$ into $g([1,1,2,0])$. These two last $\mathcal{H}_1$-normal sequences are then transformed respectively into $g([0,0,1,2])$ and $g([0,0,2,1])$ by use of $\phi[(0,1)(3,4),1^{\mathbb{Z}}]$ and $\phi[(1,2)(3,5),1^{\mathbb{Z}}]$ that are $K^{\mathbb{Z}}$-equivalences of the first kind. As a result the four codes $g(\underline{b})\mathcal{A}_1$ specified by $\underline{b} = [0,1,2,2]$, $\underline{b} = [0,2,1,1]$, $\underline{b} = [0,0,1,2]$ and $\underline{b} = [0,0,2,1]$ are

$\mathcal{H}_1$-codes that are $K^{\mathbb{Z}}$-equivalent or equivalent by reciprocity. Hence they have the same minimum symbol distance.

In table 10.1, we first give the list of the 39 $\mathcal{H}_1$-normal sequences $g$ of the form (10.6) satisfying $1 \leq m \leq 3$, $b(0) = 0$ and $b(i) \neq \infty$ for $1 \leq i \leq m$. These sequences are divided into 16 classes containing 1, 2 or 4 sequences. As mentioned after theorem 7.24, we say that an $\mathcal{H}_1$-normal sequence $g$ is catastrophic when the bases of the $F$-space $g\mathcal{A}_1$ are catastrophic convolutional encoders. It follows from problem 8.1 that if $g$ is catastrophic then so are all $\mathcal{H}_1$-normal sequences in the same class as $g$. In table 10.1 these catastrophic classes are marked by $*$.[4] For the noncatastrophic classes we give the minimum symbol distance of the ideals $g\mathcal{A}_1$ generated by the sequences $g$ of these classes. Since the degree of these sequences $g$ is small, the minimum symbol distance is easily computable by the modified Viterbi algorithm described by Forney [37] and mentioned in section 3.1. This computation can be simplified owing to the facts that, in a sequence of $g\mathcal{A}_1$, any nonzero word has an even symbol weight, and that the initial and final nonzero words of a finite length nonzero sequence have their symbol weight equal to 4.

Along the lines described in section 3.1, we can obtain upper bounds $\overline{\mathrm{sd}}(m)$ on the minimum symbol distance of $(6, 2, m)$ binary codes. These bounds are $\overline{\mathrm{sd}}(1) = 8$, $\overline{\mathrm{sd}}(2) = 12$, $\overline{\mathrm{sd}}(3) = 16$ and $\overline{\mathrm{sd}}(4) = 18$. No class of the table achieves this bound with equality for $m = 3$ (see, however, section 10.4). Besides the $\mathcal{H}_1$-normal sequences of degree $\leq 3$, we give also in table 10.1 the three classes of $\mathcal{H}_1$-normal sequences $g$ of degree 4 that achieve with equality the upper bound $sd(g\mathcal{A}_1) \leq 18$.

---

[4]Since $A_1$ does not satisfy all conditions of section 9.3, the tools developed in that section cannot be used here. Hence the verification that an encoder is noncatastrophic needs the computation of all its $2 \times 2$ minors.

**Table 10.1** : Some (6,2) $\mathcal{H}_1$-codes.

| Class | Elements of the class | $sd[g(b)\mathcal{A}_1]$ |
|-------|----------------------|------------------------|
| 1 | $[0,0]$ | $*$ |
| 2 | $[0,1]\,[0,2]$ | 8 |
| 3 | $[0,0,0]$ | $*$ |
| 4 | $[0,0,1]\,[0,0,2]\,[0,1,1]\,[0,2,2]$ | 12 |
| 5 | $[0,1,0]\,[0,2,0]$ | 12 |
| 6 | $[0,1,2]\,[0,2,1]$ | $*$ |
| 7 | $[0,0,0,0]$ | $*$ |
| 8 | $[0,0,0,1]\,[0,0,0,2]$ $[0,1,1,1]\,[0,2,2,2]$ | 12 |
| 9 | $[0,0,1,0]\,[0,0,2,0]$ $[0,1,0,0]\,[0,2,0,0]$ | 14 |
| 10 | $[0,0,1,1]\,[0,0,2,2]$ | $*$ |
| 11 | $[0,0,1,2]\,[0,0,2,1]$ $[0,1,2,2]\,[0,2,1,1]$ | 14 |
| 12 | $[0,1,0,1]\,[0,2,0,2]$ | $*$ |
| 13 | $[0,1,0,2]\,[0,2,0,1]$ $[0,2,1,2]\,[0,1,2,1]$ | 14 |
| 14 | $[0,1,1,0]\,[0,2,2,0]$ | $*$ |
| 15 | $[0,1,1,2]\,[0,2,2,1]$ | $*$ |
| 16 | $[0,1,2,0]\,[0,2,1,0]$ | 14 |
| 17 | $[0,1,0,0,1]\,[0,2,0,0,2]$ $[0,1,1,0,1]\,[0,2,2,0,2]$ | 18 |
| 18 | $[0,1,1,0,2]\,[0,2,2,0,1]$ $[0,2,1,1,2]\,[0,1,2,2,1]$ | 18 |
| 19 | $[0,1,1,2,0]\,[0,2,2,1,0]$ $[0,2,1,1,0]\,[0,1,2,2,0]$ | 18 |

## 10.2 Codes of length 7

Let $\mathcal{H}^{(0)}$ be the cyclic group of order $n$ generated by an element $\lambda$ satisfying $\lambda^n = 1$ and $\lambda^r \neq 1$ for $r < n$. The group $\text{Aut}(\mathcal{H}^{(0)})$ is the set of permutations of $\mathcal{H}^{(0)}$ induced by $\lambda \mapsto \lambda^r$ with $r$ satisfying $1 \leq r \leq n-1$ and relatively prime with $n$. Choose $n = 7$. In this case $\text{Aut}(\mathcal{H}^{(0)})$ has order six; hence there are six different groups $\mathcal{H}_\alpha = <\mathcal{H}^{(0)}, \alpha>$ with $\alpha$ in $\text{Aut}(\mathcal{H}^{(0)})$. Any group $\mathcal{H}_\alpha$ is isomorphic to $\mathcal{H}^{(0)}$ and it is generated by the element $x$ of $(\mathcal{H}^{(0)})^{\mathbb{Z}}$ that satisfies

$$x^{(i)} = \lambda^{\alpha^i} \; ; \text{all } i \in \mathbb{Z} . \tag{10.8}$$

For $F = GF(2)$, the algebra $\mathcal{A}_\alpha = F\mathcal{H}_\alpha$ is semi-simple and it can be written as a direct sum $A_\alpha = I_0^{(\alpha)} \oplus I_1^{(\alpha)} \oplus I_3^{(\alpha)}$ of minimal ideals $I_j^{(\alpha)} = e_j^{(\alpha)} A_\alpha$ where the idempotents $e_j^{(\alpha)}$ are given by

$$e_0^{(\alpha)} = 1 + x + x^2 + x^3 + x^4 + x^5 + x^6 ,$$

$$e_1^{(\alpha)} = 1 + x + x^2 + x^4 ,$$

$$e_3^{(\alpha)} = 1 + x^3 + x^6 + x^5 .$$

The formal expression of the idempotents $e_j^\alpha(x)$ does not depend on $\alpha$, but, in this formal expression, $x$ depends on $\alpha$ according to (10.8). The $F$-dimension of the ideal $I_0^{(\alpha)}$ is 1 and the $F$-dimension of the ideals $I_1^{(\alpha)}$ and $I_3^{(\alpha)}$ is 3.

It follows from theorem 9.6 that the $\mathcal{H}_\alpha$-normal sequences generating ideals of dimension 3 in $\mathcal{A}_\alpha := A_\alpha((D))$ have the form

$$g = \sum_{j=0}^{m} (a_j e)^{\alpha^j} D^j \; ; \; a_j \in A_\alpha , \tag{10.9}$$

where $e$ is $e_1^{(\alpha)}$ or $e_3^{(\alpha)}$ and $a_0 e$ is nonzero. Since $\mathcal{H}^{(0)}$ is a cyclic group (hence an Abelian group), the algebras $A_\alpha$ are commutative and in (10.9) one has $a_j e = e a_j$ for all $j$ and all $\alpha$. Three of the six algebras $A_\alpha$ contain no ideal that can be a proper convolutional code. Indeed, if $\alpha$ is induced by one of the mappings $\lambda \mapsto \lambda$, $\lambda \mapsto \lambda^2$ or $\lambda \mapsto \lambda^4$, all ideals in $A_\alpha$ remain invariant under $\alpha$ and, in this case, any basis $G = \sum_{j=0}^{m} G_j D^j$ of the $F$-space $gA_\alpha$ has the property that all nonzero $F$-matrices $G_j$ generate the same $F$-space. Then obviously $E(G)$ is the Laurent extension of $E_0(G_0)$ and it cannot be a proper convolutional code.

Among the last three automorphisms $\alpha$ of $\mathcal{H}^{(0)}$, we consider first the one induced by

$$\lambda^\alpha := \lambda^{-1}. \tag{10.10}$$

This automorphism $\alpha$ permutes the two idempotents $e_1^{(\alpha)}$ and $e_3^{(\alpha)}$. As it will be seen below, the bases $G$ of the $F$-spaces $gA_\alpha$ associated with an $\mathcal{H}_\alpha$-normal sequence $g$ will often be noncatastrophic encoders of proper convolutional codes. We shall investigate these codes by using methods that are similar to the ones of the preceding section. We shall first divide the $\mathcal{H}_\alpha$-codes into classes such that all codes of a given class have the same minimum symbol distance, and thereafter we shall analyze in detail one member of each class. To make this partition, we shall use the tools introduced in chapter 8 and specialized in section 9.4. In particular we shall make use of the normalizer $N_K[R(\mathcal{H}^{(0)})]$ of the right regular representation of $\mathcal{H}^{(0)}$ in the group $K = S(\mathcal{H}^{(0)})$, which is the symmetric group of order 7! and degree 7 in its action by permutation on $\mathcal{H}^{(0)}$. As mentioned in chapter 6, this normalizer is the semi-direct product of $R(\mathcal{H}^{(0)})$ and $\mathrm{Aut}(\mathcal{H}^{(0)})$. For ease of representation we shall often label the seven coordinates of $F^7$ by the integers $0, 1, \cdots, 6$ rather than by the elements $1, \lambda, \cdots, \lambda^6$ of $\mathcal{H}^{(0)}$. In this notation the group $R(\mathcal{H}^{(0)})$, which coincides here with $L(\mathcal{H}^{(0)})$, is a cyclic permutation group of order 7 generated by the permutation $(0, 1, 2, 3, 4, 5, 6)$ and $\mathrm{Aut}(\mathcal{H}^{(0)})$ is a cyclic group of order 6 generated by the permutation $(1, 3, 2, 6, 4, 5)$.

Let us now enumerate the equivalences of $\mathcal{H}_\alpha$-codes that preserve the minimum distance. With $g$ written as in (10.9), we denote by $\mathcal{D}_i$ (for $i = 1$

and $i = 3$), the set of codes $g\mathcal{A}_\alpha$ that are obtained when one uses $e = e_i^{(\alpha)}$.

**Theorem 10.4 :** $\phi[(1,6)(2,5)(3,4),\, 1^z]$ is a convolutional $K^z$-equivalence that maps $\mathcal{D}_3$ onto $\mathcal{D}_1$.
**Proof :** We verify that $\phi^{-1}GR(\mathcal{H}_\alpha)\phi$ equals $GR(\mathcal{H}_\alpha)$ and that $g\mathcal{A}_\alpha \in \mathcal{D}_3$ implies $g\phi\mathcal{A}_\alpha \in \mathcal{D}_1$. $\square$

On the basis of this theorem we shall only analyze the class $\mathcal{D}_1$ and we shall always use $e = e_1^{(\alpha)}$ in the expression (10.9) of $\mathcal{H}_\alpha$-normal sequences.

It turns out that the set $Ae$ is nothing but the set $\{ex^b \mid 0 \le b \le 6$ and $b = \infty\}$, where $ex^\infty$ denotes the zero polynomial. Thus we can rewrite (10.9) as

$$g = \sum_{j=0}^{m} (ex^{b(j)})^{\alpha^j} D^j, \tag{10.11}$$

which makes clear that $g$ is specified as soon as the $(m+1)$-tuple $\underline{b} = [b(0), \cdots, b(m)]$ is given. It is then seen that the $F$-space $g\mathcal{A}_\alpha$ consists of the eight sequences $gx^r = \sum_{j=0}^{m}(ex^{b(j)+r})^{\alpha^j} D^j$ with $r = 0, 1, \cdots, 6, \infty$.

We shall now explicitly describe some $K^z$-equivalences of the codes $g\mathcal{A}_\alpha$ in terms of the $(m+1)$-tuple $\underline{b}$ that specifies the $\mathcal{H}_\alpha$-normal sequence $g$ given by (10.11).

**Theorem 10.5 :** The $(m+1)$-tuples $\underline{b}$ and $2\underline{b} = [2b(0), \cdots, 2b(m)]$ (with $2b(i)$ computed modulo 7) specify $K^z$-equivalent convolutional codes.
**Proof :** Use the convolutional $K^z$-equivalence of the first kind $\phi = \phi(\phi^{(0)}, 1^z)$, with $\phi^{(0)} = (1, 2, 4)(3, 6, 5)$. If $g$ is specified by $\underline{b}$, then $g\phi$ is specified by $2\underline{b}$. $\square$

**Theorem 10.6 :** The $(m+1)$-tuple $\underline{b} = [b(0), \cdots, b(m)]$ and the $(m+1)$-tuple $\underline{b}'$ given by

$$b'(i) = b(i) \text{ for even } i, \quad b'(i) = b(i) + 1 \text{ for odd } i,$$

specify $K^z$-equivalent convolutional codes.

**Proof :** Use the convolutional $K^{\mathbb{Z}}$-equivalence of the first kind $\phi = \phi(1, y)$, where $y$ is the element of $GR(\mathcal{H}_\alpha)$ satisfying $y^{(0)} = (0, 6, 5, 4, 3, 2, 1)$. If $g$ is specified by $\underline{b}$, then $g\phi$ is specified by $\underline{b}'$. $\square$

Consider an $\mathcal{H}_\alpha$-normal sequence $g$ of the form (10.11) and write it as $g = \sum_{j=0}^{m} g_j D^j$ where $g_m$ is assumed to be nonzero. Remark that one has $\hat{\mathcal{H}}_\alpha = \mathcal{H}_\alpha$. As a consequence of corollary 7.22, it follows that $\hat{g} = \sum_{j=0}^{m} g_{m-j} D^j$ is also an $\mathcal{H}_\alpha$-normal sequence and that it generates a minimal ideal $\hat{C} = \hat{g}\mathcal{A}_\alpha$, which is the reciprocal code of $C$. However, starting from a polynomial $g$ that has the form (10.11) (implying that $g\mathcal{A}_\alpha$ is in $\mathcal{D}_1$), we obtain a sequence $\hat{g}$ producing a code $\hat{g}\mathcal{A}_\alpha$ in $\mathcal{D}_1$ for even $m$ and in $\mathcal{D}_3$ for odd $m$.

**Theorem 10.7 :** Let $g$ be the sequence (10.11) and define

$$\tilde{g} := \sum_{j=0}^{m} (ex^{\hat{b}(j)})^{\alpha^j} D^j,$$

with $\hat{b}(j) = b(m - j)$. The convolutional codes $g\mathcal{A}_\alpha$ and $\tilde{g}\mathcal{A}_\alpha$ have the same minimum symbol distance.

**Proof :** The code $\hat{g}\mathcal{A}_\alpha$ is the reciprocal of $g\mathcal{A}$ and hence has the same minimum symbol distance. If $m$ is even, we have $\tilde{g} = \hat{g}$ whence $\tilde{g}\mathcal{A}_\alpha = \hat{g}\mathcal{A}_\alpha$. If $m$ is odd, we have $\tilde{g}\mathcal{A}_\alpha = \hat{g}\phi\mathcal{A}_\alpha$ where $\phi = \phi\ ((1,6)(2,5)(3,4),\ 1^{\mathbb{Z}})$ is a convolutional $K^{\mathbb{Z}}$-equivalence of the first kind. $\square$

**Remark 10.8 :** Since $g\mathcal{A}_\alpha$ coincides with $(gx)\mathcal{A}_\alpha$, the $(m + 1)$-tuples $[b(0), \cdots, b(m)]$ and $[1 + b(0), \cdots, 1 + b(m)]$ specify the same code.

Using the upper bounds on the minimum symbol distance mentioned in chapter 3, we find that the minimum symbol distance of any $(7, 3)$ binary convolutional code of span $m$ is at most $4(m + 1)$ for $m \leq 7$.[5] Let us try to find codes in $\mathcal{D}_1$ that achieve this bound. We shall first use a low

---

[5] This follows from the well-known Plotkin bound [87].

cost sieve method that rejects several polynomials $g$ of the form (10.11) satisfying $sd(g\mathcal{A}_\alpha) < 4(m+1)$. We remark that if some $b(j)$ specifying $g$ is $\infty$, then the minimum symbol distance of the code $C = g\mathcal{A}_\alpha$ is at most $4m$ so that it cannot achieve the upper bound $4(m+1)$. Thus, for $m \leq 7$, a "good" $\mathcal{H}_\alpha$-normal sequence $g$ cannot be specified by an $(m+1)$-tuple $\underline{b}$ having some entries equal to $\infty$. Consider now the sequences of the form $g(1 + x^s D)D^t x^u$, for $t$ and $u$ in $\mathbb{Z}$. The symbol weight of such a sequence is the same as the symbol weight of $g(1 + x^s D)$. Associating to $g$ its $(m+1)$-tuple $\underline{b} = [b(0), \cdots, b(m)]$, we can represent this sequence $g(1 + x^s D)$ by the $2 \times (m+2)$ matrix

$$\begin{pmatrix} b(0) & b(1) & b(2) & \cdots & b(m) & \infty \\ \infty & b(0)+s & b(1)+s & \cdots & b(m-1)+s & b(m)+s \end{pmatrix}. \quad (10.12)$$

To determine its symbol weight we construct a $7 \times 7$ matrix $\Delta$ whose $(i,j)$-entry is the symbol weight $\Delta_{i,j}$ of the word $ex^i + (ex^j)^\alpha = (x^i + x^{i+1} + x^{i+2} + x^{i+4}) + (x^{-j} + x^{3-j} + x^{6-j} + x^{5-j})$ for $0 \leq i, j \leq 6$, These $\Delta_{i,j}$ satisfy the equalities

$$\Delta_{0,j} = \Delta_{0,2j}, \quad \Delta_{i,j} = \Delta_{0,i+j}, \quad \Delta_{i,j} = \Delta_{j,i}. \quad (10.13)$$

Thus it is sufficient to compute $\Delta_{0,0} = 6$, $\Delta_{0,1} = 4$ and $\Delta_{0,3} = 2$ to obtain the complete matrix $\Delta$, which is given in figure 10.1.

Now write $g(1 + x^s D) = \sum_{r=0}^{m+1} v_r D^r$ with $v_r$ in $A_\alpha$. For $1 \leq r \leq m$, the symbol weight of the word $v_r$ is then equal to $\Delta_{b(r), b(r-1)+s}$ for even $s$, and to $\Delta_{b(r-1)+s, b(r)}$ for odd $s$. In both cases it follows from (10.13) that it is equal to $\Delta_{s, b(r-1)+b(r)}$. Thus the symbol weight $w_s$ of $g(1 + x^s D)$ satisfies

$$w_s = 8 + \sum_{r=1}^{m} \Delta_{s, b(r-1)+b(r)} \quad (10.14)$$

since the first and the last nonzero word of $g(1 + x^s D)$, being nonzero words of one of the (7,3) binary block codes $eA_\alpha$ or $e^\alpha A_\alpha$, have their

| $i$ $j$ | 0 | 1 | 2 | 3 | 4 | 5 | 6 |
|---|---|---|---|---|---|---|---|
| 0 | 6 | 4 | 4 | 2 | 4 | 2 | 2 |
| 1 | 4 | 4 | 2 | 4 | 2 | 2 | 6 |
| 2 | 4 | 2 | 4 | 2 | 2 | 6 | 4 |
| 3 | 2 | 4 | 2 | 2 | 6 | 4 | 4 |
| 4 | 4 | 2 | 2 | 6 | 4 | 4 | 2 |
| 5 | 2 | 2 | 6 | 4 | 4 | 2 | 4 |
| 6 | 2 | 6 | 4 | 4 | 2 | 4 | 2 |

**Figure 10.1** : The matrix $\Delta$ where $\Delta_{i,j}$ is the symbol weight of
$$x^i e + (x^j e)^\alpha .$$

symbol weight equal to 4. Denote by $W$ the column 7-tuple having $w_s$ as
its $s^{\text{th}}$ component for $0 \leq s \leq 6$. Equality (10.14) shows that one obtains
$W$ by summing $m$ columns of $\Delta$ and adding 8 to all components of the
result. A necessary condition for $g\mathcal{A}_\alpha$ to satisfy $sd(g\mathcal{A}_\alpha) = 4(m+1)$ is
that all components of $W$ be at least equal to $4(m+1)$. Equation (10.14)
suggests that we use the numbers

$$c(r) := b(r-1) + b(r) \bmod 7; \ 1 \leq r \leq m,$$

to specify which columns of $\Delta$ should be used to compute $W$. The knowledge of $b(0)$ and of the $m$-tuple $\underline{c} = (c(1), \cdots c(m))$ is clearly equivalent to

the knowledge of the $(m+1)$-tuple $\underline{b}$.

**Theorem 10.9 :** The two convolutional $\mathcal{H}_\alpha$-codes generated by the two sequences $g$ of the form $(10.11)$, that are specified respectively by $(b(0) = 0, \underline{c})$ and by $(b(0) = a, \underline{c})$ are $K^{\mathbb{Z}}$-equivalent.

**Proof :** The two corresponding $(m+1)$-tuples $\underline{b}$ are respectively $\underline{b}_0 = [0, b(1), b(2), b(3), \cdots]$ and $\underline{b}_a = [a, b(1) - a, b(2) + a, b(3) - a, \cdots]$. By remark 10.8, it is seen that $\underline{b}_a$ specifies the same code as $\underline{b}^* = [0, b(1) - 2a, b(2), b(3) - 2a, \cdots]$ and, by repeated application of theorem 10.6, the code specified by $\underline{b}^*$ is found to be $K^{\mathbb{Z}}$-equivalent to the code specified by $\underline{b}_0$. $\square$

This theorem shows that if two $\mathcal{H}_\alpha$-codes generated by two $\mathcal{H}_\alpha$-normal sequences $g$ are not $K^{\mathbb{Z}}$-equivalent, then the $m$-tuples $\underline{c}$ associated with these two sequences have to be different. Thus we can restrict the enumeration of $\mathcal{H}_\alpha$-normal sequences $g$ to sequences specified by *different* $m$-tuples $\underline{c}$. However, among all these $m$-tuples $\underline{c}$, some do correspond to generators $g$ of codes that are $K^{\mathbb{Z}}$-equivalent or equivalent by reciprocity. For this reason it is interesting to express the $K^{\mathbb{Z}}$-equivalences of theorems 10.5 and 10.6, the equivalence by reciprocity of theorem 10.7 and the remark 10.8 in terms of the $m$-tuples $\underline{c}$ rather than in terms of the $(m+1)$-tuples $\underline{b}$.

**Theorem 10.10 :** The $\mathcal{H}_\alpha$-normal sequences specified respectively by $\underline{c} = (c(1), \cdots, c(m))$ and $2\underline{c} = (2c(1), \cdots, 2c(m))$ generate convolutional codes that are $K^{\mathbb{Z}}$-equivalent, independently of the value of $b(0)$.

**Theorem 10.11 :** Let $1^m$ be the all ones $m$-tuple. All $g$ specified by $\underline{c}$ and by $\underline{c} + 1^m$ generate $K^{\mathbb{Z}}$-equivalent codes.

**Theorem 10.12 :** For arbitrary $b(0)$, specify $g$ by $\underline{c} = (c(1), \cdots, c(m))$ and $\hat{g}$ by $\hat{\underline{c}} = (c(m), \cdots, c(1))$. Then the codes $g\mathcal{A}_\alpha$ and $\hat{g}\mathcal{A}_\alpha$ have the same minimum symbol distance.

**Remark 10.13 :** The $m$-tuple $(c(1), \cdots, c(m))$ and the $(m+1)$-tuple $(2 + c(1), \cdots, 2 + c(m))$ specify codes having the same minimum symbol distance, independently of $b(0)$.

We note that this last remark can also be obtained by iterated application of theorem 10.11.

Table 10.2 shows several examples of application of the statements above. The first column gives triples $\underline{c} = (c(1), c(2), c(3))$, the second column mentions some of the theorems stated above and the last column gives the triples deduced from the triples of the first column by use of the theorems mentioned in the second column. Thus corresponding triples in the first and third columns specify two generator polynomials $g_1$ and $g_2$ (of the form (10.11) for an arbitrary $b(0)$) having the property that the minimum symbol distance of the convolutional codes $g_1 \, \mathcal{A}_\alpha$ and $g_2 \, \mathcal{A}_\alpha$ are equal.

**Table 10.2 :** Examples of triples $\underline{c}$ specifying polynomials of degree 3 over $\mathcal{A}_\alpha$ that generate codes having the same minimum symbol distance.

| Initial triple | Applied theorem | Obtained triple |
|:---:|:---:|:---:|
| $(4, 5, 0)$ | Theorem 10.11 | $(1, 2, 4)$ |
| $(1, 2, 4)$ | Theorem 10.11 | $(0, 1, 3)$ |
| $(0, 1, 3)$ | Theorem 10.10 | $(0, 2, 6)$ |
| $(0, 2, 6)$ | Theorem 10.10 | $(0, 4, 5)$ |
| $(0, 1, 3)$ | Theorem 10.12 | $(3, 1, 0)$ |
| $(3, 1, 0)$ | Theorem 10.11 | $(0, 5, 4)$ |
| $(0, 5, 4)$ | Theorem 10.10 | $(0, 3, 1)$ |

We shall now use the properties above to obtain for $1 \leq m \leq 5$, the nonequivalent generator polynomials $g$ of $D$-degree equal to $m$, that specify $\mathcal{H}_\alpha$-codes achieving $sd(g\,\mathcal{A}_\alpha) = 4(m+1)$. We see from (10.14) that we first have to find all nonequivalent collections of $m$ (not necessarily distinct) columns of $\Delta$ whose sum has no component strictly smaller than $4(m+1) - 8 = 4(m-1)$. In this case, we shall say that the collection of columns achieves the *weight condition*. To any ordering of the elements of such a collection, there corresponds a $(7,3)$ convolutional $\mathcal{H}_\alpha$-code generated by a polynomial $g$ of degree $m$ over $A_\alpha$ having the property that all sequences $g(1 + x^s D)$ have symbol weight at least equal to $4(m+1)$. For $1 \leq m \leq 5$ we now give all nonequivalent $m$-tuples $\underline{c}$ that satisfy this condition and, for each such $\underline{c}$, the unique $(m+1)$-tuple $\underline{b}$ "achieving" this $\underline{c}$ with $b(0) = 0$.

- $m = 1$. In this case, the weight condition is trivially satisfied and all $\underline{c}$ are equivalent to $\underline{c} = (0)$. A pair $\underline{b}$ achieving this $\underline{c}$ is $\underline{b} = [0, 0]$. The corresponding $g$ is such that any basis of the $F$-space $gA_\alpha$ is a noncatastrophic convolutional encoder. Indeed, applying the statements of section 9.3, we see that $\boldsymbol{\Gamma} = [1, 1]$ is trivially a $1 \times 2$ noncatastrophic encoder over $GF(2^3)$.

- $m = 2$. There are two inequivalent pairs $\underline{c}$, namely $\underline{c} = (0, 0)$ and $\underline{c} = (0, 1)$, and both achieve the weight condition. The corresponding triples $\underline{b}$ are respectively $\underline{b} = [0, 0, 0]$ and $\underline{b} = [0, 0, 1]$. The two associated polynomials $g$ are such that any basis of the $F$-space $gA_\alpha$ is a noncatastrophic convolutional encoder. Indeed $\boldsymbol{\Gamma}_1 = [1+D, 1]$ and $\boldsymbol{\Gamma}_2 = [1+\beta D, 1]$, with $\beta$ a primitive element of $GF(2^3)$, are noncatastrophic encoders.

- $m = 3$. We have to find the collections of three columns of $\Delta$ satisfying the weight condition, i.e., the components of their sums are $\geq 8$. There are only two inequivalent such collections, namely $\{0, 1, 2\}$ and $\{0, 1, 3\}$. For example, the collection $\{1, 5, 6\}$ also satisfies the weight condition but two repeated applications of theorem 10.11 show that it is equivalent to $\{0, 1, 3\}$. To each of the two unordered triples $\{0, 1, 2\}$ and $\{0, 1, 3\}$ there correspond six ordered triples $\underline{c}$. These twelve ordered triples are respectively $(0, 1, 2)$, $(0, 2, 1)$, $(1, 0, 2)$, $(1, 2, 0)$, $(2, 0, 1)$, $(2, 1, 0)$, $(0, 1, 3)$, $(0, 3, 1)$, $(1, 0, 3)$, $(1, 3, 0)$, $(3, 0, 1)$, $(3, 1, 0)$. Making then use of theorem 10.12, we find that only six of these twelve triples may specify codes that are in-equivalent by reciprocity. For example, the codes specified by $c = (2, 1, 0)$ and by $c = (0, 1, 2)$ are equivalent by reciprocity. The six ordered triples $c$ we are left with are $(0, 1, 2)$, $(0, 2, 1)$, $(1, 0, 2)$, $(0, 1, 3)$, $(0, 3, 1)$ and $(1, 0, 3)$. However, the three last of them specify equivalent codes. Denoting indeed by $\simeq_n$ the equivalence of two triples $c$ under theorem $(10.n)$, we have

$$(0, 1, 3) \simeq_{13} (3, 1, 0) \simeq_{12} (0, 5, 4) \simeq_{11} (0, 3, 1)$$

and

$$(1, 0, 3) \simeq_{12} (0, 6, 2) \simeq_{11} (0, 3, 1).$$

There finally remain only four inequivalent classes of codes. They are associated with the ordered triples $c = (0, 1, 2)$, $c = (0, 2, 1)$, $c = (1, 0, 2)$ and $c = (0, 1, 3)$. A 4-tuple $b$ corresponding to $c = (0, 1, 2)$ is easily found to be $[0, 0, 1, 1]$. According to theorem 9.7, any basis of the $F$-space $gA_\alpha$ with $g$ specified by this $b$ is a catastrophic encoder. Indeed the $(2, 1)$ encoder $\boldsymbol{\Gamma} = [1 + \beta D, \; 1 + \beta D]$, with $\beta$ a primitive element of $GF(2^3)$, is obviously a catastrophic convolutional encoder over $GF(2^3)$. A four-tuple $b$ specifying a code in the class of each of the three remaining triples $c$ is given by $b = [0, 0, 2, 6]$, $b = [0, 1, 6, 3]$, $b = [0, 0, 1, 2]$, respectively. The bases of the corresponding $F$-spaces $gA_\alpha$ are noncatastrophic convolutional encoders as it follows from theorem 9.7.

• $m = 4$. We have to find collections of four columns of $\Delta$ satisfying the weight condition, in the sense that the components of their sums are all $\geq 12$. There are only two such inequivalent collections, namely $\{0, 1, 2, 4\}$ and $\{0, 1, 2, 5\}$, which produce $2 \times 4! = 48$ different 4-tuples $c$. Many of those $c$ are however equivalent, as follows from theorems 10.10, 10.11 and 10.12. It turns out that only eight of these 4-tuples $c$ specify generators of codes that are equivalent neither by $K^z$-equivalence nor by reciprocity.

The 8 inequivalent 4-tuples $\underline{c}$ can be chosen to be $(0, 1, 2, 4)$, $(0, 1, 4, 2)$, $(1, 0, 2, 4)$, $(1, 0, 4, 2)$, $(0, 1, 2, 5)$, $(0, 1, 5, 2)$, $(0, 2, 1, 5)$ and $(0, 5, 1, 2)$. To $\underline{c} = (0, 2, 1, 5)$ corresponds the 5-tuple $\underline{b} = [0, 0, 2, 6, 6]$ and, according to theorem 9.7, any basis of the $F$-space $g\mathcal{A}_\alpha$, for $g$ specified by this $\underline{b}$, is a catastrophic convolutional encoder. Indeed, the encoder $\Gamma = [1 + \beta^2 D + \beta^6 D^2, \ 1 + \beta^6 D]$ over $GF(2^3)$ is catastrophic since one has $1 + \beta^2 D + \beta^6 D^2 = (1 + \beta^6 D)(1 + D)$. The seven remaining classes correspond to noncatastrophic and nonequivalent $(7, 3)$ $\mathcal{H}_\alpha$-codes. We now give one 5-tuple $\underline{b}$ in each of these classes: $\underline{b} = [0, 0, 1, 1, 3]$, $\underline{b} = [0, 0, 1, 3, 6]$, $\underline{b} = [0, 1, 6, 3, 1]$, $\underline{b} = [0, 1, 6, 5, 4]$, $\underline{b} = [0, 0, 1, 1, 4]$, $\underline{b} = [0, 0, 1, 4, 5]$ and $\underline{b} = [0, 0, 5, 3, 6]$.

• $m = 5$. We have to find collections of five columns of $\Delta$ satisfying the weight condition, in the sense that the components of their sums are all $\geq 16$. It is seen that one column of $\Delta$ must appear twice in this collection and that all collections of five columns are equivalent to the one given by $\{0, 0, 1, 2, 4\}$. There are $5!/2! = 60$ different permutations of these five columns, to which correspond sixty different 5-tuples $\underline{c}$. However the equivalences of theorems 10.10, 10.11 and 10.12 reduce the number of nonequivalent 5-tuples $\underline{c}$ to 10. These 5-tuples are

$$\underline{c} = (0, 0, 1, 2, 4), \ \underline{c} = (0, 0, 1, 4, 2), \ \underline{c} = (0, 1, 0, 2, 4),$$

$$\underline{c} = (0, 1, 0, 4, 2), \ \underline{c} = (0, 1, 2, 0, 4), \ \underline{c} = (0, 1, 4, 2, 0)$$

$$\underline{c} = (1, 0, 0, 2, 4), \ \underline{c} = (1, 0, 0, 4, 2), \ \underline{c} = (0, 1, 2, 4, 0)$$

$$\underline{c} = (1, 0, 2, 0, 4).$$

For example, we can check that among the sixty 5-tuples mentioned, all of the type $\underline{c} = (0, c(2), c(3), c(4), 0)$ are equivalent when the $K^Z$-equivalence and the equivalence by reciprocity are taken into account. Also the twelve 5-tuples of the forms $(0, 0, c(3), c(4), c(5))$ and $(c(1), c(2), c(3), 0, 0)$ are equivalent to one of the 5-tuples $(0, 0, 1, 2, 4)$ and $(0, 0, 1, 4, 2)$. Each 5-tuple $\underline{c}$

represents a class of seven $\mathcal{H}_\alpha$-normal sequences $g$ generating equivalent codes $g\mathcal{A}_\alpha$. Representatives of the 10 nonequivalent classes are specified by the 10 following 6-tuples:

$$\underline{b} = [0,0,0,1,1,3], \quad \underline{b} = [0,0,0,1,3,6], \quad \underline{b} = [0,0,1,6,3,1],$$

$$\underline{b} = [0,0,1,6,5,4], \quad \underline{b} = [0,0,1,1,6,5], \quad \underline{b} = [0,0,1,3,4,5],$$

$$\underline{b} = [0,1,6,1,1,3], \quad \underline{b} = [0,1,6,1,3,6], \quad \underline{b} = [0,0,1,1,3,4],$$

$$\underline{b} = [0,1,6,3,4,0].$$

All corresponding bases of $g\mathcal{A}_\alpha$ are noncatastrophic convolutional encoders, as can be seen by application of theorem 9.7.

Let us now describe how to find the minimum symbol distance of all these codes. We find it useful to generalize the representation (10.12) of the code sequences of length $m + 2$ to code sequences of any length. With $g$ an $\mathcal{H}_\alpha$-normal sequence of the form (10.11), we represent any sequence $g(D)u(D)$ of $g\mathcal{A}_\alpha$ by $g(D)[u_e(D^2) + u_0(D^2)D]$ where $u_e(D)$ and $u_0(D)$ are in $\mathcal{A}_\alpha$, and we call the sequences $u_e(D^2)$ and $u_0(D^2)D$ the even part and the odd part of the information sequence $u(D) = u_e(D^2) + u_0(D^2)D$. Without essential loss of generality we choose del $u_e = 0$ and del $u_0 \geq 0$. Consider now a sequence of the form $g(D)u_e(D^2)$. In such a sequence, it is clear that the coefficients of the even powers of $D$ are elements of the ideal $e\mathcal{A}_\alpha$ and that the coefficients of the odd powers of $D$ are in the ideal $e^\alpha\mathcal{A}_\alpha$. The converse statement holds true for $g(D)u_0(D^2)D$. Thus we can write

$$g(D)u_e(D^2) = \sum_{j=0}^{\infty} (ex^{f(j)})^{\alpha^j} D^j; \quad f(j) \in \{0, 1, \cdots, 6, \infty\} \qquad (10.15)$$

and

$$g(D)u_0(D^2)D = \sum_{j=1}^{\infty} (ex^{g(j)})^{\alpha^{j+1}} D^j; \quad g(j) \in \{0, 1, \cdots, 6, \infty\} . \qquad (10.16)$$

We call the sequence $g(D) u_e(D^2)$ the even part of the encoded sequence $v$ and we call the sequence $g(D) u_o(D^2)D$ the odd part of $v$. It is clear that any sequence $v = gu$ in $g\mathcal{A}_\alpha$ is equal, within postmultiplication by some power of $D$, to the sum of its even part (10.15) and of its odd part (10.16). Generalizing the representation (10.12) of the sequences $g(1 + x^s D)$, we represent any polynomial sequence $v = gu$ of delay zero in $g\mathcal{A}_\alpha$ by a $2 \times (m + \ell + 1)$ matrix where $\ell$ is the degree of $u$. This matrix has one of the forms

$$\Omega = \begin{pmatrix} f(0) & f(1) & f(2) & \cdots & f(j) & \cdots & f(m+\ell-1) & f(m+\ell) \\ \infty & g(1) & g(2) & \cdots & g(j) & \cdots & g(m+\ell-1) & \infty \end{pmatrix}$$
$$(10.17)$$

or

$$\Omega = \begin{pmatrix} f(0) & f(1) & f(2) & \cdots & f(j) & \cdots & f(m+\ell-1) & \infty \\ \infty & g(1) & g(2) & \cdots & g(j) & \cdots & g(m+\ell-1) & g(m+\ell) \end{pmatrix}$$
$$(10.18)$$

where $f(0)$, $f(m+\ell)$ and $g(m+\ell)$ are not equal to $\infty$, and where the column $(f(j), g(j))^T$ represents $ex^{f(j)} + (ex^{g(j)})^\alpha$ for even $j$ and $(ex^{f(j)})^\alpha + ex^{g(j)}$ for odd $j$.

Since we are only interested in the symbol weight of the sequences represented by (10.17) and (10.18), we may postmultiply these sequences by $x^{-f(0)}$, thus subtracting $f(0)$ from all entries of this matrix, without modifying their symbol weight. Equivalently we may suppose that $f(0)$ is equal to 0. If, for some $j$, neither $f(j)$ nor $g(j)$ are $\infty$, then it follows from figure 10.1 that the coefficient of $D^j$ in $gu$ has a symbol weight equal to 2, 4 or 6. If exactly one of these two exponents $f(j)$ and $g(j)$ is $\infty$, the symbol weight of the coefficient of $D^j$ is 4. If both are $\infty$, the coefficient of $D^j$ is zero.

Let us now explain how to use (10.17) and (10.18) to check if the minimum symbol distance of the $(7, 3)$ code $g(\underline{b})\mathcal{A}_\alpha$ specified by the $(m+1)$-tuple $\underline{b}$ is equal to $4(m + 1)$. The basic idea of the argument is as follows.

In $v = gu$ written as $v = \sum_{j=0}^{m+\ell} v_j D^j$ with $v_0 \neq 0$ and $v_{m+\ell} \neq 0$, the symbol weight of $v_0$ and $v_{m+\ell}$ is equal to 4, and the symbol weight of any other nonzero word is at least 2. It follows that the symbol weight of any sequence containing at least $2m$ nonzero words is at least equal to $4+2(2m-2)+4 = 4(m+1)$, which is equal to the upper bound on $sd(g\mathcal{A}_\alpha)$. For this reason, we first enumerate all even sequences $g(D)\,u_e(D^2)$ in $g\,\mathcal{A}_\alpha$ that have delay zero, satisfy $f(0) = 0$ and contain at most $2m-1$ nonzero words. Maybe the easiest way to do that is to exploit the isomorphism mentioned in section 9.3 between the even sequences of the $(7,3)$ codes under investigation and the sequences of the $(2,1)$ codes over $GF(2^3)$, and then to use a modified Viterbi algorithm [37] to enumerate all sequences of symbol weight $\leq 2m - 1$ and delay zero in the $(2,1)$ convolutional code over $GF(2^3)$ that is associated with the $(7,3)$ convolutional code specified by $g$.

As an example, we specify a generator polynomial $g$ by the 5-tuple $\underline{b} = [0,1,6,5,4]$, which corresponds to $m = 4$. The $(2,1)$ encoder over $GF(2^3)$ associated with $g$ is $[1+\alpha^6+\alpha^4,\ \alpha+\alpha^5]$ with $\alpha$ a zero of $x^3+x+1$, and using this $(2,1)$ encoder, we can enumerate all even sequences of $g\mathcal{A}_\alpha$ containing at most seven nonzero words, having delay zero and specified by an $(m+\ell+1)$-tuple $[f(0), \cdots, f(m+\ell)]$ in which the first component $f(0)$ is zero. These even sequences are listed in table 10.3. In an even sequence, all nonzero words have symbol weight equal to 4. Thus it follows from table 10.3 that the nonzero even sequences of the code cannot have symbol weight $< 20$, since all of them contain at least five nonzero words. As an odd sequence is nothing but an even sequence multiplied by $D$, the same property holds true for odd sequences.

It remains to be checked that all general sequences (with a nonzero even part *and* a nonzero odd part) have also a symbol weight $\geq 20$. To achieve this goal, we shall use as follows the sequences listed in table 10.3. Let us consider for example the two even sequences $[0,1,1,1,\infty,3,2]$ and $[0,1,3,\infty,6,2,1]$ appearing in this table, and let us construct from these two sequences some matrices $\Omega$ having the form (10.17) or (10.18). We call such a matrix $\Omega$ a *matching*. For example, two possible matchings of $[0, 1, 1, 1, \infty, 3, 2]$ and $[0, 1, 3, \infty, 6, 2, 1]$ are

$$\Omega = \begin{pmatrix} 0 & 1 & 3 & \infty & 6 & 2 & 1 & \infty \\ \infty & 0 & 1 & 1 & 1 & \infty & 3 & 2 \end{pmatrix}$$

and

$$\Omega = \begin{pmatrix} 0 & 1 & 1 & 1 & \infty & 3 & 2 & \infty & \infty & \infty \\ \infty & \infty & \infty & 0 & 1 & 3 & \infty & 6 & 2 & 1 \end{pmatrix}.$$

**Table 10.3 :** Even sequences containing at most 7 nonzero words in the code specified by $\underline{b} = [0,1,6,5,4]$.

| 5 nonzero words | 6 nonzero words | 7 nonzero words |
|---|---|---|
| $[0, 1, 6, 5, 4]$ | $[0, 1, \infty, 4, 0, 4, 3]$ | $[0, 1, 2, 6, 3, 5, 4]$ |
| | $[0, 1, 3, \infty, 6, 2, 1]$ | $[0, 1, 5, 3, 5, 6, 5]$ |
| | $[0, 1, 1, 1, \infty, 3, 2]$ | $[0, 1, 0, 2, 2, 0, 6]$ |
| | | $[0, 1, 4, 0, 1, 1, 0]$ |
| | | $[0, 1, 3, \infty, \infty, 6, 6, 4, 3]$ |
| | | $[0, 1, 5, 3, \infty, \infty, 0, 3, 2]$ |
| | | $[0, 1, 4, 0, \infty, 4, \infty, 6, 5]$ |
| | | $[0, 1, 3, \infty, 5, \infty, 3, 6, 5]$ |
| | | $[0, 1, 3, \infty, 0, 5, \infty, 0, 6]$ |
| | | $[0, 1, \infty, 4, \infty, 2, 4, 5, 4]$ |
| | | $[0, 1, \infty, 4, 1, \infty, 5, 1, 0]$ |
| | | $[0, 1, \infty, 4, 5, 0, \infty, 2, 1]$ |
| | | $[0, 1, \infty, 4, \infty, 2, \infty, \infty, 6, 2, 1]$ |

However, as follows from the remarks made after (10.18), a matching containing at least $8 (= 2m)$ columns with no $\infty$ entry describes a code sequence of symbol weight $\geq 20$. In other words, only the matchings with at most 7 columns containing no $\infty$ entry can specify code sequences of symbol weight $< 20$. It turns out that, among all matchings obtainable from $[0, 1, 1, 1, 1, \infty, 3, 2]$ and $[0, 1, 3, \infty, 6, 2, 1]$, only one has this property, namely

$$\Omega(0) = \begin{pmatrix} 0 & 1 & 1 & 1 & \infty & 3 & 2 & \infty \\ \infty & 0 & 1 & 3 & \infty & 6 & 2 & 1 \end{pmatrix}. \tag{10.19}$$

On the other hand, to each sequence listed in table 10.3 there correspond seven code sequences; indeed, if $\underline{f} = [f(0), \cdots, f(m + \ell)]$ represents a code sequence, then $[f(0) + i, \cdots, f(m + \ell) + i]$ also represents a code sequence for $0 \leq i \leq 6$. Hence, besides (10.19), we have to consider the matrices

$$\Omega(i) = \begin{pmatrix} 0 & 1 & 1 & 1 & \infty & 3 & 2 & \infty \\ \infty & i & i+1 & i+3 & \infty & i+6 & i+2 & i+1 \end{pmatrix} \tag{10.20}$$

for $1 \leq i \leq 6$. However, as mentioned above, it is not necessary to add an integer $j$ to the elements of the *first* row of $\Omega(i)$, because the sequences resulting from such an operation (which amounts to postmultiplication by $x^j$) have the same symbol weight as the sequences represented by (10.20).

For a given $i$, the symbol weight $\Delta^*(i)$ of the sequence represented by (10.20) is given by $\Delta^*(i) = 4 + \Delta_{i,1} + \Delta_{1,i+1} + \Delta_{i+3,1} + \Delta_{i+6,3} + \Delta_{2,i+2} + 4$ where $\Delta_{i,j}$ is the $(i, j)$ entry of the matrix $\Delta$ in figure 10.1. Using (10.13), we see that $\Delta^*(i)$ is equal to $8 + \Delta_{i,1} + 2\Delta_{i,2} + 2\Delta_{i,4}$. When $i$ goes from 0 to 6, the seven values of $\Delta^*(i)$ are the entries of the column 7-tuple obtained by summing column 1, twice column 2 and twice column 4 of the matrix $\Delta$, and by adding 8 to all components of this sum. The result of this computation is the column 7-tuple $(28, 20, 22, 28, 22, 30, 26)^T$. Since all components of this 7-tuple are $\geq 20$, it is possible that the code specified by $\underline{b} = [0, 1, 6, 5, 4]$ has minimum symbol distance 20. To be sure that this minimum distance is actually 20, we should check in the same way

all possible matchings associated with the pairs of sequences appearing
in table 10.3. There are 17 sequences in this table, but there are only
a few column 7-tuples to compute, because most pairs of sequences in
table 10.3 cannot be matched so as to describe code sequences containing
at most 7 nonzero words. In particular, the matching of two sequences
containing seven nonzero words always produces a sequence containing at
least 8 nonzero words.

The reader may check that the only matchings that may lead to a low
weight ($< 20$) sequence are in one of the following sets:

$$\Omega_1(i) = \begin{pmatrix} 0 & 1 & 6 & 5 & 4 & \infty \\ \infty & i & i+1 & i+6 & i+5 & i+4 \end{pmatrix},$$

$$\Omega_2(i) = \begin{pmatrix} 0 & 1 & 2 & 6 & 3 & 5 & 4 \\ \infty & i & i+1 & i+6 & i+5 & i+4 & \infty \end{pmatrix},$$

$$\Omega_3(i) = \begin{pmatrix} 0 & 1 & 5 & 3 & 5 & 6 & 5 \\ \infty & i & i+1 & i+6 & i+5 & i+4 & \infty \end{pmatrix},$$

$$\Omega_4(i) = \begin{pmatrix} 0 & 1 & 0 & 2 & 2 & 0 & 6 \\ \infty & i & i+1 & i+6 & i+5 & i+4 & \infty \end{pmatrix},$$

$$\Omega_5(i) = \begin{pmatrix} 0 & 1 & 4 & 0 & 1 & 1 & 0 \\ \infty & i & i+1 & i+6 & i+5 & i+4 & \infty \end{pmatrix},$$

$$\Omega_6(i) = \begin{pmatrix} 0 & 1 & 1 & 1 & \infty & 3 & 2 & \infty \\ \infty & i & i+1 & i+3 & \infty & i+6 & i+2 & i+1 \end{pmatrix},$$

$$\Omega_7(i) = \begin{pmatrix} 0 & 1 & 3 & \infty & 6 & 2 & 1 & \infty \\ \infty & i & i+1 & \infty & i+4 & i & i+4 & i+3 \end{pmatrix},$$

for $0 \leq i \leq 6$. The 7 matchings $\Omega_1(i)$ were already taken into account
in the preselection procedure described after (10.14) and the 7 matchings
$\Omega_6(i)$ were discussed after (10.20).

As explained after (10.20), to each 7-tuple $[\Omega_r(0), \cdots, \Omega_r(6)]$ of matchings, there corresponds a column 7-tuple $\Delta_r^* = [\Delta_r^*(0), \cdots, \Delta_r^*(6)]^T$ obtained by summing some columns of $\Delta$ and adding 8 to all components of the result. These column 7-tuples are

$$\Delta_1^* = (26, 20, 20, 22, 20, 22, 22)^T,$$

$$\Delta_2^* = (24, 24, 24, 24, 24, 24, 32)^T,$$

$$\Delta_3^* = (22, 28, 22, 22, 26, 28, 28)^T,$$

$$\Delta_4^* = (30, 26, 20, 28, 22, 20, 30)^T,$$

$$\Delta_5^* = (20, 28, 30, 28, 22, 22, 26)^T,$$

$$\Delta_6^* = (28, 20, 22, 28, 22, 30, 26)^T,$$

$$\Delta_7^* = (24, 22, 24, 26, 26, 26, 28)^T.$$

Since the minimum value of the entries of these 7-tuples $\Delta_r^*$ is 20, the minimum symbol distance of the code specified by $\underline{b} = [0,1,6,5,4]$ is equal to 20, which reaches the upper bound mentioned above.

**Table 10.4** : $\mathcal{H}_\alpha$-codes ($\alpha : \lambda \mapsto \lambda^{-1}$) achieving $sd = 4(m+1)$ for $m \leq 5$.

| $m$ | $\underline{b}$ |
|---|---|
| 1 | $[0,0]$ |
| 2 | $[0,0,0], [0,0,1]$ |
| 3 | $[0,0,2,6], [0,1,6,3], [0,0,1,2]$ |
| 4 | $[0,1,6,5,4], [0,0,1,1,4], [0,0,1,4,5]$ |
| 5 | $[0,0,1,1,3,4]$ |

The same procedure can be used to compute the minimum symbol distance of the inequivalent noncatastrophic encoders associated with the $(m+1)$-tuples $\underline{b}$ mentioned above for $m = 1, 2, 3, 4, 5$. In table 10.4, we give the list of all $(m+1)$-tuples $\underline{b}$ specifying a polynomial $g$ such that the bases of the $F$-space $g\mathcal{A}_\alpha$ are noncatastrophic encoders and $sd(g\mathcal{A}_\alpha)$ equals $4(m+1)$. In the case $m=5$ the result of this analysis was corroborated by Conan [23], who used a computer program to check that 24 is the true value of the minimum symbol distance of the code specified by $\underline{b} = [0,0,1,1,3,4]$.

This concludes our study of the codes that are ideals in the algebra $\mathcal{A}_\alpha$ with $\alpha$ satisfying $\lambda^\alpha = \lambda^{-1}$ for $\lambda \in \mathcal{H}^{(0)}$.

Let us now consider the two algebras $\mathcal{A}_\alpha$ that are specified by $\lambda^\alpha = \lambda^{-2}$ and $\lambda^\alpha = \lambda^{-4}$. We remark that if a code is an ideal in one of these algebras, then its reciprocal is an ideal in the other. Since the reciprocal of a code has the same minimum symbol distance as the original code, we shall be satisfied with studying ideals in the algebra $\mathcal{A}_\alpha$ specified by $\lambda^\alpha = \lambda^{-2}$. In this case $\mathcal{H}_\alpha$ is the set of $x \in (\mathcal{H}^{(0)})^{\mathbb{Z}}$ satisfying $x^{(i)} = \lambda^{(-2)^i}$ for all $i \in \mathbb{Z}$. An $\mathcal{H}_\alpha$-normal sequence generating a minimal ideal of dimension 3 in $\mathcal{A}_\alpha$ has the form given in (10.11) where $e$ is $e_1^{(\alpha)}$ or $e_3^{(\alpha)}$, but the meaning of $\alpha$ is different. Let us denote by $\mathcal{D}_i$ the set of codes $g\mathcal{A}_\alpha$ that are generated by a normal sequence $g$ corresponding to the choice $e = e_i^{(\alpha)}$. We would like to find the $(m+1)$-tuples $\underline{b}$ that specify polynomials $g$ such that the codes $g\mathcal{A}_\alpha$ have the same minimum symbol distance. We remark first that theorems 10.4 and 10.5 and remark 10.8 hold true for ideals in the algebra $\mathcal{A}_\alpha$, while theorem 10.6 has to be replaced by the following statement.

**Theorem 10.14 :** The $(m+1)$-tuple $\underline{b} = [b(0), \cdots, b(m)]$ and the $(m+1)$-tuple $\underline{b}'$ given by

$$b'(i) = b(i) \text{ for } i \equiv 0(6), \quad b'(i) = 3 + b(i) \text{ for } i \equiv 1(6),$$

$$b'(i) = 5 + b(i) \text{ for } i \equiv 2(6), \quad b'(i) = 4 + b(i) \text{ for } i \equiv 3(6),$$

$$b'(i) = 1 + b(i) \text{ for } i \equiv 4(6), \quad b'(i) = 6 + b(i) \text{ for } i \equiv 5(6),$$

specify $K^{\mathbb{Z}}$-equivalent codes.

**Proof :** Use the convolutional $K^{\mathbb{Z}}$-equivalence $\phi(1,y)$ where $y$ is the element of $GR(\mathcal{H}_\alpha)$ satisfying $y^{(0)} = (0,1,2,3,4,5,6)$ (with $i$ denoting the coordinate indexed by $x^i$). This $\phi$ has the following properties. $\phi^{(i)}$ is the identity for $i \equiv 0(6)$, $\phi^{(i)} = y^{(0)}$ for $i \equiv 1(6)$, $\phi^{(i)} = (y^{(0)})^6$ for $i \equiv 2(6)$, $\phi^{(i)} = (y^{(0)})^3$ for $i \equiv 3(6)$, $\phi^{(i)} = (y^{(0)})^2$ for $i \equiv 4(6)$, $\phi^{(i)} = (y^{(0)})^4$ for $i \equiv 5(6)$. Since any $x$ in $\mathcal{H}_\alpha$ satisfies $x^\alpha = x^{-2}$, it follows that $g = \sum_{i=0}^m (ex^{b(i)})^{\alpha^i} D^i$ satisfies $g\phi = \sum_{i=0}^m g_i D^i$ with $g_i = (ex^{b'(i)})^{\alpha^i}$ where $b'(i)$ is defined as above. $\square$

It follows from theorems 10.4, 10.5 and 10.14 and from remark 10.8 that any $(m+1)$-tuple $\underline{b} = [b(0), \cdots, b(m)]$ specifies a code that is $K^{\mathbb{Z}}$-equivalent to a code specified by an $(m+1)$-tuple of the form $\underline{b}' = [0, 0, b'(2), \cdots, b'(m)]$ where the first nonzero $b'(i)$ is 2 or 6. Conversely, two different $\underline{b}'$ of this form specify nonequivalent codes.

**Table 10.5 :** $\mathcal{H}_\alpha$-codes $(\alpha : \lambda \mapsto \lambda^{-2})$ achieving $sd = 4(m+1)$ for $m \leq 4$.

| $m$ | $\underline{b}$ |
|---|---|
| 1 | $[0,0]$ |
| 2 | $[0,0,0], [0,0,2], [0,0,6]$ |
| 3 | $[0,0,2,0], [0,0,2,3], [0,0,2,4], [0,0,2,5]$ |
|   | $[0,0,6,0], [0,0,6,2], [0,0,6,5], [0,0,6,6]$ |
| 4 | $[0,0,2,0,4], [0,0,2,2,3], [0,0,2,3,5]$ |
|   | $[0,0,2,4,4], [0,0,6,0,1], [0,0,6,0,5]$ |
|   | $[0,0,6,5,5], [0,0,6,6,2]$ |

The techniques we use to compute the minimum symbol distance of the convolutional codes $C = g\mathcal{A}_\alpha$, with $g$ specified by a given $\underline{b}$, are quite the same as the ones used above in the case of the algebra specified by $\lambda^\alpha = \lambda^{-1}$. We omit the details and we give in table 10.5 the results of this analysis. For small values of $m$, the table lists all $(m+1)$-tuples $\underline{b}$

that specify a polynomial $g = \sum_{j=1}^{m}(ex^{b(j)})^{\alpha^j}D^j$ for which the bases of the $F$-spaces $gA_\alpha$ are noncatastrophic encoders and $sd(gA_\alpha)$ equals $4(m+1)$.

Let us emphasize that the $(m+1)$-tuple $\underline{b}$ in table 10.5 does not represent the sequence $\sum_i e^{\alpha^i}x^{(-1)^i b(i)}D^i$ but the sequence $\sum_i(ex^{b(i)})^{\alpha^i}D^i$. In the first algebra $A_\alpha$ considered above, based on $\lambda^\alpha = \lambda^{-1}$, these two expressions did denote the same sequence. This is not the case in the algebra $A_\alpha$ specified by $\lambda^\alpha = \lambda^{-2}$, where the second sequence can now be written as $\sum_i e^{\alpha^i}x^{(-2)^i b(i)}D^i$.

## 10.3  Codes of length 9

Let $\mathcal{H}^{(0)}$ be the elementary Abelian group of order 9 generated by symbols $\lambda$ and $\mu$ that satisfy $\lambda^3 = \mu^3 = 1$ and $\lambda\mu = \mu\lambda$. Specify the automorphism $\alpha$ of $\mathcal{H}^{(0)}$ by $\lambda^\alpha = \lambda^2$, $\mu^\alpha = \mu\lambda$, and define $\mathcal{H}_\alpha :=< \mathcal{H}^{(0)}, \alpha >$. Since the automorphism $\alpha$ is an involution of $\mathcal{H}^{(0)}$ (which means $\nu^{\alpha^2} = \nu$ for all $\nu \in \mathcal{H}^{(0)}$), the group $\mathcal{H}_\alpha$ coincides with its reciprocal $\hat{\mathcal{H}}_\alpha$ and the reciprocal $\hat{C}$ of any $\mathcal{H}_\alpha$-code $C$ is still an $\mathcal{H}_\alpha$-code.

Let $x$ and $y$ be the elements of $\mathcal{H}_\alpha$ that satisfy $x^{(0)} = \lambda$ and $y^{(0)} = \mu$. With $F = GF(2)$, the algebra $A_\alpha = F\mathcal{H}_\alpha$ is semi-simple. This algebra can be expressed as a direct sum $A_\alpha = I_0 \oplus I_1 \oplus I_2 \oplus I_3 \oplus I_4$ of five minimal ideals $I_j = e_j A_\alpha = A_\alpha e_j$, with $0 \leq j \leq 4$, where the $e_j$ are the idempotents given by

$$e_0 = (1 + x + x^2)(1 + y + y^2),$$

$$e_1 = (x + x^2)(1 + xy + x^2 y^2),$$

$$e_2 = (x + x^2)(1 + y + y^2),$$

$$e_3 = (x + x^2)(1 + x^2 y + xy^2),$$

$$e_4 = (y + y^2)(1 + x + x^2).$$

These idempotents satisfy $e_0^\alpha = e_0$, $e_1^\alpha = e_2$, $e_2^\alpha = e_1$, $e_3^\alpha = e_3$, $e_4^\alpha = e_4$. The $F$-dimension of the $F$-space $e_0 A_\alpha$ is equal to 1, and the $F$-dimensions of the $F$-spaces $e_j A_\alpha$ with $1 \leq j \leq 4$ are all equal to 2.

For $e = e_1$, consider then the set of sequences $g$ of the form

$$g = \sum_{j=0}^{m} (ex^{b(j)})^{\alpha^j} D^j \; ; \quad b(j) \in \{0, 1, 2, \infty\}, \quad b(0) \neq \infty \, , \qquad (10.21)$$

where $x^\infty$ means zero. When $b(j)$ runs over the set $\{0, 1, 2, \infty\}$, the element $ex^{b(j)}$ runs over the 2-dimensional ideal $I_1 = e_\alpha$. Since $\mathcal{H}_\alpha$ is an Abelian group, (10.21) is the general form of the elements of $\mathcal{A}_\alpha := A_\alpha((D))$ that are polynomial $\mathcal{H}_\alpha$-normal sequences and have their initial word in $A_\alpha e = eA_\alpha$. For $b(j) \neq \infty$, the element $ex^{2b(j)}$ of $I_1$ is equal to $ex^{2b(j) \bmod 3}$. For this reason, we shall identify the integer $2b(j)$ with its residue mod 3. Like in the preceding sections, we shall exhibit several equivalences for the codes generated by $\mathcal{H}_\alpha$-normal sequences of the form (10.21). To that end we need a characterization of the permutation groups $R[\mathcal{H}^{(0)}]$, $L[\mathcal{H}^{(0)}]$, $\mathrm{Aut}(\mathcal{H}^{(0)})$ and $N_K[R(\mathcal{H}^{(0)})]$ with $K$ the symmetric group of order 9! and degree 9 acting on the group $\mathcal{H}^{(0)}$. Since $\mathcal{H}^{(0)}$ is Abelian we have $R[\mathcal{H}^{(0)}] = L[\mathcal{H}^{(0)}]$.

The permutation group $R[\mathcal{H}^{(0)}]$ is given in table 10.6 where, in the second column, the element $\lambda^i \mu^j$ of $\mathcal{H}^{(0)}$ is denoted for convenience by the integer $3j + i$ ; thus, for example, 5 represents $\lambda^2 \mu$ and 7 represents $\lambda \mu^2$.

The group $\mathrm{Aut}(\mathcal{H}^{(0)})$ is characterized as follows. Any element of $\mathcal{H}^{(0)}$ can be written as $\lambda^{r_1} \mu^{r_2}$ with $0 \leq r_1, r_2 \leq 2$. Consider $r_1$ and $r_2$ as elements of $GF(3)$ and let $P$ be a $2 \times 2$ matrix over $GF(3)$. From the pair $r = (r_1, r_2)$ over $GF(3)$ we obtain the pair $s = rP$ over $GF(3)$ and we write it as $s = (s_1, s_2)$. One can verify that the mapping $\lambda^{r_1} \mu^{r_2} \mapsto \lambda^{s_1} \mu^{s_2}$ is a permutation of $\mathcal{H}^{(0)}$ if and only if $P$ is a nonsingular matrix over $GF(3)$. Moreover it is not difficult to verify that this permutation is an automorphism of $\mathcal{H}^{(0)}$ and that a given automorphisms of $\mathcal{H}^{(0)}$ is uniquely representable in this way. Hence, the order of $\mathrm{Aut}(\mathcal{H}^{(0)})$ is equal to the number of nonsingular $2 \times 2$ matrices over $GF(3)$, which is $(3^2-1)(3^2-3) = 48$. For example the matrix $\begin{pmatrix} 2 & 0 \\ 0 & 2 \end{pmatrix}$ represents the automorphism of $\mathcal{H}^{(0)}$ induced by $\lambda \mapsto \lambda^2$, $\mu \mapsto \mu^2$, and it acts as the permutation $(1,2)(3,6)(4,8)(5,7)$. In the same way the matrix $\begin{pmatrix} 2 & 0 \\ 1 & 1 \end{pmatrix}$ represents the automorphism induced by $\lambda \mapsto \lambda^2$, $\mu \mapsto \lambda\mu$, and it acts as the permutation $(1,2)(3,4)(6,8)$. The group $N_K[R(\mathcal{H}^{(0)})]$ is then easily obtained as the semi-direct product of the groups $R(\mathcal{H}^{(0)})$ and $\mathrm{Aut}(\mathcal{H}^{(0)})$ (see subsection 6.1.2).

**Table 10.6 :** The group $R[\mathcal{H}^{(0)}]$ with $\mathcal{H}^{(0)}$ the elementary Abelian group of order 9.

| $h^{(0)}$ | $r(h^{(0)})$ |
|:---:|:---:|
| 1 | $(0)(1)(2)(3)(4)(5)(6)(7)(8)$ |
| $\lambda$ | $(0,1,2)(3,4,5)(6,7,8)$ |
| $\lambda^2$ | $(0,2,1)(3,5,4)(6,8,7)$ |
| $\mu$ | $(0,3,6)(1,4,7)(2,5,8)$ |
| $\lambda\mu$ | $(0,4,8)(1,5,6)(2,3,7)$ |
| $\lambda^2\mu$ | $(0,5,7)(1,3,8)(2,4,6)$ |
| $\mu^2$ | $(0,6,3)(1,7,4)(2,8,5)$ |
| $\lambda\mu^2$ | $(0,7,5)(1,8,3)(2,6,4)$ |
| $\lambda^2\mu^2$ | $(0,8,4)(1,6,5)(2,7,3)$ |

We now consider the problem of finding which $(m+1)$-tuples $\underline{b}$ specify $\mathcal{H}_\alpha$-normal sequences $g$ of the form (10.21), that generate $K^{\mathbb{Z}}$-equivalent $(9,2)$ binary convolutional codes.

**Theorem 10.16 :** The $(m+1)$-tuples $\underline{b} = [b(0), \cdots, b(m)]$ and $2\underline{b} = [2b(0), \cdots, 2b(m)]$ specify $K^{\mathbb{Z}}$-equivalent $\mathcal{H}_\alpha$-codes.

**Proof :** Use the $K^Z$-equivalence of the first kind

$$\phi = \phi[(1,2)(3,6)(4,8)(5,7),1^Z].$$

If $g$ is specified by $\underline{b}$, then $g\phi$ is specified by $2\underline{b}$. $\square$

**Theorem 10.17 :** The $(m+1)$-tuple $\underline{b} = [b(0),\cdots,b(m)]$ and the $(m+1)$-tuple $\underline{b}'$ given by $b'(i) = b(i)$ for $i \equiv 0(2)$ and $b'(i) = 1 + b(i)$ for $i \equiv 1(2)$ specify $K^Z$-equivalent $\mathcal{H}_\alpha$-codes.

**Proof :** Use the $K^Z$-equivalence of the first kind $\phi = \phi(1,x)$. If $g$ is specified by $\underline{b}$, then $g\phi$ is specified by $\underline{b}'$. $\square$

**Theorem 10.18 :** The $(m+1)$-tuple $\underline{b} = [b(0),\cdots,b(m)]$ and the $(m+1)$-tuple $\underline{b}'$ given by $b'(i) = i + b(i)$ for $0 \leq i \leq m$, specify $K^Z$-equivalent $\mathcal{H}_\alpha$-codes.

**Proof :** Use the $K^Z$-equivalence of the first kind $\phi = \phi(1,x^2y)$. If $g$ is specified by $\underline{b}$ then $g\phi$ is specified by $\underline{b}'$. $\square$

**Theorem 10.19 :** Let $b(0)$ and $b(m)$ be $\neq \infty$. The $\mathcal{H}_\alpha$-normal sequences $g = \sum_{j=0}^{m}(ex^{b(j)})^{\alpha^j}D^j$ and $\tilde{g} = \sum_{j=0}^{m}(ex^{b(m-j)})^{\alpha^j}D^j$ specify $\mathcal{H}_\alpha$-codes $g\mathcal{A}_\alpha$ and $\tilde{g}\mathcal{A}_\alpha$ that have the same minimum symbol distance.

**Proof :** The proof is the same as that of theorem 10.7. If necessary (i.e., if $m$ is odd), use the convolutional $K^Z$-equivalence of the first kind $\phi[(1,2)(3,4),(6,8),1^Z]$. $\square$

Let us remark that the two sequences $g$ and $gx^{-b(0)}$ specified respectively by $\underline{b} = [b(0),\cdots,b(m)]$ and $\underline{b}' = [0,b(1) - b(0),\cdots,b(m) - b(0)]$ generate the same code. For this reason the component $b(0)$ of $\underline{b}$ may always be chosen equal to 0.

On the basis of the theorems above we can construct classes of $(m+1)$-tuples $\underline{b}$, with $b(0) = 0$, that specify codes having the same minimum symbol distance. As an example, we check that, for $m = 3$, the $(m+1)$-tuples $\underline{b}$ having $b(0) = 0$ and no $b(j)$ equal to $\infty$ are in only two classes

(by the $K^{\mathbb{Z}}$-equivalences of theorems 10.16 to 10.18 and by reciprocity).
The first of these classes contains the following nine 4-tuples $[0,0,0,0]$,
$[0,0,1,1]$, $[0,0,2,2]$, $[0,1,0,1]$, $[0,1,1,2]$, $[0,1,2,0]$, $[0,2,0,2]$, $[0,2,1,0]$ and
$[0,2,2,1]$. All $\underline{b}$ in this class specify $\mathcal{H}_\alpha$-normal sequences $g$ having the
property that any basis of the $F$-space $gA_\alpha$ is a catastrophic convolutional
encoder. Indeed the $(2,1)$ encoder $\Gamma = [1+D, 1+D]$ over $GF(2^2)$ associated
with $\underline{b} = [0,0,0,0]$ is obviously catastrophic. From problems 2.1 and 8.1, it
follows then that all $(m+1)$-tuples $\underline{b}$ in the same class specify catastrophic
bases. The second class contains the 18 other 4-tuples $\underline{b}$ over $\{0,1,2\}$
satisfying $b(0) = 0$. A representative of this class is $\underline{b} = [0,0,0,1]$. Since
the associated encoder $\Gamma = [1+D, 1+\alpha D]$ over $GF(2^2)$, with $\alpha$ a primitive
element of $GF(2^2)$, is noncatastrophic, these eighteen 4-tuples $\underline{b}$ specify
noncatastrophic generators $g$.

**Table 10.7** : Upper bounds on the minimum symbol distance of (9,2) binary
convolutional codes.

| $m$ | 1 | 2 | 3 | 4 | 5 | 6 | 7 |
|-----|----|----|----|----|----|----|----|
| $\overline{sd}$ | 12 | 18 | 24 | 28 | 32 | 38 | 42 |

After having collected the generator polynomials and the corresponding
codes into equivalence classes, we analyze one representative of each class.
Since we are only interested in finding the "best" codes, we list in table
10.7 the best available upper bounds $\overline{sd}$ on the minimum symbol distance
of $(9,2)$ binary convolutional codes for $m \leq 7$. These upper bounds were
obtained by the techniques explained in chapter 3.

The method we apply to find the $\mathcal{H}_\alpha$-codes that are as close as possible
to these bounds is very similar to the one we have applied to the codes that
are ideals in the first algebra $\mathcal{A}_\alpha$ discussed in section 10.2. The automorphism $\alpha$ used to specify $\mathcal{H}_\alpha = < \mathcal{H}^{(0)}, \alpha >$ is indeed again an involution
(which means that $\alpha^2$ is the identity when acting on $\mathcal{H}^{(0)}$). Therefore, we

can write any sequence $v = ga$ of $g\mathcal{A}_\alpha$ as the sum of an *even* part and of an *odd* part, and we can represent it by a $2 \times (m + \ell + 1)$ matrix of the form (10.17) or (10.18), with $\ell = \deg a$. In fact the analysis is even simpler because the symbol weight of $x^i e + (x^j e)^\alpha$ has the constant value 4, for $0 \le i, j \le 2$. For that reason, if neither $f(j)$ nor $g(j)$ is $\infty$ for given $j$, the coefficient of $D^j$ in the represented sequence will have symbol weight equal to 4. If $f(j)$ and $g(j)$ are both equal to $\infty$, this symbol weight is zero, and in the remaining case, this symbol weight is equal to 6.

Consider for example the code $C = g\mathcal{A}_\alpha$ where $g$ is specified by $\underline{b} = [0,0,0,1,2]$. We make the following remarks.

**(i)** From table 10.7, one deduces $sd(g\mathcal{A}_\alpha) \le 28$.

**(ii)** The first and last nonzero words of any sequence in $g\mathcal{A}_\alpha$ have symbol weight equal to 6.

Hence, if a code sequence contains $s$ nonzero words, its symbol weight is at least equal to $6 + 4(s-2) + 6$ which is $4 + 4s$ and $\ge 28$ for $s \ge 6$. Stated otherwise, only code sequences containing at most five nonzero words can have a symbol weight $< 28$. By the same method as the one summarized in table 10.3 for a specific $(7,3)$ code, it is easily seen that the only nonzero sequences of $C = g\mathcal{A}_\alpha$ containing at most five nonzero words have the form $gx^r D^s$ with $r$ in $\{0, 1, 2\}$ and $s$ in $\mathbb{Z}$. Since the symbol weight of these sequences is 30, the minimum distance of $C = g\mathcal{A}_\alpha$ is actually 28.

Let us now go through the set of nonequivalent binary $\mathcal{H}_\alpha$-codes.

• $m = 1$. All $\underline{b}$ are equivalent to the pair $[0,0]$. This pair specifies a generator polynomial $g$ for which any basis of $g A_\alpha$ is a noncatastrophic encoder. Moreover one has $sd(g\mathcal{A}_\alpha) = 12$, which is optimal as follows from table 10.7.

• $m = 2$. All $\underline{b}$ are equivalent to the triple $[0,0,0]$. This triple specifies a generator polynomial $g$ for which any basis of $g A_\alpha$ is a noncatastrophic encoder. Moreover one has $sd(g\mathcal{A}_\alpha) = 18$, which is optimal as it follows from table 10.7.

- $m = 3$. As shown above there are basically two inequivalent 4-tuples $\underline{b}$, which can be chosen to be $\underline{b} = [0,0,0,0]$ and $\underline{b} = [0,0,0,1]$. The first one specifies a generator polynomial $g$ for which any basis of $g\mathcal{A}_\alpha$ is a catastrophic encoder. The second one specifies an optimal noncatastrophic generator $g$ satisfying $sd(g\mathcal{A}_\alpha) = 24$, thus achieving the upper bound of table 10.7.

- $m = 4$. There are four inequivalent 5-tuples $\underline{b}$. The first one, $\underline{b} = [0,0,0,1,0]$, leads to catastrophic encoders. With $\beta$ a primitive element of $GF(2^2)$, $1 + \beta D$ is indeed a divisor of $1 + D + D^2$. The second one, $b = [0,0,0,0,0]$, specifies a generator $g$ that satisfies $sd(g\mathcal{A}_\alpha) \leq 24$. The last two 5-tuples are $\underline{b} = [0,0,0,1,2]$ and $\underline{b} = [0,0,0,0,1]$. They specify generators $g$ satisfying $sd(g\mathcal{A}_\alpha) = 28$, which achieves the upper bound of table 10.7.

- $m = 5$. There are 10 inequivalent 6-tuples $\underline{b}$. The first three of these, $\underline{b} = [0,0,0,0,1,1]$, $\underline{b} = [0,0,0,1,0,2]$ and $\underline{b} = [0,0,0,0,0,0]$, lead to catastrophic encoders. For example, the two polynomials $1 + D + D^2$ and $1 + \beta D + \beta^2 D^2$ over $GF(2^2)$, which are associated with $\underline{b} = [0,0,0,1,0,2]$, are divisible by $1 + \beta^2 D$. Two other ones, $\underline{b} = [0,0,0,0,0,1]$ and $\underline{b} = [0,0,0,0,1,0]$, specify codes with a minimum symbol distance not exceding 30. The five remaining 6-tuples $\underline{b}$ specify generator polynomials $g$ satisfying $sd(g\mathcal{A}_\alpha) = 32$, which is the bound of table 10.7. These 6-tuples are $\underline{b} = [0,0,0,0,1,2]$, $\underline{b} = [0,0,0,1,0,0]$, $\underline{b} = [0,0,0,1,1,0]$, $\underline{b} = [0,0,0,1,1,1]$ and $\underline{b} = [0,0,0,1,2,1]$.

- $m = 6$. In this case the upper bound on the minimum symbol distance is 38, but this bound cannot be reached by $\mathcal{H}_\alpha$-codes. Indeed if the 7-tuple $\underline{b}$ specifying an $\mathcal{H}_\alpha$-normal sequence $g$ contains at least one $b(j)$ equal to $\infty$, then the symbol weight of $g$ is at most 36, and if no entry $b(j)$ of $\underline{b}$ is $\infty$, then the symbol weight of $g$ $(1+x^i D)$ is exactly 36 for $0 \leq i \leq 2$. Thus we have to restrict our search to generator polynomials $g$ satisfying $sd(g\mathcal{A}_\alpha) = 36$. To make the selection more drastic, we introduce the additional requirement that any nonzero sequence should contain at least 7 nonzero words. It turns out that there are 25 nonequivalent classes of 7-tuples $\underline{b}$ with no entry $b(j)$ equal to $\infty$. Six of these classes lead to catastrophic encoders. Among the 19 remaining classes, only 5 specify codes $g\mathcal{A}_\alpha$ achieving $sd(g\mathcal{A}_\alpha) = 36$ and satisfying the additional requirement above. Representative 7-tuples of each of these five classes are $\underline{b} = [0,0,0,0,1,2,2]$, $\underline{b} = [0,0,0,1,0,0,1]$, $\underline{b} = [0,0,0,1,0,2,2]$, $\underline{b} = [0,0,0,1,1,0,1]$, $\underline{b} = [0,0,0,1,1,1,0]$.

• $m = 7$. We consider only the example $\underline{b} = [0,0,\infty,0,0,1,2,1]$. This 8-tuple $\underline{b}$ specifies an $\mathcal{H}_\alpha$-normal sequence $g$ having the property that the minimum symbol weight of $g\mathcal{A}_\alpha$ is 42, which is optimal in view of table 10.7.

**Table 10.8** : Noncatastrophic generators of binary convolutional
$\mathcal{H}_\alpha$-codes with large minimum symbol distance.

| $m$ | $\underline{b}$ | $sd$ |
|---|:---:|---|
| 1 | $[0,0]$ | 12 |
| 2 | $[0,0,0]$ | 18 |
| 3 | $[0,0,0,1]$ | 24 |
| 4 | $[0,0,0,1,2]\ [0,0,0,0,1]$ | 28 |
| 5 | $[0,0,0,0,1,2]\ [0,0,0,1,0,0]$ | 32 |
|   | $[0,0,0,1,1,0]\ [0,0,0,1,1,1]$ | |
|   | $[0,0,0,1,2,1]$ | |
| 6 | $[0,0,0,0,1,2,2]\ [0,0,0,1,0,0,1]$ | 36 |
|   | $[0,0,0,1,0,2,2]\ [0,0,0,1,1,0,1]$ | |
|   | $[0,0,0,1,1,1,0]$ | |
| 7 | $[0,0,\infty,0,0,1,2,1]$ | 42 |

## 10.4    Codes of length 10

Let $\mathcal{H}^{(0)}$ be the dihedral group $D_5$ (of order 10) generated by the symbols $\lambda$ and $\mu$ satisfying $\lambda^5 = \mu^2 = 1$, $\mu\lambda = \lambda^4\mu$. The group algebra $A^{(0)} := F\mathcal{H}^{(0)}$ of $\mathcal{H}^{(0)}$ over $F = GF(2)$ is not semi-simple, and the dimension of its socle $S^{(0)}$ as a vector space over $F$ is equal to 9. This socle contains one minimal ideal $I_0^{(0)}$ of $F$-dimension 1 and five minimal ideals $I_i^{(0)}$, $1 \le i \le 5$, of $F$-dimension 4. The ideal $I_0^{(0)} = n_0^{(0)} A^{(0)}$ generated by $n_0^{(0)} = (1 + \mu)(1 + \lambda + \lambda^2 + \lambda^3 + \lambda^4)$ is nilpotent. For $1 \le i \le 5$, the ideal $I_i^{(0)} = e_i^{(0)} A^{(0)}$ is generated by the idempotent

$$e_i^{(0)} = e_i^{(0)}(\lambda, \mu) = \lambda + \lambda^2 + \mu(\lambda^i + \lambda^{i+1}). \tag{10.22}$$

Moreover the socle $S^{(0)}$ of $A^{(0)}$ can be written as $S^{(0)} = I_0^{(0)} \oplus I_i^{(0)} \oplus I_j^{(0)}$ for any $i$ and $j$ with $1 \le i, j \le 5$.

It turns out that the group $\mathrm{Aut}(\mathcal{H}^{(0)})$ has order 20. In fact, any $\alpha \in \mathrm{Aut}(\mathcal{H}^{(0)})$ is induced by one of the mappings $\lambda \mapsto \lambda^\alpha = \lambda^r$, $\mu \mapsto \mu^\alpha = \mu\lambda^s$, for $1 \le r \le 4$ and $0 \le s \le 4$. Hence there exist 20 groups $\mathcal{H}_\alpha = < \mathcal{H}^{(0)}, \alpha >$.

Define $A_\alpha := F\mathcal{H}_\alpha$ and $\mathcal{A}_\alpha := A_\alpha((D))$, and divide the set of algebras $\mathcal{A}_\alpha$ into two classes. The first of these classes, denoted by $\mathcal{D}_1$, contains the 10 algebras $\mathcal{A}_\alpha$ associated with the automorphisms $\alpha$ satisfying $\lambda^\alpha = \lambda$ or $\lambda^\alpha = \lambda^{-1}$, and the second class, denoted by $\mathcal{D}_2$, contains the 10 algebras associated with the automorphisms $\alpha$ satisfying $\lambda^\alpha = \lambda^2$ or $\lambda^\alpha = \lambda^{-2}$. It turns out that the socles of all algebras $\mathcal{A}_\alpha$ in $\mathcal{D}_1$ are $K^\mathbb{Z}$-equivalent (with $K = S(\mathcal{H}^{(0)})$) in the sense that, for $\mathcal{A}_\alpha$ and $\mathcal{A}_\beta$ in $\mathcal{D}_1$, any minimal ideal in $\mathcal{A}_\beta$ is transformed into a minimal ideal in $\mathcal{A}_\alpha$ by means of a suitable convolutional $K^\mathbb{Z}$-equivalence $\phi(1, z)$ for some $z \in \mathcal{H}_\beta$. The same statements can be made concerning the socles of the algebras in $\mathcal{D}_2$ and the minimal ideals therein. The discussion of these properties is suggested in problems 10.2 and 10.3.

As an example, choose $\alpha$ to be the identity automorphism $\alpha = 1$. The algebra $\mathcal{A}_1$ is in the class $\mathcal{D}_1$. In $\mathcal{H}_1$, we define $x$ and $y$ to be the elements that satisfy $x^{(i)} = \lambda$ and $y^{(i)} = \mu$ for all $i \in \mathbb{Z}$. We define then the idempotent $e$ in $A_1 := F\mathcal{H}_1$ by $e := e_1^{(0)}(x, y)$ with $e_1^{(0)}$ as given in (10.22). The $\mathcal{H}_1$-normal sequences having their initial word in $A_1e$ have the form

$$g = \sum_{j=0}^{m}[(1 + x)^{b(j)}e]D^j \,; \quad b(j) \in \{0, 1, \cdots, 14, \infty\}, \tag{10.23}$$

since the elements of the *left* ideals $A_1e$ can be identified with the 16 elements $(1 + x)^b e$ with $b \in \{0, 1, \cdots, 14, \infty\}$. As before, $(1 + x)^\infty$ stands for 0.

It is not difficult to verify that the $\mathcal{H}_1$-normal sequences $g$ specified by $\underline{b} = [0, 1]$ and $\underline{b} = [0, 1, 5]$ satisfy respectively $sd(g\mathcal{A}_\alpha) = 8$ and $sd(g\mathcal{A}_\alpha) = 12$. These values are lower than the corresponding upper bounds on $sd$ mentioned in chapter 3.

We shall not continue our discussion of the codes that are ideals in some of the algebras $\mathcal{A}_\alpha$ mentioned in this section. The comments made above may be of some help for the reader interested in further investigation.

## 10.5 Codes over $GF(2^\ell)$ and concatenated binary codes

In this section we study $(2, 1)$ convolutional codes over the field $F^* = GF(2^\ell)$ and we use these codes to construct good semiregular $(2\ell, \ell - 1)$ binary convolutional codes.

Consider first a $1 \times 2$ convolutional encoder $G = [g_1(D), g_2(D)]$ where $g_i(D)$ is a polynomial of degree $m$ over $F^*$. Given a primitive element $\beta$ of $F^*$ we can write

$$g_i(D) = \sum_{j=0}^{m} \beta^{b(i,j)} D^j, \tag{10.24}$$

where $b(i, j)$ is an element of the set $\{0, 1, \cdots, 2^\ell - 2, \infty\}$ and where $\beta^\infty$ denotes zero. Thus the pair $(\underline{b}^{(1)}, \underline{b}^{(2)})$ of the two $(m + 1)$-tuples $\underline{b}^{(1)} =$

$[b(1,0), \cdots, b(1,m)]$ and $\underline{b}^{(2)} = [b(2,0), \cdots, b(2,m)]$ specifies the encoder $G$.

Denote by $K$ $(= M_2)$ the monomial group of the $2 \times 2$ matrices over $F^*$ with a unique nonzero element in each row and each column, and denote by $I_2$ the $2 \times 2$ identity matrix. Define then $h_s$ to be the element of $K^{\mathbb{Z}}$ satisfying $h_s^{(i)} = \beta^s I_2$, for all $i$ in $\mathbb{Z}$. The set $H := \{h_s \mid 0 \leq s \leq 2^l - 2\}$ is a subgroup of $K^{\mathbb{Z}}$. For any $h_s \in H$ and any $v \in [F^*((D))]^2$, one has $vh_s = \beta^s v$, and, since $C = E(G)$ is an $F^*$-space, $v \in C$ implies $vh_s \in C$. As a consequence, $H$ is a subgroup of $\mathrm{Aut}_K(C)$.

Note that $H^{(0)}$ is a normal subgroup of $K$. Thus, with any $\phi^{(0)} \in K$ and any $h \in H$, we can associate a convolutional $K^{\mathbb{Z}}$-equivalence $\phi(\phi^{(0)}, h)$ of $C = E(G)$. These $K^{\mathbb{Z}}$-equivalences can be used to construct classes of encoders $G$ in such a way that $sd[E(G)]$ has the same value for all $G$ in the same class.

Consider now the specific case $F^* = GF(2^2)$. The following theorems show that certain classes of $1 \times 2$ convolutional encoders $G = [g_1, g_2]$ over $F^*$ specify codes with the same minimum symbol distance.

**Theorem 10.20 :** Suppose that the entries of $G$ are given by (10.24). For $i = 1, 2$, define $\bar{g}_i(D) := \sum_{j=0}^m \beta^{j+b(i,j)} D^j$. Then, for $\overline{G} := [\bar{g}_1(D), \bar{g}_2(D)]$, the codes $E(G)$ and $E(\overline{G})$ are $K^{\mathbb{Z}}$-equivalent convolutional codes.
**Proof :** Use the convolutional $K^{\mathbb{Z}}$-equivalence $\phi(1, h_1)$. $\square$

**Theorem 10.21 :** Suppose that the entries of $G$ are given by (10.24). For $i = 1, 2$, define $\bar{g}_i(D) := \beta^{s(i)} g_i(D)$ with $s(i) \in \{0, 1, 2\}$. Then, for $\overline{G} := [\bar{g}_1(D), \bar{g}_2(D)]$, the codes $E(G)$ and $E(\overline{G})$ are $K^{\mathbb{Z}}$-equivalent convolutional codes.
**Proof :** Use the convolutional $K^{\mathbb{Z}}$-equivalence $\phi(\phi^{(0)}, 1)$, with $\phi^{(0)} = \begin{pmatrix} \beta^{s(1)} & 0 \\ 0 & \beta^{s(2)} \end{pmatrix}$. $\square$

**Theorem 10.22 :** If we replace $\beta$ by $\beta^2$ in (10.24), the new encoder $G$

generates a code having the same minimum symbol distance as the initial one.

**Theorem 10.23 :** Replacing the encoder $(g_1, g_2)$ by $(g_2, g_1)$ does not modify the minimum symbol distance.

**Theorem 10.24 :** The reciprocal encoder $\hat{G}$ of $G$ generates a code $E(\hat{G})$ with the same minimum symbol distance as $E(G)$.

The proofs of theorems 10.22, 23 and 24 are omitted.

In all these cases the modified encoder is catastrophic if and only if the initial encoder is catastrophic.

When using these 5 theorems, we obtain several classes of encoders with the property that, in each class, all encoders generate codes having the same minimum symbol distance and all of them are simultaneously catastrophic or noncatastrophic. We discuss here first the case of encoders specified by polynomials $g_i$ of degree 3 over $F^*$. For one representative $G = [g_1, g_2]$ in each class, we verify the symbol weight of the sequences of the type $G(1 + \beta^s D)$ for $s \in \{0, 1, 2, \infty\}$. This verification shows that only six classes of encoders are noncatastrophic and may correspond to codes $C$ achieving $sd(C) = 8$, which is the maximum possible value. The pairs $(\underline{b}^{(1)}, \underline{b}^{(2)})$ specifying these classes are

$$([0,0,0,1],[0,1,0,2])\,,\ ([0,0,0,1],[0,2,0,2])\,,\ ([0,0,0,1],[0,2,1,2])\,,$$

$$([0,0,1,1],[0,1,0,2])\,,\ ([0,0,1,0],[0,0,2,0])\,,\ ([0,0,1,0],[0,1,0,0])\,.$$

A computer search using the modified Viterbi algorithm [37] has shown that only the first of these encoders generates a code of minimum symbol distance 8 and that the five remaining encoders generate codes of minimum symbol distance 7.

To construct binary codes from these quaternary codes, we apply a concatenation procedure; we replace the symbols over $F^*$ in the code sequences by binary triples, according to the rule

$$0 \mapsto 000, \ 1 \mapsto 011, \ \beta \mapsto 101, \ \beta^2 \mapsto 110.$$

As follows from [34], the resulting code is a $(6, 2)$ binary code (with $m = 3$) and its minimum symbol distance is twice the minimum symbol distance of the original code over $F^*$. Applying this concatenation to the first of the $(2, 1)$ codes over $F^*$ given above, we obtain a binary code (denoted here by $C$) with minimum symbol distance equal to 16. According to the results of section 3.1, this value is best possible. (We note that this optimum value of the minimum symbol distance was not achievable by the $(6, 2)$ codes with $m = 3$ that were described in section 10.1). A generator matrix of the code $C$ is given in figure 10.2. This code $C$ is an example of a semiregular $\mathcal{H}$-code with $\mathcal{H} = < \mathcal{H}^{(0)}, \alpha >$, where $\mathcal{H}^{(0)}$ is the cyclic group of order 3 generated by the element $\xi$ satisfying $\xi^3 = 1$, and $\alpha$ is the identity automorphism. Define $A := F\mathcal{H}$ and $\mathcal{A} := A((D))$ and let $x$ be the element of $\mathcal{H}$ that satisfies $x^{(0)} = \xi$. Then consider the polynomial

$$g := (e, e) + (e, xe)D + (e, e)D^2 + (xe, x^2e)D^3$$

over $\mathcal{A}^2$, where $e$ denotes $x + x^2$. It is not difficult to check that $C$ is nothing but the (irreducible) $\mathcal{A}$-submodule $g\mathcal{A}$ of $\mathcal{A}^2$.

$$\begin{bmatrix} D^3 & 1+D+D^2 & 1+D+D^2+D^3 & D+D^3 & 1+D^2+D^3 & 1+D+D^2 \\ 1+D+D^2+D^3 & D^3 & 1+D+D^2 & 1+D+D^2 & D+D^3 & 1+D^2+D^3 \end{bmatrix}$$

**Figure 10.2 :** A generator matrix of a $(6, 2)$ binary convolutional code with the largest possible minimum symbol distance.

A similar method can be used to obtain $(10, 4)$ convolutional codes that are better than the ones mentioned in section 10.4. This method is more flexible than the method of section 10.4 and it gives (at low cost) several binary codes achieving the upper bound on $sd$. The resulting codes remain invariant under a group of order 5.

Let $\mathcal{H}^{(0)}$ be the cyclic group of order 5 generated by the symbol $\xi$ satisfying $\xi^5 = 1$, define $\mathcal{H} :=< \mathcal{H}^{(0)}, \alpha >$ with $\alpha$ the identity automorphism, and let $x$ be the element of $\mathcal{H}$ satisfying $x^{(0)} = \xi$. With $F = GF(2)$, the algebra $A = F\mathcal{H}$ is semi-simple and it contains the minimal ideal $I = eA$ (of $F$-dimension 4) that is generated by the idempotent $e = x + x^2 + x^3 + x^4$. Since $I$ is a minimal ideal in a semi-simple commutative algebra, it is isomorphic to a field $F^*$, which in the present case is $GF(2^4)$. In this isomorphism, $e$ is identified with the element 1 of $F^*$ and $(1 + x)e$ is identified with some primitive element $\beta$ of $F^*$. Furthermore, we can verify that the symbol weight of the polynomial $(1 + x)^b e$ in $I$ is equal to 4 if $b$ is divisible by 3 and to 2 in the other cases. We consider then the $1 \times 2$ encoder $G = (1, 1) + (\beta, \beta^2)D$ over $F^*$. This encoder is noncatastrophic and it obviously satisfies $sd[E(G)] = 4$. Using the isomorphism between $F^*$ and $eA$, we associate with $G$ the $\mathcal{H}$-normal sequence

$$g = (e, e) + ((1 + x)e, (1 + x)^2 e)D.$$

The remarks made above are useful to prove that the irreducible module $C = g\mathcal{A}$, with $\mathcal{A} := A((D))$, satisfies $sd(C) = 10$, which is an upper bound for the minimum symbol distance of the $(10, 4)$ binary codes generated by encoders all entries of which have degree at most 2.

It seems that the general class of convolutional codes $g\mathcal{A}$ is quite promising and could be analyzed without great difficulty.

## 10.6 Longer binary codes

Let $\mathcal{H}^{(0)}$ be the cyclic abstract group of order $n$ and for an automorphism $\alpha$ of $\mathcal{H}^{(0)}$ define $\mathcal{H} :=< \mathcal{H}^{(0)}, \alpha >$. Let then $F$ be the finite field $GF(q)$ with $q$ relatively prime with $n$ so that the group algebra $A = F\mathcal{H}$ is semisimple. Any minimal ideal $I$ in $A$ is generated by a primitive idempotent $e$, i.e., an element such that the set of all $(ea)^r = ea^r$ for $r = 0, 1, \cdots, q^k - 2$, is the set of the $q^k - 1$ nonzero elements of $I$.

Assume that the automorphism $\alpha$ of $\mathcal{H}^{(0)}$ maps the ideal $I = eA$ on *another* minimal ideal $I^\alpha = e^\alpha A$, thus satisfying $I \cap I^\alpha = \{0\}$. In this case the $\mathcal{H}$-normal sequence $g = e + (ea^r)^\alpha D$ generates in $\mathcal{A} = A((D))$ the ideal $J = g\mathcal{A}$ that is a proper convolutional code.

Obviously the first nonzero word of any finite nonzero sequence in $J$ is a word of the block code $I = eA$ while the last nonzero word is in $I^\alpha$. Since the block codes $I$ and $I^\alpha$ are permutation equivalent, the symbol minimum distance $sd(J)$ is at least two times the symbol minimum distance $sd(I)$ of the block code $I$. In some cases however, it can be larger. To make this explicit we denote the direct sum $I \oplus I^\alpha$ by $I_0$.

Consider a nonzero sequence of finite length $\geq 3$ in $J$. Besides its first and last nonzero word, any such sequence contains at least one nonzero word in $I_0$ and, as a consequence, its symbol weight is at least equal to

$$d_3 = sd(I) + sd(I_0) + sd(I^\alpha). \tag{10.25}$$

As for the nonzero sequences of length $\leq 2$, they have the form $ga^b = ea^b + (ea^{r+b})^\alpha D$ for some $b$, and their symbol weight is at least equal to

$$d_2(r) = \min_b [sw(ea^b) + sw(ea^{r+b})] \tag{10.26}$$

since $\alpha$ does not modify the weight of a word. Therefore, if we can find a value of $r$ such that $d_2(r) \geq d_3$, then $sd(J)$ will be at least equal to $d_3$.

Here we shall illustrate by a simple example how to find such an $r$. In our example, we choose $\mathcal{H}^{(0)}$ to be the abstract cyclic group of order 17:

$$\mathcal{H}^{(0)} = \{1, \lambda, \cdots, \lambda^{16}\}; \ \lambda^{17} = 1.$$

Then we define the automorphism $\alpha$ of $\mathcal{H}^{(0)}$ by

$$\alpha \ : \ \lambda \mapsto \lambda^3,$$

and we define $\mathcal{H} = < \mathcal{H}^{(0)}, \alpha >$. Let $x$ be a generator of $\mathcal{H}$, choose $F = GF(2)$, define $A := F\mathcal{H}$ and

$$e := x^3 + x^6 + x^{12} + x^7 + x^{14} + x^{11} + x^5 + x^{10}.$$

| b | 0 | 1 | 2 | 3 | 4 | 5 | 6 | 7 | 8 | 9 | 10 | 11 | 12 | 13 | 14 | 15 | 16 | w |
|---|---|---|---|---|---|---|---|---|---|---|----|----|----|----|----|----|----|---|
| 0 | . | . | . | 1 | . | 1 | 1 | 1 | . | . | 1 | 1 | 1 | . | 1 | . | . | 8 |
| 1 | . | . | . | 1 | 1 | 1 | . | . | 1 | . | 1 | . | . | 1 | 1 | 1 | . | 8 |
| 2 | . | . | . | 1 | . | . | 1 | . | 1 | 1 | 1 | 1 | . | 1 | . | . | 1 | 8 |
| 3 | 1 | . | . | 1 | 1 | . | 1 | 1 | 1 | . | . | . | 1 | 1 | 1 | . | 1 | 10 |
| 4 | . | 1 | . | 1 | . | 1 | 1 | . | . | 1 | . | . | 1 | . | . | 1 | 1 | 8 |
| 5 | 1 | 1 | 1 | 1 | 1 | 1 | . | 1 | . | 1 | 1 | . | 1 | 1 | . | 1 | . | 12 |
| 6 | 1 | . | . | . | . | . | 1 | 1 | 1 | 1 | . | 1 | 1 | . | 1 | 1 | 1 | 10 |
| 7 | . | 1 | . | . | . | . | 1 | . | . | . | 1 | 1 | . | 1 | 1 | . | . | 6 |
| 8 | . | 1 | 1 | . | . | . | 1 | 1 | . | . | 1 | . | 1 | 1 | . | 1 | . | 8 |
| 9 | . | 1 | . | 1 | . | . | 1 | . | 1 | . | 1 | 1 | 1 | . | 1 | 1 | 1 | 10 |
| 10 | 1 | 1 | 1 | 1 | 1 | . | 1 | 1 | 1 | 1 | 1 | . | . | 1 | 1 | . | . | 12 |
| 11 | 1 | . | . | . | . | 1 | 1 | . | . | . | . | 1 | . | 1 | . | 1 | . | 6 |
| 12 | 1 | 1 | . | . | . | 1 | . | 1 | . | . | . | 1 | 1 | 1 | 1 | 1 | 1 | 10 |
| 13 | . | . | 1 | . | . | 1 | 1 | 1 | 1 | . | . | 1 | . | . | . | . | . | 6 |
| 14 | . | . | 1 | 1 | . | 1 | . | . | . | 1 | . | 1 | 1 | . | . | . | . | 6 |
| 15 | . | . | 1 | . | 1 | 1 | 1 | . | . | 1 | 1 | 1 | . | 1 | . | . | . | 8 |

**Figure 10.3 :** The 17-tuples $(1+x)^b e$ and their weights

for $b = 0, 1, \cdots, 15$.

In this case, $I = eA$ is a minimal ideal in $A$ of dimension 8 over $F$ and, with $a = (1 + x)$, the element $a$ is primitive in $I$. When applied to $e$, the automorphism $\alpha$ produces

$$e^\alpha = x^9 + x + x^2 + x^4 + x^8 + x^{16} + x^{15} + x^{13},$$

and the ideal $I^\alpha = e^\alpha A$ is isomorphic to $I$. The sum of these two ideals is direct and $I_0 = I \oplus I^\alpha$ is nothing but the set of the $2^{16}$ even weight elements of $A$.

Consider now the elements of the form $g = e + (ea^r)^\alpha D$ in $\mathcal{A} = A((D))$. It is well known (see for example [6]) that the symbol minimum weight of $I$ and $I^\alpha$ is equal to 6; hence $d_3$ is equal to $6 + 2 + 6 = 14$. In order for $J$ to have symbol minimum distance $\geq 14$, we select $r$ so that $d_2(r)$ be $\geq 14$, thus larger than $sd(I) + sd(I^\alpha) = 12$. To do that we give in figure 10.3 the representation as 17-tuples of the 16 polynomials $(1 + x)^b e$ for $b = 0, 1, \cdots, 15$, and we denote $sw(ea^b)$ by $w(b)$. Then we remark that we

have $(1 + x)^{15}e = x^{-1}e$, which implies that for $b = 0, 1, \cdots, 254$, $w(b)$ is
equal to $w(b \bmod 15)$. Thus we have

$$d_2(r) = \min_{0 \le b \le 14} [w(b) + w(b + r)]. \tag{10.27}$$

In the case $r = 5$, we give in table 10.9 the 15 values (for $b = 0, 1, \cdots, 14$)
of $w(b)$, $w(b + r)$ and $sw(ga^b) = w(b) + w(b + r)$. As it appears from this
figure, the quantity $d_2(5)$ given by $(10.27)$ is equal to 14. Hence the $(17, 8)$
binary convolutional code generated by

$$g = e + [(1 + x)^5 e]^\alpha D$$

has symbol minimum distance *equal* to 14, and it follows from section 3.1
that this is the largest possible value. Also $r = 10$ leads to $sd(g\mathcal{A}) = 14$
but the other values of $r \bmod 15$ specify codes with a symbol minimum
distance equal only to 12.

The principles of the method go back to [45] and its applicability to
the construction of good convolutional codes, all degrees $m(i)$ of which are
equal to 1, was suggested in [90].

**Table 10.9 :** Some weights useful to compute $sd(g\mathcal{A})$.

| $b$ | 0 | 1 | 2 | 3 | 4 | 5 | 6 | 7 | 8 | 9 | 10 | 11 | 12 | 13 | 14 |
|---|---|---|---|---|---|---|---|---|---|---|---|---|---|---|---|
| $w(b)$ | 8 | 8 | 8 | 10 | 8 | 12 | 10 | 6 | 8 | 10 | 12 | 6 | 10 | 6 | 6 |
| $w(b + r)$ | 12 | 10 | 6 | 8 | 10 | 12 | 6 | 10 | 6 | 6 | 8 | 8 | 8 | 10 | 8 |
| $w(ga^b)$ | 20 | 18 | 14 | 18 | 18 | 24 | 16 | 16 | 14 | 16 | 20 | 14 | 18 | 16 | 14 |

## 10.7   Comments

In this chapter we have described several methods to construct convolutional codes that have a strong algebraic structure, and to select among them those having the largest minimum symbol distance. The code investigated in the first three sections of the chapter were treated in depth while the codes considered in the three last sections would certainly deserve further study. Some references related to these questions are [30, 89, 91, 93].

### PROBLEMS

**10.1** Let $\mathcal{H}^{(0)}$ be the elementary Abelian group of order 9 generated by $\lambda$ and $\mu$ (with $\lambda^3 = \mu^3 = 1$, $\lambda\mu = \mu\lambda$). Define $\mathcal{H} := < \mathcal{H}^{(0)}, \alpha >$ and $A := F\mathcal{H}$, with $\alpha$ satifying $\lambda^\alpha = \mu^2$, $\mu^\alpha = \lambda$. Analyze in detail some binary $\mathcal{H}$-codes of dimension 4 that are the direct sum of two minimal ideals $g_1 A((D))$ and $g_2 A((D))$ generated by two $\mathcal{H}$-normal sequences $g_1$ and $g_2$.

**10.2** Construct explicitly the automorphism group of the dihedral group $D_5$.

**10.3** Determine the $K^{\mathcal{Z}}$-equivalences between the algebras in each of the two classes considered in section 10.4.

**10.4** Analyze in more detail the construction method of binary (10,4) convolutional codes that is suggested in section 10.5.

**10.5** Extend the approach of section 10.6 to codes that are a direct sum of minimal ideals.

**10.6** Let $g = g_0 + g_1 D$ be an $\mathcal{H}$-normal sequence. Show that $d_3$, given by (10.25), is only a lower bound on the symbol weight of the sequences of length $\geq 3$ in $C = g\mathcal{A}$ and try to find a generator $g$ such that $sd(g\mathcal{A}) > d_3$.

# Chapter 11

# Convolutional codes that are good for some nonstandard criteria

In this chapter we shall no longer use the minimum symbol distance as the quality criterion for convolutional codes; we shall replace it by the minimum word distance, the distance repartition and other criteria introduced below.

In section 11.1 we shall discuss a class of codes having a large minimum word distance. These codes are well matched to channels producing clustered errors separated by periods of noiseless transmission. In the second section we investigate in further detail some codes that were introduced in chapter 10. These codes are shown to have a good distance repartition so that they can be efficiently used for channels producing clustered errors and independent symbol errors. In the third section we extend to convolutional codes the concept of unequal error protection (or UEP) originally defined for block codes in [14, 32, 44]. Then we give some examples of how the construction techniques described in chapter 10 can be used to construct convolutional codes with good UEP properties. Finally in the fourth section we introduce the concept of channel error correcting codes, we present a rather simple construction of such codes and we give some information on their use.

# 11.1 Binary word error correcting convolutional codes

The goal of this section is to construct word error correcting convolutional codes. As mentioned in chapter 3, it is reasonable to measure the error correcting capability of such a code $C$ by means of the parameter $wd(C)$. In the sequel we first give an algebraic framework in which our codes can be defined. Then we discuss two families of word correcting codes: the codes generated by free encoders and the codes generated by reduced encoders.

## 11.1.1 Representation of a class of binary convolutional codes

We consider the situation where a source delivers, at each time unit $j \in Z$, an information $a_j$ that is representable by a polynomial $a_j(x)$ of formal degree $k-1$ over the finite field $F = GF(2)$. Assuming that this information sequence has finite delay, we represent it as

$$a = \sum_{j=r}^{\infty} a_j(x) D^j. \tag{11.1}$$

To encode this information sequence $a$, we use a two-variable generator polynomial $g$ represented by

$$g = \sum_{j=0}^{m} g_j(x) D^j, \tag{11.2}$$

where the nonzero $g_j(x)$ are polynomials in $x$ over $F$. The encoding of the information $a$ by means of the generator polynomial $g$ consists of computing the sequence $v = ga$. This sequence $v$ can be written as

$$v = \sum_{j=r}^{\infty} v_j(x)D^j, \qquad (11.3)$$

where $v_j(x)$ is a polynomial of formal degree $n-1$ over $F$. The value of the integer $n$ is $k + e_M$, where $e_M$ denotes the maximum degree of the nonzero polynomials $g_j(x)$. The encoding mapping $a \mapsto v = ga$ presents some similarities with the encoding described in section 10.2 but the multiplication $ga$ of section 10.2 induces the structure of an ideal for the code generated by $g$, which will not be the case here.

We shall specialize as follows the form (11.2) of the generator polynomials $g(x, D)$. We assume first that, for $0 \le j \le m$, there exist integers $e(j)$ satisfying $0 \le e(j) \le e_M$ and such that $g_j(x)$ is given by

$$g_j(x) = x^{e(j)}. \qquad (11.4)$$

We assume in addition that the integers $e(j)$ have the form

$$e(j) = (j - r)(j - r - 1)/2 \,;\; 0 \le j \le m, \qquad (11.5)$$

for some arbitrary $r \in \mathbb{Z}$. Thus, in the particular case $r = 2$, $m = 4$, the corresponding generator polynomial is given by

$$g(x, D) = x^3 + xD + D^2 + D^3 + xD^4. \qquad (11.6)$$

Beside the representation $a \mapsto v = ga$ of the encoding, in which $a$ has formal degree $k - 1$ in $x$, we can also use a matrix representation. In this case the information $a$ is a $k$-tuple over $\mathcal{F}$, the encoder $G$ is a $k \times n$ matrix over $F[D]$ (with $n = k + e_M$) and $v$ is the $n$-tuple over $\mathcal{F}$ given by $v = aG$. Thus, the encoder $G$ associated with the polynomial $g(x, D)$ given in (11.6) has the property that its $i^{\text{th}}$ row is the element of $F^n[D]$ represented by the two-variable polynomial $x^{i-1}g(x, D)$ when the $n$ columns of $G$ (and also the $n$ coordinates of any $v \in E(G)$) are indexed successively by the $n$ monomials $1, x, \cdots, x^{n-1}$. In the same way, the information sequence $a = [a^1(D), \cdots, a^k(D)]$ is the element of $\mathcal{F}^k$ such that $a(x, D)$ given in (11.1) satisfies $a(x, D) = \sum_{i=0}^{k-1} x^i a^{i+1}(D)$. For example if we associate the $3 \times 6$ encoder $G$ with the polynomial $g$ given by (11.6), its representation as a $3 \times 6$ matrix over $F[D]$ is

$$G = \begin{bmatrix} D^2 + D^3 & D + D^4 & 0 & 1 & 0 & 0 \\ 0 & D^2 + D^3 & D + D^4 & 0 & 1 & 0 \\ 0 & 0 & D^2 + D^3 & D + D^4 & 0 & 1 \end{bmatrix}. \tag{11.7}$$

In the present context, we can also represent $G$ as a $k \times (m + 1)$ matrix having as its $(i, j)$-entry the coefficient $x^{i-1+e(j)}$ of $D^j$ in $x^{i-1}g(x, D)$. The representation of the encoder $G$ above is then

$$G = \begin{bmatrix} x^3 & x & 1 & 1 & x \\ x^4 & x^2 & x & x & x^2 \\ x^5 & x^3 & x^2 & x^2 & x^3 \end{bmatrix}. \tag{11.8}$$

We call the encoding procedure described by $a \mapsto v = ga$, with $g$ satisfying (11.2), a *free* encoding procedure. The corresponding encoder $G$ is then called a free encoder.

The next subsection is devoted to proving the word correcting properties of the codes $C = E(G)$ when $G$ is a free encoder constructed according to (11.4) and (11.5).

## 11.1.2 Error correcting properties of the codes generated by free encoders

In this subsection we assume that (11.4) and (11.5) hold everywhere and we answer the following questions.

(i)  When is the encoder $G$ derived from $g(x, D)$ a catastrophic encoder?

(ii) What is the minimum word distance $wd(C)$ of $C = E(G)$?

The first of these questions is answered by the following theorem.

**Theorem 11.1 :** Let $g$ be constructed according to (11.4) and (11.5) and let $G$ be the associated encoder. This encoder $G$ is catastrophic if and only if $m$ is odd and $r$ is equal to $(m - 1)/2$.

**Proof :** If both conditions of the theorem are satisfied, $e(s)$ equals $e(m-s)$ and the first row of $G$ can be represented by

$$g(x, D) = \sum_{j=0}^{r} x^{e(j)} \left( D^j + D^{m-j} \right).$$

The informati⁄n sequence $a = [(1 + D)^{-1}, 0, \cdots, 0]$ satisfies $sw(a) = \infty$, but $v = aG$ can be written as

$$v(x, D) = \sum_{j=0}^{r} x^{e(j)} \left( \sum_{\ell=j}^{m-1-j} D^\ell \right),$$

so that it satisfies $sw(v) < \infty$. As a consequence the encoder $G$ is catastrophic.[6]

Suppose now that at least one of the conditions of the theorem is not satisfied. In this case, there is a unique value of $s$ (either 0 or $m$) for which $e(s)$ reaches its maximum value : $e(s) = e_M$. For any $a = \sum_{j=r}^{\infty} a_j(x) D^j$ satisfying $sw(a) = \infty$, we denote by $i_M$ the largest integer such that $x^{i_M}$ appears with a nonzero coefficient in infinitely many $a_j(x)$. It follows that $x^{i_M + e_M}$ appears with a nonzero coefficient in infinitely many words $v_j(x)$ of $v = \sum_j v_j(x) D^j$, thus implying that the symbol weight of $v$ is infinite. As a consequence, if $sw(a)$ equals $\infty$, then so does $sw(ga)$, and the encoder $G$ is noncatastrophic. $\square$

In connection with question (ii), we now prove that, whenever $G$ is a noncatastrophic encoder constructed according to the rules of subsection

---

[6]In this case each row of $G$ is a catastrophic encoder of rate $1/n$.

11.1.1, the word distance $wd(C)$ of the convolutional code $C = E(G)$ is equal to $m + 1$. This is of course the maximum possible value since all entries $g_{ij}(D)$ of the matrix $G$, written as in (11.7), have degree $\leq m$. Thus, under the hypothesis that $G$ is a noncatastrophic encoder, we have to prove that $v(x, D) = g(x, D) a(x, D)$ contains at least $m + 1$ nonzero words $v_j(x)$ for any nonzero $a(x, D) = \sum_j a_j(x) D^j$ containing a finite number of nonzero words $a_j(x)$. Without real loss of generality we assume that the information $a$ is a nonzero polynomial sequence

$$a(x, D) = \sum_{j=0}^{t-1} a_j(x) D^j \tag{11.9}$$

of polynomials $a_j(x)$ of degree at most equal to $k - 1$, but, instead of using the notation (11.9), we represent $a$ as a $t$-tuple $\mathbf{a} = [a_0(x), \cdots, a_{t-1}(x)]$ of polynomials $a_j(x)$. In the same way we represent the corresponding encoded sequence $v(x, D) = \sum_{j=0}^{m+t-1} v_j(x) D^j$ as an $(m + t)$-tuple $\mathbf{v} = [v_0(x), \cdots, v_{m+t-1}(x)]$. With this notation, the relation between $\mathbf{a}$ and $\mathbf{v}$ can be expressed in matrix form by

$$\mathbf{v} = \mathbf{a} \, \boldsymbol{\Phi}, \tag{11.10}$$

where $\boldsymbol{\Phi}$ is a $t \times (m + t)$ polynomial matrix constructed as follows. For $1 \leq i \leq t$ and $0 \leq j \leq m + t$, the $(i, j)$-entry of $\boldsymbol{\Phi}$ is $x^{e(j-i)}$ if $j - i$ is in $[0, m]$, and it is zero otherwise. Thus, the matrix $\boldsymbol{\Phi}$ has the form

$$\boldsymbol{\Phi} = \begin{bmatrix} x^{e(0)} & x^{e(1)} & \cdots & \cdots & x^{e(m)} & 0 & \cdots & 0 \\ 0 & x^{e(0)} & \cdots & \cdots & x^{e(m-1)} & x^{e(m)} & \cdots & 0 \\ \vdots & \vdots & \vdots & \vdots & \vdots & \vdots & \cdots & \vdots \\ 0 & 0 & \cdots & x^{e(0)} & \cdots & \cdots & \cdots & x^{e(m)} \end{bmatrix} . \tag{11.11}$$

To prove $wd(C) = m + 1$ amounts to showing that in (11.10), no nonzero $t$-tuple $\mathbf{a}$ can produce an $(m+t)$-tuple $\mathbf{v}$ with $t$ (or more) zero components

$v_j(x)$, or, equivalently, that no $t \times t$ submatrix of $\boldsymbol{\Phi}$ (considered as a matrix over $F(x)$) can have a nonzero determinant.

To prove that all $t \times t$ submatrices of $\boldsymbol{\Phi}$ have a nonzero determinant, we define $\boldsymbol{\Phi}^*$ to be the $t \times (m+t)$ matrix having $x^{f(j-i)}$ in position $(i,j)$ where $f(s) = (s-r)(s-r-1)/2$. In all positions $(i,j)$ where $\boldsymbol{\Phi}$ contains a nonzero monomial, the matrices $\boldsymbol{\Phi}$ and $\boldsymbol{\Phi}^*$ have the same entry, but in all positions where $\boldsymbol{\Phi}$ contains zero, $\boldsymbol{\Phi}^*$ contains a nonzero monomial. For $1 \le i \le t$, let us multiply the $i^{\text{th}}$ row of both $\boldsymbol{\Phi}$ and $\boldsymbol{\Phi}^*$ by $x^{f(m+t-1)-f(m+t-i)}$ and, for $1 \le j \le m+t$, let us multiply the $j^{\text{th}}$ column of these matrices by $x^{-f(j-1)}$. We denote by $\boldsymbol{\Psi}$ and $\boldsymbol{\Psi}^*$ the two matrices resulting from $\boldsymbol{\Phi}$ and $\boldsymbol{\Phi}^*$ via these transformations. It is not difficult to see that the matrix $\boldsymbol{\Psi}^*$ is a Vandermonde matrix [72, 87], i.e., a matrix having in position $(i,j)$ the $(i-1)^{\text{st}}$ power of the element in position $(1,j)$. In the present case this element in position $(1,j)$ is $x^{m+t-j}$. As for the matrix $\boldsymbol{\Psi}$, it coincides with the matrix $\boldsymbol{\Psi}^*$ except that it has some zero entries in the lower left and in the right upper corner. We are now ready to prove the following lemma.

**Lemma 11.2 :** Any $t \times t$ submatrix of $\boldsymbol{\Phi}$ has a nonzero determinant.

**Proof :** Proving that a $t \times t$ submatrix of $\boldsymbol{\Phi}$ has a nonzero determinant is equivalent to proving that the corresponding $t \times t$ submatrix of $\boldsymbol{\Psi}$ has a nonzero determinant. Let $\boldsymbol{\Omega}$ be any $t \times t$ submatrix of $\boldsymbol{\Psi}$ and let $\boldsymbol{\Omega}^*$ be the corresponding submatrix of $\boldsymbol{\Psi}^*$. This matrix $\boldsymbol{\Omega}^*$ can be written as

$$\boldsymbol{\Omega}^* = \begin{bmatrix} 1 & 1 & \cdots & 1 \\ x^{r(t)} & x^{r(t-1)} & \cdots & x^{r(1)} \\ x^{2r(t)} & x^{2r(t-1)} & \cdots & x^{2r(1)} \\ \vdots & \vdots & & \vdots \\ x^{(t-1)r(t)} & x^{(t-1)r(t-1)} & \cdots & x^{(t-1)r(1)} \end{bmatrix}, \qquad (11.12)$$

with $r(t) > r(t-1) > \cdots > r(1)$. The matrix $\Omega$ coincides with $\Omega^*$ in all positions except possibly in the lower left and the upper right corners where it may contain zeros. In any case, independently of which $t$ columns are chosen to construct $\Omega$ and $\Omega^*$, all elements of the main diagonal of $\Omega$ are nonzero.

Let us now prove that $\det \Omega^*$ is nonzero. The value of this determinant is given by $\sum_\pi x^{\sum_{i=1}^{t} r(i)\pi(i-1)}$ [72, 87], where the $\pi$-sum is taken over all permutations $\pi : \ j \mapsto \pi(j)$ of the set $\{0, 1, \cdots, t-1\}$. From $r(t) > r(t-1) > \cdots > r(1)$ it follows that the permutation $\pi$ achieving the minimum of $\sum_{i=1}^{t} r(i)\pi(i-1)$ is unique and is given by $\pi(i) = t-1-i$. As a consequence, the monomial of smallest degree in $\det \Omega^*$ appears with coefficient 1 and is the product of all diagonal elements of $\Omega^*$. Since no diagonal element of $\Omega$ is zero, this product is one of the monomials the sum of which is $\det \Omega$. Since the set of monomials that are added up to obtain $\det \Omega$ is a subset of the monomials that are added up to obtain $\det \Omega^*$, and since the (unique) lowest degree monomial of $\det \Omega^*$ appears also in $\det \Omega$, it follows that $\det \Omega$ is also nonzero. $\square$

According to the remarks made after (11.11), lemma 11.2 yields the following result.

**Theorem 11.3 :** Let $g(x, D)$ be a two-variable polynomial satisfying (11.4) and (11.5), and let $G$ be the $k \times n$ matrix the $i^{\text{th}}$ row of which is represented by $x^{i-1}g(x, D)$. If $G$ is a noncatastrophic encoder, then one has $sw[E(G)] = m+1$ holds.

## 11.1.3 Properties of the codes generated by reduced encoders

The codes generated by the free encoders described in subsection 11.1.2 have a redundancy $m-k$ equal to the maximum value $e_M$ of the numbers $e(j)$ specifying the generator polynomial $g(x, D)$. When these numbers satisfy (11.5), $e_M$ is either equal to $e(0) = r(r+1)/2$ or to $e(m) = (m-$

$r)(m - r - 1)/2$. In particular, for even values of $m$, which correspond to odd values of $wd[E(G)]$, $e_M$ is at least equal to $m(m+2)/8$.

In this subsection we describe a modification of this encoding procedure that may produce encoders $G$ having lower redundancy but still satisfying $wd[E(G)] = m + 1$. First we describe how these encoders are constructed.

Let us choose any $(m+1)$-tuple $[e(0), \cdots, e(m)]$ of nonnegative integers $e(j)$, and let us associate with this $(m+1)$-tuple the two-variable polynomial over $F$ given by

$$g(x, D) = \sum_{j=0}^{m} x^{e(j)} D^j. \qquad (11.13)$$

In addition, let us choose a polynomial

$$\mu(x) = 1 + \sum_{j=1}^{n-1} \mu_j x^j + x^n \qquad (11.14)$$

with coefficients in $F$, having no multiple factor. Given an information sequence $a(x, D) = \sum_{j=r}^{\infty} a_j(x) D^j$ of $x$-degree $\leq k - 1$, with $k < n$, we encode it into the sequence $v$ given by

$$v(x, D) = g(x, D) a(x, D) \bmod \mu(x). \qquad (11.15)$$

This means that the word $v_j(x)$ in $v(x, D) = \sum_{j=r}^{\infty} v_j(x) D^j$, is the residue mod $\mu(x)$ of the coefficient of $D^j$ in the product $ga$. To obtain the $k \times n$ encoder that represents the mapping (11.15), we replace all powers of $x$ in $x^{i-1} g(x, D)$ by their residues modulo $\mu(x)$. We thus write

$$x^{i-1} g(x, D) = \sum_{j=1}^{n} \gamma_i^j(D) x^{j-1} \bmod \mu(x); \quad i = 1, 2, \cdots, k, \qquad (11.16)$$

where $\gamma_i^j(D)$ is a polynomial over $F$. Then we define the $n \times n$ polynomial matrix $G$ to be the matrix having $\gamma_i^j(D)$ as its $(i, j)$ entry, and we denote by $G^{[k]}$ the $k \times n$ matrix of the $k$ first rows of $G$. The matrix representation of

(11.15) for sequences $a(x, D)$ of $x$-degree $\leq k - 1$ is then given by $v = aG^{[k]}$ with $a \in \mathcal{F}^k$ and $v \in \mathcal{F}^n$.

Let us now discuss the conditions for $G^{[k]}$ to be a noncatastrophic encoder. We first consider the $n \times n$ matrix

$$
M = \begin{bmatrix}
0 & 1 & 0 & \cdots & 0 & 0 \\
0 & 0 & 1 & \cdots & 0 & 0 \\
\vdots & \vdots & \vdots & & \vdots & \vdots \\
0 & 0 & 0 & \cdots & 0 & 1 \\
-1 & -\mu_1 & \mu_2 & & -\mu_{n-2} & -\mu_{n-1}
\end{bmatrix}, \qquad (11.17)
$$

over $F = GF(2)$, which is called the *companion matrix* of the polynomial $\mu(x)$. The $n \times n$ matrix $G$ is then easily shown to satisfy

$$
G = \sum_{j=1}^{n} \gamma_1^j(D) \, M^{j-1}, \qquad (11.18)
$$

where $M^0 = I_n$. As it is a polynomial of degree $n$ over $F$, the polynomial $\mu(x)$ has $n$ zeros in some extension field $F^*$ of $F$ and, since it has no multiple factor, all these zeros are different. We denote by $Z(\mu) = \{\alpha_1, \alpha_2, \cdots, \alpha_n\}$ the set of these zeros and we define $A$ to be the $n \times n$ diagonal matrix with $\alpha_j$ in position $(j, j)$. With $V$ the $n \times n$ matrix having $(\alpha_j)^{i-1}$ in position $(i, j)$ we have

$$
MV = VA. \qquad (11.19)
$$

The equality (11.19) is indeed trivially true regarding the first $(n-1)$ rows; as for the last row equality, it simply expresses the relation $\mu(\alpha_i) = 0$ for $i = 1, \cdots, n$. Using (11.18) and (11.19) we can then write

$$
G = V \left[ \sum_{j=1}^{n} \gamma_1^j(D) \, A^{j-1} \right] V^{-1}, \qquad (11.20)
$$

which leads to

$$G^{[k]}V = V^{[k]}\Gamma(D), \tag{11.21}$$

where $V^{[k]}$ denotes the matrix of the first $k$ rows of $V$ and where $\Gamma(D)$ is the diagonal $n \times n$ matrix having $g(\alpha_j, D)$ as its $(j, j)$ entry. Let us make the following remarks.

(i) The matrix $V$ is a Vandermonde matrix [72]. Since all $\alpha_j$ are different, $V$ is nonsingular. This implies that the encoders $G^{[k]}$ over $F$ and $G^{[k]}V$ over $F^*$ have the same Hermite form (2.28); hence they are simultaneously catastrophic or noncatastrophic.

(ii) Since all $k \times k$ minors of $V^{[k]}$ are nonzero, the g.c.d. of the $k \times k$ minor of the right hand side of (11.21) is the g.c.d. of the polynomials $\tau^J(D)$ $:= \prod_{\alpha \in J} g(\alpha, D)$ with $J$ an arbitrary subset of cardinality $k$ of $Z(\mu)$.

(iii) For given $k$, the g.c.d. of the polynomials $\tau^J(D)$, with $|J| = k$, is a polynomial over $F$ (within a nonzero factor in $F^*$). This follows from the fact that if $\tau^J(D) = \sum_i \tau_i^J D^i$, with $\tau_i^J \in F^*$, is a polynomial in this class, then so is $\sum_i (\tau_i^J)^2 D^i$, since the property $\alpha \in Z(\mu)$ implies $\alpha^2 \in Z(\mu)$ for any polynomial $\mu$ over $GF(2)$.

**Theorem 11.4 :** The encoder $G^{[k]}$ is basic if and only if the polynomials $\tau^J(D)$, with $|J| = k$, are relatively prime.

**Proof :** From corollary 2.36 we know that an encoder is basic if and only if the g.c.d. of its $k \times k$ minors is in $F$. Relation (11.21) and remark (i) above imply that the g.c.d. of the $k \times k$ minors of $G^{[k]}$ is equal to the g.c.d. of the $k \times k$ minors of $V^{[k]}\Gamma$, which, by remark (ii), is equal to the g.c.d. of the polynomials $\tau^J(D)$ with $|J| = k$. $\square$

**Theorem 11.5 :** If $G^{[k]}$ is a basic encoder, then so is $G^{[i]}$ for all $i \leq k$.

**Proof :** Denote by $\tau_i(D)$ the g.c.d. of the polynomials $\tau^J(D)$ with $J$ satisfying $|J| = i$. The theorem is then a direct consequence of the fact that, for $i \leq k$, the polynomial $\tau_i(D)$ is a divisor of $\tau_k(D)$. $\square$

Let us now give an example showing how to apply these theorems. We define

$$g(x, D) = 1 + D + xD^2 + x^3 D^3 + x^7 D^4 , \qquad (11.22)$$

$$\mu(x) = 1 + x^2 + x^5 . \qquad (11.23)$$

The polynomial $\mu(x)$ is irreducible over $F$, and the set of its zeros has the form $Z(\mu) = \{\alpha, \alpha^2, \alpha^4, \alpha^8, \alpha^{16}\}$. Let us denote $g(\alpha^{2^i}, D)$ by $g_i(D)$ for $0 \le i \le 4$. We verify that $g_0(D)$ is relatively prime with $g_1(D)$ and $g_2(D)$, and it is not difficult to see that this implies that the polynomials $g_i(D)$ and $g_j(D)$ are relatively prime for all $i \ne j$. Denote $\prod_{i=0}^{4} g_i(D)$ by $g(D)$. For $|J| = 4$, the polynomials $\tau^J(D)$ are nothing but the polynomials $g(D)/g_i(D)$ for $i \in [0, 4]$; hence they are relatively prime. As a consequence the encoder

$$G^{[4]} = \begin{bmatrix} 1+D & D^2 & D^4 & D^3 & D^4 \\ D^4 & 1+D & D^2+D^4 & D^4 & D^3 \\ D^3 & D^4 & 1+D+D^3 & D^2+D^4 & D^4 \\ D^4 & D^3 & 0 & 1+D+D^3 & D^2+D^4 \end{bmatrix}$$

$$(11.24)$$

and its subencoders $G^{[3]}$, $G^{[2]}$ and $G^{[1]}$ are basic.

Unfortunately, it seems that the computation of the minimum word distance of the codes generated by these reduced encoders $G^{[k]}$ cannot be simplified by use of their algebraic structure. In fact, a computer program was necessary to compute the word distance of these codes. The first encoders we have analyzed in this way are the encoders $G^{[k]}$ associated with the pair $(g, \mu)$ specified by (11.22) and (11.23). The results are shown in tables 11.1 and 11.2, which give not only $wd[E(G^{[k]})]$ but also the parameter $\Delta(G^{[k]})$ expressing the speed at which $wd[E(G^{[k]})]$ is reached. This parameter $\Delta(G^{[k]})$ is defined to be the smallest integer $t$ such that the minimum value of $ww(aG^{[k]} \bmod D^t)$, taken over all nonzero information sequences $a$ of delay zero, is equal to $wd[E(G^{[k]})]$

**Table 11.1** : Word distance of some codes of length 5
associated with (11.22) and (11.23).

| $k$ | $wd[E(G^{[k]})]$ | $\Delta(G^{[k]})$ |
|---|---|---|
| 1 | 5 | 6 |
| 2 | 5 | 8 |
| 3 | 5 | 14 |
| 4 | 4 | 24 |

**Table 11.2** : Other convolutional codes with a large
minimum word distance.

| $n$ | $\mu(x)$ | $[e(0),\cdots,e(m)]$ | $k$ | $wd[E(G^{[k]})]$ | $\Delta(G^{[k]})$ |
|---|---|---|---|---|---|
| 3 | $x^3 + x + 1$ | $[3,1,0,0,1]$ | 2 | 5 | 18 |
| 4 | $x^4 + x^3 + x^2 + x + 1$ | $[6,3,1,0,0]$ | 2 | 5 | 10 |
|  |  |  | 3 | 5 | 23 |
|  | $x^4 + x + 1$ | $[0,1,3,6,10,0,6]$ | 2 | 7 | 17 |
| 5 | $x^5 + x^4 + x^2 + x + 1$ | $[1,3,6,10,15]$ | 4 | 5 | 28 |
|  |  | $[66,55,45,36,28]$ | 4 | 5 | 27 |
|  | $x^5 + x^3 + x^2 + x + 1$ | $[6,3,1,0,0,1,3]$ | 3 | 7 | 21 |
|  | no reduction | $[0,1,3,2,0,3,0,2,0]$ | 2 | 9 | 17 |
| 6 | $x^6 + x + 1$ | $[3,1,0,0,1]$ | 4 | 5 | 15 |
|  | $x^6 + x^4 + x^2 + x + 1$ | $[6,3,1,0,0,1,3]$ | 3 | 7 | 21 |
| 7 | no reduction | $[2,0,1,0,2]$ | 5 | 5 | 18 |

Other examples are given in table 11.2. In this table, the third item
is the $(m + 1)$-tuple $[e(0),\cdots,e(m)]$ of exponents $e(j)$ that specifies the

generator $g$. Many of these $(m + 1)$-tuples are still constructed according to equations (11.4) and (11.5), but this construction is then followed by a reduction modulo $\mu(x)$. For two codes of the table, no reduction mod $\mu(x)$ has to be performed.

## 11.2 Codes for compound channels

Consider the following communication model. At each time unit $i \in \mathbb{Z}$, an encoder produces an $n$-tuple $v_i$ over $F = GF(2)$, and transmits it over a channel. The channel can have two different actions on $v_i$. For some integers $i$, it acts on $v_i$ as a binary symmetric channel $BSC(p)$, and for the remaining integers $i$, it transforms $v_i$ into a special signal $\omega$ that is not a binary $n$-tuple; the latter action is often called an *erasure*. Thus the output of the channel has the form

$$w = \sum_i w_i \, D^i; \quad w_i \in F^n \cup \{\omega\}, \tag{11.25}$$

where the event $w_i = \omega$ informs the receiver that, at time $i$, *some* $v_i$ was transmitted, but gives no information on *which* $v_i$ was transmitted. A channel having these characteristics we call a (binary) compound channel. To characterize it completely, we should give the probability $p$ together with the probabilistic model that generates the output $w_i = \omega$, but we shall not consider this point of view here.

Let us assume that we use a convolutional code $C$ of length $n$ over a compound channel, and that $b$ words $v_i$ of the encoded sequence $v$ are received as $w_i = \omega$. The consequence is that the amount of symbol distance available to the decoder to produce an estimate $\hat{v}$ of $v$ can become temporarily as small as the quantity $sd(C|b)$ introduced in section 3.1, at least if the $b$ erased words are sufficiently "close" to each other. This shows the importance of using a code $C$ with a good distance repartition $dr(C)$ when the channel is a compound channel. In this section we determine the parameter $dr(C)$ of several codes $C$ introduced in chapter 10.

## 11.2.1   The distance repartition of some binary (7,3) convolutional codes

Let $A_\alpha$ and $\mathcal{A}_\alpha$ be the algebras introduced in section 10.2 and corresponding to the automorphism $\alpha$ defined by (10.10). In the same section it was mentioned that, when $g$ is a generator polynomial of the form (10.9), specified by its $(m+1)$-tuple $\underline{b} = [b(0), \cdots, b(m)]$, the convolutional code $C = g\,\mathcal{A}_\alpha$ has to satisfy

$$sd(C) \leq 4(m+1) . \tag{11.26}$$

Extending the Plotkin argument [87] leading to this bound, we see that, for $0 \leq s \leq m$, the minimum symbol distance $sd(C|s)$ of order $s$ of $C$ satisfies

$$sd(C|s) \leq 4(m+1-s) . \tag{11.27}$$

All inequivalent codes $C = g\,\mathcal{A}_\alpha$ that reach the bound (11.26) for $m \leq 5$ were listed in table 10.4. Here we explain how to determine the corresponding values of $sd(C|s)$ for $0 \leq s \leq m$.

Let us first remark that it follows from the results of section 10.2 that all codes listed in table 10.4 satisfy $wd(C) = m+1$. Let us make two other observations.

**(i)** The symbol weight of a nonzero word in any sequence of one of these codes is equal to 2,4 or 6 (see figure 10.1).

**(ii)** The first and last nonzero words of a code sequence have symbol weight equal to 4.

For a given $v \in g\,\mathcal{A}_\alpha$, denote $ww(v)$ by $w$. From the two observations above we have

$$sw(v|1) \geq 2w , \quad sw(v|s) \geq 2(w - s); \ s \geq 2 . \tag{11.28}$$

This makes it obvious that, if $C$ does not satisfy $sd(C \mid 1) = 4m$, then there exists a nonzero sequence $v$ in $C$ satisfying $ww(v) \leq 2m - 1$. More generally, if $C$ does not satisfy $sd(C \mid s) = 4(m + 1 - s)$ for $s \geq 2$, then there exists a nonzero sequence $v$ in $C$ satisfying $ww(v) \leq 2m - (s - 1)$.

We use these facts to compute $dr(C)$ when $C = g\mathcal{A}_\alpha$ is generated by the polynomial $g$ of $D$-degree 4 specified by $\underline{b} = [0, 1, 6, 5, 4]$. The even nonzero sequences $v$ of $C$ satisfying $ww(v) \leq 2m - 1 = 7$ were listed in table 10.3. Since their nonzero words have symbol weight equal to 4, and since they contain at least 5 nonzero words, all these sequences $v$ satisfy $sw(v|s) \geq 20 - 4s$. Moreover, this bound is achieved by the generator polynomial $g$. It remains to verify whether the general code sequences $v$ (with a nonzero even part $and$ a nonzero odd part) for which $ww(v) \leq 7$ holds satisfy

$$sw(v|s) \geq 20 - 4s; \quad 1 \leq s \leq 4. \tag{11.29}$$

As in section 10.2 we represent these general sequences by matchings $\Omega_r(i)$. All matchings that specify code sequences of word weight $\leq 7$ were given in this section 10.2; to prove (11.29) we shall have to analyze them more in detail.

Let us consider for example the seven matchings

$$\Omega_4(i) = \begin{pmatrix} 0 & 1 & 0 & 2 & 2 & 0 & 6 \\ \infty & i & i+1 & i+6 & i+5 & i+4 & \infty \end{pmatrix} ; \quad 0 \leq i \leq 6, \tag{11.30}$$

and let us construct the $7 \times 7$ matrix $U_4$ that has the symbol weight of the word represented by the $j^{\text{th}}$ column of $\Omega_4(i)$ in position $(i + 1, j)$. This matrix is given by

$$U_4 = \begin{bmatrix} 4 & 4 & 4 & 4 & 6 & 4 & 4 \\ 4 & 4 & 4 & 4 & 4 & 2 & 4 \\ 4 & 2 & 2 & 2 & 4 & 2 & 4 \\ 4 & 4 & 4 & 4 & 2 & 6 & 4 \\ 4 & 2 & 2 & 2 & 4 & 4 & 4 \\ 4 & 2 & 2 & 2 & 2 & 4 & 4 \\ 4 & 6 & 6 & 6 & 2 & 2 & 4 \end{bmatrix} .$$

We compute then the $7 \times 5$ matrix $W_4$ whose $(r, s)$-entry is the sum of the $8 - s$ smallest integers of the $r^{\text{th}}$ row of $U_4$; the result is

$$
W_4 = \begin{bmatrix}
30 & 24 & 20 & 16 & 12 \\
26 & 22 & 18 & 14 & 10 \\
20 & 16 & 12 & 8 & 6 \\
28 & 22 & 18 & 14 & 10 \\
22 & 18 & 14 & 10 & 6 \\
20 & 16 & 12 & 8 & 6 \\
30 & 24 & 18 & 12 & 8
\end{bmatrix} .
$$

Obviously, the $(r, s)$-entry of $W_4$ is the value of $sw(v|s-1)$ associated with the sequence $v$ specified by $\Omega_4(r-1)$. As a consequence, $sw(C|s-1)$ is equal to the minimum of $20 - 4(s-1)$ (which is the value obtained above by considering the even sequences) and of the entries in the $s^{\text{th}}$ column of the seven matrices $W_r$ for $1 \le r \le 7$. Beside $W_4$, the other matrices $W_r$ associated with $\underline{b} = [0, 1, 6, 5, 4]$ are

$$
W_1 = \begin{bmatrix}
26 & 20 & 16 & 12 & 8 \\
20 & 16 & 12 & 8 & 4 \\
20 & 16 & 12 & 8 & 4 \\
22 & 16 & 12 & 8 & 4 \\
20 & 16 & 12 & 8 & 4 \\
22 & 16 & 12 & 8 & 4 \\
22 & 16 & 12 & 8 & 4
\end{bmatrix} , \quad
W_2 = \begin{bmatrix}
24 & 20 & 16 & 12 & 8 \\
24 & 20 & 16 & 12 & 8 \\
24 & 18 & 14 & 10 & 6 \\
24 & 20 & 16 & 12 & 8 \\
24 & 18 & 14 & 10 & 6 \\
24 & 18 & 14 & 10 & 6 \\
32 & 26 & 20 & 16 & 12
\end{bmatrix} ,
$$

$$
W_3 = \begin{bmatrix}
22 & 18 & 14 & 10 & 6 \\
28 & 22 & 18 & 14 & 10 \\
22 & 18 & 14 & 10 & 6 \\
22 & 18 & 14 & 10 & 6 \\
26 & 20 & 14 & 10 & 6 \\
28 & 22 & 18 & 14 & 10 \\
28 & 22 & 18 & 14 & 10
\end{bmatrix} , \quad
W_5 = \begin{bmatrix}
20 & 16 & 12 & 8 & 4 \\
28 & 22 & 16 & 12 & 8 \\
30 & 24 & 18 & 14 & 10 \\
28 & 24 & 20 & 16 & 12 \\
22 & 18 & 14 & 10 & 6 \\
22 & 18 & 14 & 10 & 6 \\
26 & 20 & 16 & 12 & 8
\end{bmatrix} ,
$$

$$W_6 = \begin{bmatrix} 28 & 24 & 20 & 16 & 12 \\ 20 & 16 & 12 & 8 & 6 \\ 22 & 18 & 16 & 12 & 8 \\ 28 & 22 & 16 & 12 & 8 \\ 22 & 18 & 14 & 10 & 6 \\ 30 & 24 & 18 & 14 & 10 \\ 26 & 20 & 16 & 12 & 8 \end{bmatrix}, \ W_7 = \begin{bmatrix} 24 & 20 & 16 & 12 & 8 \\ 22 & 18 & 14 & 10 & 6 \\ 24 & 18 & 14 & 10 & 6 \\ 26 & 20 & 16 & 12 & 8 \\ 26 & 20 & 16 & 12 & 8 \\ 26 & 20 & 16 & 12 & 8 \\ 28 & 22 & 18 & 14 & 10 \end{bmatrix}.$$

The analysis of these matrices yields the result $dr(C) = [20, 16, 12, 8, 4]$. Table 11.3 contains the distributions $dr(C)$ of all codes listed in table 10.4; the asterisk means that the components of $dr(C)$ reach the upper bound (11.27).

**Table 11.3** : The distance repartition of the codes listed in table 10.4.

| $m$ | $\underline{b}$ | $dr(C)$ |
|---|---|---|
| 1 | $[0, 0]$ | $*$ |
| 2 | $[0, 0, 0]$ | $*$ |
|   | $[0, 0, 1]$ | $*$ |
| 3 | $[0, 0, 2, 6]$ | $*$ |
|   | $[0, 1, 6, 3]$ | $*$ |
|   | $[0, 0, 1, 2]$ | $*$ |
| 4 | $[0, 1, 6, 5, 4]$ | $*$ |
|   | $[0, 0, 1, 1, 4]$ | $[20, 14, 10, 6, 4]$ |
|   | $[0, 0, 1, 4, 5]$ | $[20, 14, 10, 6, 4]$ |
| 5 | $[0, 0, 1, 1, 3, 4]$ | $[24, 18, 14, 10, 6, 4]$ |

## 11.2.2   The distance repartition of some binary convolutional codes of length 9

Let us first analyze the distance repartition of some of the $(9,2)$ codes that were considered in section 10.3. These codes have a generator polynomial $g$ of the form (10.21), and they are ideals $g \mathcal{A}_\alpha$ in $\mathcal{A}_\alpha$. Since the generators $g$ satisfy $sw(g|s) = 6(m+1-s)$, the component $sd(g \mathcal{A}_\alpha|s)$ of $dr(g \mathcal{A}_\alpha)$ is bounded from above by $6(m+1-s)$. Now consider now an arbitrary even polynomial sequence $v = \sum_j v_j D^j$ in $g \mathcal{A}_\alpha$. As mentioned in section 10.3, it satisfies $ww(v) \geq m+1$. Since each nonzero $v_j$ satisfies $sw(v_j) = 6$, the inequality $sw(v|s) \geq 6(m+1-s)$ remains true for any even polynomial sequence $v$ in $g \mathcal{A}_\alpha$.

Consider a general finite length sequence of $v \in g \mathcal{A}_\alpha$ having a nonzero even part *and* a nonzero odd part. The specific properties of such a sequence $v$ are the following.

**(i)** It contains at least $m+2$ nonzero words.

**(ii)** Its first and last nonzero words have symbol weight equal to 6, and the other nonzero words have symbol weight at least equal to 4.

These properties imply

$$sw(v|0) \geq 4m + 12, \quad sw(v|1) \geq 4m + 6, \quad sw(v|2+s) \geq 4(m-s); \quad s \geq 0.$$
$$(11.31)$$

All bounds (11.31) are achieved with equality by the sequence $g + gD$.

The computation of $dr(g \mathcal{A}_\alpha)$ is now an easy matter. Consider for example the generator polynomial $g$ specified by $\underline{b} = [0,0,0,0,1,2]$. The even sequences $v$ of $g \mathcal{A}_\alpha$ satisfy $sw(v|s) = 6[ww(v) - s]$, which is at least equal to $36 - 6s$, and this last bound is satisfied with equality by $g$ itself. On the other hand, a general sequence $v \in g \mathcal{A}_\alpha$ satisfies (11.31) with $m = 5$, and this bound is achieved by $v = g + gD$. As a consequence we have

$$sd(g \mathcal{A}_\alpha \mid 1) \;=\; \min(30, 26) = 26,$$

in positions where a code sequence of symbol weight 5 has all its symbols equal to 1, the minimum distance Viterbi decoder will choose an estimate $\hat{a}_1$ that is not equal to $a_1$. Thus, the information $a_2$ is better protected against noise than the information $a_1$.

To find encoders that exhibit this U.E.P. property, we use the techniques developed in chapter 10. First, let $\mathcal{H}^{(0)}$ be the cyclic group of order 7 generated by $\lambda$, let $\mathcal{H}$ be $< \mathcal{H}^{(0)}, \alpha >$ where $\alpha \in \text{Aut}\,(\mathcal{H}^{(0)})$ satisfies $\lambda^\alpha = \lambda^{-1}$, let $A$ be $F\mathcal{H}$ with $F = GF(2)$, and let $\mathcal{A}$ be $A((D))$. The cyclic group $\mathcal{H}$ is generated by the element $x$ satisfying $x^{(0)} = \lambda$, and the algebra $A$ contains three minimal idempotents, namely $e_0 = 1 + x + x^2 + x^3 + x^4 + x^5 + x^6$, $e_1 = 1 + x + x^2 + x^4$ and $e_3 = 1 + x^{-1} + x^{-2} + x^{-4}$. The two sequences $g_0 = e_0$ and $g_1 = e_1 + e_1^\alpha D + (e_1 x)^\alpha D^2$ are $\mathcal{H}$-normal, the ideals $g_0 \mathcal{A}$ and $g_1 \mathcal{A}$ in $\mathcal{A}$ are minimal and the sum $C$ of these ideals is direct. This sum is a $(7, 4)$ binary convolutional code, for which we choose the encoder

$$G_7 = \begin{bmatrix} 1 & 1 & 1 & 1 & 1 & 1 & 1 \\ 1+D & 1+D^2 & 1+D^2 & D+D^2 & 1 & D+D^2 & D \\ 0 & 1 & 1+D+D^2 & 1+D^2 & D+D^2 & 1+D & D+D^2 \\ D^2 & D & 1 & 1+D+D^2 & 1+D+D^2 & D+D^2 & 1 \end{bmatrix},$$

$$(11.37)$$

thus numbering the coordinates of $C$ in the order $1, x, x^2, \cdots, x^6$. The first row of $G_7$ is $g_0$ and the $i^{\text{th}}$ row of $G_7$ is $g_1 x^{i-2}$ for $i = 2, 3, 4$. To compute the parameters $sd^{[i]}(G_7)$ for $1 \le i \le 4$, we can use techniques similar to the ones described in section 10.2. However instead of using the matrix $\Delta$ of figure 10.1, we shall use a matrix $\Delta'$ that is deduced from $\Delta$ as follows. The $(i, j)$-entry of $\Delta'$ is equal to the minimum of $\Delta_{i,j}$ and $7 - \Delta_{i,j}$, which corresponds to the possibility of complementing in a code sequence all symbols of any word having symbol weight $\ge 4$, by addition to this word of the first row of $G_7$. As a result one obtains $sd^{[1]}(G_7) = 7$ and $sd^{[i]}(G_7) = 9$ for $2 \le i \le 4$.

Next, let $\mathcal{H}^{(0)}$ be the elementary Abelian group of order 9, generated by $\lambda$ and $\mu$ satisfying $\lambda^3 = \mu^3 = 1$, $\lambda\mu = \mu\lambda$, and let $\alpha$ be the element of $\mathrm{Aut}(\mathcal{H}^{(0)})$ that satisfies $\lambda^\alpha = \mu$ , $\mu^\alpha = \lambda$. Define $\mathcal{H} := < \mathcal{H}^{(0)}, \alpha >$, $A := F\mathcal{H}$ with $F = GF(2)$, and $\mathcal{A} := A((D))$, and denote by $x$ and $y$ the elements of $\mathcal{H}$ satisfying respectively $x^{(0)} = \lambda$ and $y^{(0)} = \mu$. Consider then the $\mathcal{H}$-normal polynomials $g_0 = (1 + x + x^2)(1 + y + y^2)$, $g_1 = (x + x^2)(1 + xy + x^2y^2)$, $g_2 = (x + x^2)(1 + x^2y + xy^2)$, $e = (x + x^2)(1 + y + y^2)$ and $g_3 = e + e^\alpha D + e^{\alpha^2} D^2$. The four sequences $g_i$ are $\mathcal{H}$-normal and they generate minimal ideals $g_i \mathcal{A}$ in $\mathcal{A}$. The sum $C = \sum_{i=0}^3 g_i \mathcal{A}$ of these four ideals is a direct sum, and is a $(9, 7)$-convolutional code over $F = GF(2)$.

A minimal encoder $G_9$ for $C$ is given by

$$G_9 = \begin{bmatrix} 1 & 1 & 1 & 1 & 1 & 1 & 1 & 1 & 1 \\ 0 & 1 & 1 & 1 & 0 & 1 & 1 & 1 & 0 \\ 1 & 0 & 1 & 1 & 1 & 0 & 0 & 1 & 1 \\ 0 & 1 & 1 & 1 & 1 & 0 & 1 & 0 & 1 \\ 1 & 0 & 1 & 0 & 1 & 1 & 1 & 1 & 0 \\ 0 & 5 & 5 & 2 & 7 & 7 & 2 & 7 & 7 \\ 7 & 2 & 7 & 5 & 0 & 5 & 7 & 2 & 7 \end{bmatrix}. \tag{11.38}$$

for the order $1$, $x$, $x^2$, $y$, $yx$, $yx^2$, $y^2$, $y^2x$, $y^2x^2$ of the coordinates. In the matrix (11.38), polynomials are represented in octal notation; for example, $1$, $2$, $5$ and $7$ represent $1$, $D$, $D^2 + 1$ and $D^2 + D + 1$. It turns out that the 7-tuple $[sd^{[1]}(G_9), \cdots, sd^{[7]}(G_9)]$ is equal to $[3, 3, 3, 3, 3, 6, 6]$. As a conclusion, the two encoders $G_7$ and $G_9$ guarantee more protection to the last components of the information sequence than to the first ones.

We go back for a while to a definition introduced in chapter 3, with the aim of refining the concept of minimum symbol distance $sd(C|s)$ of order $s$ of the convolutional code $C$. Given an encoder $G$ of $C$ we define the integer

$$sd^{[i]}(G|j) := \min_{a_i \neq 0} sw(aG|j),$$

where $a_i$ denotes the $i^{\mathrm{th}}$ component of the information sequence $a = (a_1, \cdots, a_k) \in \mathcal{F}^k$. If the maximum degree of the entries of $G$ is equal to $m$, we associate then with $G$ the $k \times (m+1)$ matrix $Dr(G)$ having as its $(i, j + 1)$-entry, the quantity $sd^{[i]}(G|j)$ defined above. This matrix $Dr(G)$ gives some information on the amount of symbol minimum distance that remains available to estimate any component $a_i$ of the information $a$ when $j$ words of $v = aG$ are erased. The matrices $Dr(G_7)$ and $Dr(G_9)$ associated with the matrices given in (11.37) and (11.38) are computed rather easily. The $4 \times 3$ matrix $Dr(G_7)$ has $(3, 0, 0)$ as its first row and $(9, 6, 3)$ as its last two rows; the $7 \times 3$ matrix $Dr(G_9)$ has $(3, 0, 0)$ as its five first rows and $(6, 4, 2)$ as its last two rows.

## 11.4 Channel correcting convolutional codes

In this section we consider the situation where $n$ channels are simultaneously available to transmit information and where some of them may be very noisy for long periods. The storage of binary digits along the tracks of a magnetic tape is an example of such a situation. To face the possibility of errors on these $n$ channels, we represent the information by a $k$-tuple $a = (a_1, \cdots, a_k)$ over $\mathcal{F}$ and we encode it into the $n$-tuple $v = (v_1, \cdots, v_n)$ over $\mathcal{F}$ given by $v = aG$, where $G$ is a basic $k \times n$ convolutional encoder over $F$. The length of the encoded sequence $v$ is assumed to be finite; thus, without loss of essential generality, we can represent it as a polynomial, i.e., as an element of $F^n[D]$. Each component $v_i$ of $v$ is transmitted on one of the $n$ available channels, and received as an element $u_i$ of $\mathcal{F}$. The channel model we consider is as follows. Most of the time the symbols of $u_i$ are equal to the corresponding symbols of $v_i$. However there is a reasonably small probability that, during the transmission of $v$, some of the channels will fail. If the $i^{\text{th}}$ channel fails then the quantity $sw(v_i - u_i)$ will be large. We would like to use an encoder $G$ that would make it possible for the receiver to recover the transmitted information $a$ even if some of the $n$ received sequences $u_i$ are erroneous.

In subsection 11.4.1 we introduce the concept of minimum channel distance and we obtain an upper bound on this quantity. In subsection 11.4.2 we give a general method producing convolutional codes for which this bound is reached. Finally in subsection 11.4.3 we suggest a method to decode these convolutional codes.

## 11.4.1   MDS codes over the field of Laurent series

Let us first give some definitions.

**Definitions 11.6 :** The channel weight $chw(v)$ of the sequence $v = (v_1, \cdots, v_n) \in \mathcal{F}^n$ is defined to be the number of nonzero entries $v_i$ of $v$. The channel distance $chd(u, v)$ between the elements $u$ and $v$ of $\mathcal{F}^n$ is defined to be $chw(v - u)$. The minimum channel distance $chd(C)$ of $C = E(G)$ is defined by $chd(C) := \min chd(v, u)$ where the minimum is over all $u, v \in C$ satisfying $u \neq v$. Since $C$ is an $F$-space, this definition is equivalent to

$$chd(C) := \min chw(v); \ v \in C, \ v \neq 0 . \tag{11.39}$$

The practical importance of $chd(C)$ is easily understood. Given a received sequence $u = (u_1, \cdots, u_n)$ in $\mathcal{F}^n$, there exists at most one sequence $v = (v_1, \cdots, v_n)$ in $C$ that satisfies $chd(u, v) \leq (chd(C) - 1)/2$. This merely follows from the fact that $chd(u, v)$ is actually a distance function (see chapter 3). As a result, if $v \in C$ is transmitted over the $n$ channels (one component $v_i$ over each channel) and if at most $(chd(C) - 1)/2$ components of the received sequence $u$ contain errors, then it is theoretically possible to recover the transmitted sequence, just by estimating it to be the code sequence $v$ that minimizes $chd(u, v)$.

Let $G$ be a convolutional $k \times n$ encoder and let $J$ be a $k$-tuple of integers $j_1, j_2, \cdots, j_k$, with $1 \leq j_1 < \cdots < j_k \leq n$, having the property that the $k \times k$ submatrix formed by the columns of indes $j_1, \cdots, j_k$ of $G$ is nonsingular. Define $G^* := (G^J)^{-1}G$. Obviously, any row $g^*$ of $G^*$ satisfies

$chw(g^*) \leq n - k + 1$, which implies

$$chd(C) \leq n - k + 1 \qquad (11.40)$$

for the code $C = E(G)$. By analogy with the terminology used for block codes [71], we call a convolutional code $C$ that achieves the bound (11.40), a maximum distance separable (or MDS) convolutional code.

## 11.4.2 A simple method to construct MDS convolutional codes

Let $F$ be the field $GF(q)$ with $q$ any prime power, and let $G$ be a $k \times n$ convolutional encoder over $F$ having the property that, for any ordered $k$-tuple $J = \{j_1, \cdots, j_k\}$ with $1 \leq j_1 < \cdots < j_k \leq n$, det $G^J$ is a nonzero element of $F[D]$. We call such an encoder $G$ a totally nonsingular (or TN) matrix. In this case, for any nonzero $a \in \mathcal{F}^k$, the "partial sequence" $a\,G^J$ is nonzero for *all* $k$-tuples $J$. This implies $chw(aG) \geq n - k + 1$ and, as a consequence $C = E(G)$ satisfies (11.40) with equality. A converse result is stated below in lemma 11.7. Thus, to construct a $k \times n$ encoder that generates an MDS convolutional code amounts to constructing a $k \times n$ TN-matrix over $F[D]$. This can be done as follows.

Let $\pi(D)$ be an irreducible polynomial over $F$, of degree $m + 1$ in the indeterminate $D$. Let $F^*$ be the set of polynomials of formal degree $m$ over $F$, endowed with the natural addition and the multiplication modulo $\pi(D)$. These two operations give $F^*$ the structure of the finite field $GF(q^{m+1})$. For $n \leq q^{m+1}$, we choose $n$ different elements $g_1, \cdots, g_n$ of $F^*$, and we define $G^*$ to be the $k \times n$ $F^*$-matrix having the element $(g_j)^{i-1}$ in position $(i, j)$. (If one of the $g_j$ is zero, we use the convention $0^0 = 1$.) In this case det $(G^*)^J$ equals $\prod_{j>i,\ i,j \in J} (g_j - g_i)$ [71] and it is nonzero since no two $g_j$ are equal. We denote now by $G$ the matrix $G^*$ interpreted as a matrix over $F[D]$ rather than over $F^*$; although the entries of $G^*$ are considered as elements of $F^*$ and the entries of $G$ as elements of $F[D]$, both matrices are formally identical. For a given $k$-tuple $J$, det $(G^*)^J$ is the element of $F^*$ identified with the residue modulo $\pi(D)$ of the element det $G^J$ of $F[D]$. Therefore, the fact that det $(G^*)^J$ is nonzero implies that det $G^J$ is also nonzero. On the other hand, if we premultiply the $k \times n$ $F^*$-matrix $G^*$ by a $k \times k$ nonsingular matrix $T$ over $F^*$, the resulting matrix $G_1^* :=$ $TG^*$ has the property that all its $k \times k$ minors are nonzero. The matrix $G_1$ formally identical to $G_1^*$ but considered as a matrix over $F[D]$ has the same property. The same result holds for the $F[D]$-matrix $G_2$ formally identical to $G_2^* := G^*S$ with $S$ an $F^*$-matrix having exactly one nonzero element in each row and in each column.

We conclude that, when its entries are interpreted as elements of $F[D]$, any matrix of the form $TG^*S$, with $T$ nonsingular and $S$ as described above, is an encoder of an MDS convolutional code. Let $G$ be a basic $k \times n$ TN encoder. The code $C = E(G)$ is then an MDS convolutional code and the dual code $C^\perp$ of $C$ is also an MDS convolutional code. Indeed, it follows from lemma 2.40 that any basic encoder $G^\perp$ of $C^\perp$ is a TN encoder.

Let us now discuss some examples. Let $F$ be the field $GF(2)$ and let $F^*$ be its extension field $GF(2^3)$ represented as the set of polynomials over $F$ modulo $\pi(D) = D^3 + D + 1$. Define then $G^*$ to be the $F^*$-matrix having $D^{(j-1)(i-1)}$ as $(i, j)$ entry, that is

$$G^* = \begin{bmatrix} 1 & 1 & 1 & 1 & 1 & 1 & 1 \\ 1 & D & D^2 & 1+D & D+D^2 & 1+D+D^2 & 1+D^2 \\ 1 & D^2 & D+D^2 & 1+D^2 & D & 1+D & 1+D+D^2 \\ 1 & 1+D & 1+D^2 & D^2 & 1+D+D^2 & D & D+D^2 \end{bmatrix},$$

and define two $F^*$-matrices $T_1$ and $S$ by

$$T_1 := \begin{bmatrix} 1 & 1 & 0 & 1 \\ D & D^2 & 0 & D+D^2 \\ D^2 & D+D^2 & 0 & D \\ 0 & 0 & 1 & 0 \end{bmatrix}$$

and

$$S := \text{diag}(1, D, D^2, D^3, D^4, D^5, D^6).$$

Computing the $F^*$-matrix $G_1^* = T_1 G^* S$ and interpreting it as an encoder $G_1$ over $F[D]$, we obtain

$$G_1 = \begin{bmatrix} 1 & 0 & 0 & 1 & 0 & 1 & 1 \\ 0 & 0 & 1 & 0 & 1 & 1 & 1 \\ 0 & 1 & 0 & 1 & 1 & 1 & 0 \\ 1 & 1+D & 1+D^2 & D^2 & 1+D+D^2 & D & D+D^2 \end{bmatrix}.$$

We know that the code $C_1 = E(G_1)$ and its dual $C_1^\perp$ are MDS convolutional codes. In passing we note that $G_1$ is a minimal encoder and that a minimal encoder of $C_1^\perp$ is

$$G_1^\perp = \begin{bmatrix} 1 & 1 & 1 & 1 & 1 & 1 & 1 \\ 1+D & 0 & D & 0 & 1 & 1 & D \\ 1 & 1 & D & 1+D & 0 & D & 0 \end{bmatrix}.$$

Next, define

$$T_2 = \begin{bmatrix} D^3 & D^5 & D^3 & D^4 \\ D^4 & 0 & D^3 & D^6 \\ D & D^2 & 0 & D^4 \\ D & D^4 & D^3 & D^5 \end{bmatrix},$$

and compute the matrix $G_2^* = T_2 G^* S$ over $F^*$. Then interpreting the elements of $G_2^*$ as elements of $F[D]$ we obtain the matrix

$$G_2 = \begin{bmatrix} 1 & 0 & 0 & 0 & 1+D & 1+D^2 & 1+D+D^2 \\ 0 & 1 & 0 & 0 & D & 1+D^2 & D+D^2 \\ 0 & 0 & 1 & 0 & 1 & 1 & 1 \\ 0 & 0 & 0 & 1 & 1+D & D^2 & D+D^2 \end{bmatrix}.$$

This is a systematic (hence basic) encoder but it is not minimal. A minimal encoder of the code $C_2 = E(G_2)$ is

$$
G_2' = \begin{bmatrix}
1 & 0 & 0 & 1 & 0 & 1 & 1 \\
0 & 1 & 0 & 1 & 1 & 1 & 0 \\
0 & 0 & 1 & 0 & 1 & 1 & 1 \\
0 & 0 & 0 & 1 & 1+D & D^2 & D+D^2
\end{bmatrix},
$$

and a minimal encoder of the dual code $C_2^{\perp}$ is

$$
G_2^{\perp} = \begin{bmatrix}
1 & 1 & 1 & 1 & 1 & 1 & 1 \\
D & 1+D & 0 & D & 0 & 1 & 1 \\
0 & D & 0 & 1 & 1 & D & 1+D
\end{bmatrix}.
$$

## 11.4.3 Decoding methods for channel correcting convolutional codes

Let us first introduce the concept of an $(n, t)$-covering of the $n$ coordinates of $\mathcal{F}^n$. We index these coordinates by the elements of the set $\{1, 2, \cdots, n\}$ and we denote by $K(n, t)$ a set of subsets $\mathcal{Y}_1, \mathcal{Y}_2, \cdots, \mathcal{Y}_r$ of $\{1, 2, \cdots, n\}$ such that each $\mathcal{Y}_i$ has cardinality $2t$. We call the set $K(n, t)$ an $(n, t)$-covering of $\{1, 2, \cdots, n\}$ if each subset of cardinality $t$ of $\{1, 2, \cdots, n\}$ is included in at least one subset $\mathcal{Y}_j$ for $1 \leq j \leq r$. Consider, for example, the set $K(8, 2)$ of the 6 subsets $\mathcal{Y}_j$ of $\{1, 2 \cdots, 8\}$ given by

$$
\mathcal{Y}_1 = \{1, 2, 3, 4\}, \ \mathcal{Y}_2 = \{1, 2, 5, 6\}, \ \mathcal{Y}_3 = \{1, 2, 7, 8\},
$$

$$
\mathcal{Y}_4 = \{3, 4, 5, 6\}, \ \mathcal{Y}_5 = \{3, 4, 7, 8\}, \ \mathcal{Y}_6 = \{5, 6, 7, 8\}. \tag{11.41}
$$

Since any 2-subset of $\{1, 2, \cdots, 8\}$ is included in at least one of the six 4-subsets above, the set $K(8, 2)$ is an $(8, 2)$-covering of the set $\{1, 2, \cdots, 8\}$.

Here is a general method for constructing $(n, t)$-coverings of reasonably small cardinality $r$. For even $n$, we divide $\{1, 2, \cdots, n\}$ into $n/2$ disjoint

2-subsets, namely $\{1,2\}$, $\{3,4\}$, $\cdots$, $\{n-1,n\}$, for example, and with any choice of $t$ of these 2-subsets we associate the $2t$-subset $\mathcal{Y}$ formed by their union. There are $\begin{pmatrix} n/2 \\ t \end{pmatrix}$ such $2t$-subsets $\mathcal{Y}$ of $\{1,2,\cdots,n\}$ and the set $K(n,t)$ of them is obviously an $(n,t)$-covering of $\{1,2,\cdots,n\}$. For odd $n$, we first construct an $(n+1,t)$ covering $K(n+1,t)$ of $\{1,2,\cdots,n,n+1\}$ by the method above and we replace in any $2t$-set $\mathcal{Y}$ of $K(n+1,t)$ the element $n+1$ by any other element of $\{1,2,\cdots,n\}$ that is not yet $\mathcal{Y}$. This construction does not minimize the cardinality of $K(n,t)$ for all $n$ and $t$, but it gives a reasonable solution in all cases.

Let us now go back to $(n,k)$ MDS convolutional codes. We can specify such a code $C$ either by a $k \times n$ encoder $G$ or by an $(n-k) \times n$ parity check matrix. The next lemma contains the converse of a result given in subsection 11.4.2.

**Lemma 11.7 :** If $C$ is an $(n,k)$ MDS convolutional code, any $k \times n$ encoder $G$ and any $(n-k) \times n$ parity check matrix $H$ of $C$ are TN-matrices.

**Proof :** If $G$ is not a TN-matrix, let $G^J$ be a singular $k \times k$ submatrix of $G$. There exists a nonzero $a \in \mathcal{F}^k$ satisfying $aG^J = 0$, hence $chw(aG) \leq n-k$. Similarly, if $H$ is not a TN-matrix, let $J$ be an $(n-k)$-subset of $\{1,2,\cdots,n\}$ for which one has det $(H^J) = 0$. There exists a nonzero $v = (v_1,\cdots,v_n) \in \mathcal{F}^n$ satisfying $vH^T = 0$ and $v_j = 0$ for all $j \notin J$. This $v$ would be a nonzero sequence of $C$ satisfying $chw(v) \leq n-k$ so that $C$ would not be an MDS code. $\square$

As a second point of this subsection, we discuss some properties of the $(n-k) \times n$ parity check matrices $H$ of an $(n,k)$ MDS convolutional code $C$. Choose $n$ and $k$ such that $n-k$ is even and write $n-k = 2t$. A consequence of lemma 11.7 is that for any $2t$-subset $\mathcal{Y}$ of $\{1,2,\cdots,n\}$, we can choose a parity check matrix $H$ of $C$ such that $H^{\mathcal{Y}}$ is a diagonal (nonsingular) matrix. Denote by $\overline{\mathcal{Y}}$ the complementary set of $\mathcal{Y}$ in $\{1,2,\cdots,n\}$.

**Lemma 11.8 :** Let $\mathcal{Y}$ be an $(n-k)$-subset of $\{1,2,\cdots,n\}$. If the parity

check matrix $H$ of the MDS convolutional code $C$ is such that $H^{\mathcal{Y}}$ is
diagonal, then all minors (of any order) of $H^{\overline{\mathcal{Y}}}$ are nonzero.

**Proof :** Since $H^{\mathcal{Y}}$ is a diagonal matrix any minor of $H^{\overline{\mathcal{Y}}}$ is a factor of
some (nonzero) $(n-k) \times (n-k)$ minor of $H$. $\square$

Let us now consider the decoding of an $(n, k)$ MDS convolutional code
$C$. Assume that the sequence $v = (v_1, \cdots, v_n) \in C$ transmitted over an
$n$-tuple of separate channels is received as $u = (u_1, \cdots, u_n) \in \mathcal{F}^n$ and that
the error sequence $e := v - u$ satisfies

$$chw(e) \le (n-k)/2. \tag{11.42}$$

Assume then that $\mathcal{Y}$ is a subset of $\{1, 2, \cdots, n\}$ satisfying

$$e_j \ne 0 \Rightarrow j \in \mathcal{Y}.$$

In this case we say that the error $e$ is covered by $\mathcal{Y}$.

**Theorem 11.9 :** Let $\mathcal{Y}$ be an $(n-k)$-subset of $\{1, 2, \cdots, n\}$. If the error
$e$ satisfies (11.42) and if $H^{\mathcal{Y}}$ is a diagonal matrix, then one has

$$chw(e\,H^T) \le (n-k)/2 \tag{11.43}$$

if and only if $e$ is covered by $\mathcal{Y}$.

**Proof :** If $e$ is not covered by $\mathcal{Y}$ write $e = e_1 + e_2$ with $e_1$ covered by
$\mathcal{Y}$ and $e_2$ covered by $\overline{\mathcal{Y}}$. Lemma 11.8 yields $chw(e_2\,H^T) \ge n - k + 1 - chw(e_2)$. Furthermore, since $e_1$ is covered by $\mathcal{Y}$, one has $chw(e_1\,H^T) = chw(e_1)$. From $chw(e\,H^T) \ge |chw(e_2\,H^T) - chw(e_1\,H^T)|$ we obtain then
$chw(e\,H^T) \ge n - k + 1 - chw(e_1) - chw(e_2)$, and since $chw(e) = chw(e_1)$
$+ chw(e_2)$ is assumed to be $\le (n-k)/2$, it follows that (11.43) cannot be
true. The converse property is immediate. $\square$

This theorem leads to the following decoding algorithm for an MDS
convolutional code $C$ of length $n$ and dimension $k$, used over an $n$-tuple
of channels as described in the beginning of section 11.4. Let $K(n, t) =$

$\{\mathcal{Y}(j) \mid 1 \leq j \leq r\}$ be an $(n,t)$-covering of $\{1,2,\cdots,n\}$ and let $H$ be a parity check matrix of $C$; thus one has $E(H) = C^{\perp}$. For $1 \leq j \leq r$, compute the matrix $H_j := (H^{\mathcal{Y}(j)})^{-1}H$, which in general is not a polynomial matrix but a matrix over the field $F(D)$ of rational fractions over $F$. Suppose that the transmitted code sequence $v = (v_1,\cdots,v_n)$ and the received sequence $u = (u_1,\cdots,u_n)$ are polynomials that satisfy $chw(v-u) \leq t = (n-k)/2$. In this case it follows from theorem 11.9 that at least one of the syndromes $s_j := uH_j^T$ will satisfy $chw(s_j) \leq t$. The decoding estimate $\hat{v}$ is then given by

$$
\begin{aligned}
\hat{v}^{\overline{\mathcal{Y}}(j)} &= u^{\overline{\mathcal{Y}}(j)} \\
\hat{v}^{\mathcal{Y}(j)} &= (u^{\overline{\mathcal{Y}}(j)})(H_j^{\overline{\mathcal{Y}}(j)})^T .
\end{aligned}
\tag{11.44}
$$

Obviously $\hat{v}$ is a code sequence, since it satisfies $\hat{v}H_j^T = 0$. Moreover it satisfies $cwd(\hat{v} - u) \leq t$.

In [96] the situation is considered where the number of *simultaneously* erroneous components $v_i$ of $v$ is $\leq t$ but the $n - t$ correct components are not necessarily the same during the whole transmission. Specific encoding and decoding methods are described for this situation. For further details, the reader is referred to the original paper.


## 11.5   Conclusion

This chapter has been devoted to the description of convolutional codes that can be used in nonclassical situations. It illustrates how our algebraic approach can also be efficient in these cases. More information on the subject of sections 11.1 and 11.4 can be found in [97] and [96]. Other references on word correcting convolutional codes include [6, 54, 88]. The contents of sections 11.2 and 11.3 are new.

## PROBLEMS

**11.1** Let $g(x, D)$ be constructed in agreement with (11.4) and (11.5) for $m = 2r + 1$. In this case the encoder $G$ associated with $g$ is catastrophic. Prove that $ww(ag) = m + 1$ still holds for any *polynomial* sequence $a$.

**11.2** If $G$ is a free encoder constructed in agreement with (11.4) and (11.5), can $sd[E(G)]$ be large? Same question if $G$ is a reduced encoder.

**11.3** Analyze in detail the code $C_3$ of subsection 11.2.2.

**11.4** Construct an encoder $G$ for an $(n, k)$ convolutional code $C$ as follows. First find a nonzero polynomial $g_1^*$ of $C$ that minimizes $sw(g_1^*)$ and define the first row $g_1$ of $G$ by $g_1 := g_1^*/d_1$ where $d_1$ is the g.c.d. of the entries of $g_1^*$. Then choose another polynomial of $C$ of minimal symbol weight among all code polynomials outside $E(g_1)$ and use the result of problem 3.1 to obtain a basic encoder $G^{[2]} = \begin{bmatrix} g_1 \\ g_2 \end{bmatrix}$ of the code generated by $g_1$ and $g_2^*$. Continue in this way up to obtaining the encoder $G = G^{[k]}$ of $C$. Prove that $G$ is an optimal distance ordered encoder of $C$.

**11.5** Prove that an $(n, t)$-covering $K(n, t)$ satisfies $|K(n, t)| \geq \binom{n}{t} / \binom{2t}{t}$. Estimate the efficiency of the construction of section 11.4.3 with respect to this bound.

# References

1  M.J. Aaltonen, Linear programming bounds for tree codes, *IEEE Trans. Inform. Theory*, **25**, pp. 85-90, 1979.

2  L.R. Bahl, C.D. Cullum, W.D. Frazer and F. Jelinek, An efficient algorithm for computing the free distance, *IEEE Trans. Inform. Theory*, **18**, pp. 437-439, 1972.

3  L.R. Bahl and F. Jelinek, Rate 1/2 convolutional codes with complementary generators, *IEEE Trans. Inform. Theory*, **17**, pp. 718-727, 1971.

4  L.R. Bahl and F. Jelinek, On the structure of rate $1/n$ convolutional codes, *IEEE Trans. Inform. Theory*, **18**, pp. 192-196, 1972.

5  C. Berge, *Théorie des Graphes et ses Applications*, Dunod, Paris, 1963.

6  E.R. Berlekamp, Note on recurrent codes, *IEEE Trans. Inform. Theory*, **10**, pp. 257-258, 1964.

7  E.R. Berlekamp, *Algebraic Coding Theory*, McGraw-Hill Book Company, New York, 1968.

8  S.D. Berman, Semisimple cyclic and Abelian codes, *Cybernetics*, **3**, pp. 17-23, 1967.

9  S.D. Berman, On the theory of group codes, *Cybernetics*, **3**, pp. 25-31, 1967.

10  R.E. Blahut, *Theory and Practice of Error Control Codes*, Addison-Wesley, Reading, Mass., 1983.

11  I.F. Blake and R.C. Mullin, *The Mathematical Theory of Coding*, Academic Press, New York, 1975.

12  R.C. Bose and D.K. Ray-Chaudhury, On a class of error correcting binary group codes, *Information and Control*, **3**, pp. 68-79, 1960.

13  R.C. Bose and D.K. Ray-Chaudhury, Further results on error correcting binary group codes, *Information and Control*, **3**, pp. 279-290, 1960.

**14** I.M. Boyarinov and G.L. Katsman, Linear unequal error protection codes, *IEEE Trans. Inform. Theory*, **27**, pp. 168-175, 1981.

**15** J.J. Bussgang, Some properties of binary convolutional codes generators, *IEEE Trans. Inf. Theory*, **11**, pp. 90-100, 1965.

**16** R.D. Carmichael, *Introduction to the Theory of Groups of Finite Order*, Dover Publications, New York.

**17** W.G. Chambers, *Basics of Communication and Coding*, Clarendon Press, Oxford, 1985

**18** P.R. Chevillat and D. Costello, A multiple stack algorithm for erasurefree decoding of convolutional codes, *IEEE Trans. Commun.*, **23**, pp. 638-651, 1975.

**19** P.R. Chevillat and D. Costello, Distance and computation in sequential decoding, *IEEE Trans. Commun.*, **24**, pp. 440-447, 1976.

**20** P.R. Chevillat and D. Costello, An analysis of sequential decoding for specific time-invariant convolutional codes, *IEEE Trans. Inform. Theory*, **24**, pp. 443-451, 1978.

**21** G.C. Clark, Jr., and J.B. Cain, *Error-Correction Coding for Digital Communictions*, Plenum Press, New York, 1981.

**22** J. Conan and D. Haccoun, Reduced-state Viterbi decoding of convolutional codes, Proc. 14th Allerton Conf. Circuit and Syst. Theory, pp. 695-703, September 1976.

**23** J. Conan, Private communication.

**24** D. Costello, Construction of convolutional codes for sequential decoding, Ph.D. Thesis, Univ. of Notre Dame, Notre Dame, 1969.

**25** D. Costello, Jr., A construction technique for random-error-correcting convolutional codes, *IEEE Trans. Inform. Theory*, **15**, pp. 631-636, 1969.

**26** D. Costello, Jr., Free distance bounds for convolutional codes, *IEEE Trans. Inform. Theory*, **20**, pp. 356-365, 1974.

**27** C.W. Curtis and I. Reiner, *Representation Theory of Finite Groups and Associative Algebras*, J. Wiley & Sons, New York, 1962.

**28** Ph. Delsarte, Automorphisms of Abelian codes, *Philips Res. Repts*, **25**, pp. 389-402, 1970.

**29** Ph. Delsarte, On subfield subcodes of modified Reed-Solomon codes, *IEEE Trans. Inform. Theory*, **21**, pp. 575-576, 1975.

30  Ph. Delsarte and Ph. Piret, Semiregular convolutional codes : definition, structure and examples, *Information and Control*, **33**, pp. 56-71, 1977.

31  Ph. Delsarte and Ph. Piret, Automorphisms of convolutional codes, *SIAM J. Appl. Math.*, **34**, pp. 616-629, 1978.

32  L.A. Dunning and W.E. Robbins, Optimal encoding of linear block codes for unequal protection, *Inform. Contr.*, **37**, pp. 150-177, 1978.

33  R.M. Fano, A heuristic discussion of probabilistic decoding, *IEEE Trans. Inform. Theory*, **9**, pp. 64-74, 1963.

34  G.D. Forney, *Concatenated Codes*, MIT Press, Cambridge, Mass. 1966.

35  G.D. Forney, Convolutional codes I : Algebraic structure, *IEEE Trans. Inform. Theory*, **16**, pp. 720-738, 1970.

36  G.D. Forney, Correction to "Convolutional codes I : Algebraic structure", *IEEE Trans. Inform. Theory*, **17**, p. 360, 1971.

37  G.D. Forney, Use of sequential decoders to analyze convolutional code structure, *IEEE Trans. Inform. Theory*, **16**, pp. 793-795, 1970.

38  G.D. Forney, Maximum likelihood sequence estimation of digital sequences in the presence of intersymbol interference, *IEEE Trans. Inform. Theory*, **18**, pp. 363-378, 1972.

39  G.D. Forney, The Viterbi algorithm, *Proceedings of the IEEE*, **61**, pp. 268-278, 1973.

40  G.D. Forney, Structural analysis of convolutional codes via dual codes, *IEEE Trans. Inform. Theory*, **19**, pp. 512-518, 1973.

41  G.D. Forney, Convolutional codes II : Maximum likelihood decoding, *Inform. Control*, **25**, pp. 222-266, 1974.

42  G.D. Forney, Convolutional codes III : Sequential decoding, *Inform. Control*, **25**, pp. 267-297, 1974.

43  R.G. Gallager, *Information Theory and Reliable Communication*, J. Wiley & Sons, New York, 1968.

44  W.J. van Gils, Two topics on linear unequal error protection codes : bounds on their length and cyclic codes classes, *IEEE Trans. Inform. Theory*, **29**, pp. 866-876, 1983.

45  J.M. Goethals, Analysis of weight distribution in binary cyclic codes, *IEEE Trans. Inform. Theory*, **12**, pp. 401-402, 1966.

46  V.D. Goppa, A new class of linear error correcting codes, *Probl. of Inform. Transmission*, **6**, pp. 207-212, 1970.

**47** D. Haccoun and M.J. Ferguson, Generalized stack algorithms for decoding convolutional codes, *IEEE Trans. Inform. Theory*, **21**, pp. 638-651, 1975.

**48** M. Hall, Jr, *The Theory of Groups*, The Macmillan Company, New York, 1959.

**49** F. Harary, *Graph Theory*, Addison-Wesley, Reading, Mass., 1971.

**50** H.J. Helgert and R.D. Stinaff, Minimum-distance bounds for binary linear codes, *IEEE Trans. Inform. Theory*, **19**, pp. 344-356, 1973

**51** H.J. Helgert, Alternant codes, *Inform. Control*, **26**, pp. 369-380, 1974.

**52** F. Hemmati and D. Costello, Truncation error probability in Viterbi decoding, *IEEE Trans. Commun.* **25**, pp. 530-532, 1977.

**53** F. Hemmati and D. Costello, Asymptotically catastrophic convolutional codes, *IEEE Trans. Inform. Theory*, **26**, pp. 298-34, 1980.

**54** Y. Iwadare, A class of high-speed decodable burst-correcting codes, *IEEE Trans. Inform. Theory*, **18**, pp. 817-821, 1972.

**55** F. Jelinek, A fast sequential decoding algorithm using a stack, *IBM J. Res. Dev.*, **13**, pp. 675-685, 1969.

**56** R. Johannesson, Robustly-optimal rate one-half binary convolutional codes, *IEEE Trans. Inform. Theory*, **21,** pp. 464-468, 1975.

**57** R. Johannesson, Some rate one-half binary convolutional codes with an optimum distance profile, *IEEE Trans. Inform. Theory*, **22**, pp. 629-631, 1976.

**58** R. Johannesson, Some rate 1/3 and 1/4 binary convolutional codes with an optimum distance profile, *IEEE Trans. Inform. Theory*, **23**, pp. 281-283, 1977.

**59** R. Johannesson and E. Paaske, Further results on binary convolutional codes with an optimum distance profile, *IEEE Trans. Inform. Theory*, **24**, pp. 264-268, 1978.

**60** J. Justesen, New convolutional codes constructions and a class of asymptotically good time-varying codes, *IEEE Trans. Inform. Theory*, **19**, pp. 220-225, 1973.

**61** J. Justesen, An algebraic construction of rate $1/\nu$ convolutional codes, *IEEE Trans. Inform. Theory*, **21**, pp. 577-580, 1975.

**62** G. Kowalevski, *Einführung in die Determinantentheorie Einschiesslich der Fredholmschen Determinanten*, Chelsea Publishing Company, New York, 1948.

**63** K.J. Larsen, Short convolutional codes with maximal free distance for rates 1/2, 1/3 and 1/4, *IEEE Trans. Inform. Theory*, **19**, pp. 371-372, 1973.

**64** K.J. Larsen, Comments on : An efficient algorithm for computing the free distance, *IEEE Trans. Inform. Theory*, **19**, pp. 577-579, 1973.

65  J. Layland and R.J. McEliece, An upper bound on the free distance of a tree code, Jet Prop. Lab., Space Program Summary, 37-62, **3**, pp. 63-64.

66  R. Lidl and H. Niederreiter, *Introduction to Finite Fields and their Applications*, Cambridge University Press, Cambridge, 1986.

67  S. Lin and D. Costello, Jr., *Error Control Coding : Fundamentals and Applications*, Prentice-Hall, Englewood Cliffs, 1983.

68  J.H. van Lint, *Introduction to Coding Theory*, Springer-Verlag, New York, 1982.

69  S. MacLane and G. Birkhoff, *Algebra*, The Macmillan Company, New York, 1967.

70  F.J. MacWilliams, Binary codes which are ideals in the group algebra of an Abelian group, *Bell Syst. Tech. J.*, **49**, pp. 987-1011, 1970.

71  F.J. MacWilliams and N.J.A. Sloane, *The Theory of Error Correcting Codes*, North-Holland Publishing Company, Amsterdam, 1977.

72  M. Marcus and H. Minc, *A Survey of Matrix Theory and Matrix Inequalities*, Allyn & Bacon, Boston, 1964.

73  C.W. Marshall, *Applied Graph Theory*, Wiley-Interscience, New York, 1971.

74  J.L. Massey, *Threshold Decoding*, MIT Press, Cambridge, Mass., 1963.

75  J.L. Massey and R.W. Liu, Application of Lyapounov's direct method to the error-propagation effect in convolutional codes, *IEEE Trans. Inform. Theory*, **10**, pp. 248-250, 1964.

76  J.L. Massey, Implementation of burst-correcting convolutional codes, *IEEE Trans. Inform. Theory*, **11**, pp. 416-422, 1965.

77  J.L. Massey, Uniform codes, *IEEE Trans. Inform. Theory*, **12**, pp. 132-134, 1966.

78  J.L. Massey, Some algebraic and distances properties of convolutional codes, *Proc. 1968 Symp. on Error-Correcting-Codes*, Univ. of Wisconsin, Madison, 1968.

79  J.L. Massey and M.K. Sain, Inverses of linear sequential circuits, *IEEE Trans. on Computers*, **17**, pp. 330-337, 1968.

80  J.L. Massey and D. Costello, Nonsystematic convolutional codes for sequential decoding in space applications, *IEEE Trans. Commun. Technol.*, **19**, pp. 806-813, 1971.

81  J.L. Massey, Variable-length codes and the Fano metric, *IEEE Trans. Inform. Theory*, **18**, pp. 196-198, 1972.

82  J.L. Massey, D. Costello and J. Justesen, Polynomial weights and code construction, *IEEE Trans. Inform. Theory*, **19**, pp. 101-110, 1973.

**83** H.F. Mattson and G. Solomon, A new treatment of Bose-Chaudhuri codes, *Journal Soc. Indust. Appl. Math.*, **9**, pp. 654-669, 1961.

**84** R.J. McEliece, *The Theory of Information and Coding*, Addison-Wesley, Reading, Mass., 1977.

**85** T.N. Morrissey, A unified Markovian analysis of decoders for convolutional codes, Technical report No. EE-687, Department of Electrical Engineering, Univ. of Notre Dame, 1968.

**86** E. Paaske, Short binary convolutional codes with maximal free distance, for rates 2/3 and 3/4, *IEEE Trans. Inform. Theory*, **20**, p. 683, 1974.

**87** W.W. Peterson and E.J. Weldon, *Error Correcting Codes*, 2nd ed., MIT Press, Cambridge, Mass., 1972.

**88** Ph. Piret, Some optimal type $B_1$ convolutional codes, *IEEE Trans. Inform. Theory*, **17**, pp. 355-356, 1971.

**89** Ph. Piret, On a class of alternating cyclic convolutional codes, *IEEE Trans. Inform. Theory*, **21**, pp. 64-69, 1975.

**90** Ph. Piret, Structure and constructions of cyclic convolutional codes, *IEEE Trans. Inform. Theory*, **22**, pp. 147-155, 1976.

**91** Ph. Piret, Some optimal AMC codes, *IEEE Trans. Inform. Theory*, **22**, pp. 247-248, 1976.

**92** Ph. Piret, Algebraic properties of convolutional codes with automorphisms, Doctoral thesis, Université catholique de Louvain, 1977.

**93** Ph. Piret, Generalized permutations in convolutional codes, *Inform. Contr.*, **38**, pp. 213-239, 1978.

**94** Ph. Piret, Addendum to "Generalized permutations in convolutional codes", *Inform. Contr.*, **40**, pp. 332-334, 1979.

**95** Ph. Piret, On the number of divisors of a polynomial over $GF(2)$, in *Applied algebra, algorithmics and error-correcting codes*, ed. by A. Poli, Lecture notes in computer science, vol. 228, Springer-Verlag, 1986.

**96** Ph. Piret and T. Krol, MDS convolutional codes, *IEEE Trans. Inform. Theory*, **29**, pp. 224-232, 1983.

**97** Ph. Piret, Word-error correcting convolutional codes, *IEEE trans. Inform. Theory*, **30**, pp. 637-644, 1984.

**98** V. Pless, *Introduction to the Theory of Error-Correcting Codes*, J. Wiley & Sons, New York, 1982.

**99** I.S. Reed and G. Solomon, Polynomial codes over certain finite fields, *IEEE Trans. Inform. Theory*, **8** pp. 300-304, 1962.

**100** W.J. Reitsema, A lower bound on the free distance of convolutional codes related to cyclic codes, *IEEE Trans. Inform. Theory*, **27**, pp. 638-639, 1981.

**101** J.P. Robinson and A.J. Bernstein, A class of binary recurrent codes with limited error propagation, *IEEE Trans. Inform. Theory*, **13**, pp. 106-113, 1967.

**102** J.P. Robinson, Error propagation and definite decoding of convolutional codes, *IEEE Trans. Inform. Theory*, **14**, pp. 121-128, 1968.

**103** C. Roos, On the structure of convolutional and cyclic convolutional codes, *IEEE Trans. Inform. Theory*, **25**, pp. 676-683, 1979.

**104** W.J. Rosenberg, Structural properties of convolutional codes, Ph.D. Thesis, Univ. of California, Los Angeles, 1971.

**105** W.J. Rosenberg, Consecutive zeros in convolutional codewords, *Discrete Math.*, **3**, pp. 247-264, 1972.

**106** L.D. Rudolph, Generalized threshold decoding of convolutional codes, *IEEE Trans. Inform. Theory*, **16**, pp. 739-745, 1970.

**107** D.E. Rutherford, *Introduction to Lattice Theory*, Oliver & Boyd, 1965.

**108** J.P.M. Schalkwijk and A.J. Vinck, Syndrome decoding of convolutional codes, *IEEE Trans. Commun.*, **23**, pp. 789-792, 1975.

**109** J.P.M. Schalkwijk, A.J. Vinck and K.A. Post, Syndrome decoding of binary rate $k/n$ convolutional codes, *IEEE Trans. Inform. Theory*, **24**, pp. 553-562, 1978.

**110** G. Seguin, On a class of convolutional codes, *IEEE Trans. Inform. Theory*, **29**, pp. 215-223, 1983.

**111** C.E. Shannon, A mathematical theory of communication, *Bell Syst. Tech. Journal*, **27**, pp. 379-423 and 623-656, 1948.

**112** G. Solomon and H.C.A. van Tilborg, A connection between block and convolutional codes, *SIAM J. Appl. Math.*, **37**, pp. 358-369, 1979.

**113** A.J. Viterbi, Error bounds for convolutional codes and an asymptotically optimum algorithm, *IEEE Trans. Inform. Theory*, **13**, pp. 260-269, 1967.

**114** A.J. Viterbi, Convolutional codes and their performance in communication systems, *IEEE Trans. Communications*, **19**, pp. 751-772, 1971.

**115** A.J. Viterbi and J.K. Omura, *Principles of Digital Communications and Coding*, McGraw-Hill Book Company, New York, 1979.

**116** H. Wielandt, *Finite Permutation Groups*, Academic Press, New York, 1964.

**117** K. Zigangirov, Some sequential decoding procedures, *Probl. Pered. Inf.* **2**, pp. 13-25, 1966.

**118** K. Zigangirov, New asymptotic lower bounds on the free distance for time-constant convolution codes, *Probl. Inform. Transm.*, **22**, pp. 104-111, 1986.

# INDEX